FROM DOLORES 2/24/05

D1226540

THE ASTOR ORPHANS
A PRIDE OF LIONS

OTHER BOOKS BY LATELY THOMAS

The Vanishing Evangelist

A Debonair Scoundrel

Sam Ward: King of the Lobby

Delmonico's: A Century of Splendor

The First President Johnson

Between Two Empires

The Mayor Who Mastered New York

Storming Heaven

A Pride of Lions

When Even Angels Wept

THE ASTOR ORPHANS
A PRIDE OF LIONS

LATELY THOMAS

Washington Park Press. Ltd.
Albany, New York

An earlier version of part of this material was published as *A Pride of Lions* by Lately Thomas.
Grateful acknowledgment was given to Houghton Mifflin Company for permission to quote from
John Jay Chapman and His Letters, edited by M.A. DeWolfe Howe, and to Harvard University
Press for permission to quote from *The Letters of Theodore Roosevelt*, edited by Elting E. Morison.

Washington Park Press Ltd.
7 Englewood Place
Albany, New York 12203
PH: (518) 465-0169
FX: (518) 427-9217

Library of Congress Cataloging-in-Publication Data

Thomas, Lately.
    The Astor orphans : a pride of lions / by Lately Thomas.
        p. cm.
    Based on a planned three volume work, with additional previously
unpublished materials.
    Includes index.
    ISBN 1-881324-03-6
    1. Astor family.   2. Chanler, Margaret Astor Ward--Family.
3. Chanler family.   4. Chanler, John W. (John Winthrop), 1826-1877--
Family.   5.   Upper class--New York (State)--New York.   6. New York
(State)--History--19th century.   7. New York (State)--History--20th
century.   I. Thomas, Lately. Pride of lions.   II. Title.
CT274.A86T56   1999
929'.2'0973--dc21   99-44718
                                                                         CIP

Book and Cover Design: Peggy Conway/Media Logic
Typography: Word Management
Printing: Thomson-Shore, Inc.

"Step in and enjoy the turmoil," the colorful, quotable Chanler Chapman used to say, and indeed *The Astor Orphans* opens the door wide to reveal the pageant and frolic that made up the lives of the Chanlers, eight rich, socially connected orphans who lived from the mid-nineteenth century to the 1960s.

Strong roots deep in the ancestral home soil, a rambunctious childhood spent mainly in the company of servants and each other, erratic education at home and abroad formed adults possessed of undoubted ability, means, good looks, charm, and pugnacity. But there was also a maverick strain that occasionally flowered into dramatic eccentricity. Famous for their "monumental disputes and fantastic reconciliations," the siblings also engaged in extravagant international derring-do and enjoyed an extraordinary range of acquaintance among the famous and the notorious of their time. Although they disparaged it, they were members of New York's social elite, the Four Hundred, whose leader, Mrs. Astor, was their great-aunt.

The author of this entertaining saga used the pen name Lately Thomas; his real name was Robert van Pauling Steele. Born in 1898, this talented writer enjoyed an entire career in journalism before beginning a second, prolific career in 1959 as a biographer.

The genesis of *The Astor Orphans* dates back to 1962. At the suggestion of Robert Lescher, then his editor (later his agent and the agent of his literary estate), Steele undertook a biography of Samuel Ward, one of the most scintillating, versatile, and endearing figures in nineteenth-century America. In pursuit of his subject he contacted the only person still living who had met and remembered Ward — Ward's granddaughter, and my grandmother, Margaret Livingston Chanler Aldrich. Then in her early nineties, Margaret Aldrich placed at Steele's disposal the archives at Rokeby, the Chanler family home on the Hudson River.

Steele's investigations continued after Margaret Aldrich died in 1963, at which time I became his principal contact with the extended Chanler family. *Sam Ward: King of the Lobby* was published by Houghton Mifflin in 1965, to wonderful reviews and brisk sales. It is a marvelously detailed, engaging work, and the Ward descendants (all of them children and grandchildren of Sam Ward's Chanler grandchildren) were delighted that "wicked Sam Ward," the family outcast, had made a triumphal comeback.

The family thereupon decided to ask Steele whether he would consider undertaking a thorough biographical treatment of the Chanler brothers and sisters. He was astounded. All his life, Steele said, he had wanted to write a book about these cut-ups, but he had assumed that the family would make it impossible. He agreed on the spot to undertake the project, although he had to complete other contracted books first.

Over the next six years I ransacked family attics and closets, borrowing, photocopying, organizing, and shipping books, correspondence, clippings, photographs, etc. for Steele's use in San Francisco, and arranging for Steele's interviews in the East with relatives and friends. William Morrow agreed to publish *A Pride of Lions*, but Steele and I were extremely disappointed when they decided to break the work into three volumes, which they planned to produce in sequence. This meant that the first volume stopped abruptly, midway through the story, leaving readers hanging (Archie had just disappeared from the lunatic asylum). As it turned out, Morrow decided not to proceed with the remaining volumes.

Although Steele undertook to revise the remaining material into a single sequel, his health began to fail. In his last letters to me he said that he hoped I would work with his wife, Frances, and with Robert Lescher to see the project through. He also expressed the hope that the book's publication would help buttress our beleaguered efforts to finance the preservation of Rokeby. He died in 1976.

For many years my own family responsibilities and career diverted my attention, but in 1997 I decided to renew my efforts to get the entire tale into print. Washington Park Press in Albany, a distinguished publisher of books of regional interest, promptly agreed to take up the project provided that we could condense the entire work into a single volume.

I am deeply indebted to Jedediah Steele (acting for the heirs of Robert Steele) and to Robert Lescher (acting for the Literary Estate of Lately Thomas) for their unstinting cooperation in this venture and their willingness to assign the book's royalties toward the preservation of Rokeby. Publication of *The Astor Orphans* will further strengthen the argument that Rokeby offers an interesting, documented story, and that despite the ravages of time, its preservation is possible and in the public interest.

It is unusual for a newly published book to be thirty-five years in gestation, yet the story has not suffered. It contains fascinating social history and ample character study, but the book should chiefly be read for pleasure because this is a fantastic tale, told with gusto, about the incredible commotions and irrepressible revels of a madcap brood.

"Step in and enjoy the turmoil."

July 1999

John Winthrop Aldrich
Rokeby
Barrytown, New York

Forebears of John Winthrop Chanler

In 17th century England, some Chanlers spelled their name Chaloner.

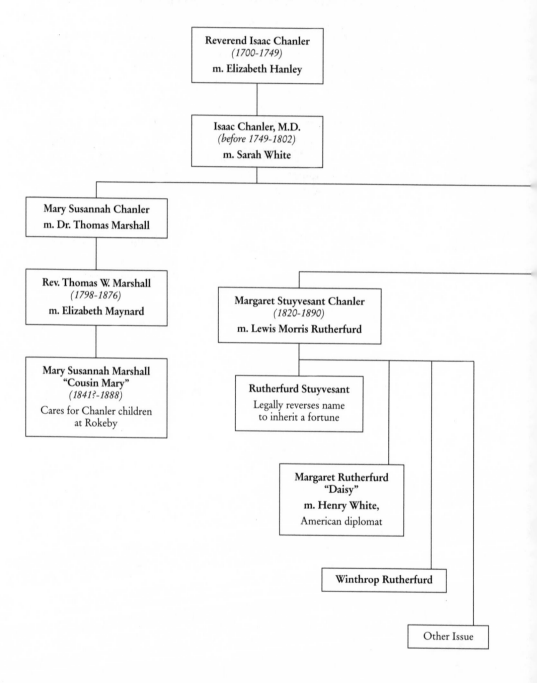

Reverend Isaac Chanler
(1700-1749)
m. Elizabeth Hanley

Isaac Chanler, M.D.
(before 1749-1802)
m. Sarah White

Mary Susannah Chanler
m. Dr. Thomas Marshall

Rev. Thomas W. Marshall
(1798-1876)
m. Elizabeth Maynard

Margaret Stuyvesant Chanler
(1820-1890)
m. Lewis Morris Rutherfurd

Mary Susannah Marshall
"Cousin Mary"
(1841?-1888)
Cares for Chanler children
at Rokeby

Rutherfurd Stuyvesant
Legally reverses name
to inherit a fortune

Margaret Rutherfurd
"Daisy"
m. Henry White,
American diplomat

Winthrop Rutherfurd

Other Issue

Reverend John White Chanler
(1787?-1853)
m. Elizabeth Shireff Winthrop

Elizabeth Winthrop Chanler
(1824-1904)
m. Dr. Octavius A. White

John Winthrop Chanler
(1826-1877)

m. 1862
Margaret Astor Ward
(1838-1875)

Helen Sarah White Chanler
(1828-1887)

Issue

Forebears of Margaret Astor Ward

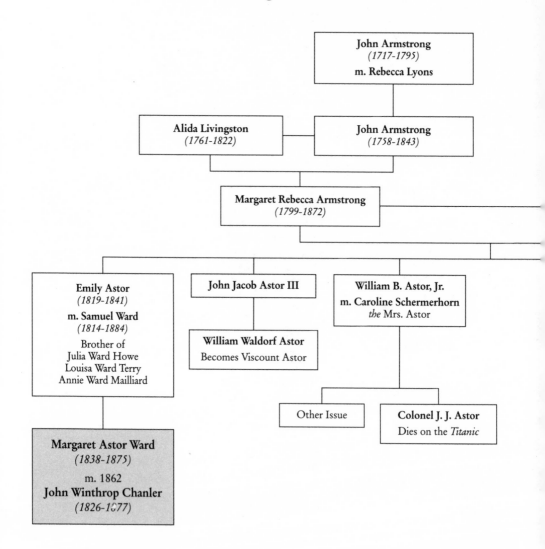

John Armstrong
(1717-1795)
m. Rebecca Lyons

Alida Livingston
(1761-1822)

John Armstrong
(1758-1843)

Margaret Rebecca Armstrong
(1799-1872)

Emily Astor
(1819-1841)

m. Samuel Ward
(1814-1884)

Brother of
Julia Ward Howe
Louisa Ward Terry
Annie Ward Mailliard

John Jacob Astor III

William B. Astor, Jr.
m. Caroline Schermerhorn
the Mrs. Astor

William Waldorf Astor
Becomes Viscount Astor

Other Issue

Colonel J. J. Astor
Dies on the *Titanic*

Margaret Astor Ward
(1838-1875)

m. 1862
John Winthrop Chanler
(1826-1877)

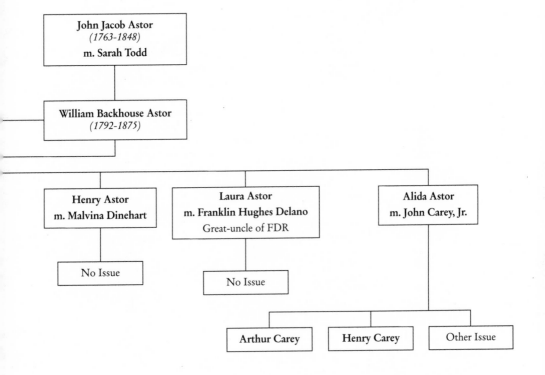

John Winthrop Chanler
(1826-1877)

John Armstrong Chanler
"Archie"
(later Chaloner)
(1862-1935)

m. 1888 Amélie Rives
(1863-1945)
Divorced 1895

Emily Astor Chanler
(1864-1872)

William Astor Chanler
"Willie"
(1867-1934)

m. 1903 Beatrice Ashley
(1886?-1946)

No Issue

Winthrop Astor Chanler
"Wintie"
(1863-1926)

m. 1886 Margaret Terry
"Daisy"
(1862-1952)

Elizabeth Winthrop Chanler
"Queen Bess"
(1866-1937)

m. 1898 John Jay Chapman
"Jack"
(1862-1933)

1. Laura Astor Chanler
   (1887-1984) m.
   Lawrence Grant White

2. John Winthrop Chanler II
   (1889-1894)

3. Beatrice Margaret Mary
   Chanler (1891-1974) m.
   Pierre Francis Allegaert

4. Hester Marion Chanler
   (1893-1990) m. Edward
   Motley Pickman

5. Marion Winthrop Chanler
   (1895-1931)

6. May Margaret Gabrielle
   Chanler (1897-1958) m.
   Porter Ralph Chandler

7. Hubert Winthrop Chanler
   (1900-1974)

8. Theodore Ward Chanler
   (1902-1961) m. Maria
   deAcosta (Sargent)

Children:

1. Girl (1899)

2. Chanler Armstrong
   Chapman (1901-1982) m.
   1. Olivia James

   2. Helen Riesenfeld

   3. Ida Holzberg
      (Wagman)

Stepchildren:
(Chapman's sons with Minna)
1. Victor Emmanuel
   Chapman (1890-1916)

2. John Jay Chapman, Jr.
   (1892-1903)

3. Conrad Chapman
   (1896-1989)

1. William Astor Chanler, Jr.
   (1904-) m.
   Innes G. James

2. Sidney Ashley Chanler
   (1907-1994) m.
   1. Princess Maria Antonia
      de Bragança

   2. Helen Brown
      (Coggeshall)

   3. Barbara Stone (Thayer)

Margaret Astor Ward
(1838-1875)

Marion Ward Chanler
(1868-1883)

Margaret Livingston Chanler
(1870-1963)

m. 1906 Richard Aldrich
(1863-1937)

Alida Beekman Chanler
(1873-1969)

m. 1896 Christopher Temple Emmet
(1868-1957)

Lewis Stuyvesant Chanler
(1869-1942)

m. 1890 Alice Chamberlain
(1868-1955)

Divorced 1921

m. 1921 Julia Olin (Benkard)
(1882-1961)

1. Richard Chanler Aldrich
(1909-1961)
m. Susan Kean Cutler

2. Margaret Astor Chanler Aldrich (1910-) m.
1. Christopher Temple Emmet Rand
2. Byron DeMott

1. Elizabeth Winthrop Emmet (1897-1934)
m. Edwin D. Morgan, Jr.

2. Margaret Chanler Emmet (1899-1970) m.
1. Francis H. Kinnicutt
2. John Benton Prosser

3. Christopher Temple Emmet, Jr. (1900-1975)

4. Hester Alida Emmet (1902-1965) m.
Louis Bancel LaFarge

5. Egerton (died as baby)

6. Jane Erin Emmet (1908-1997)

7. Winthrop Stuyvesant Emmet (1910-) m.
1. Marian de F. Clark
2. Evelyn Bigelow Clark (Hitt)
3. Elsie Wilmerding (Taylor)
4. Mary-Jane McGuckin (Laidlaw)

8. William Patten Emmet (1911-1977)

9. Thomas Addis Emmet (1915-1990) m.
Princess Eleanore Maria von Schoenberg

Children of Lewis Chanler and Alice Chamberlain:

1. Lewis Stuyvesant Chanler, Jr. (1891-1963) m.
1. Leslie Murray
2. Mary Kroehle (Dabney)

2. Alida Chanler (1894-1983) m.
William Christian Bohn

3. William Chamberlain Chanler (formerly William Astor Chanler, 2nd) (1895-1981) m. Frances Randall Williams (Rogers)

4. Alice Ruth Chanler (1907-1908)

Robert Winthrop Chanler "Bob"
(1872-1930)

m. 1893 Julia Chamberlain
(1872-1936)

Divorced 1907

m. 1910 Natalina Cavalieri
(1874-1944)

Divorced 1912

Children of Robert Chanler and Julia Chamberlain
1. Dorothy Chanler (1898-1948) m. Julian Twells Trenholm

2. Julia Chanler (1905-1977) m.
1. George Beach
2. Gabriel Laurin
3. Marchese Carlo Spinola

Egerton White Chanler
(1874-1882)

Shaded boxes represent the original Astor Orphans.

TABLE OF CONTENTS

PART I:

WILD SEEDS PLANTED

1 | A FOOTHOLD IN TIME

To the little girl in the carriage, the great white house appeared suddenly, emerging from the dim screen of trees, solid and sedate against the blue spring sky. As the wheels crunched to a halt on the gravel her father lifted her down, and she clutched his hand tightly for reassurance. Together they walked toward the broad stone steps sweeping up in a double curve to the wide veranda that stretched across the front of the house and jutted out at either end. Squarely in the center of this veranda, both leaves of the lofty entrance door stood open, waiting. Looking up at the somnolent dwelling, with its observant windows, which she was seeing for the first time, Alida had a premonition that she was going to live in this house for a long time. It was May 1876, the centennial year of the nation.

Three-year-old Alida Beekman Chanler was the youngest — except for baby Egerton — of the ten new owners of Rokeby, this manor house with its four hundred acres of surrounding park and farmland situated high on the eastern bank of the Hudson River. From its prominence the house overlooked a broad reach of the river and commanded a sweeping view westward to the Catskill Mountains, looming mistily in the blue distance.

The children's mother, Margaret Astor Ward Chanler, who had died six months earlier, had bequeathed Rokeby to all her children, "share and share alike." Within a year of settling in, the children, now spread in age from fifteen to three, lost their father, John Winthrop Chanler, as well. The band of lively, headstrong brothers and sisters were truly parentless, truly orphans. Under the direction of benign, but distant guardians, theirs was to be a privileged but unusual upbringing, out of which the young Chanlers, the "Astor orphans," emerged into extraordinary and highly individual lives.

Of the many reasons why the lives of the Chanler children are worth telling, the most obvious is that they are fascinating stories. But there are other reasons too, which have to do with the evolution of American social structure and the ways in which the Chanlers illustrated its successive transformations.

Born into the class of inherited wealth, privilege, and assured social position, in many ways they adhered to the conventions of their surroundings, and to that extent were representative of their milieu. But again and again, impelled by an abundance of vitality, imagination, and independence of spirit, they burst through the constrictions of convention to behave in ways wholly untypical of their class.

Psychologically, they also attract considerable interest, for they grew up in a household where parental concerns did not determine the tenor of life. Left far more to their own devices than most young people of their class, they nonetheless had the financial resources and social connections to fulfill almost any desire when they became adults. What they made of this curious opportunity is itself a compelling study.

Let us first meet the individuals who made up this "pride of lions." At the time their father died, the three oldest Chanler children were at school in England.

John Armstrong Chanler, called Archie or Armstrong, had been thirteen when his mother died. Archie would, over the course of a long and eventful life, marry an extraordinarily popular novelist, experiment in paranormal and psychological phenomena, be incarcerated in a madhouse by his brothers, escape to adopt a new name and carry on a campaign against his family, yet die reconciled with them all.

Winthrop Astor Chanler, usually called Wintie, was a year younger than Archie. After attending Harvard, Wintie married an exceedingly accommodating wife, who was also an intellectual and writer, and proceeded to live an internationally peripatetic life filled with sport, travel, wit, and good company. He made brief forays into business and politics, and enjoyed the wars he got into — Spanish-American, First World War — but his heart was most truly wedded to riding and hunting.

The third child, Elizabeth Winthrop Chanler, was aptly nicknamed Queen Bess by her siblings because she was the authoritative arbiter of their behavior. Elizabeth was nine when her mother died. Shortly after beginning school in England, Elizabeth suffered a debilitating disease of the hip which ended her formal schooling. She overcame pain and crippling, but everyone expected that she would remain single. To their surprise, she married John Jay Chapman, a widower with three children. She saw her husband through a complete mental breakdown, had two children of her own, settled on an estate neighboring Rokeby. She became a successful New York hostess and active social figure.

The remaining seven children were living at Rokeby when their father died, watched over by an elderly female cousin, a male tutor, and numerous servants.

William Astor Chanler, the oldest of the group at home, was called Willie. Eight at the time of his mother's death, he relished every kind of hard physical activity. A brief stint at Harvard brought him friends for life, but Willie found his greatest satisfaction in danger and intrigue. He wrestled alligators in Florida, had adventures with criminal gangs in the Wild West, explored in East Africa, ran guns in Cuba, fought in the Spanish-American War, led revolts in North Africa, sought to influence negotiations after the First World War. An active member of Tammany Hall in New York City, Willie entered politics enthusiastically, but usually left shortly after winning office to pursue some more physically strenuous activity.

Marion Ward Chanler, the handsomest of the children, died tragically while away at St. Paul's School in New Hampshire. He was only fourteen and had survived his mother by a mere seven years.

Lewis Stuyvesant Chanler, age six when his mother died, was a quiet, sensitive boy, unlike his rowdier brothers. He became one of New York's first pro bono lawyers, defending clients unable to pay for legal representation. Lewis also entered politics, becoming, among other things, the Democratic lieutenant governor under Republican Governor Charles Evans Hughes of New York.

Margaret Livingston Chanler, in childhood called Peg, Peggy, and Muggins, was five when her mother died. A practical, no-nonsense girl of high principle, she grew up especially close to Lewis, her "twin." During the Spanish-American War she worked as a volunteer nurse, winning a medal from the government for her efforts. She served as hostess for her brother Willie when he was in politics, and she was also active in the temperance movement and the fight for women's suffrage. In her thirties she married Richard Aldrich and had two children, and it is her descendants who inhabit Rokeby today. Margaret's inflexible adherence to principle, however, cut her off from her sister Alida for forty years, and ended forever all direct contact with her brother Lewis.

Robert Winthrop Chanler, only three when his mother died, was a physically active child like all his brothers except Lewis. For years Bob seemed to have no particular direction in life, but eventually an early interest in painting matured into a riotous, moderately productive career as an artist in the early 1900s. Bob also had a brief political career serving as an immensely popular sheriff for Dutchess County. His entanglements with women were the stuff of legend — during the latter part of his life he alternated between the attentions of two accommodating mistresses.

Alida Beekman Chanler, the child who had a premonition she would live at Rokeby a long time, was regarded by her family as a fey, romantic, beautiful butterfly. She married Temple Emmet, moved to Long Island, and produced an enormous brood of children. Later in life she converted to Roman Catholicism, alienating her sister Margaret for forty years. Alida lived to be ninety-six, dying in 1969, the last surviving member of the celebrated Four Hundred.

Finally, there was Egerton White Chanler, the baby, who died of a brain tumor at the age of eight. His death caused his special playmate, Alida, such despondency that for a time her life was despaired of as well.

So before they reached adulthood, the pride had been reduced to eight, but these eight young lions — Archie, Wintie, Elizabeth, Willie, Lewis, Margaret, Bob, and Alida — went on to enjoy long, rich, and complex lives.

It is clear from their names — Winthrop, Stuyvesant, Livingston, Astor, Beekman, Armstrong, White, Ward — that the orphans belonged to America's social and economic elite. Indeed, one might even say that they were captives of the past even when they were children. But while enormous inherited wealth ensured that they need never have to earn a living, their lineage also engendered the highest expectations of them.

The children's mother, Margaret Astor Ward, brought not only the Astor money and name to her marriage, but also connections to the Livingstons and the Armstrongs, the family that had originally built Rokeby.

Sometime before 1748, one John Armstrong had immigrated to the western frontier of Pennsylvania from Northern Ireland. During the French and Indian War the settlements on that frontier suffered cruelly from scalping parties of Delaware Indians, who were allied with the French. Under Armstrong's leadership a band of three hundred men surprised the Delaware stronghold at Kittanning, killed fifty braves including the chief, and burned the community before beating a successful retreat.

The blow was disastrous to the Delawares, and since the raid brought comparative peace to the frontier, Armstrong became celebrated in the colony as "the hero of Kittanning." At the outbreak of the Revolution, he served for a year as a brigadier general under Washington and then as major general in the Pennsylvania Militia for the remainder of the conflict. Later he was elected to Congress.

His son, also named John Armstrong, was a student at what would become Princeton University when the war started. Enlisting immediately, young Armstrong worked parental connections to obtain a place on the staff first of General Mercer and then of General Horatio Gates. Gates's headquarters, however, became a hotbed of intrigue, and young Armstrong was doubtless involved in Gates's plotting to supersede Washington.

During the interval before the formal peace was signed, young Armstrong's taste for intrigue led him to write the so-called "Newburgh Letters." These "addresses," which circulated anonymously among the officers stationed at Newburgh, New York, recited the grievances of the officers, whom the Continental Congress had left without pay or adequate provisioning. They hinted at a military coup, if necessary. The letters so angered Washington that he threatened to hang their author, if he could be identified.

In later years Armstrong admitted his authorship, while Washington, on his part, conceded that the plight of the officers had not been overstated. Armstrong's extreme pugnacity was remarked by his contemporaries.

Retiring from the army, John Armstrong, Jr., attained the rank of brigadier general in Pennsylvania and then improved his social position considerably by marrying a Livingston heiress, Alida. Powerful in both state and national affairs, the Livingstons held vast land grants along the upper Hudson. They lived on these estates in feudal grandeur, and their daughters were sometimes dowered with portions of the family lands. Alida Livingston brought to her marriage the riverfront acreage in the Red Hook district of Dutchess County, north of Rhinebeck, which would later be called Rokeby.

Through his Livingston connections, John Armstrong was twice elevated to the United States Senate, and in 1804 was named to succeed his brother-in-law, Chancellor Livingston, as United States minister at the court of Napoleon. During the War of 1812 President Madison, for political as well as practical reasons, offered the post of secretary of war to Armstrong, although the two men mutually disliked and distrusted each other, and after that conflict he withdrew to private life. He wrote a half dozen books; one — a treatise on agriculture — went through three editions.

General Armstrong had set about providing his estate with a suitable manor house directly after returning from France in 1810. He wanted no mansion — nothing showy or extravagant — but a comfortable, commodious dignified gentleman's home. That was the kind of house he got, large, solid, and practical, of stuccoed fieldstone, although the interior was distinguished by touches of French taste which set the dwelling off from the other great houses along the river.

Armstrong and his wife had five sons and one daughter, named Margaret Rebecca. This daughter was expected to marry well, but her choice of a husband did not, at first, entirely please her parents. At a reception in Albany, she had met William Backhouse Astor, son of John Jacob Astor, then the richest man in America. Knickerbocker gentility looked askance upon the Astors, despite their great and growing wealth, for John Jacob's father had been the village butcher in Waldorf, Germany.

Because Margaret Rebecca Armstrong was a Livingston, and the Livingstons were immensely influential socially and politically, the advantages to the Astors of the match were obvious. William B. lost no time falling in love. There was some backing and filling, aimed, on the Astor side, at safeguarding their fortune from rapacious in-laws, but an understanding was finally reached, and the couple was married in 1818. Eventually, in 1836, William purchased the Rokeby property for the formidable sum of $50,000, but old General Armstrong continued to sit at the head of the table whenever he came to Rokeby, until he died in 1843 at eighty-five years of age.

It was at Rokeby — a name chosen by Margaret after reading the fashionable poem of the same name by Sir Walter Scott — that their first child was born, a girl named Emily. Five more children followed — John Jacob III, William B., and Henry, and two daughters Laura and Alida. Two other children died as infants.

Both the Astors were assiduous readers, Margaret's taste running to romances and works of piety, while her husband perused encyclopedias. He had been educated at Heidelberg and Göttingen Universities, where he often conversed with a moody classmate named Arthur Schopenhauer. On his return home William had bowed to his father's wish that he enter the family business, but he never lost his taste for scholarship and persuaded his father to establish what is now the New York Public Library.

A steady accumulation of books in the house led to the addition of Rokeby's octagonal tower, the lower floor of which became the main library. And the growing family, requiring extra attendants, caused Astor to add a third story to the house, under a mansard roof. By this means eight bedrooms were added, while an entire wing was built at the back to house a larger kitchen, offices, and a laundry.

Although William B. Astor had deep affection for his family, his habitual expression was dour and morose. He was as parsimonious with words as he was with money; old John Jacob having summed him up exactly when he said, "William will never make a dollar, but he will never lose one that he has."

In New York City, their social life was colorless and correct; Margaret Armstrong Astor was too country-bred to take on city glitter, and William's demeanor as a host was dismayingly funereal. Rokeby, where an air of provinciality and eighteenth-century formality pervaded, was hardly more cheerful.

Into this somber respectability their daughter Emily Astor brought a bit of sunlight. She inherited the delight in music and jolly, witty company so marked in her grandfather, John Jacob, at least when he wasn't doing business. She had a clear soprano voice of exceptional range and brilliance and her grandfather doted on her singing of old German songs. Emily was easily John Jacob's favorite, and she could look forward to receiving a handsome dowry upon her marriage.

That event occurred in 1838. Emily's husband was Samuel Ward, Jr. Sam's family tree included two governors, Revolutionary patriots, and the Marions of South Carolina. Sam was witty, gay, and rich. Apparently blessed with every gift and talent, he was a fluent linguist, a more than passable writer, and a brilliant mathematician, as well as a polished dancer. He had traveled widely in Europe, where he seemed to have met everybody who counted, from youthful Henry Wadsworth Longfellow, to the Duchesse d'Abrantès, Liszt, Paganini, and the astronomer-physicist François Arago. He had been honored by learned societies, and was already a gourmet and connoisseur of wines. As the eldest son of the most prominent banker in New York, he was prospectively a millionaire.

Sam was a decided catch for the Astors. Emily and he fell blissfully in love, and Emily's dropsical old grandfather found young Sam the most obliging of possible sons-in-law, although their views on matters of money did not coincide. To the younger Astor sisters, Laura and Alida, Sam Ward appeared as a knight-rescuer from boredom.

Summers found Emily and Sam at Rokeby, and the second summer they brought with them their first-born, a girl whom they had named Margaret Astor Ward for her grandmother. That summer Rokeby echoed with unaccustomed laughter when Sam's three sisters, Julia, Louisa, and Annie Ward, came visiting. The contrast between the lively Ward temperament and the stiff reticence of the Astors was not lost upon keen-witted, fun-loving Julia, who would become Julia Ward Howe.

Sam and Emily's halcyon days lasted less than three years. Emily died in childbirth, and motherless Margaret was brought back to Rokeby. From then on the child, called "Maddie," would live with the Astors.

Estranged already, the Astors and Sam Ward parted ways entirely after Sam fell in love with Medora Grymes, about whom scandal hovered, and married her. The Astors regarded it as a desecration of Emily's memory and severed all connection. They even threatened legal action regarding Maddie's inheritance, so rather than jeopardize his daughter's prospects, Sam relinquished the child to her maternal grandparents.

Thereafter Sam compounded his turpitude, in Astor opinion, by losing his fortune. It is true that he went on to win and lose two fortunes more, and to scintillate through a career of friendships and adventures incomprehensible to his first wife's family, but the breach was never healed.

Maddie Ward's girlhood was not gay. Thrown into the company of elderly cousins and uncles, she had few friends of her own age. Now and then she was permitted to see her scapegrace father briefly, but only in the severe custody of Nancy Richards, her mother's nurse, and she was never able to establish any satisfactory relationship with him. Her upbringing was largely in the hands of Nancy, a daughter of the carpenter who had built Rokeby. Maddie's was a feudal upbringing, filled with duties and the rigid enforcement of social gradations. She was drilled in Mrs. Astor's rubric of good manners, reserve, and decorum, many of the rules being vestiges of the previous century.

Two breaks in the dreary regularity of those years came with the marriages of her mother's younger sisters. Laura married Franklin Hughes Delano in the dining room at Rokeby. The match so pleased old John Jacob Astor that he gave the bride $200,000 in trust as a wedding present. Alida, the youngest Astor daughter, finally chose to marry John Carey, Jr.

Gentle and serious-minded, Alida became distressed over the plight of orphaned or neglected girls in the county and begged her father to endow a home. St. Margaret's home for girls was established in nearby Red Hook, where it figured largely in Chanler charitable concerns and was maintained as a privately supported charity until well into the twentieth century.

As Maddie herself grew old enough to marry, her grandparents guarded her with watchful solicitude, fending off fortune hunters. Maddie herself felt that the more sensitive young men of her acquaintance shrank from an Astor alliance, disliking to be suspected of casting covetous eyes upon their wealth.

John Winthrop Chanler, a very proper and serious-minded New York lawyer with excellent family connections, suffered from no such inhibition, but he was not immediately attracted to Miss Ward. His sister brought them together and employed her influence to predispose Maddie's grandparents to the match. In the autumn of 1861 the couple's betrothal was announced.

Chanler's family had originally spelled their name Chaloner and were presumably Norman-French, settled in England. Family stories had it that in Cromwell's time three Chaloners had sat in the Long Parliament, and at the trial of Charles I, one had voted to acquit the king, one to behead him, and the third, sniffing danger on both sides, had walked out without voting. After the Restoration, the royalist was advanced in favor, the regicide disappeared, and the abstainer withdrew into prudent obscurity. True or not, the story illustrated an abiding family trait to disagree violently among themselves out of strong convictions.

The first Chanler to reach America, the Reverend Isaac Chanler, was a Baptist divine who settled in Charleston, South Carolina, where he prospered, published theological works, and fathered a son, named Isaac also.

This son earned a medical degree at the University of Edinburgh, writing a thesis bearing the prophetic title of "Hysteria, Its Causes and Aspects." Returning to South Carolina, he served as a surgeon in the Continental Army during the Revolutionary War. While studying abroad this Isaac had joined the Church of England, and his son, John White Chanler, became an Episcopal clergyman. A graduate of Yale College, John White Chanler was invited to New York by a classmate named

Winthrop. There Chanler met his friend's sister, Elizabeth Shirreff Winthrop, and eventually they married. On her father's side Elizabeth Chanler traced her family to the Winthrops of Massachusetts, while her mother, born Judith Stuyvesant, was closely related to the Livingstons and Beekmans and was an heiress of the Stuyvesant real estate holdings in lower Manhattan.

John Winthrop Chanler, this couple's only son, graduated from Columbia College, and after a visit to Europe was admitted to the bar. Politics attracted him, and in 1858 and 1859 he was elected to the New York State Assembly from a Tammany district. In 1860 he was defeated in a bid for election to Congress, and upon the outbreak of the Civil War he was called up for three months of military service. He then returned home and in 1862 won election to Congress as Tammany's candidate in the Third Congressional District of New York City.

His betrothal to Margaret Astor Ward, therefore, came at the outset of what gave every indication of being a fine, perhaps even brilliant career. The match was not a flighty one: Chanler was thirty-five and his fiancée was twenty-three. The wedding took place in the Astor home on Lafayette Place, just after New Year's 1862.

In March 1863 the new congressman took his seat as a member of the Democratic minority and thereafter dutifully fulfilled the role of a minority member. The couple purchased a residence close to the Capitol and there entertained decorously. In addition to pursuing his political activities, Chanler became something of a connoisseur and collector of paintings.

Chanler was reelected in 1864 and 1866. Meanwhile, Maddie's children were arriving almost annually. John Armstrong Chanler, was born on October 10, 1862. Winthrop Astor Chanler followed a year later on October 14, 1863, and then a daughter, named Emily for Maddie's mother, born in 1864. A second daughter, Elizabeth Winthrop Chanler, arrived on February 23, 1866, and William Astor Chanler, the third son, on June 11, 1867, at Newport, where the Chanlers maintained a summer home called Cliff Lawn. One more child was born during Chanler's congressional tenure — Marion Ward Chanler on July 27, 1868 — followed by Lewis Stuyvesant Chanler on September 24, 1869.

The four eldest — Armstrong, Winthrop, Emily, and Elizabeth — made their bow in society at the celebrated children's Christmas ball that President Andrew Johnson gave for his grandchildren at the White House on December 29, 1868. Winthrop Chanler remembered that event all his life. He and Armstrong became lost amid the forest of crinolines billowing around them and were found in a corner, clutching hands, in tears.

When Chanler was defeated in the 1868 election, owing to his opposition to Tammany's boss Tweed, it effectively ended his office holding, although he continued to be politically active.

In the autumn of 1870 the Chanlers moved into a home in New York City, a spacious brownstone at 192 Madison Avenue between 34th and 35th Streets, later the site of Altman's store. Margaret Livingston Chanler, who was born here on October 31, 1870, remembered the place as vast and gloomy, heavy with dark woods and cavernous rooms. The location of the house reflected the northward drift of fashion in the city; although the older aristocracy, the Fishes, Stuyvesants, Rutherfurds, and their offshoots, clung to lower Second Avenue, Stuyvesant Square, and Gramercy Park, already Fifth Avenue was being lined with the homes of the rich. The Chanler home had been erected on Astor property, as a matter of course: the family's holdings were scattered all over Manhattan, with a heavy concentration in midtown Manhattan. Three family townhouses, all built as gifts by William B. Astor, occupied half the blockfront along Madison Avenue — the homes of the Chanlers, the Delanos, and the Careys. Thus Maddie's much-loved Aunts Laura and Alida were her next-door neighbors.

The Chanlers produced yet another son, Robert Winthrop Chanler, on February 22, 1872, but later that year they suffered their first bereavement when Emily, the eldest daughter, died of scarlet fever before her eighth birthday. Maddie felt her loss poignantly; her children were a joy to her, and she insisted that there could never be too many. Maternal responsibilities she accepted lightly, almost gaily. One time at a gathering of ladies she took out her knitting and announced cheerfully that she was starting on her winter quota of seventy-two pairs of children's stockings.

The year of Emily's death brought a second grief to Maddie when old Mrs. Astor died, cutting a link with a world that already was alien to the bustling, dollar-scrambling New York of 1872. The arrival of a new daughter, Alida Beekman Chanler, on June 22, 1873, partially eased the pain of Emily's loss. A year later, in November 1874, the Chanlers' eleventh child was born and given names from Winthrop and Southern branches of the family, Egerton White Chanler.

In one respect the Chanler household differed radically from the home of William B. Astor. The Chanlers all talked, and often they all talked at the same time. Chanler himself favored this; he excelled at conversation, and never excluded his children from discussions of business or politics or other grown-up concerns.

In 1875, on the day before Thanksgiving, William B. Astor died, aged eighty-two. Since the death of his wife he had lived humorlessly, devoting all his time to business. Funeral services were held in Grace Church, the stronghold of Gotham society, and afterward the long procession of carriages wound through rain-swept streets to Trinity Cemetery far uptown.

The newspapers estimated that William B. Astor had left an estate of more than $100,000,000, "even at the present depressed values of real estate." When the will was opened on December 7, therefore, the public craned to see what would become of the largest fortune in America.

The bulk of the estate, it developed, was left to two of Astor's sons, John Jacob Astor III and William B. Astor, Jr., with John Jacob, the eldest, receiving the lion's share. Henry Astor, the third son, was essentially disowned because of an inappropriate marriage. After the two sons, the chief beneficiary was Maddie Chanler. Altogether she was left property worth about $5,000,000, including the house at 192 Madison Avenue, and Rokeby and its contents. She received in addition improved property to the value of $175,000; the income from $375,000 held in trust; three houses and lots on Fifth Avenue at the corner of 34th Street; other improved property to the value of $40,000; $30,000 in cash; one-third of another sum of $50,000; and so forth, the list rolling on and on.

The acquisition of Rokeby delighted Maddie, and she anticipated eagerly returning there in the spring. But the long, tiring drive in her grandfather's funeral procession, in blustery, raw weather, had induced a chill, which speedily became pneumonia. Immediately after Astor's funeral Sam Ward had called on his daughter and found her already ill. But he was shocked when a telegram reached him in Washington on December 13, stating that Maddie had died that morning. Only thirty-seven and pregnant with a twelfth child, she left a grief-distracted husband and ten children, ranging in age from thirteen to two. The saga of the Chanler pride had begun.

2 | CAST ADRIFT

Margaret Chanler's funeral was held in St. Mark's-in-the-Bouwerie, which the Chanlers deemed their family church through their descent from Peter Stuyvesant. Her coffin then traced the route that her grandfather's hearse had traversed a few weeks previously to Trinity Cemetery, where it was laid in the family vault.

As soon as she had been decently buried, the consuming topic of interest was how she had disposed of her fortune. Her will, though it dealt with a conglomeration of properties and investments, had essentially one simple intent: everything was left to her husband and ten surviving children. John Winthrop Chanler received $100,000 in cash and securities, plus some additional real estate, while the entire general estate, which included Rokeby, was bequeathed to the children collectively.

There were a few personal gifts, the largest being $6,000 left to "my faithful nurse, Nancy Richards," together with the income for life from a trust fund of $4,000. Donations were made to charities, including the mission school and chapel of St. Mark's-in-the-Bouwerie and Christ Church in Red Hook.

The children felt the death of their mother with different degrees of intensity. While their mother lay dying, the younger children had been taken Christmas shopping, in order to get them out of the house. Upon their return they were told that their mother was no more. Five-year-old Margaret felt no sorrow, but exclaimed, "She has gone to join dear Emily in heaven!" Archie and Wintie, however, would retain an impression of their mother as a tender, gentle figure, sincere in her religion, reserved in public, but capable of great gaiety in the nursery. Elizabeth, who was nine, felt that her mother's responsibilities had devolved upon her as the eldest daughter, and this role of quasi-authority her brothers and sisters deferred to.

Margaret Chanler had named her husband sole executor of her will and guardian of their children. To fulfill these cares, he retired from political activity and planned an early removal to Rokeby. An unmarried cousin from South Carolina, Mary Marshall, volunteered to assume charge of the brood. Miss Marshall's life revolved around a stern Calvinist religion of duty and inflexible principles, yet she was kind, endlessly patient, and imbued with a profound sense of family loyalty.

When Chanler applied to the court for allotment of funds, he estimated that the costs of supporting and educating the children at not less than $40,000 a year, the total including outlays for the upkeep of Rokeby, with servants, gardeners, and farmers; the salaries of a governess for the girls, and a tutor for the younger boys; boarding school for those who were older; a nurse or nurses for the babies; a housekeeper; food, fuel, lights, and medical and travel expenses. The domestic staff called for a cook, laundress, three maids, seamstress, and butler; the outside help comprised a coachman and three grooms, a gardener and three assistants, and a farmer and three helpers. Chanler called the court's attention to the children's property, valued at more than a million dollars, and to their "high social position and station in life," which made it desirable that their education "and manner of living during their minority should correspond to the position to which it is probable [they] will each occupy upon attaining his or her majority." The court concurred, and ordered that all necessary and proper expenses be paid out of their income.

The children's education was a pressing concern. Archie and Wintie were at St. John's Military Academy at Sing Sing, a school conducted by a distant cousin. While that was all very well as a start, Chanler felt that his elder sons should have a more gentlemanly education at a first-rate English school and Elizabeth, as eldest girl, should receive the benefit of European polish. Chance solved the problem of the younger boys: Wintie and Archie had brought home from school E. B. Bostwick, a young man who made such a favorable impression that he was engaged as tutor. Bostwick was pleasant, pliant, and strictly upright in his conduct; and although his educational qualifications hardly extended beyond geometry and mediocre Latin, as "Mr. Bostwick" he would remain at Rokeby for years.

In 1877 John Winthrop Chanler sailed for England with Archie, Wintie, and Elizabeth. He hoped to enter Archie in Rugby, Wintie in Eton, and

*William B. Astor, the nation's richest citizen
and great-grandfather of the Chanler children.
Photo ca. 1865.*

*Margaret Rebecca Astor, wife of William B. Astor,
daughter of General Armstrong, the builder of Rokeby,
and niece of Chancellor Robert R. Livingston.
Photo ca. 1865.*

Ward's celebrated sister Julia Ward Howe, author of the "Battle Hymn of the Republic," and mentor to her great-niece Margaret Chanler as a civic activist. Photo ca. 1890.

Samuel Ward, a scintillating, incorrigible charmer, and grandfather of the Chanlers. The Astors could banish his person but not his genes. Photo ca. 1880.

John Winthrop Chanler, the father of the Chanler children and heir to ancestral Winthrop and Stuyvesant lands in lower Manhattan, a district he later represented in Congress. Daguerreotype ca. 1850.

Margaret Astor ("Maddie") Ward, at about the time of her engagement to J.W. Chanler. The heiress lived to bear eleven children in fourteen years of marriage, and to inherit Rokeby. Photo ca. 1861.

Emily Astor Chanler, the oldest daughter, was named for her long-dead Grandmother Ward. Emily died of scarlet fever in 1872 at the age of eight.

Marion Ward Chanler died of pneumonia at fifteen in 1883 at St. Paul's School in New Hampshire.

Egerton White Chanler, the eleventh child and Alida's long-mourned playmate, died of a brain tumor at the age of eight in 1882.

*Miss Mary Marshall, John Winthrop
Chanler's spinster cousin from Charleston,
South Carolina, volunteered to serve
in loco parentis at Rokeby following
Chanler's death. Photo ca. 1880.*

*Miss Mary Meroney, Rokeby's
indispensable housekeeper and family
counselor for thirty years. Photo ca. 1885.*

*Jane Cross, a freedwoman who was a
laborer at the Washington Navy Yard
when she was hired by Maddie Chanler
as a nurse. She moved back to New York
with the family in 1869. Much loved
by the children, she died at Rokeby.
Photo ca. 1880.*

John Armstrong ("Archie") Chanler and Winthrop Astor ("Wintie") Chanler. Archie was the firstborn child, and the lifelong rivalry between these two brothers was keen. Photo ca. 1873.

Elizabeth Winthrop Chanler, posing for W. & D. Downey, "photographers to the Queen,"
in London. At about this time her hip disorder became acute. Photo ca. 1880.

William Astor ("Willie") Chanler in the uniform of St. John's Military Academy, Sing Sing, New York. Willie's competitive and martial spirit took root early. Photo ca. 1881.

Lewis Stuyvesant Chanler. Even as a young child, Lewis was playing the lawyer in household disputes at Rokeby, anticipating the career that beckoned. Photo 1880.

Margaret Livingston Chanler. The ramrod back, the firm set of the jaw, the steady gaze all suggest in this girl the strength of character that would mark the woman. Photo 1885.

Robert Winthrop ("Bob") Chanler. Lacking the education and sophistication of his older siblings, Bob was happiest with his animals and in the fields and woods of Rokeby. Photo 1880.

Cousin Mary Marshall and Alida Beekman Chanler. Dreamy and romantic, Alida matured into a "Beauty," as did her sister Elizabeth. Photo 1884.

The Astor orphans and their cousin Mary Marshall at Rokeby. From left: Willie, Alida, Archie, Elizabeth, Wintie, Cousin Mary Marshall, Lewis, Margaret and Bob. Photo ca. 1884.

The south elevation of Rokeby. In the mid-nineteenth century the Astors altered the Armstrong house by adding the eighty-foot-long piazza, mansarded third floor, and tower (at left). Photo ca. 1888.

Rokeby's west elevation. The Gothic Revival octagonal library is on the ground floor of the tower. Photo ca. 1888.

Cliff Lawn, the house the Chanlers built for summer use in Newport, Rhode Island, about 1865, starting the trend to build on the ocean bluffs.

Elizabeth in Miss Sewell's select school for young ladies on the Isle of Wight, but he ran into unexpected difficulties. Archie failed the entrance examinations at Rugby and Wintie had passed the age at which boys customarily entered Eton. Negotiation surmounted Wintie's handicap, and Archie was taken into Hillbrow, a preparatory school conducted by a Rugby master, J. W. Vecqueray. No difficulty arose in Elizabeth's case, and after seeing all three children satisfactorily bestowed, their father sailed for home by way of Paris.

Throughout the trip he had received weekly bulletins from the assiduous Mr. Bostwick — the boys were busy with their rabbits, goats, and chickens; Margaret was taken into town by Miss Marshall to have her teeth straightened; the crops were thriving despite the bothersome drought. The picture was reassuring. Reaching New York in the autumn, Chanler enrolled Willie at St. John's and proceeded on to Rokeby.

There, long serious letters arrived almost daily from Archie, and short, merry ones from Wintie. Archie's progress was disappointing: his teachers found him mentally quick, but undisciplined and neglectful. Wintie was less conspicuously good or bad, but obviously spent his time more congenially with his horse than with his books.

A letter from Archie on September 29, 1877, enclosed another indifferent report card, but dwelt on his athletic progress "Our side had the best of it at first but as the other side had a master with them they beat." The letter reached Rokeby in mid-October, simultaneously with a note from Willie at St. John's, asking "How is the farm getting on and the goats? How is my little calf getting on? How is all the family?"

Five days after the date of this letter to "Dear Papa," John Winthrop Chanler was dead. He had caught a slight cold while playing croquet on wet grass, the cold led to pneumonia, and he died, aged fifty-one, at Rokeby, on October 19, 1877. His funeral took place in St. Mark's, the mayor of New York heading an official delegation that included former Secretary of State Hamilton Fish. Then John Winthrop Chanler was borne to Trinity Cemetery and laid beside his wife in the family vault.

How to convey the shattering news to the children abroad plunged the relatives into a quandary. Finally Winthrop cousins who lived in Paris were appealed to by cable. Fifteen-year-old Archie Chanler described what happened in a carefully composed letter addressed collectively to "Willie, Marion, Lewis, Margaret, Robert, Alida, and Pedge [Egerton]:

"My dear Brothers and Sisters:

"I am very well and am trying to bear up under this great affliction, which God has seen fit to send us, as well as I can. Dear Cousin Bob sent me a telegram last Wednesday saying that he would be at Rugby that day. . . . . [Cousin Bob] first told me that he had some very [bad] news to tell me, and I asked him what, and he said that dear Papa was dead. Of course I was nearly knocked off my feet by the blow. But Cousin Bob comforted me and told me that I must be the strongest as I was the oldest, and bear up against it. . . . Cousin Bob and I went for a walk and talked it over, and he was awfully kind to me and comforted me a great deal. . . . Cousin Bob went to Shepreth on Thursday to tell Wintie but Mr. Wortham had already got a telegram so all Cousin Bob could do was to comfort him. Bob then went to the Isle of Wight but she [Elizabeth] had also been told by Miss Sewell who had received a telegram. . . . Wintie is bearing up very well, and so is Bessie. . . . We are all in perfect health, and are in as good spirits as we can afford. Give my love to Mr. Bostwick and dear Bunk [Willie] and let him read this letter as it is for him as well as for you and I only send it to Rokeby as you are nearly all there. Write to me soon. How are you all. Keep cheerful as possible.

From your loving
ARCHIE"

Wintie's letter of condolence was no less earnest, although more lightly phrased. Addressing "all the children at Rokeby," he explained that "I have not time to write to each of you, and as neither Dear Bob, Lallie [Alida] or Pedge [Egerton] could read them, I will write to all and you 'great big ones' can read it to the little ones." Winthrop then wrote:

"Remember, my dear Bunk [Willie] that you are the head of the house & what a responsibility you have, and so do your best. . . . Did all of you go to dear papa's funeral? Do poor Edgie [Egerton] and Lallie seem to understand that they are Orphans? . . . Sister Bessie, Brother Archie and Wintie are coming to you all next summer, and then we will be together again like old times, except we will not have either dear Mamma or Papa but will talk about them and try to remember them just the same as if they were with us. . . ."

In this abrupt way the Chanlers became different from other children, and because of that they realized they must cling together to draw comfort from each other. Cast adrift, denied the certainties that sustained other children, what would become of the orphans?

3 | A CURIOUS CHILDHOOD

John Winthrop Chanler's will was designed both to unite and protect the children. He had been preoccupied with heading off the remotest possibility that Sam Ward, his wife's father, might obtain any share in or control over the children's inheritance. Sam Ward had never dreamed of interfering, but Chanler had dreamed of little else for a long time. Sam was attached to his grandchildren, but was only rarely permitted to see them. The older ones remembered a few, almost clandestine calls at Cliff Lawn, in Newport, when Sam would line up the children by age and size and study them intently for family likenesses; then suddenly he would break into a smile and begin pulling presents from his capacious pockets.

Chanler's solution was to leave control of the children's upbringing, education, and material wealth in the hands of trustees and guardians, who were all as averse to Samuel Ward as he was. They included four Astors — John Jacob III and his son William Waldorf (later Viscount Astor), Laura Astor Delano, and Alida Astor Carey; Rutherfurd Stuyvesant and his wife, Mary, and his sister, Margaret S. Rutherfurd ("Daisy," later Mrs. Henry White); and Mrs. William Preston Griffin, the widowed sister of Mrs. Hamilton Fish. Mrs. Griffin was affectionately known to the Chanlers as Aunt Tiny (pronounced Teeny), an abbreviation deriving from her name, Christine. Among the executors and trustees named were Lewis Morris Rutherfurd and Franklin Hughes Delano.

In general, the estate was left in trust to the children in equal shares. In addition, Archie received the land and buildings of St. Margaret's home for girls at Red Hook, together with $50,000 to maintain the institution as a memorial to his mother and great-grandmother. He also received a farm, called Ore Lot or Ravenswood, that lay one mile south of Rokeby. The Chanler children owned Rokeby jointly already, but Archie, as the eldest son, was left the contents of the house and all the farm stock and equipment, together with $100,000 with which to maintain the property. It had been Maddie's wish that eventually Archie should own it wholly and live there, to perpetuate the Chanler name on the river.

Wintie Chanler received the contents of the Madison Avenue house, which was then rented unfurnished to others for the remainder of the Chanlers' minority, and eventually sold. Wintie also received farm property across the river from Rokeby and Cliff Lawn, the family's summer home at Newport. Each of the other children received a separate lot at Newport for his or her own use. Various friends were left minor sums, and $1,000 was left to Columbia College to endow the Chanler History Prize, still presented today, for the best student paper on a historical subject. Their mother's jewelry was to be divided among the three Chanler sisters once they had all come of age, and the entire balance of the estate was placed in trust for the benefit of the children, share and share alike, with one significant exception: the trustees were instructed to set aside $50,000 for each of the three Chanler daughters, Elizabeth, Margaret, and Alida. These funds were to be invested and the income reinvested until the girls either married or attained the age of twenty-one; thereupon the income was to be paid to them directly and unconditionally, free from control even by their husbands. Since in 1877 the sisters were eleven, seven, and four, respectively, these legacies would assure each daughter an independent income exempt from male control, something rarely found among women of wealth at that time.

Though of the highest respectability, the guardians were ill-prepared to raise a brood of high-spirited youngsters. Most were middle-aged or older, and some were childless. Nevertheless, on December 21, 1877, all but John Jacob Astor legally accepted their responsibilities and John Jacob promised to lend his counsel whenever requested. However, none of the guardians could face the prospect of taking all ten orphans into his or her home, and there was anguished debate as to how to dispose them. The very thought of being separated appalled the children, and they begged to be allowed to stay at Rokeby. Finally, after Mary Marshall consented to stay on as the household authority, this was agreed.

Her decision required courage. The Chanlers already were exhibiting more than ordinary energies, and the conditions under which they would live promised to intensify their spirit of independence. At Rokeby, knowing that they were on their own ground, and in the absence of normal parental guidance and discipline, they would be encouraged to feel that they were a special group, unique to themselves, different even from their closest relatives.

The isolation of Rokeby was more than geographical. Old ideas, remnants of a previous century, permeated the house. The visitors who drove up in stately carriages to exchange polite courtesies were mainly old relatives; old retainers manned the grounds; old ways of living were the rule. The Chanlers, too, were attached to their home by influences and impulses of which they were only dimly aware, for the land had been in ancestral possession since a grant by James II in 1688. Four generations before them had called Rokeby home; every room had associations with some forebear. In the westward-facing bedroom a Charleston relation, old Mrs. Maynard Marshall, used to sit with the girls of the household through long, hot summer afternoons, languidly reading antique romances. There was the library stacked to its vaulted ceiling with the elegantly bound volumes, including all the eighteenth and early nineteenth-century classics. And of course, there was the dining room where the specter of General Armstrong hovered at the table.

The guardians ruled benignly, but from a distance. Once a month they gathered in the parlor of "Tiny" Griffin, received Miss Marshall's monthly report, audited her accounts (always correct to the penny), laid down policy for the conduct of their wards, and authorized the necessary outlays. Governesses were engaged for the girls — three Frenchwomen in a row, and then an Englishwoman. A mousy German piano teacher made trips periodically from Vassar College, and Mr. Bostwick tutored the boys. Bills for the expenses of the three children in England required checking, payments had to be forwarded, and surplus income accruing from the funds in trust must be judiciously reinvested — not always with fortunate results despite the prestigious advice available. The children's income totaled about $80,000 annually, and the guardians had sought permission to spend $70,000 of it; but the court set a limit of $30,000 a year. In consequence, there was no luxury at Rokeby, merely an abundance of plain fare and substantial comfort.

This suited the frugal tastes of Mary Marshall. Her overriding concern was to instill high moral principles in her charges; do that, she believed, and conduct would take care of itself; but her rules for social intercourse made slight impression upon her hyperactive group. Voices resounded loudly everywhere in the great house, children talking, on all floors, at all hours, and all at once.

Each child pugnaciously challenged everything, and since the disputants seldom allowed an antagonist to finish a sentence, loud arguments pro and con could be heard simultaneously. There were rules: no hitting, no "showing off," and a third provided that "a bore must shut up." The Chanlers enjoyed their verbal battles enormously throughout their lives, though they often horrified those who witnessed them.

Tutors and governesses were teased mercilessly, whereupon the children would be dismissed, allowing them to spend the lesson time with their pets. Numberless animals lived at Rokeby — dogs, cats, chickens, rabbits, birds, goats, ponies, even the occasional raccoon or snake. Whenever the children went for a walk they were escorted by a pack of yelping hounds, bulldogs, setters, and crossbreeds. Puppies were carried cheerfully for miles. Whenever there was a sick dog, some Chanler would sit up with it. Just letting the animals in and out of the house kept small feet on the go, and there were always dogs underfoot. At mealtimes dogs scuffled under the table, getting kicked by legs of various lengths.

In their self-contained community the children tended to pair off. Lewis and Margaret, a year apart in their ages, were inseparable from the time they shared their first nursery together. Lewis teased Margaret, frightening her deliciously by saying there were bears under her bed. She would dash with pounding heart past a tall armoire that he called their lair. Alida and Egerton made another pair. Egerton, a sweet-tempered, lively boy, romped with Alida all over the grounds; together they fed the snowbirds in winter, and spotted the first snakes emerging from their torpor in the spring. Wall-eyed, and neglected by lazy nurses as a baby, Alida did not learn to walk until she was two and a half, when Margaret finally had taught her. But Alida was imaginative, as practical-minded Margaret was not.

Both Lewis and Margaret took to books when very young. Reading, either alone or aloud in a group, was a principal diversion at Rokeby and formed an important part of the children's education. They were given the run of the library. Starting with fairy tales, they read their way through Victorian children's stories, such as those by Miss Yonge and Mrs. Molesworth, *The Little Duke*, and Kingsley's *The Heroes*, and so on to Cooper, Scott, Dickens, and always Shakespeare and Plutarch. Willie reveled in Marryat, Mayne Reid, and Henty, while the girls wept over Little Nell. The Bible was read daily at morning and evening prayers.

Robert was unlike the others. Less attractive in appearance, he was difficult to control and seemed absolutely averse to learning. He played with the farm children and was rough in manner, but was passionately devoted to animals. He broke a steer to harness to pull his sled when he was very small. Impulsive and undisciplined, Robert was constantly violating the rules, coming late to meals, neglecting lessons, disappearing at church time to hunt rabbits, failing to account for how he spent his time.

Signs and portents were commonplace at Rokeby and were accepted without question, a fact that bears remembering later. Second sight was a frequent manifestation. One morning Mary Marshall calmly reported that during the night a cousin had come and stood at the foot of her bed; and nobody was surprised when word arrived that during the night that cousin had died.

In the world of Rokeby the servants exerted a stronger influence on the children than Mary Marshall could bring to bear. Most of the domestic help were Irish, recent immigrants from class-conscious Europe, and imperceptibly they imparted their concepts of caste. They had very pronounced ideas about their own position and duties, and correspondingly firm notions regarding the proper behavior for their employers. They instilled in the Chanlers a sense of superiority and self-sufficiency that would make it impossible for the children ever to doubt their own social elevation, but impossible also ever to condescend to persons of inferior rank.

At the head of the house staff was Hade, the coachman, who had been a trooper in McClellan's cavalry during the war; he would teach the Chanlers to ride and handle horses fearlessly. Of equal authority was Mary Meroney, the head nurse. Mary, with her "tread like an empress" and proud to have been born a subject of William IV, ruled the servants hall. She had made the grand tour of Europe in the service of Governor and Mrs. Hamilton Fish, and her room was filled with keepsakes from every country she had visited. Nurses, housemaids, governesses, cooks, and footmen might come and go; Mary Meroney was immovable. When the children had complaints, they took them to Mary; when they had crises, she was the one who listened and pointed the way out. It was Mary to whom the weeping sisters ran when the butler borrowed their mite-box savings and failed to repay them, an experience that gave six-year-old Margaret a lifelong mistrust of male servants.

On the third floor the housekeeper, Mrs. Redmond, lived in silent melancholy, mourning for a brother who had gone to sea and was never heard of again. Her only visitor was the Methodist minister from nearby Red Hook. At each of his calls, she would hurry down to the parlor, pathetically hoping that this time the caller was her brother. She did, however, teach Margaret Chanler all she knew about housekeeping. Coming upon the child one day playing at cleaning the furniture, Mrs. Redmond patiently showed her the correct way to dust, polish, scrub floors, clean windows, and tidy a room.

The one servant who could more or less handle the obstreperous Chanler boys was Jane Cross, a former slave whom Maddie Chanler had found working as a day laborer in the navy yard at Washington. Old Black Jane, as she was called, began as the boys' nurse at Rokeby but continued to serve and manage them long after they were grown men. Jane appreciated good manners and had a sense of the family's importance. When friction developed between a haughty French governess and the Irish kitchen help, Old Jane's tact calmed the storm. Jane could neither read nor write, though the children in relays tried to teach her. Her ghost remained attached to the house, and on the anniversary of her death anyone in the room below the billiard room was said to be able to hear Old Jane, sweeping, sweeping.

The children attended the Irish wakes held in the servants' hall. The stark, the grisly, and the supernatural were not kept from them; they experienced a full quota of childhood's shivery terrors. In the White Room, two angels with swords on a mirror frame were known to come down and dance on the floor "in a terrible manner" unless the fire on the hearth remained aglow.

Sedate and composed though she was, Mary Marshall would join in games with the children, and she saw to it that they mastered two essential accomplishments: card playing and dancing. Whist she regarded as a good school for manners and a useful curb on tempers. When snowstorms raged, the household would absorb themselves in whist, and in summer they would sprawl on the floor absorbed in bezique.

Quarrels among the children might last for years and flare up to the bewilderment of persons not in the know. If an argument grew uproarious, Mr. Bostwick would rouse himself to referee, but at times Rokeby sounded as though it was occupied by savages. In these furious word battles wounds were principally those of having been outshouted by an opponent. Throughout their lives, Chanler voices, distinctive in their projection, clarity, and diction, also registered several decibels louder than those of other people. When two or more came together, they could be heard above the ordinary conversational din, often in chorus, as they thought nothing of talking at once.

Sundays at Rokeby were dedicated to religion. Before breakfast Cousin Mary would hear each child in a short Bible reading, and then would hold family prayers. After breakfast came the ride to church; rented carriages would convey the servants to the churches of their choice. In the afternoon there was more Bible reading, singing of hymns, and prayers again at night. No child was allowed to pull a bell rope except for firewood, the servants being relieved of all but indispensable tasks. The children were told that Sundays belonged to poor people just as much as to the rich, but they did not really believe this. Nevertheless, they conformed, although the boys would sometimes set their dogs to fighting on the servants' porch, urging them on with blood-curdling yells.

Sometimes the children's sense of importance was cultivated in bizarre ways. Miss Marshall gravely sent them one by one to a popular phrenologist to have their cranial bumps examined. He wisely forecast a brilliant future for each and all: one boy bound to become a statesman another a millionaire, a third a judge or a general, while all three girls would surely marry into the nobility. The pompously florid documents were preserved, and Chanlers laughed over them in later life.

THE EDUCATION OF BESS
AND OTHER MATTERS

The three Chanlers marooned in Europe escaped such phreno-logical insights into their futures. Thrown prematurely on their own resources, all three rebounded with youthful resiliency from the numbing shock of their father's death. Though far from home, their crisis was eased by relatives who took them in during vacations and watched over their progress at school. Henry White, secretary of the United States legation in London, and his wife, Daisy, one of the children's guardians, were particularly helpful, as were the Countess de Steurs, daughter of another guardian, Alida Carey, and her husband, a Dutch diplomat stationed in Paris. But Archie, Wintie, and Elizabeth were still forced to rely on their own resources of character, and in consequence they developed a precocious self-sufficiency. And as the eldest, they also rose to their position of leadership. Two months after his father's death, Archie wrote the tribe at Rokeby:

"I got your sweet round robin yesterday and I thank you and Cousin Mary for writing it. I am awfully glad to hear that you are all well and are in good spirits again. I am very glad that you are going to spend the winter at dear old Rokeby with Cousin Mary. How I wish I could be there with you around the fire in the dear old library. But I hope to have a very pleasant winter with Mrs. Wortham and Wintie and Bessie. . . . I got a letter from Wintie and Bessie last week and they are both in excellent health and spirits. . . . Wintie is having a splendid time hunting. . . . Give my love to all the guardians and Mr. Bostwick and Cousin Mary and Aunt Betty and Aunt Margaret and give my love to dear old Hannah and to everybody that asks about me."

On the same day the ebullient Wintie wrote to his brother Marion, on mourning paper decorated with a fancifully drawn "Merry Christmas" inside a garland of holly:

"Dear Fat:

"Your very nice and well written [letter] arrived here to day and please allow me to congratulate you on having attained to that high honour of long trousers. I can well understand that you are feeling 'very big' (as Lewis or Munga [Margaret] said you did) for I know how I felt the first day that I wore long trousers! How Dear Papa took me down to Brooks & said that he did not see why I was not tall enough to wear long ones instead of knickerbockers. I was highly delighted & was looking at my legs all the way home! Hope that you are enjoying yourself tumbling about on that pond & that you have not succeeded in fracturing your skull, I remain,

Ever your affec't Brother
WINTHROP A. CHANLER"

Archie's poor showing in school — his headmaster reported him to be "indifferent at best" — was giving the guardians cause for anxiety, but Wintie exhibited verbal facility, radiant charm, and social ease. He was also already remarkable for his light-hearted determination to extract enjoyment from every moment regardless of risks or reprimands. Once he jumped through a glass door on a dare, and after being duly spanked for this, cheerfully jumped through the door again. Long, long afterward, his daughter recalled that he enjoyed only those pastimes that involved some risk to life and limb.

Elizabeth was growing into a beauty and promised to be a social belle later on, but about a year after her father's death, she developed a disease of the hip that radically altered her prospects and removed her from Miss Sewell's school. The cause and exact nature of her malady were obscure; it might have been a tubercular infection of the bone, or a mild form of poliomyelitis; the doctors sought in vain an effective treatment. She was taken to London for examination by a noted Harley Street surgeon, but his obvious bafflement was plain even to the thirteen-year-old invalid, and the meaningless banalities he murmured as he departed plunged the child into a deep depression, a gloom intensified by the drab dowdiness of her lodgings in ultra-respectable Brown's Hotel. Then suddenly her whole outlook changed, thanks to her scapegrace Grandfather Sam Ward. Unknown to her, Sam had arranged the consultation in London; he had even tried to pay the surgeon, but had been prevented by the jealous guardians. Sam was in funds just then and in high favor in England, where he had just participated in Gladstone's famous Midlothian election campaign. Because the guardians secretly believed that Elizabeth was going to die, they gave permission for Sam to see his granddaughter. The wonder of that brief meeting remained with Elizabeth all her life.

There was no tiresome conversation, no dwelling on symptoms, but a succession of marvelous grown-up presents — a ruby ring, a sumptuous traveling case lined with maroon-colored silk and fitted with cut-glass flasks capped in gilt, a camel's hair traveling robe, rolled in its straps. The whole occasion was straight out of fairyland, dispelling all her resentment and despondency.

Elizabeth traveled to Paris to spend Christmas 1880 there. The doctors in Paris resorted to heroic measures to prevent a threatened permanent curvature of the spine. For two years Elizabeth lived strapped to a board, a complete invalid. Her character crystallized during this period into a patient inflexibility that would become her dominant trait. She never whined, and she tried to spread cheerfulness to those around her. Her fortitude and dignity earned her the family title of "Queen Bess."

Elizabeth returned to New York in the autumn of 1881, and while lying strapped in her apparatus at the Brevoort House she again enjoyed a brief visit from Sam Ward and a magical rain of presents. To the end of her life Sam remained in Elizabeth's memory as someone outside the bounds of ordinary humanity. By 1882 she could walk with crutches, and gradually she dispensed even with these, although periodically she had to use a cane, and she was never strong.

Cousin Mary Marshall had fortified Elizabeth's bent toward self-abnegation by inculcating resignation to God's will. She sadly stressed that Elizabeth must never even entertain the thought of marriage. So completely was this fact accepted by the family, any suggestion to the contrary would have come as a shock.

The same year that Elizabeth was released from total invalidism, however, Egerton Chanler died of a brain tumor. He was only eight. Alida, his special playmate, was so affected that for a while she seemed destined to follow her brother. During her slow return to health she formed a habit that she kept a secret. In her loneliness she would steal upstairs to one of the guest rooms, ordinarily forbidden to the children, and from a westward-facing bedroom she would watch the gorgeous colors of sunset in the clouds over the Catskills and weave romantic imaginings.

During this period Archie, who had progressed to Rugby and had now returned from England and entered Columbia College, also became mysteriously ill. Rokeby was kept in a state of tension for weeks, until the crisis of his unexplained illness passed and he slowly regained his vigor. Then, in February 1883, the family was stricken anew when Marion Chanler died suddenly at St. Paul's School in New Hampshire. In a contest with another boy about who could eat the most Turkish delight, Marion won, but spent the night vomiting in the bitter cold dormitory, thereby contracting pneumonia. Wintie, who by then was at Harvard, hastened to his brother's bedside and found him apparently past danger; but Marion died twenty-four hours later. He was only fourteen.

The calm faith of Mary Marshall helped to carry the surviving eight Chanlers through this melancholy period. By 1884 they were back on even keel, when word came that Grandfather Sam Ward had died in Italy. With him at the end had been his well-loved nephew and niece, the novelist F. Marion Crawford and Margaret ("Daisy") Terry, whom the Chanlers had met at Newport some time before.

Margaret and Alida spent much of their formative years in New York City, attending French class, dancing class, and so forth. Their Aunt Lina, wife of William B. Astor, Jr., was the undisputed ruler of New York's "Four Hundred." A ruthless maker and breaker of reputations, she saw to it that her "dreadfully countrified" Chanler nieces became a credit to her imperious court. Assisting in the transformative process were three other Astor matrons, the girls' Aunt Alida Carey, Aunt Laura Delano, and Aunt Augusta Astor, the wife of John Jacob III. The girls struggled through it all and by force of personality were not submerged.

5 | IDYLL IN ROME

Wintie Chanler was the first of the family to plunge into the hazards of marriage. This he did with the same cheerful abandon with which he had jumped through the glass door. Reverberations at Rokeby were correspondingly shattering. Wintie had given ample notice of his intention, and the family had done its best to deflect him, but opposition was the wrong way to influence Winthrop Chanler. Naturally headstrong, he was in love, and love has a logic of its own.

Grandfather Sam Ward unintentionally set things slowly in motion when in 1879 he had arranged a reunion of his sisters — Julia Ward Howe, Annie Ward Mailliard, and Louisa Ward Terry. Louisa had come from her home in Rome with her seventeen-year-old daughter, Margaret Terry, universally called Daisy. During the summer of 1880 Daisy met her Chanler cousins, and she thought Wintie quite the nicest young man she had ever encountered. The Terrys returned to Rome, Wintie put in four years of desultory industry at Harvard, and Daisy continued her music studies.

In college Wintie set his own pace. Amos Tuck French, another freshman in the class of 1885 who became Wintie's lifelong friend and correspondent, was quite mesmerized by young Chanler's jaunty man-of-the-worldliness, his English accent, his London clothes, his nonchalance, and his sparkling wit. Upper classmen might resent Wintie's "infernal cheek," such as joining in the steeplechase races at the country club in nearby Brookline, but such daring won Wintie popularity, and he was elected to the most exclusive of Harvard clubs, the Porcellian. Regarding his studies, Wintie was not above paying impoverished students to prepare papers for him, and he managed, by charm and adroitness, to avoid flunking out.

Amos French described an encounter that captures the competitive spirit that characterized Wintie's relationship with Archie. French was visiting Wintie one evening when Archie arrived. Ignoring French completely, the brothers immediately started arguing with each other, and it ended in a wrestling match on the floor of the billiard room. French was embarrassed and mystified. Wintie seemed to have resented being subordinate to his older brother; he dearly wanted to be head of the family, and he felt that Archie at times was deficient in the role. Archie's better showing in college irritated Wintie, as did Archie's greater height and his patrician stance; Wintie was short and slight in build.

In the spring of 1884, just before Wintie's final year at Harvard, Louisa Terry learned he was in England and invited him to visit the Terrys in Rome. In June he came. He was just short of twenty-one years old, abounding in vitality, carefree, and anxious to please.

Louisa had first married Thomas Crawford, the sculptor whose heroic statue tops the dome of the Capitol in Washington, and produced three children. After Thomas Crawford died, Louisa married Luther Terry, an American painter who had traveled to Rome in 1833 and elected to remain there permanently. Two children had come of this union — Daisy and Arthur.

Luther Terry possessed sufficient talent to win some portrait commissions, but Louisa, heiress to a comfortable fortune, had been the family's financial prop. However, the panic of the 1870s swept away most of Louisa's wealth, forcing the family to move into a cramped apartment. This comedown made a deep impression on teenaged Daisy Terry. She recalled resentfully her half-sisters' elaborate wedding trousseaus, the chestfuls of dainty lingerie that contrasted so painfully with her plain cotton underthings. Daisy promised herself that as far as possible she would henceforth exclude everything from her life that was ugly and repellent and poor.

The Terry children had been born and reared in Rome. They spoke Italian from infancy and had little in common with their parents' homeland. Yet they were not truly Italian either, but existed in a condition of rootlessness, at ease in, yet slightly foreign to, both America and Europe. Daisy Terry had always lived in the midst of art and artists, so she considered them quite as normal, useful, and unexceptional as senators or priests. This point of view, of course, was incomprehensible to most Americans of the time.

Only a few weeks before Wintie's arrival, Grandfather Ward had died, and the family was in mourning, but Wintie Chanler was not equipped to mourn long, and his effect upon Daisy was instantaneous.

"Hazel eyes full of a merry light, irrepressibly curly brown hair, an air of great good breeding and courage in his handsome face, with a constant ripple of fun playing over it" — that was how Daisy saw her cousin. He did not mind any of the drawbacks of summer in the city, neither the heat nor the fleas. In search of a little coolness the family took him to Tivoli for nights of "moonlight on the cypresses, nightingales in the laurels, soft summer wind blowing the spray of waterfalls on our faces . . . days of being utterly happy in the moment — young and lazy — the sweet, warm sense of being alive." So Daisy wrote in her diary.

Wintie gaily prolonged the holiday by inviting the whole family to spend a month with him at a villa he rented at Rimini, on the Adriatic coast. There Daisy, more matured by her education and environment than her American cousin, began to feel that she was "preparing to bid farewell to youth," as she phrased it — in plain speech, she was contemplating marriage with this enchanting young man whose middle name was Astor.

Wintie, however, was simply having a wonderful time; he never looked for complications. A month of fun and off he dashed to visit relatives in Germany, then hastened back to Harvard for his final year, while Daisy waited for letters that did not come.

Two years passed before Wintie returned; but in the summer of 1886 he went abroad again. He had come of age, taken control of his personal inheritance, and was now himself a guardian for his younger brothers and sisters. With Archie for company, Wintie was doing Europe as a man of independent means, out for a good time.

At Vallombrosa the two men stopped to visit with the Terrys. There were no intrusive tourists, just a few old acquaintances of the Terrys rusticating in the country hotel. Life moved placidly, time drifting by, and it seemed like Archie was on the point of yielding to the romantic spell of the place and his cousin. But at the close of summer it was Winthrop and Daisy who became engaged.

The news was flashed to Rokeby faster than by letter, but on September 15 Wintie wrote to Mary Marshall:

"My dear Cousin Mary:
"You will have heard the news . . . so there is no need of my dwelling on it. . . . I hope you are pleased & even if you are not now, I know you will be as soon as you see & know Daisy. What a lucky man I am! . . . We intend

to be married on New Year's day if possible & then spend the rest of the winter in the south of Spain. That is all I can write now for I have so many letters to write. Love to all the kids & give us your blessing . . . By the way, you may be surprised that it is me & not Archie who is going to marry Daisy. The reason is easily explained. Archie made a mistake in his own feelings. I know I have not."

But there was an obstacle: Daisy Terry was Roman Catholic. And to compound her undesirability at Rokeby, she was a communicant of the Roman Church not by reason of birth, and hence absolved of personal predilection for gross error, but by her own choice, fervently expressed.

Wintie's announced intention to marry a Catholic created a shudder of revulsion. Catholics were tolerated in the kitchen, but in the front of the house they were definitely out of place. Wintie knew the storm his choice would raise, and he punctiliously fulfilled every family obligation in an attempt to lighten the blow. Coming home prior to the wedding especially to mollify them, he found the family sorrowful and immovable. Not only did they object to his choice, they feared his own eventual contamination. As far as Wintie was concerned, the Chanlers were Episcopalians traditionally and that settled the question. Nevertheless, when he headed back to Rome the family loaded him down with tracts bearing titles like *Plain Reasons Against Joining the Church of Rome*.

While Wintie was gone, Daisy had made her own overtures to the relatives at Rokeby, but her letters, while well meant, were stiff and self-conscious. The equally reserved responses she received did not alter her determination to marry Winthrop Chanler quickly, and Wintie was as eager as she.

Three dispensations were required: to marry during Advent, to overcome the issue of consanguinity, and to decide the faith of future children. Wintie declined to agree that all children be reared in the faith of their mother, but a compromise was reached whereby the daughters would be reared as Catholics, and the sons as Protestants. Wintie's charm and Daisy's determination succeeded in overcoming the other two obstacles, and on December 16, 1886, they were married in the French church of St. Louis in Rome. After a honeymoon that began in Algiers and wandered back across Europe, the couple traveled home to America, reaching Rokeby in June. There they were accorded a decidedly chilly welcome.

Mary Marshall was narrowly religious, but she was resolved to do injustice to no one. Rather than countenance any ill-speaking, she laid down the rule that Daisy must not be mentioned by the children among themselves. Daisy herself stood up to the ordeal of meeting her husband's embattled relatives courageously, supported by the poise which her more extensive experience of the world gave her.

To her the Chanlers seemed a race of barbarians laboring under a strange delusion about their importance in the scheme of things. Their manners were countrified, the girls dressed like dowdies, and the boys were rude and bumptious, more taken up with their barnyard pets than with things of the intellect or gracious living. To a musician with Daisy's training, the Rokeby repertory of one hundred and twenty-six songs and hymns was pathetically ludicrous, while their ignorance of contemporary political, artistic, literary, or scientific trends was appalling. Their behavior shocked her: at dinner one time Robert burst out that hairs from the English governess's wig were falling into his soup, Daisy squirmed, but nobody else paid any heed.

With regard to Daisy's religion, Miss Marshall bore her presence in prim silence. The boys paid the matter less regard; young Alida was secretly thrilled, without daring to say so; Elizabeth was smoothly polite but inwardly disapproving; but seventeen-year-old Margaret was irreconcilable. Margaret was not introspective; she was practical and expressed herself best by action. For her the barrier between herself and the superstitions of Rome was not to be explained away or talked out of existence; no sophistry could justify so gross and perverse a departure from truth.

The appearance itself of Rokeby irritated Daisy. The heavy, tasteless furniture was clumsily placed, and the finest room in the house, the drawing room, was never used except for funerals. While the family was at Lake George, Daisy carried out a rearrangement more to her own taste. She opened up the drawing room, brought in her piano, added flowers and book stands, and converted it into a pleasant sitting and music room. When the family returned, she was in possession. After their initial shock, the family generally approved the change, except for Margaret. To her the drawing room had been sacred to the memory of her parents and Daisy's innovations were a desecration. When the family gathered there of an evening for music and cards, Margaret would withdraw across the hall and sulk in the "home parlor" in silent reproach.

Wintie Chanler took both his wife's irritation and his sister's obstinacy light-heartedly. Riding, shooting, tennis, or swimming kept him occupied while he and Daisy awaited the birth of their first child. Julia Ward Howe came from Boston for the event, and under her auspices the baby arrived on September 30, 1887, and was promptly christened Laura in honor of the Chanlers' rich, childless Great-Aunt Laura Delano. But when the christening was performed by a Catholic priest, Margaret was horrified, and she told her brother Lewis that it would have been kinder to have "smothered the little creature in its innocence at birth." She refused to remain in the same room with the child, and if it were brought in, she would walk out. Yet she confessed to Elizabeth that she loved Laura more than anything the world, but couldn't show it. At night she would steal into the nursery and kiss the baby as it slept.

Daisy found one uncensorious friend at Rokeby — fifteen-year-old Bob Chanler. Bob had become something of a family problem; unruly, boisterous, erratic, he seemed incapable of formal learning, but he was discovered to have a surprising ability to draw. He was also enraptured by Daisy's piano playing. He would listen enthralled to Bach fugues as she played them over and over. When she tried to find out what fascinated him in this intricate music, which was not relished by his brothers, he stammered an explanation that it revealed to him a world of beauty. Beauty, she gathered, meant to Bob the rhythmic pattern — constant change recurring within a fixed frame. A Bach fugue meant colors to him, he said; it made him think of things he had never thought of before. Then he would dash off to hunt rabbits, unwilling or unable to tell her more.

At the approach of winter, a milder climate than Rokeby's was recommended for Daisy and little Laura, and in November the Winties moved to Washington to sample the social and intellectual atmosphere prevailing along the Potomac. For Wintie the location promised to be ideal — cosmopolitan society in town, and plenty of riding and fox hunting in the nearby Virginia hills. But in those hills was developing a drama that would involve him deeply.

6 | THE WORLD BECKONS, AND GOODBYE TO COUSIN MARY

Meanwhile, Archie Chanler had earned his MA at Columbia in 1884 and was admitted to the New York bar a year later. He had hired an impecunious but brilliant student to assist him with his studies. Michael Pepin went on to international celebrity as a scientist. In May 1885 Archie set sail for Europe as a man of independent means. The idea of practicing law bored him, and he embarked upon the grand tour as the proper finishing education for a gentleman of the *beau monde*. He had already adventured out West, where for several months he had stalked the elusive Apache chief Geronimo with the troops of General George Crook. Then wheeling about, Archie left New York for London, amply provided with introductions, fortified by awareness that he was young, rich, and privileged, and attended by a valet to take care of all the "beastly details."

In England the doors of the great world swung open to him at the touch of well-placed relatives. Also, the influence of his Grandfather Ward was still potent. With nonchalance Archie informed his brother Willie, stuck at home:

"I took some letters I had from Mr. Mailliard to Lord Rosebery. He was a great friend of Grandpa Ward's. Ld R wrote me a very nice note & I found him to be, as far as I could judge from first sight, a very pleasant & clever man. Lady R was a Miss Rothschild, enormously rich & enormously fat."

To be sought out by the elegant, fashionable, and fastidious Earl of Rosebery, dandy, dilettante, future prime minister, was a compliment falling to few transatlantic travelers, and Archie did his best to live up to the distinction. He attended a reception at the Foreign Office and saw the Prince and Princess of Wales — he a "good natured looking fat rascal & wore a gorgeous uniform. The Princess is very handsome & looks very nice."

The young women caught his eye, and he conceded that they had lovely figures, but thought they could not compare with American women in style or looks. Their coiffure he did not like. "They are doing their hair in the most unbecoming way. It looks like a coil of overgrown angle worms at the back of their head."

Day after day of delectable entertainments filled June and July, then he sped to Paris by the night train, tormented by fleas. After paying homage to the Louvre and Napoleon's tomb, he explored the Bois in a rented carriage, voting it a "very pretty place but don't equal the Central Park." The summer was topped off by a visit to the Terrys at Sorrento, swimming, sailing, and lying in the sun; the "clear metallic look" of the air reminded him of "a cool clear day at Newport."

In September 1885 he returned home, only to take off again to the West Indies and South America, in the company of Wintie, young Oliver Hazard Perry Belmont, and two others. They stopped at St. Thomas and Martinique and sampled the exotic foods of the tropics, including yams and bread fruit. "A yam cooked looks like a potato and tastes like castile soap," was Archie's verdict, while bread fruit tasted "exactly like the mash of ground corn soaked in water which we feed chickens."

After two unsatisfactory months in Mexico, the group traveled to Caracas, where Wintie and one companion took off for Europe, while the other three moved on to Panama. There the heat and primitive discomforts were too much for Belmont and his friend, and they sailed north, leaving Archie to press on to Ecuador. He made the hazardous trip inland to Quito, across mountains, through rain forests, past the forbidding peaks of Chimborazo and Cotopaxi. In Quito the hotel was clean and comfortable, the food excellent and amazingly cheap.

Then it was back to Europe and the serious business of life. Archie settled in Paris, where he attended lectures at the Sorbonne and attempted to bring his baritone voice up to concert level. Several months of strenuous endeavor convinced him that the task was futile, so he abandoned the experiment and advised his sister Margaret, who was on a similar quest, to do the same.

Returning to the United States, he dropped by Newport and Rokeby, then put in a season enjoying his numerous New York clubs — the Union, Century, Democratic, Manhattan, Tennis & Racquet, and that most socially exclusive assemblage, the Knickerbocker Club. He took up amateur boxing, for which he showed marked proficiency.

In 1887 he drifted toward Washington, where the Wintie Chanlers were establishing themselves in a house at 1347 Connecticut Avenue. While visiting in the Virginia countryside, Archie was invited to spend Christmas at Castle Hill, the ancestral seat of the Rives family, in the fashionable horse country near Charlottesville.

Archie had met the eldest Rives daughter, Amélie, at Newport during the previous summer. It had been her first season, and she had attracted much comment by her extraordinary beauty and reportedly extraordinary ways. Amélie Rives had artistic and literary talents; she had had a poem published when she was fifteen, and she was already at work on a novel; Archie was told that he would figure as the model for the hero. Shortly after Christmas, he headed back to Paris, to resume attendance at the Sorbonne.

Then on February 29, 1888, Mary Marshall died. In his diary Wintie wrote: "Cousin Mary Marshall died on Wednesday Feb 29th after an operation for gall stone. I went to New York on Thursday the first. Found the girls [Margaret and Alida] very brave, but looking pretty well worn out. Funeral on Saturday . . . On Tuesday night left New York with the two girls. We are going to keep them with us for a week or two. . . ."

Archie and Elizabeth Chanler, both in Europe, were notified by cable. All the Chanlers were keenly sensible of their loss. Cousin Mary's calm perseverance in the performance of duty, her devotion to principles, and her patient piety would remain with her charges for life; unfortunately, her death also removed one restraint on their tempestuous temperaments.

What to do with fifteen-year-old Alida, who was sentimental, and eighteen-year-old Margaret, who was practical and opinionated, posed a problem for the guardians, Wintie included. Rokeby without the presence of a chaperone was unsuitable. Temporarily the girls were placed in the care of the Rutherfurd Stuyvesants in New York, and Wintie was released to go on with a program of serious reading which he had inaugurated earlier that year.

As his diary attests, however, Wintie was distracted by the acquisition of a horse, something that would recur again and again during his life. On February 4, 1888, his first diary entry reads in part: "Today made inquiries about a horse at Burne's the feed man. He said I ought to get one for $200." And on April 16, "Bought a bay gelding . . . this A.M. for $190," only to amend this three days later: "The new horse has corns & contract hoof but goes sound. Still think he'll do."

Other notable events Wintie recorded included entertaining his great-aunt Julia Ward Howe when she came to Washington to lecture on Greek literature and a hectic weekend when Willie Chanler came down from Harvard with two friends: one "spent Sat night in jail for simple drunk," the other pal was "bounced from Kernans theater," and Willie himself was "slugged by the barkeeper for calling him Gustave."

Acquisition of a horse had been in preparation for a riding trip through western Virginia, one feature of which was to be a stopover at Castle Hill to meet the now suddenly celebrated Amélie Rives. Her novella, *The Quick or the Dead?* had just been published in *Lippincott's Magazine* and was creating a furor. Not for years had a book so shocked, scandalized, and enthralled the reading public; its sales soared. What made the story immensely important to the Chanlers, however, was that Archie really had been the model for the hero.

Wintie recorded his impressions in his diary: "Finished Amélie Rives' 'Quick or Dead.' A most sensual bit of rot. Presumably a love story but not a decent bit of love making in it. Distinctly horrid, & when one thinks it is written by a young girl it fairly makes one sick. Brog [Archie] is the hero — very well drawn. Wrote & told him my opinion of the book but reserved my opinion of the authoress. . . ."

7 | A DUBIOUS CONQUEST

Whatever Wintie thought of her writing, Amélie Rives had respectable ancestors. Her grandfather, William Cabell Rives, had studied law under Thomas Jefferson, served as a United States senator, and twice been minister to France. Her father, Alfred Landon Rives, had served as chief of engineers in the Virginia forces during the Civil War, and in 1887 and 1888 he was in Panama supervising railroad construction.

Amélie herself had been born in Richmond in the midst of the war (her godfather was Robert E. Lee). Her education had been erratic, but Amélie had a quick intelligence, great sensitivity, and an early facility with words. She would shut herself up for days and pour out a stream of poems and stories, some of which found their way into print. In 1887 a book of her tales, *A Brother to Dragons*, was published, drawing some critical acclaim. Public curiosity was piqued by the rumors of her bewitching beauty as well as her odd ways. As a small child, she was said to have frightened a playmate once by asking: "Do you think if I drank a whole cupful of warm, bubbly blood, I would see a real fairy?"

When *The Quick or the Dead?* appeared in April 1888, Amélie became a celebrity overnight. Her book was so deliciously scandalous that it sold 300,000 copies, an enormous sale for the day. The plot concerns the emotional writhings of a hysterical young widow (remarkably like the author) who is torn between orgiastic craving for the embraces of her deceased husband and carnal attraction to his flesh-and-blood cousin and physical double. The heroine swings from whimpering submission to "pantherish" paroxysms of passion in the privacy of her bedroom, while wavering between the living and the dead wooer. The setting was recognizably

Castle Hill, and the dual hero (real and spectral) was recognizably John Armstrong Chanler.

Archie Chanler had been decidedly attracted to Miss Amélie Rives at Newport in the summer of 1887, and that autumn one object of his visit to Virginia had been the hope of seeing her again. The hospitable Riveses had invited him to Castle Hill, and the acquaintance had ripened. But it is hardly surprising that the idea of having the Chanler name associated with such frenetic frothings was distasteful to Winthrop Astor Chanler.

It was with a well-settled prejudice, therefore, that Wintie and his cavalcade cantered up to the stately columns of Castle Hill to meet in person the perpetrator of all this "sensual rot." The visitors were received hospitably, and Wintie's wife, Daisy, described the effect Amélie produced, especially on the men, as "dazzling." Amélie had, she said, "the largest dark blue-grey eyes; the longest black lashes; the most wonderful halo of loosely curled ash-blonde hair; very regular features, and a shapely, well-curved mouth." The only defect that Daisy could detect was a slight lack of height, but this shortcoming was artfully concealed by the "romantic white tea gown that draped and flowed from her shoulders in the most becoming fashion." Daisy readily paid the bewitching twenty-five-year-old the tribute of calling her "a siren, a goddess, perhaps a genius. . . ."

In the Astor connection one name was never spoken: Henry Astor. Henry, the third son of William B. Astor, detested society and loathed business. A great hulking fellow, given to ungovernable rages, he liked the country and uncouth ways. For years he had lived in a gardener's cottage on the Rokeby grounds, despised by his brothers, despaired of by his parents, and avoided by his sisters, but acclaimed as a good fellow in every alehouse for miles around.

In 1871 Henry fell in love with Malvina Dinehart, the buxom daughter of a farmer across the river from Rokeby, and suddenly, without notifying his family, he married her. His brother William raced up from the city to prevent the marriage but arrived too late. Added to the ignominy of the match was the mortification that Malvina had retained her dower rights — the only woman who ever married an Astor in the direct line and kept them. The practice was to settle a handsome sum on the Astor men's brides in exchange for waiving their dower rights in the Astor estate; thereby control of the Astor wealth was kept firmly in Astor hands. Henry's action was considered as a kind of criminal defiance, and in anger his father left him a paltry $30,000 inheritance. Henry was in no way impoverished, for his grandfather, the founder of the fortune, had left him a quarter interest in a Manhattan farm which came to be valued at $20,000,000.

Henry Astor and his wife were cut off from all recognition by his immediate family. His formidable income was remitted without comment from the Astor estate office every quarter, and he would deposit the checks whenever he got around to going to the bank, which was not often. The country people liked him, though they suspected that he was crazy. Once or twice the Chanler children had been taken to gaze upon their mythical great-uncle, but the acquaintance went no further. As a consequence of Henry's actions, whenever some marriage occurred without due formality and previous family discussion, his specter would arise to haunt the entire connection.

In May 1888 Wintie began to hear rumors that his brother was seriously enamored. The truth, though Wintie did not know it, was that Amélie, having refused Archie's repeated proposals several times, had finally agreed to marry. Now that they were engaged, Archie and Amélie were debating how to break the news and avoid the rash of publicity that probably would follow.

Late in May 1888 Archie, newly returned to New York from Paris, wrote to his sister Margaret, who was at Rokeby, saying that he wished to consult her on an important matter. "Don't show this [letter] to anyone," he cautioned. "Just quietly come to town. Tell Lewis I want him to bring you. Don't tell Alida, she isn't needed. . . . Just say to the Winties & Alida (if they question you closely) that I wanted to see you in town & Lewis can bring you down."

What seventeen-year-old could resist. Proud of her brother's confidence, Margaret met him in New York and continued on with him to Castle Hill. And there she fell completely under Amélie's spell.

On June 1 a brief announcement appeared in a Richmond newspaper, was picked up by a newspaper in Baltimore, and by June 3 *The New York Times* ran the headline "Miss Amélie Rives to Marry." Her fiancé was identified, with name misspelled, as "Mr. Archie Chandler, great-grandson of John Jacob Astor." The wedding, it added, would take place in the autumn.

Meanwhile, no word from Archie arrived at Rokeby, and speculation grew feverish. Gossip had Miss Rives also engaged to a Mr. Coolidge of Boston, but then, as the column said, ". . . it has been hard to decide which of the small army with whose individual members the fair authoress, it is understood, has carried on a more or less desperate flirtation for some years, she would finally choose. . . ." A notorious and desperate flirt about to be grafted onto the family tree! This was not the sort of thing the Chanlers could face with equanimity. To make matters worse, Archie unwisely consented to be interviewed by the *New York Herald*, while snubbing other papers. This of course produced exactly the effect Archie had hoped to circumvent — a rash of highly fanciful, vulgar publicity.

The temperature at Rokeby had shot up to the boiling point when another laconic dispatch in the *Times* stated that a marriage license had been issued on June 13 at Charlottesville to "Amélie Rives, authoress, and Mr. John A. Chandler of New York." And the very next day, June 14, 1888 — without a word of notification to any Chanler, Astor, Winthrop, Stuyvesant, Rutherfurd, White, or any other blood relative of the bridegroom — the wedding was celebrated at Castle Hill.

Wintie fairly erupted when he read the newspaper accounts. These made no attempt to disguise the surprise which the hurry-up wedding had occasioned in Virginia, inasmuch as "some weeks ago it was authoritatively announced that the marriage would take place 'in the fall.'" Only one newspaper mentioned the presence of "Miss Margaret Livingston Chanler," without further identification. The bride's father was in Panama so could not attend, it was explained, but he had been informed of the wedding in a "fully descriptive cable." To the Chanlers no message had been sent.

The family was humiliated, and Wintie was too angry to trust himself to write to Archie immediately. He fumed for five days, and then wrote to Margaret, in response to a naively rapturous letter from her:

"If ever two people deserved a good spanking, those two are Brog [Archie] and you. Of course, you were but as putty in his hands, and backed him up in his absurd mysteries — but still your own commonsense, if no other feeling, should have told you that he was quite wrong, in what he did. . . . All of us at Rokeby heard it from an outsider & the daily papers."

On receipt of her pitiful letter of exculpation, he scolded her again:

"Your reasons for not letting us know are precisely what we all supposed them to have been. Of course we all knew perfectly well that you wanted to send us word & that Archie would not let you. . . . The whole trouble is that he apparently looked upon the family in the same light as the public — with a strong preference for the public. . . . In the most important epoch of his life he has made a fool of himself and hurt his wife in the eyes of the public. . . . "

Hoping to calm the strife, Daisy Chanler wrote congratulating Archie on his and Amélie's happiness, but pointing out that "you do not seem to realize in the least how very keenly we all felt your treating us as if we were mere outsiders to be classed with reporters and other noxious and inquisitive bipeds. The news of your marriage was known to hundreds of people before it reached us. Aunt Caroline Astor was here . . . and said: 'Well, I hear Archie is being married.' We naturally poohpooned the thing as a newspaper story. The next day the 'Herald,' 'Times,' etc., confirmed the fait accompli, not until Monday did we get any news from Virginia and in the meantime we had a stream of visitors who could none of them fail to be surprised at our being left so totally in the dark. . . . Mr. Bostwick has just returned from Baltimore, quite worn out with dodging questions as to why none of the family were present, and he told Wintie last night that you really ought to know how the farmers and people here are talking. . . ."

There was just one way to save the situation, Daisy advised, and that was for Archie and Amélie to put in an appearance at Rokeby quickly, and in this way counteract the talk of a family division.

When at length Wintie did write to Archie, he was bitingly sarcastic:

"Dear Brog: Just a line from an outsider to disturb the bliss of Armida's garden. Ask for and read the two letters I have written to Margaret in the name of the Rokebyites and use your own judgment about repeating the contents. Love to Armida. We don't want any cuttings from the Herald or any other of your friends the journalists.

"P.S. — The weather here is very warm, 93 in the shade today. I wonder if you wouldn't find it cool in spite of the thermometer."

To which Archie instantly replied:

"Dear Wintie: I have just received your note of June 21st, and I shall want an apology from you in writing before anything further can pass between us."

The honeymooners put off their visit to Rokeby for several weeks, not because Archie was reluctant, but because Amélie begged off. Margaret Chanler had left Castle Hill aglow with hero worship of her glamorous sister-in-law, and Amélie had posted letter after letter to her, counting her as the one firm ally in the strangers' camp. Not in fiction alone did Amélie's flawless penmanship flow in torrid, torrential phrases. Writing from Castle Hill on June 30, two weeks after the wedding, she poured out her mood to her "dear, dear Sister":

"You will never know my Margaret, the comfort your little note brought me. It was like a kiss on a bare and aching heart, and the tears came into my eyes and stayed there as I read it. God has given you to me Margaret — has given us to each other, and you do not know how humbly thankful I feel to Him, or how I think of you with almost every breath I draw. . . . God has let you save me from the very pit of gloom, and grief, and terror. . . ." And so on. In a deluge of words covering ten, fifteen, twenty-four pages, were strewn forebodings — premonitions of some desperate ordeal, "some terrific blow," that they all were going to be called upon to undergo soon. "Darling, darling Margaret — I wish your dear strong arms were tight about me. . . ." Two days later came another anguished appeal — "Oh! Margaret, pray for me!")

By the middle of July Margaret, who had sailed for Europe with Alida, was being pursued by such fears as, "How I wish you or someone who loves me could be there [Rokeby] when I first go. . . . I dread Daisy. I am not afraid of anyone, but I am afraid of treachery, oh! so tremblingly afraid. . . . I never had anything quite so distasteful to do in my life, but duties aren't to be shirked, are they dear? . . . Please write whenever you can dearest, & not on thin paper. It hurts my poor old eyes so dreadfully."

Amélie's letters to Margaret, especially, were filled with insinuations that she had given herself in thrall to a madman. Of course an acute observer on the scene would have noticed that Amélie's actual physical being seemed unaffected, her grasp on the reins being firm and emphatic when she put her stallion Usurper over a five-barred gate; yet in her letters she was a poor thing, a madonna of sorrows:

"Margaret, tell me as though you were my own sister as well as Archie's, have you ever thought in the bottom of your soul, that Archie's mind was not quite right? He laughs at me in such a dreadful way at times, until I am crying & trembling with terror. And the more I cry & beg him to stop or to tell me what is the matter, the more he laughs. Oh! Margaret, Margaret, write to me darling. Pray for me."

There had indeed been scenes between these two high-strung, sensitive, imaginative personalities. Archie's mockery at times had driven his own sisters to tears, and Amélie was not attuned to the violent horseplay of Rokeby. She had been all her life the star of a never-ending drama, supported and encouraged by her adoring relatives. Both she and Archie were strong-willed, and neither had practiced self-discipline.

A change came in August, when Amélie and Archie descended upon Newport. Young, beautiful, and author of a bestseller, she basked in a blaze of social homage. Archie was proud of her. The ordeal of Rokeby still lay ahead, and fortunately Amélie didn't know that Wintie had written his friend Amos Tuck French: "My brother J. Armstrong Amélie Rives Chanler and his consort are expected up here for a few days, and I am reading 'Titus Andronicus,' 'The Curse of Kehama,' and 'Ten Nights in a Bar Room' so as to have a little ready conversation of a literary turn."

About October 1, Amélie and Archie reached Rokeby, and her siren spell produced its usual effect: Rokeby was conquered. Wintie was still nursing his grudge against Archie, but the visit passed off famously. Far from proving a "dragon," Daisy Chanler got along excellently with her sister-in-law; both were intellectual, both were widely read, with similar cultural interests; both loved worldly society.

As for the Chanler boys, Willie and Lewis were bowled over by the sweeping eyelashes and the melting gaze, while sixteen-year-old Bob wrote to his sisters: "Amélie has arrived. She was not feeling very well & did not come to dinner; I know that I have not seen anybody that can hold a candell to her in the way of looks, & besides she being very religius, I do not know what more we can want in the way of a sister in law."

Lewis reported similarly, although with more restraint, as became a nineteen-year-old enrolled in Columbia's school of law. He had met the bridal couple in New York on their way to Rokeby, and had dined with them, Wintie, and Willie at Delmonico's.

Archie's report to those overseas was jubilant: "All goes well. Amélie has had success wherever she has been. . . . You don't know how delighted I am to be able to say that Amélie is a success with all here. It is the greatest relief to her & to me."

But the Indian summer of harmony did not last. Word came that Archie and his wife had decided to spend the winter apart. Although they both insisted that the separation would be temporary only, the tension it bespoke was apparent. Margaret got the first word, from Amélie, who wrote on November 15 from Castle Hill:

"My dearest, sweet Margaret: I am so glad to be able to tell you, that the worst is over, for the present at least. Archie agrees fully with me that for the present it is much best for him to go abroad without me. I am not going to write of him any more after this letter, because I want to be perfectly loyal to him. I had to tell you, so that you would not think me shirking my duty. . . . I am to be a prisoner (God knows a willing one!) in my old home. I have promised Archie to sign a paper to the effect that I will not go away from Castle Hill for two years, also to sign one giving him permission to remain abroad two years. . . . Never let him dream that I have told you this Margaret. Just accept his statement that I am staying here to write a book this winter for which I have been offered $25,000. It is true, but of course only part of the truth. . . ."

Archie was rather more straightforward with his sisters. He wrote on the eve of his sailing: ". . . it is undoubtedly best for Amélie to stop here this winter both on account of the rest it will be to her nerves . . . & for her writing. I ought to, and want to, see you all, so I go abroad. The rest to my nerves will be most refreshing after the strain I have been on since I first set eyes on Amélie . . . People will of course talk and say 'separation' & prophesy trouble. What people say is a matter of infinite indifference to both of us."

Of course unsought advice was showered upon the newlyweds, and Amélie's letters took on a tinge of asperity when she assured Margaret that ". . . it is disastrous and impossible for anyone, no matter how true and loving, to advise a woman in regard to her husband, or a man in regard to his wife. . . . Archie and I understand each other absolutely. You can leave our future to God and to us."

8 | THE FAMILY SCATTERS, TO TRIUMPHS AND ADVENTURES

William Astor Chanler had emerged from the chrysalis stage of growing up endowed with more energy and drive than most of his energetic clan. At restless eighteen, Willie was posing problems for his older brothers, both guardians by then. Wintie did his utmost to keep Willie in the path of virtue so deftly avoided by Wintie himself at the same age. When Willie rebelled at a summer of cramming for the Phillips Exeter examinations, Wintie lectured him roundly: "Make friends with Virgil, Homer, and Chauvenet for the next few weeks and try a little self-denial."

While Wintie went off to watch the America's Cup, Willie did apply himself — just enough to pass his tests. But a few weeks at Exeter demonstrated that the place was not for him, and in the spring of 1886 he went south to hunt in the Florida Everglades. The rigors of wilderness life he found entirely to his liking.

Certainly it was a far cry from the placidity of Rokeby, where sister Elizabeth reported such amenities as "the excitement of this week has been a fair in Mrs. Aspinwall's Sunday school house. They have some pretty things for sail [sic] & the prices, wonderful to say, are very reasonable. . . . We are reading Mansfield Park by Miss Austen & like it as much as her best."

In the Everglades, Willie wrestled alligators and longed for bigger game.

That autumn Willie passed the Harvard entrance examinations, and the guardians voted to give him the same allowance in college that Wintie had received, $1,600, plus money to furnish his rooms and pay a tutor if necessary.

When Willie left for Harvard, he took with him a fourteen-year-old lad named George E. Galvin, the son of the gardener at Steen Valetje, the Delano estate adjoining Rokeby. George's father sent him off with a simple command: "You go with Willie Chanler and do everything he says." That became young Galvin's program for living. He turned his hand to whatever was required; he slept in Willie's rooms, ran errands for him, shared in his escapades, and filled the roles of valet, secretary, and confidant.

At Harvard Willie proved a desultory student, reading for his own enjoyment and taking nothing too seriously, unless it was his developing passion for horses. He was elected to his brother Wintie's club, the Porcellian, and his collegiate ambition became to play on the college polo team, but the expense of providing horses was an obstacle. In the summer of 1887, however, he circumvented that handicap by making a trip to Arizona with his brother Archie and rounding up a carload of wild mustangs and shipping them to Boston. There they were broken to saddle, and enough were sold profitably to pay expenses.

On June 11, 1888, just three days before Archie and Amélie married, Willie became twenty-one and gained his freedom. Without ado, the sophomore bade Harvard goodbye. He was out for adventure, and in December he sailed for England at the start of a lifelong quest for danger and excitement. With him he took George Galvin.

For the Chanlers, 1888 was proving to be the year of dispersal. When Mary Marshall died, the guardians had been confronted by the problem of the four remaining minor children — Lewis, Margaret, Robert, and Alida. Elizabeth, having come of age in 1887, was on her own, accountable to nobody for the use she made of her considerable income. This was intensifying her natural self-reliance, as it would also in the case of her sisters. The guardians determined that Margaret and Alida should be entered in Miss Sewell's school on the Isle of Wight, the same that Elizabeth had attended. Archie volunteered to see his sisters safely bestowed, and in a burst of generosity the guardians allotted both girls special allowances to pay for "gloves and ribbons." Margaret was granted seventy dollars a month for this purpose, and Alida twenty dollars, but then Margaret was expected to share. Lewis Chanler, studying law at Columbia at this time, was allowed seventy dollars a month for "clothes, amusements & traveling expenses," while Robert, at home, was forced to content himself with fifty dollars.

In London Archie, Willie, Margaret, Alida, and Elizabeth all gathered for a grand family reunion at Christmas, while at Rokeby that year the outlook was rather bleak, with five members of the family absent. Daisy and Wintie were at the estate, marking time until they should return to Rome in the spring, and Robert and Mr. Bostwick were with them. Lewis came up from the city on the weekends, for he loved Rokeby and its countryside and spent only such time in New York as was unavoidable. But despite the depleted family, it was the set wish of those on hand to celebrate Christmas as it always had been celebrated there. The ritual was feudal and traditional, and to share it with those absent Wintie started a Christmas letter to the "dear girls" on December 17: "The baby is to have a small Xmas tree to which all the children on the place are to be invited. They will receive sundry presents & their parents will drink a glass of champagne, munch a slice of cake & pocket $5.00 with my blessings. . . . D[aisy] & Robert are upstairs playing billiards. Mr. B. also above reading the New York Times & trying to find out why Harrison was elected [President]. . . . Tomorrow is a guardians meeting which I attend. Jex has the mange and has been banished until cured. . . . Robert goes to church every Sunday & Lewis ditto when here. All are well & send love & greeting. Affectionately, W."

As the winter progressed, Wintie grew restless. To occupy the time, he reopened his diary: "The house in Washington is to let for 5 months. . . . We are living at Rokeby with Robert & Mr. B. The girls are in the Isle of Wight under Miss Sewell's wing. Archie & Willie are also abroad. Amélie is at Castle Hill. We, that is D[aisy] & I, go abroad in Feb. or Mar. for several months. . . . I am reading Pepys Diary which D. gave me for Xmas & have finished the first Volume."

Decidedly, country life was not gay. On January 12 Wintie wrote: "Got up at 9:30 as usual. I must contrive to rise earlier . . . Walked with D. a while & then wrote [a letter] about Cliff Lawn, which does badly, not paying expenses even. . . . After luncheon walked to Red Hook & saw Parson Lambert about the girl from the Home [St. Margaret's orphanage] & told him how inefficient & ill taught she is."

Feeling stultified by the stagnant life, Wintie and family sailed for Europe on March 30. With them was Robert, nominally in the care of Mr. Bostwick, to continue his education abroad. Robert was seventeen, big and virile. He had romped with the village and farm children all his life, and his popularity, especially with the girls, had caused comment. There had been whispers, quickly squelched, connecting him with one of the farmers' daughters who had been married off with suspicious suddenness and had produced an early child. The family was uneasy: there must be no more misalliances like Henry Astor's.

Though scattered, the family remained in close touch with each other. Margaret and Alida were at Miss Sewell's, while Elizabeth stayed with the Henry Whites in London. Through White, Elizabeth was presented to Queen Victoria at one of the queen's last drawing rooms, and her "very American" disregard of etiquette made a minor stir in diplomatic circles. Each debutante, as she was named, was supposed to step forward, curtsey to the queen, and pass across to the other side of the room. Elizabeth intensely disliked to be jostled or touched. The presentation line was moving slowly, and at her turn a court functionary nudged her and hissed, "Hurry!" Instantly Elizabeth froze, and forgetting all she had rehearsed, strode across the room, omitting the curtsey. Fortunately at the same moment Elizabeth stepped forward, Victoria's veil became disarranged, and her ladies moved to screen her while repairs were made, and the courtiers glanced aside. Thus the American girl's omission either passed unnoticed or was put down to consummate tact. The story brightened diplomatic gossip and even reached Rokeby, where Lewis wrote excitedly, "Just think, I heard it was in Town Topics!"

Archie had moved on to Paris, but shortly headed back to the United States. At Castle Hill he found all calm, the heat generated by clashing temperaments having dissipated, and in early April 1889 Amélie and Archie sailed for England.

From the moment they landed, they were caught up in a whirl of social activity. Amélie was the sensation of the season, the brightest literary, political, and artistic lights competing for her smiles. Hardy took her aside to congratulate her personally on her new novella, *Virginia of Virginia*; Meredith declared her eyes of a blue so deep as to suggest purple. Oscar Wilde was infatuated by the fair Virginian and gave her a copy of *The Happy Prince* inscribed: "London — a rose-red July, '89."

The incense being burned in honor of his wife sometimes irritated the nostrils of Archie Chanler; he deemed it in excessively bad taste. Week after week he found himself at dinners and receptions, all but ignored, while Amélie was the center of attention. When Henry James urged Amélie to settle in England, where her talent would be better recognized and rewarded, she was inclined to agree, but Archie objected; he would not live abroad permanently, he said. There were scenes in private, and by the end of the London season both husband and wife were ready for a rest cure at Bad Kissingen, in Bavaria.

The two then left for Algiers, where a new cause of friction developed. Archie wished Amélie to devote herself to painting for which he believed she had a natural gift superior to her literary talent. He engaged an instructor, but she treated the experiment lightly, confiding to Margaret that "between you and me and Queen Bess & the gate post," it was of no use. She sent her love to "pretty Alida, gadding about in her sweet, thoughtless way."

And soon Amélie was writing again about Archie's "coldness. . . . He is like that with everyone. . . . It is his nature to be indifferent & silent and I don't think it will ever change." Archie, for his part, did not allude to the tense situation in his letters.

All this while Willie Chanler had been blazing his own trail. Strikingly handsome, with bold, arrogant features, hypnotic eyes, and perfect self-assurance, Willie made friends at every social level. He felt that nothing lay beyond his powers. Taking off with Elizabeth for bandit-ridden Sicily, he lingered there several weeks in hope of meeting some outlaws. When the hope proved vain, he talked the hotelkeeper at Palermo into letting them depart without settling their bill in full, for the two had run short of cash. This would occur frequently with Willie. Nonchalantly he informed sister Margaret that she could settle the account when she reached Sicily.

But civilized travel failed to satisfy Willie Chanler's robust appetite for adventure. For more than a year he had been talking about hunting big game in Africa. Lewis had openly scoffed at the notion, telling his sisters not to worry about Willie, because "in the first place he cant get into Africa & if he could he has too much sense to go very far." Willie, however, was determined.

To get into the hinterland of East Africa, where he proposed to hunt, was not easy for an American; the rival colonial powers there were jealous of their secrets and suspicious of foreigners generally. But Willie succeeded in obtaining a lieutenant's commission in the German East African Ivory Patrol that would at least procure him entrance into the backcountry. Hastening to Brindisi, he embarked for Port Said, Aden, and Zanzibar, taking with him George Galvin, who was not yet sixteen. During the voyage he revised his plans and decided to hunt independently through the lion and elephant country around Mount Kilimanjaro.

At Zanzibar he wrote to Margaret on March 20, 1889:

"The troubles here add to the amusements of the place somewhat, for if we were not hearing every now and then of fights with the natives I don't know what we'd do.... The rascally Germans are making all the trouble and doing nearly all the fighting. The English are simply putting down the slave trade with as little bloodshed as possible. . . . I am learning the language (Swahili) and do not find it hard. The climate is not so deadly after all, but I suffer very much from an exaggerated sort of prickly heat. I think I shall start for Kilimanjaro about the end of May. . . . I am having a great deal of difficulty in getting my men together but think I shall succeed."

Luck favored the young adventurer, and in May the expedition, numbering 120 men and captained by Willie, with George Galvin as second in command, embarked by dhow for Mombasa, and from there headed inland. They followed the old Uganda trail westward to Tsavo, in the heart of the lion country, then turned southwest and made for Taveta, the headquarters of the Arab slave traders. From Taveta, turning westward again, the safari reached the lower slopes of Kilimanjaro, and finding at a place called Nkiri Nkubwa a well-built "boma," or permanent camp, they settled there for an extended stay. Game was plentiful, the buffalo were vicious and aggressive, and the rhinoceros the same. One night two rhinos charged right through the boma, smashing everything but luckily injuring nobody. There were other narrow escapes, and a constant lookout had to be maintained against the hostile Masai, whose territory lay to the north.

Although the region had been fairly well explored, portions were still unknown, and Willie was the first American to hunt there. He loved the life, although he exasperated a German explorer, Hans Meyer, by explaining that his only motive was to "have fun." The cool daring of this twenty-three-year-old sportsman, roaming country that the great Stanley had called unsafe to enter "even with a thousand rifles," seconded only by a sixteen-year-old boy, perturbed the serious-minded German.

At home the newspapers carried occasional reports of his progress, and Wintie reassured his sisters that there was little or no fever in the uplands around Kilimanjaro. When Willie at length emerged from the interior safe and sound, Wintie relayed the news to Amos Tuck French: "He says he had fine sport, though he doesn't mention what kind. He pretends to like the life and says he is not coming home for a year or two. . . . He has his Irish groom with him and says he is a great success. I can't imagine at what." Wintie was a little envious of Willie's freedom, and when his brother returned to Europe around Christmas time and failed to pass through Rome and render a first-hand account of his adventures, Wintie was nettled.

Wintie was also bored. He seemed to do nothing but laze away the days. And he confessed to his friend French, not altogether mockingly, "Mere luxuries don't please me at all — oh, no — I must have excitement." Without, of course, forfeiting the crowning luxury of an intelligent and affectionate wife. But Daisy wisely let him have scope to ramble now and then.

Wintie believed that leisure was given to mortals to enjoy. To extract contentment from the passing moment, to be good-humored, jolly, well-mannered, and witty — that was the thing. He was not formed to muck and moil, but to pass his time merrily, within the limits of good form. Friends might choose to work — Amos French was in a bank, commuting between Wall Street and Tuxedo Park — but Wintie refused to be ensnared by any dull grind. He was under no compulsion to do anything especially; he had no profession. If he was hard up today — and he often was pressed for cash — tomorrow would bring another check. If a bill could not be paid, why, send it to the family lawyer to settle. Wintie's eye would gleam as he pictured the discomfiture of that often-harassed retainer upon receiving an account demanding immediate settlement. "This will make him sit up!" he would gloat.

When the Chanler children reached maturity, at age twenty-one, each took direct control of his or her inheritance. But except for Archie after 1900, they all left their financial affairs in the hands of the Chanler Estate, which was managed by the law office of Henry Lewis Morris on Exchange Place, a block from Wall Street. Mr. Morris, who was some years older than his obstreperous clients, was a distant relative and a man of substantial property himself. His specialty was the management of New York City investment realty for inheritors who had little capacity or interest in managing such complex and vulnerable assets, many of which were owned jointly with siblings. The presence of this prudent, entirely trustworthy, avuncular figure in their lives helped insulate the Chanlers to a large degree from business-related acrimony within the family. It also insulated them from some of the normal aggravations of bill-paying citizens. Mr. Morris held a power of attorney to act on behalf of his clients in matters relating to the management of the Estate. The three sisters, especially, relied on him for advice and cautionary counsel, even after their marriages, and Margaret went so far as to name the by-then elderly and ailing Morris to be her daughter's godfather in 1911. Shortly after, the firm evolved into Morris and McVeigh, and at the close of the twentieth century it continues to perform estate planning and management functions for many of the Chanler descendants.

Theoretically, upon coming of age, each of the eight Chanlers enjoyed the income yielded by approximately $800,000. In the late nineteenth century, this meant each received about $20,000 a year, collected and disbursed as needed, or reinvested, by Mr. Morris. The Chanlers' income increased following the deaths of Laura Astor Delano in 1902 and her brother Henry Astor in 1917. Laura left each one the income from $500,000 placed in trust, and from Henry each received the proceeds outright from the sale of city real estate amounting to approximately $200,000. Gradually over the decades in the early part of the twentieth century, the Estate shifted assets from realty to portfolios of stocks and bonds.

Elizabeth and Margaret were by far the most prudent of the eight when it came to living within their means. Margaret lived by an admonition she must have heard from Mr. Morris: at all costs avoid debt and avoid the invasion of capital. The two sisters also followed the Astor and Morris custom of utilizing intervivos and testamentary trusts, with the Morris firm as trustee, to preserve capital. The other Chanlers, to a greater or lesser extent, often found that their style of living demanded expenditures that exceeded what Mr. Morris considered prudent or sometimes even possible.

PART II:

PURSUIT OF HAPPINESS

9 | FROM LEWIS TO ARCHIE
TO TEDDY

While his sisters and brothers were scattering about Europe, Lewis Stuyvesant Chanler shuttled between Rokeby and New York, where he was completing his law studies at Columbia. Lewis was especially attached to the homestead, in this respect resembling Margaret, his "twin" of nursery days. In both appearance and temperament he was decidedly different from his elder brothers; he had shot up to six feet four inches in height, and like Robert he was dark, in contrast to the fair complexions of Archie, Wintie, and Willie. The extreme elegance of his clothes moved his brothers to protest that he overdressed. His nature was gentler, more sensitive, and more altruistic than theirs. Significantly, he had no "Astor" in his name.

As a boy he had summoned brothers or sisters to the court of Mr. Bostwick to answer charges of failure to repay a loan of twenty-five cents, or of infringing upon the plaintiff's right to occupancy of a rabbit hutch, all in strict legal form. He was also a born speechmaker. When his unenthusiastic family drove him out of the house, he would roam Rokeby woods and frighten the crows with his oratory instead.

It was inevitable that Lewis should eye political life, and he took the family tradition of Democratic leadership very seriously. In 1888, at age nineteen, he reported exuberantly to Margaret:

"Tonight I made my maiden speech at Barrytown. Everybody turned out to see what I would do and there must have been fifty or sixty at least there; it was the first regular meeting of the [Democratic] Club & of course I presided; it was altogether a success as far as the meeting went."

The hold that Rokeby held upon his affections appeared repeatedly in Lewis's letters to those abroad. "I had no idea when I decided to go to Law School how hard it would be to know that I was only 3 hours from

Rokeby & yet as far away as though I were at Cambridge," he told Margaret.

The Democratic defeat in the national elections of 1888 filled him with foreboding for the nation, but a more cheerful prospect opened in June of 1889, when Lewis sailed for a vacation in England. The guardians voted him $300 extra to pay for the trip.

Lewis chafed under the supervision of his three older brothers, who had become guardians on reaching their majority. He pushed his law studies and practiced patrician activities at such establishments as Delmonico's and Tiffany's, where the cautious guardians sanctioned modest charge accounts. During their minority, cash-strapped Chanlers sometimes turned their Delmonico's account into a resource by ordering dinners that were not served, but were billed to the guardians. Friends of the family said that all their lives the Chanler men would settle any annoying monetary crisis by proposing, "Let's have dinner at Del's."

In June 1890 Lewis sailed again for England, and while in London shocked the family by announcing his engagement; his twenty-first birthday was only three months away, in September.

Lewis's courtship had been quiet, and he made clear that he preferred to keep the wedding equally simple. The bride-to-be was well known to the Chanlers. She was Alice Chamberlain, a former Dutchess County neighbor, who had played with the Chanlers as a child. Her father, the heir of a successful shipping merchant, was deceased, and his strong-willed widow had taken Alice and her younger sister, Julia, to Europe for their education.

Lewis was self-conscious about springing his surprise on the family without prior consultation, but the match was suitable on both sides and he was finished with explaining his actions to his guardian-brothers.

Wintie and Willie got the news upon their return to New York from a hunting trip to Colorado. Wintie had casually accepted the invitation while in London, and had sailed off, without ado, leaving Daisy and his two children stranded in England, where she knew no one and where the cold and fog chilled her Roman blood. Disconsolately she had beaten a retreat to Italy.

Wintie sent her a vivid account of their train stalling high in the Rockies and passing most of the night in the open. "What a journey! Half an hour out of Leadville the train came to a standstill at the telegraph station. It seems that there was a train wrecked lower down on the road & that we must wait till it was cleared away. . . . Well, we stayed there until nearly 10 o'clock. The passengers built a huge bonfire & sang hymns at first & then more appropriate songs. . . .

I never saw a better-natured crowd in my life. There we were in the middle of a howling wilderness, most of us supperless, yet no grumbling & all as jolly as sand boys. . . ." Roam as he did, Wintie was never far in spirit from Daisy, and she, clever woman, understood his restlessness and seldom held him back.

Wintie received the news about Lewis's marriage "not disagreeably." Willie looked forward to meeting Alice shortly, and added mischievously that he was "advertising for a wife, but unfortunately the requirements for that august position are difficult to fulfill & as yet the numerous applicants I have received with a cold dismissal. There are many with money, some with good looks, but alack! few with brains."

Meanwhile Archie's marriage was not going well, ostensibly due to friction over Archie's view of where Amélie's real talent lay. He charged her with indolence, asserting she would rather sit and write than stand and paint; she spurned the accusation. But the basic cause lay deeper. Fundamentally uncongenial, both were prone to excitability and were readily gripped by nervous tensions. In his calmer moments, Archie Chanler might have stepped out of a novel by Jane Austen, but Amélie prided herself on being "advanced" and "enlightened." Their problems were aggravated by Amélie's celebrity, for Archie could not help being jealous.

The Chanler sisters, who lived with Archie and Amélie in Paris through two winters, were aware of the growing conflict. As homemaker, housekeeper, or hostess, Amélie was incompetent. Amélie failed repeatedly to appear at occasions after accepting invitations, so hostesses dropped her from their lists. Nor did she discharge the reciprocal obligations of entertaining those who had entertained them. Domestic arrangements mystified Amélie. A sadly disillusioned Margaret guessed that her sister-in-law really wanted to live surrounded by her relatives, idolized and pampered, and that she had simply used Archie to gain entry to a luxurious social circle. Amélie's mother, sisters, and women cousins were much in the Paris house. Archie's temper became uneven; he brooded and began to exhibit odd behavior, but he never spoke a derogatory word about his wife.

At this time Amélie was also, with or without medical sanction, experimenting with morphine. It may have been prescribed to relieve her excruciating headaches, but it had become an addiction. There were days when she remained in her bedroom, invisible to everyone except her mother, supposedly ill but really under the influence of the drug. A novel she wrote in Paris recounted the heroine's suicide by an injection of morphine, and preceding chapters dealt in clinical detail with the sensations the drug produced.

During his years abroad, Archie had been struck by the need of promising American artists who could not afford to complete their art education in Europe. In the United States there were few art schools, few instructors of merit, so that an ambitious American painter or sculptor was forced to seek instruction abroad. Interested in the arts, Archie Chanler evolved a plan.

Early in 1890 he returned alone to New York to raise an endowment fund to provide scholarships for gifted Americans artists. He proposed to award five-year grants, through selective competition, to support artists in reasonable comfort in Paris or another European art center; recipients would pledge to give a portion of their time to teaching upon their return to the United States. In this way Archie hoped that eventually it would be unnecessary for American artists to go abroad for their training.

His proposal was in advance of its time, but the newspapers gave it generous support, praising both Chanler's initiative and his plan of organization. There would be two boards; a jury, composed of artists, to select the recipients, and a board, of business men and bankers, to handle the money and make the payments. Neither group could interfere with the other. At first the scheme would be confined to New York City, but Archie hoped that in time similar funds would be established in other major cities.

He first approached his relatives and rich acquaintances, but met with skepticism. Several cousins flatly refused to donate a nickel to "support some young riffraff in Parts for five years doing nothing." But Archie persisted, priming the pump with a first contribution of $13,500 from his own pocket. Great-Aunt Laura Delano gave $1,000, and Elizabeth Chanler the same amount. Cousin Harry Carey in Boston was more open-handed, giving $5,000, which Uncle William Astor followed with $2,500. Gradually the fund grew. One evening at dinner Archie made his cousin Harry Carey a sporting proposition: whichever of the two, both young and healthy men, died first would leave $25,000 to the prize fund.

"Done," assented Carey; and on his death two years later, the $25,000, although not expressly provided for in the will, was paid by his heir and brother. And in 1891 the Paris Art Fund was launched with an initial endowment of more than $50,000. Two artist friends of Archie's — Stanford White, the architect, and Augustus Saint-Gaudens, the sculptor — were active in support of the prize, and the first winner was soon selected and sent to Paris for five years with a guaranteed annual income of $900, an ample allowance for that day. Since that time, the fund, now called the Chaloner Art Prize or the Concours Chaloner, has continued to assist American artists and American art. Archie later endowed an annual artist's fellowship at the American Academy in Rome which likewise continues to fulfill his purpose today.

The plan having been securely launched, Archie returned to Europe, and a few weeks later was back, this time with Amélie, whose obscure derangements were growing worse. They went directly to Castle Hill, where the hectic, unreal, dreamlike pattern of her turbulent adolescence was revived. The Winthrop Chanlers and Wintie's three sisters were staying in New York, and reports of affairs at Castle Hill became so contradictory that it was deemed advisable to send an observer. Elizabeth volunteered to go, and her report painted a grotesque picture indeed.

Castle Hill was swarming with visitors and cousins, although in one darkened room the lady of the house lay apparently near death. Elizabeth reported her sister-in-law "much weaker . . . altogether worn to a thread of endurance . . . a shadow of her former self. Her hands have great hollows along their backs her face is long and dragged. But she is tranquil & at peace & Archie is very clear & sweet. . . ."

The attendant household — Elizabeth thought every one of them was a relative — was "divided into drawing-room & bedroom detachments," one being always on duty in the sick room. Meanwhile, elsewhere in the house social life went on uninhibited. Elizabeth recounted spending "a delightful hour round the dining-room table comparing pages of Paradise Lost with pages of the Agamemnon & Virgil. . . . We screamed and gesticulated to our entire satisfaction." The scene was Rokeby transported to Virginia.

Archie did everything in his power to halt his wife's wasting away, without success. She could not bear daylight. Sometimes she wished to be read to, but for hours she would lie inert, pallid, undoubtedly in pain yet obviously self-dramatizing also.

As a last resort the doctors suggested placing her in Dr. S. Weir Mitchell's clinic for nervous diseases in Philadelphia. Mitchell was pioneering in the diagnosis and treatment of mental and psychosomatic ills. After anxious debate, Amélie was placed under the direct care of Mitchell's chief of clinic, Dr. J. Madison Taylor. Her commitment was kept a secret from all except her family and the Chanlers, and the latter were discreet.

The weekly visits to Philadelphia brought Archie into close association with Dr. Taylor, and a personal intimacy developed between them. Several times the doctor was a guest at Castle Hill, where he came to enjoy Archie's peculiarities, such as his adoption of a semivegetarian diet. Archie felt that his health had improved since he gave up eating red meats, and the subject of diet interested him greatly. Dr. Taylor predicted that Chanler would go further in his dietary scruples.

During this time Archie engaged in a maze of business promotions. Although he declined to practice himself, he set up a law firm in New York City with two partners, W. G. Maxwell and Harry Van Ness Philip, and told Wintie with immense pride that the firm had earned $10,000 in fees during its first eight months.

Then Archie turned to the promotion of patented inventions, including a self-threading needle for sewing machines. Elated by the success of his Paris Art Prize, he had in mind founding bigger and better philanthropies in neglected fields, schemes that would require large endowments, and he counted on his business ventures to bring in the money needed. Wintie took a hand in several of these projects, investing and acting as salesman for the products among his wealthy friends, especially pushing a fire-resistant paint which he urged they use on their horse barns.

Wintie and Daisy had moved back to Washington, where in February 1891, Daisy was stricken with measles. Consequently she was unable to attend the wedding of Wintie's cousin, John Jacob Astor IV, the son and heir of Uncle William and Aunt Caroline Astor, to Ava Lowle Willing, of Philadelphia. Wintie had looked forward to the wedding with keen interest and Daisy insisted that he go along without her. He had been regaling his sisters with advance gossip about how "poor Jack," who "had not a friend in the wide world," had at last found a young lady who is willing to marry him" — thanks entirely to his mother, *the* Mrs. Astor.

"It is amusing to see how Aunt Caroline has managed the whole affair," he wrote to Margaret. "It may be that Aunt C. went to some society caterer and gave him *carte blanche*. At all events, the friendless Jack goes to the altar . . . A day or two before the wedding he is to give a farewell (it is his first as well as his last) bachelor supper to his *friends* at the Knickerbocker. Delicious, isn't it? Not one of the men would cross the street to shake hands with him for his own sake. But the mother is such a social power & has done so much for them that they are only too glad of the chance."

The "Golden Caliban" was what they were calling Jack Astor in Philadelphia, said Wintie as he launched into his narrative of the wedding:

"Well! Jack has got his Jill at last! Let its hope there will be no 'vinegar & brown paper' required for some time to come. The wedding was really beautiful. The bride is a lovely girl. Tall, dark, clear white skin with well coloured cheeks. Beautiful expressive eyes & charming change of expression & play of features. Perfect manner. Self-possessed & ready of wit. If she does not make something of Jack nobody can. Poor girl! They tell me in Philadelphia that she has been perfectly desperate about the whole business. Has left a puddle of tears on every parlour floor in the town. Her family which is very rich & quite the *fine fleur* of Phil, has forced her into it. Up to the last moment her friends feared that she would rebel & break loose — but she did not. They seldom do!

"The wedding took place in the Willing house. About 150 people were asked for the ceremony & about 50000 for the reception afterwards. You of course know from the papers who the ushers & bridesmaids were, so I shan't stop to tell them off. The maids were all in *couleur de rose* & were the prettiest lot of girls I have ever seen at such a ceremony. Just before the time came for the service I went up stairs to see Jack & cheer him up. He was up stairs surrounded by his ushers & best man. To my surprise he was not a bit scared or (apparently) nervous. He asked for a Prayer Book just to see 'what he had to say.' I told him it did not matter a single dam what he said now, for the Parson would only & could only understand him in one way. That seemed to brace him up. Then I went down stairs & squeezed myself in among the family at the right of the altar, just behind Uncle William. Best place in the room where I could see everything. The music started up & they all came. First the ushers & bridesmaids; then Jack & Stewart [the best man]. Jack wagged (he *can't* bow) his head at the Parson, who was a huge, unctuous man with a blonde beard. Then came the bride (first time I had even seen her except once across the house at the Opera in N.Y.) on her father's arm. She looked like death, trembling & in a state of seemingly hopeless despair. They stood under a sort of sounding-board of lilies & greens in a bow window opening on the street. Then the service began. After each sentence that fell from the Parson's lips, by some curious coincidence, the crowd of people outside in the street hoorayed & bawled. Just as if the thing was being done in the open air. Of course the window was shut & the blinds down but the mob yelled as if they were in the room. The effect was ludicrous in the extreme.

"Jack answered up like a man. The girl whispered her responses below her breath. She trembled & cried a little, so that I felt as if I were attending a sale in a slave market. Aunt Caroline & Uncle W were both nervous. We all cried, as did all the members (female) of the Willing clan. The end soon came & we made our congratulations.

"Jack never appeared as well. For the first time in his life he did not behave like a fool. In spite of his ridiculous appearance & manners he was really dignified & at his ease. Had a word for everyone, looked happy & sell-possessed. She also braced up, like one who has had a long dreaded cold douche & is delighted & surprised to find it not half so bad as it was supposed to be.

"Then came the breakfast. All the bridesmaids, ushers, bride & groom were at a big round table beautifully decorated with flowers. The effect was charming. Jack & his Ava were opposite one another & not side by side. There was only one other table in the room at which the fathers, mothers, Parsons & aged aunts sat. The rest of us were fed in various troughs in different rooms. I sat with the sisters & brothers in front of Jack & we had a very jolly time. I have a very nice box of cake, which I shall send you. The bride wore very few jewels. A beautiful diamond love knot with a huge brilliant as pendant. Given by Uncle W. Said to have belonged to Mazarin. A jewel in diamonds (I think a tiara — *fleur de lis*) from Jack and that's all. It was all over by 4 o'clock. At 4.41 my train left & here I am. Yrs. W."

So ended Wintie's blithe account of one of the era's most fashionable, unhappy, and in the end ill-fated marriages.

A long-standing friendship, dating back to Harvard days, had existed between Wintie and Theodore Roosevelt and over the years this had ripened into intimacy. The two had similar tastes, adored the outdoor life, and Roosevelt was charmed by Wintie's liveliness and debonair wit. They were fellow Porcellians and fellow members of the Boone & Crockett Club, a group of sportsmen, big game hunters, founded in 1887 by Roosevelt and George Bird Grinnell.

A tight circle of congenial spirits clustered around Roosevelt and Wintie Chanler. It included Owen Wister, who had not yet produced *The Virginian*, the first Western in American literature, but was already infatuated with the West; the Cabot Lodges; the English diplomat Cecil Spring-Rice; and, later, Henry Adams, who, although older, sympathized with the enthusiasms of the younger set. Like Roosevelt, Wister had known Wintie at Harvard, and they were also linked by the close friendship between Daisy Chanler's parents, the Terrys, and Wister's awesome grandmother, the majestic Fanny Kemble. The English actress once coached Daisy in a children's play how "to walk like a queen."

One year Roosevelt was unable to make arrangements for the annual reunion of Boone & Crockett Club members so he reluctantly entrusted the arrangements to Wintie. The date drew near, and Roosevelt became nervous over Chanler's apparent neglect of the job. Teddy dashed off a peremptory note:

"Dear Winty,

"You unsatisfactory cuss, what do you mean by saying that you may not be at the dinner, and that is all there is about it? More than that, I can't make out from your letter if you have engaged or will engage, the rooms at the Knickerbocker Club. Please attend to this at once, as I don't want to have a hungry crowd of hunters gathered and no fare for them.

"Give my love to your wife, and answer this in the affirmative at once.

Cordially yours,
THEODORE ROOSEVELT"

To which Wintie replied with lines scratched out in the office of Archie's law firm:

THE WORM TURNETH

Keep your shirt on little Teddy
And don't get in a stew.
The dinner will be ready,
The room is ordered too.
But I must know how many
Can be counted on to dine,
Ere I venture upon any-
Thing concerning food or wine.
I am willing & I'm able
To do my level best,
To arrange & set the table,
Kick the waiters & the rest.
You enumerate the Crocketts,
I'll their appetites indulge,
Till their eyeballs from their sockets
Do incontinently bulge.
And when the matter's ended
And laid upon the shelf,
You may know that I intended
From the first to come myself.

10 | THAT MAVERICK BOB

Willie Chanler's experience of the West was far rowdier and more lawless than Wintie's. Willie had, at various times, fraternized with members of the "Hole in the Wall" gang of bank robbers in Wyoming, and he and Butch Cassidy would meet surreptitiously again in New York. Willie had explored San Francisco's Barbary Coast, and made a particularly close friendship, involving uproarious and sometimes disorderly practical jokes, with Jack Follansbee, a cousin of William Randolph Hearst who managed the vast Hearst ranches in California and Mexico.

Lewis Chanler was introduced to the West in a different way, and for him it held no attraction whatever. Lewis, Jr., known as Stuyve, was born in 1891, and his father had had to cut short an auspicious legal start to take his wife and baby son to Colorado Springs for their health, where they lived in virtual quarantine for weeks. When they returned, Lewis resumed his interrupted career.

He had chosen to specialize in criminal practice, a branch of the profession then disdained by attorneys with genteel backgrounds. In the 1890s legal tricksters preyed on the unfortunates caught up in the criminal process in New York City. Lewis created a stir by taking cases that he deemed meritorious and defending them vigorously, whether the client could pay or not. Most of his clients were too poor to afford counsel, so Lewis paid all costs out of his own pocket. He employed two clerks to attend each reading of the calendar and, whenever no defense counsel appeared, to inform the court that the defense would be assumed by Lewis Chanler. Lewis was aware that the scales of justice were weighted heavily against the poor and ignorant, and he contributed his talents toward righting them. In addition, he greatly enjoyed the practice.

Once Lewis accepted a case, he prosecuted it with zeal, and frequently won. Prosecutors, although baffled by his motives, came to respect his ability, while his clients found him not only a skillful counselor, but a sympathetic friend. For a while a "Chanler Club," composed mostly of murderers, flourished in the Tombs, New York's infamous jail, and was provided with a turkey at Thanksgiving and Christmas, along with tobacco and other small comforts, by its counsel.

The family approved of Lewis's ambition, although not always of his way of expressing it. Wintie confided to his friend French that he hoped his brother would "stick to it for the next two or three years." But the family found Lewis's pompous earnestness grating.

At Rokeby one day, Wintie, Willie, and Bob opened an attack on Lewis, ridiculing him as a self-important windbag, a "professional man," who actually worked in an office and vastly overrated his public services, and was incapable of ever smiling at himself. The attack went on for more than an hour, in language so violent that Wintie's daughter, Laura, a child, was shocked. Lewis took the chiding meekly, made no effort to defend himself, and when eventually the storm subsided, all was easy and friendly again. Such were the tempests of Rokeby, apparently enjoyed by all.

Elizabeth, Margaret, and Alida were now established in a house on Murray Hill in New York City that they rented jointly. There they entertained and were entertained in turn as full-fledged members of the rarefied society presided over by Aunt Caroline Astor. The older two were now mistresses of their persons and their fortunes, answerable for their actions only to themselves, and Alida came of age in June 1894.

Independence exactly suited Margaret; she wrote to brother Willie that their first season had been an "idyl — we three quite on our own feet socially. 200 people eat with us in 4 months. . . . Alida was the belle at dances & came home covered with favors like a Xmas tree. We kept well & happy. I pray God next year may be as peaceful, but of course not one of us is by way of getting married. Oh, no!"

Alone among these family members, Robert was the maverick whose strangeness was causing misgivings. Well over six feet tall, Bob was not handsome as a boy or young man — he had a perpetually sulky expression — yet he was fumblingly appealing. He craved affection, but was unsure of himself, and seemed hardly educated at all. For these reasons, Wintie felt that his youngest brother would benefit by a sojourn abroad. Daisy Chanler agreed, but her reasons were slightly different from those of her husband: she sensed qualities in Bob that might be better cultivated in artistic Europe than the rusticity of the Hudson River valley.

The guardians' European plan for Bob called for travel and language study, but far from mastering any foreign tongue, Robert's facility in English seemed to deteriorate during the next year or two. His correspondence — sentimental, affectionate, and erratic — gave evidence of a sensitive nature reaching toward something faintly glimpsed.

In Paris he went to stay with Amélie and Archie, writing to Margaret: "Amélie & Archie are as nice as they can be to me — I am just beginning to feel as if I knew her. . . . Tomorrow Archie is going to take me to Madame Galadvaize, she is the wife of the gentilman we are going to be with at Blois: she does not speak any English so I will have to whip up my French. . . . Archie took Mr. B. [Bostwick, the tutor] & I to the Louvre, & showed us the Venus of Milo, it is very beautiful, after you have seen one or two like it, the modern marbles are horrible, at least that is the way it affects me. . . . I had a long letter from Timpson [a Red Hook neighbor] yesterday and he picked some violets at Rokeby & sent them to me, was it not sweet of him. I have put them in my Bible, it made me so homesick, that I had to go and ask Amélie for a book to read. . . . I went to church on Sunday, it was what they call an American Chapple — I got there late, & what was my astonishment when I saw to men in the pulpit all in black. I looked & found it was a kind of Methodist affair, but I did not care & lissend to the sermon which was very long & pretty good. . . . Tonight I go to Romio, by Gounhou, I have not the least idea how to spell his name but knowing you to be a kind & sweet sister you will for give it. I must stop now much love & many kisses from your devoted br. Bob."

Bob was bewitched by Amélie and defended her strongly to his sisters: "Poor Amélie has got neuralger, at a most unfortunate time. Archie had given us a bully dinner at a cafe, & in the midst of it Amélie had an attack of neuralger. I brougt her home & left Archie & Mr. B. to finish the dinner. If you knew how much Amélie wanted to be with you, you would feel ashamed of having thought anything against her."

Too close association with Amélie began to go to Bob's head. Virile and without guile, he floundered toward an avowal the nature of which he did not suspect, and in bewilderment he translated his inner confusion into religious questioning. He struggled to sublimate his conflict by applying himself to a book titled *Why I Am a Christian, or Reasons for Believing in Christianity.* ("What a wonderful little work it is — just think of its being translated into Jappanies.") After much soul-searching, Bob concluded that the meaning of life was inscrutable.

Nevertheless, to avert a possible scandal, Bob was packed off to live with a French family near Blois where it was hoped he would at least acquire proficiency in spoken French. The country folk living around the village impressed Bob as "very stuppid & ignorant" but "very happy & good," and he liked them. However, the move failed to settle either Bob's seething emotions or his orthography.

The nub of Bob's letters usually dealt with esthetic reactions to sights or his tumultuous emotions, rather than accounts of events. In contrast with his brothers and sisters, who dealt with things factual, tangible, and visible, Robert groped introspectively. By 1891 he was sketching, and finding satisfaction in it. "I went into the garden of the Pettit Trianon sketched & I liked mine immensely," he reported. "I got the broad effect well."

His letters thereafter are peppered with sketches. Writing from Milan, he recollected a "doctor who used to rinkle up his face when he came in to see me meaning to look happy and pleased, but made me think that his wife was accustomed to greet him 'd'autrement.'" And there was a sketch of the little doctor, hat in hand, diving into a room.

Bob's emotional disturbance at length became so intense that he suffered what was then termed "nervous prostration," and complete rest — far from Amélie — was prescribed. The summer of 1891 he spent on a farm in Wales, in a remote spot devoid of excitements. His hosts were congenial, but the furnishings of their house moved him to esthetic groaning: "O dear me the pictures & the conflomerations of furniture of every age, Egyptian mumies down to New Town chairs."

Enforced idleness and physical lassitude led him for the first time to apply himself to reading, and he discovered that he liked books. He read haphazardly — Motley's *Dutch Republic,* Greek and Roman history, *Elsie Venner, The Story of an African Farm,* Amélie's *A Brother to Dragons,* and cousin Marion Crawford's *Khaled* — all in a jumble.

Two months later he was granted permission to return to the Continent. That winter he spent at St. Moritz, flirting, tobogganing, and resolving to do something in this world. He told Margaret: "I am sure I shall loath New Port

& U.S.A. . . . I shall live over here until I become an artist & then go over with sanguin philanthropic ideas about elevating art."

But his affections and instincts were still deeply rooted in the family, and he was confident of their continued solidarity. He confided to Margaret: "If we all work out our lives in large great works how sound will be our connecting links! We will not have any fear of outgrowing each others tastes & ideas. I think so far we bid fair to be a fine family, & one that our parents would have been proud of. Old Wintie will in turn do something when his family grows to such great proportions that he must support them."

This last observation had pertinence, since Daisy Chanler was expecting another child in three months, her third. John Winthrop Chanler II, who was to live only four years, had been born in 1889.

Soon after this Bob took the plunge, and from a studio in Rome he announced that he was formally embarked upon a career as an artist, always providing that his talent should prove substantial enough. His situation, however, had nothing of the starving Bohemian about it:

"My bed is kingly, exactly like a royal bed one sees in old palaces. We have two servants, a German woman of good repute, & our boy Remo, who speaks Italian only. Jack says our apartments are the best he has seen in Rome. He comes around every morning & talks & smokes a friendly pipe."

"Jack" was John Elliott, the painter husband of Julia Ward Howe's youngest daughter. He had agreed to start Bob's instruction, the latter said, and "when he goes & even now will get Villagos the great Spanish painter & Coleman the great animal & landscape painter to come & help me. Also I am learning modelling & have been offered [a] place in the studio of Benluri, the great sculptor who did Grand Pa Ward's bust, & all this for nothing. O I am happy. . . ."

Jose Villegas had painted Sam Ward's portrait in Rome during the last year of Sam's life. Mariano Benlliure y Gil had done a sparkling bust of Sam at the same time, admirably catching the old man's vitality and infectious twinkle. So Sam Ward was still opening doors and providing opportunities for the grandchildren whose company he had been denied. They were constantly being made to feel this remote beneficence: again and again people would come up to the brothers or sisters and speak of their warm affection for Sam Ward. Since Sam had traveled Europe for decades, his name was an open sesame in unexpected places.

Elliott tried conscientiously not to be lenient in judging young Chanler's ability. He wrote his wife:

"Of course, he is very anxious to know if I think he has talent, which is a difficult thing for me to answer as I don't want to mislead him. I think he certainly has a great deal of facility which may mean something and may not. As a rule it is rather against a man than otherwise but his ideas are so good that if he can only be made to study seriously, I think he will amount to something. . . ."

Regarding Bob's character, Elliott was puzzled. He seemed excessively, even dangerously, pliant and open to suggestions: "This evening I went to see Bob who is a dear boy, and I think I did him some good. He is more susceptible to good impressions than to bad ones as far as I can see . . . Still I fear if he were to fall into bad hands he would probably go to bits for he is easily convinced."

Although Bob settled into work, there was still one reservation that stuck in Elliott's mind. Bob, he still felt, was far too apt to be "influenced by the last person who has made some plausible remark to him. He is like a compass and people act on him like magnets, but when he is left alone he points in the right direction."

Delightfully settled in Rome, Bob had no longing for America and Rokeby. Rather, he professed to look back on his years there with positive distaste. He knew his direction now, and in February, 1893, he wrote Margaret that Stanford White had been urging him to study in Paris; he added his own conclusion, based on sound instinct, that he was "not calm enough yet to stand the life, & the work in a studio with forty other enthusiastic students. The competition & keenness would be too much for me. Perhaps in two years I shall go & work at drawing there. . . . The artists here are not proud but talk & treat a student as an equal. So you see now my reasons for staying."

But Margaret did not see the validity of the reasons he produced. She could not grasp why he should be so absorbed in art, although Bob tried to explain: "To me an artist is the most peaceful man alive, peaceful & sometimes joyfully happy & nearly every day sad. . . . And their ways of thinking are not given to the world except by pictures so the world calls them fools & empty. But they are deep-souled high minded & brave. . . ."

At long last, on February 22, 1893, Robert Winthrop Chanler became twenty-one, and he could finally dispense with explanations to his elders. Five weeks after that day of liberation, a cablegram was delivered at Lewis Chanler's law office in New York City, reading:

ENGAGED TO JULIE HURRAH
TELL FAMILY RETURN SHORTLY
BOB

The news threw the clan into a Chanler tizzy. Nobody had been consulted, and marriage called for preliminary study. Wintie hurried into town for a meeting at Delmonico's. Alida and Elizabeth were recalled from visiting relatives in Charleston, and Lewis suffered, Margaret wrote Willie, "a series of nervous shocks, culminating in silent hysterics. Brog [Archie] on the other hand has reason to believe that Bob has an artistic future — *et ça suffit pour lui.*"

Clearly the majority of the family was not satisfied, but the preponderance of opinion was that the more speedily he was married, the better. This idea he had of devoting his life to painting was nonsense, of course; art was a suitable avocation for a man, but to speak of adopting it as a profession was ridiculous.

The girl whom Bob had chosen was no stranger — she was Julia Remington Chamberlain, the younger sister of Alice Chanler, Lewis's wife. She had been her father's favorite, but had been kept under the thumb of her domineering mother. The Chanlers did not know that Bob had won her on the rebound from an unhappy love affair.

Twenty-year-old Julia had fallen in love with a socially eligible young man with no fortune. Her mother ruthlessly broke up the romance. Bob Chanler being at hand and eligible with regard to both wealth and family position, the mother had engineered the match without either of the principals quite knowing how it came about.

Bob's mentor, Jack Elliott, looked upon the match with foreboding; he wrote his wife that he hoped it wouldn't be a case of marrying in haste and repenting at leisure. To his wife Elliott wrote: "I think I can give you material for a chapter or so of your next novel on match-making mothers, coy daughters and opinionated not-to-be-caught-by-chaff youths, most interesting and pathetic. I am an old bird but I never saw a matrimonial race so jockeyed. . . ."

Alida and Elizabeth left New York on the first available ship; Margaret followed four days later, having stayed to shut up their New York house. But a storm drove her ship two hundred miles off course, and she reached

London one day late for the wedding. She wrote her great-aunt Julia Ward Howe about the ceremony and noted that "Bessie says they are frantically, seethingly in love with each other, that Julie is humbly undertaking to try to soothe him. She thinks him the greatest genius alive, wants him to work 4 years in Rome, 'knows she isn't clever' and hopes she can take care of him."

To Willie Chanler, who had gone back to East Africa, Margaret insisted that Bob was "madly in love," and the bridal couple were "as happy as people of that age and temperament most always are under like circumstances . . . Bob is 'quite mad,' but loveable, in spite of his ridiculous personal vanity & other eccentricities. Julie seems a good wholesome armful with no nerves & otherwise healthy. . . ."

Never was Margaret Chanler more mistaken. Julia was conventional, self-effacing, and shy in company. She dressed beautifully and was equipped to play the role of hostess deftly. But as a mate for Robert Chanler she was a total misfit. Underneath her surface coolness and reserve she was a woman of excessive timidity, shrinking from whatever was rowdy, bold, dogmatic, irresponsible, impulsive, rash, and above all loud. Alas! These were the very qualities she saw personified in the Chanlers.

The newlyweds arrived in New York directly from their wedding and were whisked by Wintie to his home in Tuxedo Park. There they made acquaintance with the latest addition to Daisy's family — a girl, christened Hester Marion. Wintie reported the couple "well & noisy," but admitted he was relieved when they talked about going to Bar Harbor. "Bully place for them," was his opinion. "Cool, conventional, & a long way off."

The pair stopped at Rokeby to be scrutinized, then moved on to Maine. But Julia could not feel at ease in America; the mere energy of the people exhausted her. Bob, too, was longing for Rome, so in the autumn of 1893 they sailed back to Europe.

11 | BASHAWS AND BOREDOM

Just prior to Bob's wedding Wintie Chanler had emerged from a harum-scarum adventure in Morocco. His brother Willie had heard rumors of an unexploited oil field in Morocco and had instantly become fired with the idea of locating it. If it proved to be as rich as supposed, he intended to obtain a concession from the sultan of Morocco and make a packet working it.

He was, however, deep in preparations for an expedition to explore in British East Africa, and he could not afford to leave London. He approached Wintie, who jumped at the chance to go to Morocco and bring back samples of the oil. Willie told Wintie that mission would have to be carried out with utmost secrecy to avoid arousing international suspicions.

For the trip Wintie teamed with Stephen Bonsal, a roving correspondent for the *New York Herald*, as reckless a daredevil as Willie Chanler. Wintie and Bonsal attached themselves unofficially to a British diplomatic party being sent to negotiate a trade treaty with the sultan, saying that they intended to hunt lions. In the guise of sportsmen they reached Fez without serious hindrance; but there they got into a fight with a mob of Muslim fanatics, who had been incited by the bashaw, or governor of the city. They barely escaped with their lives. Assuming a lofty tone, the two young Americans demanded redress from the sultan, who hated the bashaw anyway, so he ordered the bashaw to humble himself publicly before the Americans and pay a heavy fine.

The ceremony of abasement was staged impressively, and the bashaw paid the fine, which the lordly Americans flung to the crowd of beggars clamoring at the gate. Thereafter, however, the adventurers decided that Fez was too hot for safety, and they struck out with all speed for the coast. For three days they rode through blazing hot, danger-filled country — sustaining themselves with Veuve Cliquot drunk at desert temperatures — and reached Tangiers, where they learned that they had been reported slain, and their families had already ordered coffins to transport their remains to America.

But they did bring back samples of oil from Willie's field. These were smuggled past several customs barriers and were submitted to two different chemists for separate analyses. The German chemist unhesitatingly identified the oil as taken from low-grade deposits in the Harz Mountains, while the Englishman just as positively said it came from a worthless outcropping in Derbyshire. So that ended that episode which had kept Daisy Chanler on tenterhooks of anxiety. To compensate, Wintie meekly allowed himself to be led to Bayreuth for seven days of Wagnerian opera. "It took a lot of beer but I got through it," he noted.

By this time Willie Chanler was on his way to Zanzibar. A London newspaper account had carried his brother Wintie's Harvard class photograph as "a recent likeness of the daring young explorer," prompting Wintie to complain: "I have already been married to Amélie Rives and now I have made extensive explorations in the Dark Continent." Then off he set for America, vowing: "This is the last time I take my kids out of the country for five years at least. They have broke me flat."

A stay at Newport soon set him yawning: "The poor dear millionaires are trying their damnest to have a good time. But the wind won't blow for the yachts & it rains whenever there is a particularly good polo game. Internecine strife divides society; many people don't speak, bow, or breathe the same air with others. The small fry are all as poor, or poorer, than usual. There is no good, cheerful, reeking scandal to comfort the women. The old men are all prophesying 'trouble in the Street.'"

With the advent of autumn Wintie retreated to the house he had acquired in Tuxedo Park, a place he had discovered through his friend Amos Tuck French. "Most beautiful and healthy," he had assured Daisy, "only forty miles from New York & with every kind of comfort. Lake to sail on & fish in — forty-two miles of roads through the woods. Tennis, swimming, etc. . . ." It was forty miles from civilized conversation, Daisy was inclined to think, and cut off from theaters, music, and socializing. But having paid $30,000 for the house, Wintie proposed to enjoy it.

The newspaper accounts about brother Willie's progress in Africa gave Wintie particular satisfaction because they centered public attention on somebody in the family besides Amélie Rives. When the society column listed

Alida as "receiving" at Mrs. Astor's ball, Wintie wrote gleefully to Margaret that she had been identified as "the sister of the African explorer, and not as the sister-in-law of the novelist."

Wintie's spirits were never low for long, nor was he capable of being bored at length. He interspersed the aimless drift of his life with bursts of activity, but these were usually short-lived and led to nothing further. Hunting and horses bound the horizon of his serious interests outside of family; he adorned with style the social life provided by his wife, but he would leave it in an instant to hunt mouflon in Sardinia or chamois in the Alps.

12 | EASTWARD HO!

In some respects Willie Chanler was a model — and in sport he was a match — for his intense admirer, Theodore Roosevelt. Teddy, who was aggressively spreading the gospel of the "strenuous life," liked both Wintie and Willie Chanler, but he regarded the brothers in different lights. Wintie he loved for his wit and urbanity, indoors or out, while he looked upon Willie with a touch of awe. Willie would perform with nonchalance the sort of feats that Teddy worked himself up to by verbal breastbeating. Tough, primitive, and singleminded, Willie's capacity for action was enormous; dawdling or irresolution he despised.

Willie had made friends in England with a coterie of hard-bitten cavalry officers of the hunting set, and pending his return to Africa had been amusing himself by riding in breakneck steeplechases against the best gentlemen jockeys and winning consistently. His success did not sit well with some of his rivals, a number of whom wanted to see him taken down a peg.

Finally a match race was proposed — Willie against the best of his English competitors. The stakes were substantial and the wagering was so heavy that some bettors determined to win by eliminating Willie altogether. The following story, though undocumented like many stories revolving around William Astor Chanler, was long told in London sporting circles.

A few days before the match, two of the plotters were riding with Willie in a hunt. At a jump, they closed in on him from each side, lifted him clear of the saddle, and dropped him behind his horse. The tactic was well known, but frowned upon because such falls could be fatal. Willie escaped with a minor hip fracture, but it seemed more than enough to keep him out of the race. His competitors had misjudged Willie, however. On the appointed day he rode up to the starting line, strapped in the saddle, his hip in a cast, and went on to win.

This did not end the episode. Willie Chanler once described himself as "too mediaeval a person" to tolerate an insult. Singling out the instigator, he found his chance for revenge during a cross-country run. Just as his rival's horse rose to a fence, Chanler crashed his own mount into it. Both horses and riders went down in a tangle of lashing hooves. Willie sustained fresh injuries, but his opponent never rode again.

But Willie's attention was fixed upon serious matters also — the preparation of his expedition into unexplored British East Africa. He would be going at the head of a well-equipped party, bent upon obtaining scientific information about a region that his friend Stephen Bonsal called "the last *terra incognita* of the habitable globe."

At this time the ideal American man was Richard Harding Davis — glamorous foreign correspondent and man-about-town. Chivalrous, bold, and brave, Davis crashed through barriers impassable for ordinary mortals; he was petted by society and cheered along Broadway, and he was so good-looking that he set the standard of masculine beauty for the age. Yet Richard Harding Davis was merely the copy of an original, his friend William Astor Chanler.

Davis and Chanler had met in New York before they encountered each other again in London in the summer of 1891, when Willie revealed his plans for Africa. Davis was enormously impressed, both by Chanler's preparations and by his expertise. Willie's conversation did not "teem with treks and Soudanese porters, and anecdotes of the slave trade and the quick effectiveness of jungle fever," Davis reported in *Harper's Magazine*. "So little given is Chanler to any one topic, that it was amusing, after he had interested those about him with anecdotes of Harvard or the boulevards, to ask him for a story of the land of the Masai, and to watch the faces of his hearers as the worldly, idle, and conscientiously dressed youth of the minute before told how men look who are dying of thirst, or how an elephant is liable to act when you fire at it."

Willie had to obtain government permission to enter the territory and assemble a bewildering variety of arms and equipment. He needed a working knowledge of photography, medicine, nutrition, agriculture, surveying geography, military codes, cartography. Chanler's own refinements delighted Davis. To impress those natives who had never seen a white man, he had George Galvin coached by a professional magician in sleight-of-hand tricks. Chanler was taking a dozen pairs of flesh-colored rubber gloves, intending, while negotiating with tribal chiefs, to peel these off as if skinning himself. The entire cost of the expedition, of course, was being borne by Willie personally.

Willie needed to secure the right associate for his safari, which was expected to take two years and traverse a three-thousand-mile route through regions that were mere blanks on existing maps. His choice fell upon a lieutenant in the Austrian navy, Ludwig von Höhnel.

In 1888 von Höhnel had been the cartographer on the expedition of Count Teleki, the Hungarian explorer, that struck northward from East Africa almost to Abyssinia, and discovered Lakes Rudolph and Stephanie. His brilliantly accurate maps had drawn Chanler's attention. Early in 1891 Chanler wrote to the lieutenant, asking whether he would care to join a scientific expedition into East Africa. His laconic note gave no details, and von Höhnel had never even heard the name Chanler, but the invitation attracted him. When he sounded out his naval superiors on whether he could obtain another extended leave of absence, Admiral Baron von Sterneck, the commander of the Austrian navy, said that he would have to meet this Mr. Chanler before making a decision. Willie telegraphed from Sicily that he would arrive in Vienna in a few days.

On the morning von Höhnel and Willie met, thirty-five-year-old von Höhnel was favorably impressed by this young man eleven years his junior. Chanler's frank, unconstrained manner appealed to him, and as Willie rapidly outlined his plans, von Höhnel realized that he was a master of his subject. Together they drove off to meet with Baron von Sterneck at the Admiralty.

Chanler began to explain his proposals regarding Africa to the admiral with a total lack of self-consciousness that embarrassed von Höhnel, accustomed as he was in his world to a minute observance of rank, yet somehow the effect seemed just right. After a few moments, Chanler casually rested an elbow on a high desk at his side; this reminded the admiral that he had not invited his callers to be seated, and rectifying the omission, he led the way to a sofa. All three sat there while Chanler expounded his plans for an hour.

One point puzzled von Sterneck: why had Chanler hit upon von Höhnel as his choice of associate? Willie explained that when he was returning from his Kilimanjaro hunting trip, he became friendly with the captain of the Austrian corvette, the *Aurora*. The neatness, discipline, and cleanliness aboard the *Aurora* had greatly impressed him, Willie said, and then at Zanzibar he had found everybody talking about the brilliantly successful Teleki expedition and praising Lieutenant von Höhnel.

Greatly pleased, the admiral granted the lieutenant indefinite leave to accompany the Chanler expedition. The next day, after arranging to meet within the year for final consultation, Willie left Vienna — but not before dropping in for dinner at Vienna's famous Sacher restaurant and making friends with Madame Sacher for life.

Months went by and von Höhnel heard nothing further. At first he suspected that Chanler had been sidetracked by some love affair, but then heard that Willie was in England amusing himself by fox hunting. The lieutenant went to London at Willie's invitation and confirmed that Willie was hunting all right, but also that he had not neglected the preparations for the expedition. Supplies had reached such quantities that the nervous outfitter had inquired at the American embassy regarding Chanler's financial responsibility: was he good for the money? He was assured: "If Mr. Chanler does not return alive from Africa, you will have your account settled promptly by the estate. If Mr. Chanler does come back, you may have to wait."

On June 11, 1892 — his twenty-fifth birthday — Willie left London for Marseilles, where he took ship for Port Said en route to Zanzibar. George Galvin was left to follow with the expedition's trading goods and other supplies. Von Höhnel left Vienna at the same time with the scientific and military equipment he had collected there. The two explorers met at Port Said, where Chanler reported in high spirits to his family that his companion had brought, "4 savage Illyrian dogs, 200 rifles, and 35,000 cartridges." His health, he said, was excellent.

From Aden, Chanler impatiently pushed on ahead, leaving von Höhnel to purchase camels and hire Somali drivers for them. Von Höhnel also engaged twelve Sudanese soldiers to serve as escort.

Chanler was busy at Zanzibar rounding up the porters required for the safari. The supply of available men had been almost cornered by a missionary caravan, and Willie had to offer high wages to recruit bearers. He finally collected 130 men, but when von Höhnel saw them he was dismayed. Many were slaves rented out by their masters; others were too young to be able to carry the standard 80 to 100 pound load for twelve hours a day. None had any experience in trackless country, or any notion of the harsh conditions they were certain to encounter, or of the fatigues and hardships of African travel.

Since the success and safety of the caravan would depend on the loyalty and efficiency of its porters, von Höhnel protested against so unreliable a lot. He especially mistrusted the headmen, Hamidi and Mohamadi. But these were the only porters available, said Chanler, who felt confident that he could whip them into shape.

Embarking his bearers on a leaky Arab dhow, Chanler conveyed them to the mainland and to a base camp at Mkonumbi, about twenty miles inland, where George Galvin was waiting. Galvin amazed von Höhnel. Rather short, strongly built, cool-headed, calm in emergencies, George met every demand with practical handiness, and he had a definite knack with the men, being able to get cooperation without bullying or harshness.

The explorers had laid out their route with care. From Mkonumbi they were to ascend the Tana River in the direction of Mount Kenya, then push north as far as the southern tip of Lake Rudolph. After exploring the country between that lake and Lake Stephanie, the caravan would turn eastward and march through hundreds of miles of unknown territory to the Juba (Giuba) River, descend that stream to the coast, and come out near Kismayu in Somaliland. Stephen Bonsal had called this "a land without a name — but the Swaheli traders shudder as they call it 'the land of thirst and emptiness.'"

Willie wrote to Elizabeth from the Mkonumbi camp:

"I will write you as often as possible during the journey; but don't feel frightened if you don't hear from me for 18 months as I am not certain that communication will be open to the coast from the interior. Now I may as well tell you that if any expedition can travel with safety it is mine. It is perfectly armed & equipped in every way. . . . Lieut. von Höhnel is a wonderful fellow. . . . If we are only moderately successful this journey should be attended with such valuable scientific results that it will make us famous. . . . You may be glad to hear that I have never been in better health. . . . Tell George's people that he is very well & happy & is of the greatest service to me. Now I must stop for the sun is out of sight and it is getting dark. Love to Margaret & Alida to Lewis and Archie in fact to every one not forgetting Mr. Morris [the family lawyer]. I shall keep your last letter always with me.
Your absolutely devoted & loving brother
WILLIE"

13 | "THE LAND OF THIRST AND EMPTINESS"

On September 18, 1892, Chanler marched out of Mkonumbi at the head of one hundred and sixty men. The pack train included fifteen camels and load-carrying donkeys, as well as oxen, sheep, and goats. The two explorers rode two Somali horses, but von Höhnel's "fierce Illyrian dogs" had turned out to be two retrievers and a scrappy fox terrier. The expedition was not without civilized amenity: in Willie's personal kit were half a dozen pints of champagne, a well-thumbed Plutarch, and Browning's poems.

Willie sent a jaunty letter of farewell to Margaret, in which he also expressed his opinion of the region's inhabitants: "The intellect of these children of the tropics is pitiably weak, and their morals of the lowest possible order. This is a dreadful place for slaves. The most popular occupation is selling one another to the Somalis, a neighboring warlike people who keep slaves. There are many instances where men have sold their sons, & brothers sell one another if the opportunity offers. These Swahili have been a great race. One may see ruins of their towns many hundreds of years ago abandoned & now half-buried ruins. Now the Swahili are perfectly depraved & have no ambition above eating and pleasure. It is time they made room for others more enterprising." In his assessment and conclusions, Willie was a man of his times.

From the start the caravan progressed slowly. Von Höhnel's misgivings proved well founded. The first man to disappear took with him a load of ammunition which was never recovered. Others threw away their loads and slipped into the bush. Chanler tried reasoning with them and invoked strict disciplinary measures, to no avail. In desperation he finally called the porters together at the end of a day's march, and told them that any who wished to return to the coast could go provided they set out at once; but starting with the next day, any man who tried to desert would do so at the risk of his life.

The next day a porter tried to desert, but was caught. Chanler ordered him to be marched in front of his Sudanese captor. At a favorable moment the prisoner darted into the bushes. Acting according to the rules of caravan discipline then in place, Chanler had the porter shot.

Despite these discouragements, the expedition forged ahead. At Hameye, on the Tana River, they took a two-day rest, and Chanler sent five worthless bearers back to the coast under a headman, who was instructed to bring back replacements. Since the round trip would take at least five weeks, Chanler and von Höhnel decided to make a side journey to locate, if possible, Lake Lorian, a large body of water into which the Guaso Nyiro (Ewaso Ngiro) River was thought to empty. No white man had seen the lake, but local people placed it somewhere northeast of Hameye.

The explorers also hoped to find a nomadic people called Rendille, who were said to inhabit a wide area nearby, from whom they hoped to obtain food and additional beasts of burden to replace those that were succumbing to the tsetse fly.

On December 5 the two companions set out from Hameye with eighty men and ten donkeys; twenty-one-year-old George Galvin remained in charge of the main supplies and the camels. Heading north, the explorers crossed a flat desert, dotted with flowers and butterflies brought out by recent rains. They then came to a rocky, hilly country where the going was rough, and at length reached a range of mountains covered with forests, which they named the Jombeni (today the Nyambeni Hills). They saw much game — zebra, oryx, rhinoceros, and now and then elephants — but no human inhabitants.

On the fourth day they sighted a range of blue hills stretching far into the distance to the north and surmised that these might be the southern outcropping of the General Mathews range. As Chanler stood examining these peaks, his gun bearer cried excitedly: "Look, master! Down there is a large mountain! I think it is Kenya!" Chanler turned his glasses and beheld, standing nobly clear of the clouds, the snow-clad slopes of Kilimanjaro's mighty rival. At this proof that he was really in new country, Willie felt, he said, "as joyous as Moses when he viewed the promised land.'

Day after day the explorers' elation rose higher. They shot game to feed the men, hippopotamus meat being specially popular. Chanler developed fever, but he would permit no pause. Coming to a river which they identified as the Mackenzie, they followed it to within fifteen miles of the distant hills and could see on their slopes the smoke of countless fires. Could those be the fires of the Rendille?

Cutting their way through nearly impenetrable bush, the party emerged on a grassy plain where the going was painful because of the irregular-shaped blocks of lava that lay under the tall grass, tripping one at almost every step. Frequently the caravan was charged by rhinos.

On December 17 the expedition had its first encounter with unfriendly local people. While investigating a forested hillside, they came upon a cultivated clearing where men and women were cutting brush. These ran off, and soon several hundred warriors came running, shouting and brandishing spears and poisoned arrows. They seemed to understand neither Masai nor Swahili, and Chanler, acting swiftly, seized several warriors who ventured close and indicated by signs that they would answer as hostages. The uproar increased, and Chanler, overcome by fever, collapsed in delirium. Lying on the ground he kept yelling, "Attack! Attack! Cut them down!" terrifying von Höhnel. Then a tall man stalked out of the excited throng, speaking Swahili, and through him von Höhnel nervously negotiated a retreat. The interpreter came along, volunteering to act as the expedition's guide.

Named Motio, he had lived among various peoples in the mountains and spoke their dialects. The people who had blocked the safari's passage were called Embu, he said, and he seemed to know all about Lake Lorian and the Rendille. The lake could be reached, he said, by three days' march northward to the Guaso Nyiro River, and the Rendille were close by.

Von Höhnel hastened to set out. Chanler, much of the time unconscious, was carried in a hammock. Motio warned that the route lay across a waterless desert, and four days later they were crossing an almost treeless wasteland. The heat by day was intense, and the cold at night was bitter. They had drunk the last of their water, and the porters were combating thirst by chewing raw meat when at last they sighted the river on Christmas Eve. Jubilant because the course to Lake Lorian was now plain, Willie and von Höhnel relaxed over a Christmas feast that included a pint of champagne.

The day after Christmas they came upon a major waterfall, where the river, tumbling in two streams over a lava precipice fifty or sixty feet high, churned away through a chasm filled with spray. This waterfall they named Chanler Falls, and pushed on. The terrain was rough; their feet were bruised by the lava rocks strewn along the river bank, and the glare of the sun was blinding. Von Höhnel wrenched a knee and could not help hunt for food. They caught fish, only to discover that they were alive with worms. Swarms of mosquitoes and flies made sleep almost impossible. The horses sickened, and von Höhnel's died. Motio kept assuring them that Lake Lorian was not far off, that they would see it from a high plateau just ahead.

On December 30 the caravan reached the plateau (Merti Plateau), which rose 500 feet above the plain on the opposite bank of the river. Chanler and von Höhnel crossed over, and after a struggle up the nearly vertical side, attained the top. From there they saw the river winding away for miles through a boundless desert, but no lake.

The next day they marched four miles along the base of the plateau and climbed to the top again, this time to behold, shimmering in the northeast, a large body of water — Lake Lorian! Von Höhnel estimated the lake must be at least sixty miles long, and Chanler tried to calculate the number of days it would take to reach it.

From then on the march became even more harrowing. Following the river, they passed through wooded areas teeming with rhinoceros that charged again and again. Chanler had several narrow brushes, and his tent boy was severely gored; Chanler put him on his horse and walked. The porters muttered about entering so perilous a country; both explorers suffered from fever intermittently; a bearer dying of dysentery had to be carried in a sling; others were very ill. The ground grew soggy, and at night it exhaled dank vapors that cut into the body like cold knives. For days there was no firewood, the river winding through tall grass, and the meat had to be eaten barely warmed over fitful grass blazes. Chanler urged the men on, promising them rest and plenty to eat as soon as they reached the lake.

On January 12 they sighted a tall sycamore across the river, which had narrowed to less than ten feet in width and was only a foot deep; it seemed to be drying up, or sinking into the muddy soil. Climbing the tree, Chanler and von Höhnel peered out anxiously for a glimpse of the lake. All they could see, as far as the view extended, was a vast swamp covered with papyrus and water grass. The bitter truth was borne in on them: there was no Lake Lorian. The shimmer they had seen from the plateau had been a mirage; the Guaso Nyiro drained into a vast mud hole.

The return journey was a nightmare of thirst, hunger, and constant danger. The supply of dried corn and beans was wormy and about exhausted; the men were sickening on their unaccustomed diet of meat. The nearest food supply lay in the Jombeni Mountains, where the inhabitants cultivated grain and vegetables. To reach Jombeni in time required forced marches. They followed the river bank, cutting their way through high grass that screened the crocodiles basking at the stream's edge. The trickle of food except for meat, grew smaller and smaller. Men died. But on the ninth day they regained their Christmas camp site. Resting there only a day, the weary caravan struck out for the Jombeni hills, which Motio was sure they could reach in four days of hard marching. But it was not until January 29 that the emaciated train reached a village of the Wamsara (Meru) people on the Jombeni western slope. That night they camped, buoyed by the prospect of trading the next morning for fresh milk, vegetables, and goat's meat.

But during the night the Wamsara set up a war chant. One of Chanler's porters died that night and had to be buried by stealth, in order not to reveal their desperate condition. The next morning several hundred fighting men milled angrily around the camp. Chanler's men were starving, and the shortest route back to the base camp at Hameye lay directly across the Jombeni range through the Wamsara territory. In the enfeebled condition of the caravan, it was folly to think of making a long detour through the desert.

Realizing that he must risk a fight, Chanler aroused the groaning men at two o'clock in the morning and distributed ammunition. At five o'clock, in bright moonlight, the caravan got under way. Chanler led with five Sudanese and Motio. To guard against treachery, Motio was bound with a rope tied around his waist, a husky porter holding the end of the rope in one hand and carrying an American flag in the other. Von Höhnel, with the remaining Sudanese guard and the camel drivers, brought up the rear.

Almost at once the sentinels posted by the Wamsara shouted the alarm from hill to hill. Since they had been discovered, Chanler ordered an advance until, shortly after daybreak, they were rushed by some 200 screaming warriors.

Driven back by point-blank volleys, the attackers charged again and again. Three porters were killed and twelve were wounded, some with poisoned arrows. By eleven o'clock the attack had been repelled and the spearmen drew back. Profiting by the lull, Chanler rounded up all the food supplies he could commandeer in the adjacent villages, and soon had enough goats, cattle, and grain to support the caravan for eight days. Driving the captured livestock before them, the explorers resumed the march, harried by warriors hovering on the flanks.

Chanler pushed on, hoping to gain the crest of the ridge where Motio said the territory of the Wamsara ended and that of the Embu began. The Embu might be friendly. Several times the column was ambushed and fought its way clear. About six o'clock they reached the peak and set up camp on open ground. Twenty goats were slaughtered, the cows were milked, and all through the night the exhausted men feasted while Chanler and von Höhnel treated the wounded.

At daybreak, fearing a renewal of the attack, Chanler distributed the last rounds of ammunition and resumed the journey. But after two hours of unmolested marching they passed the crest of the summit, and a reception committee of Embu came forward to greet the caravan. It was evident that the chiefs wished to hurry the interlopers along, but a rest was imperative for the wounded.

In an attempt to placate the Embu, both explorers submitted to a ceremony of blood brotherhood, but then learned that the bond applied only to that valley. Soon they glimpsed bands of armed men scurrying to a rallying point somewhere on the path ahead, indicating an ambush. An attempt was made to poison the explorers with a pot of doctored honey, and Motio warned of worse to come. So the caravan set out again, and although there was a brush with some of the Embu's fighting men, the explorers suffered no further casualties.

On February 10, 1893, the base camp at Hameye came into sight, with the Stars and Stripes floating over it. "What news?" Willie shouted as George Galvin came running to meet him.

"Pretty good," came the answer, "All the oxen are dead — only three cattle are left — only five camels — and the donkeys are dying fast."

With flag flying and drum beating, Chanler entered the camp from which he had set out sixty-five days before. In the interval he had traversed 600 miles of unknown territory, discovered a range of mountains, exploded the myth of Lake Lorian, and had bestowed the family's name upon a major waterfall. And he was only twenty-five.

Both the Chanler family and the press in Europe and America had been receiving occasional, not always reliable rumors about Willie's progress. Direct reports arrived soon after his return to Hameye. What neither the public nor his family realized, however, was that Willie was desperately ill. For two weeks he could hardly leave his cot; nevertheless, he insisted that preparations go forward for resumption of travel as soon as he regained strength. He still had to find the Rendille and to make his way through the unknown north back to the coast.

Ten men had died on the trip to the Lorian Swamp, and ten more deserted at Hameye after hearing the survivors' tales. The loss of most of the donkeys and all of the camels crippled the expedition's transport; nevertheless,

Chanler was determined to push on. Before doing so he forwarded to the Royal Geographic Society in London a precise report on the Lorian exploration, with a map that von Höhnel had drawn.

On March 9 he set out, hobbling at the head of the caravan, supported by a stick. Then began a period of silence, and only months later would the story of Chanler's struggle with privations, treachery, and disaster become known.

He was dogged by hard luck. For weeks he was tied down by rains, his messengers drowned or were eaten by crocodiles. A fire wiped out the camp, and he rebuilt it, meanwhile sending the headman Hamidi back to the coast to recruit a new force of reliable, experienced bearers for the big push into the northern country.

He found the Rendille, whom he described as never having even heard of a European, as well as a group named the Samburu, who were subject to the Rendille. In parleys he learned the Rendille's customs, but he was rebuffed in his attempts to buy camels and donkeys from them. He collected for shipment back to the Smithsonian Institution in Washington, the American Museum of Natural History in New York, and the Imperial Museum in Vienna hundreds of specimens of the wildlife of the regions he was passing through, the game, the lepidoptera and coleoptera. A new species of antelope he identified was later named Chanler's reedbuck, *Cervicapra chanlerlii*. He took hundreds of photographs with a camera equipped with a rare telescopic lens.

Then August 24 brought a major calamity. Von Höhnel was gored by a charging rhinoceros, and the caravan had to retrace its route to the Daitcho camp, carrying the wounded man in a hammock. The nearest medical aid was 250 miles away, but George Galvin volunteered to get von Höhnel to it, and set out. Expecting Hamidi with fresh bearers, Chanler waited impatiently until October, but when Hamidi did reappear, he brought eighty callow, unseasoned men instead of the strong, experienced porters Chanler needed. Rains kept him marooned until December, when Galvin returned with his own hair-raising tales. Despite the loss of von Höhnel, Willie gave orders to press on, whereupon Hamidi and the entire force of bearers deserted, leaving only one Somali and the Sudanese soldiers faithful.

Stranded hundreds of miles in the interior, without means of transport, surrounded by restive local peoples who had been kept pacified only by constant parleying and ruses, on January 7, 1894, Chanler bowed to the inevitable and abandoned the expedition.

A portion of the trading goods was distributed as presents to the Embu at Daitcho, and the rest destroyed along with the surplus ammunition and rifles, out of consideration for future travelers that way. Then with Galvin and the Sudanese, Chanler struck out for the coast. Marching eleven hours a day, through forests, swamps, and jungles, crossing rain-swollen rivers, they reached Mombasa half-famished on February 10 — one year to the day after Chanler's triumphant return to Hameye from the trip to the Lorian Swamp.

Willie was most eager to get news of von Höhnel, who he learned had received medical treatment and been shipped home. The prognosis for his recovery was favorable. A lasting affection had been formed between the two men, so dissimilar in temperament, and Willie had been able to open his heart to this friend as he could to no one else. The news that greeted Chanler in Mombasa aroused all the combativeness in Willie's combative nature. Hamidi and the absconding porters had flocked back to Zanzibar with accounts of the frightful cruelties they had suffered at the hands of Chanler. They claimed that men had been shot for sport, flogged to death, starved, and subjected to revolting barbarities. Public opinion in Zanzibar had been inflamed, and Chanler found awaiting him a letter from Sir Lloyd Mathews, the sultan's prime minister, curtly advising him to instruct his agents to pay off the porters and disappear from Africa as speedily and secretly as possible. Sir Lloyd said that he could not answer for Chanler's life, should he show up in Zanzibar.

Willie's reaction was instant. He cabled the prime minister:
RENT ME A VILLA. INTEND TO STAY IN ZANZIBAR TWO MONTHS.

And five days later he sailed. With him went the Sudanese and one Somali camel driver who had remained loyal. On reaching Zanzibar, these men went before the American consul and unanimously refuted the porters' charges. Chanler offered to pay the customary blood money to the family of the man who had been shot while trying to desert and also offered to allow Mathews to bring suit on the porters' behalf in the United States consular court.

Sir Lloyd would have none of this, insisting that the suit must be heard in the British court. He refused to listen to testimony by the Sudanese, informing the American consul he had "formed his opinion and quite understood the case." Reporting to the State Department, the consul termed the treatment of Willie "outrageous in the extreme."

Political currents were at work of which Chanler gradually became cognizant. The Imperial British East Africa Company, which claimed a trading monopoly throughout the area that Chanler had explored, had become suspicious, and had stirred up the Colonial Office in London to question the motives of the young American who was carrying the American flag through territory over which Great Britain had hopes of exercising a protectorate. The cards were stacked against Chanler; and so, having remained for the promised two months, on April 3 Chanler sailed without concealment for Aden, and then on to Trieste.

At Trieste, von Höhnel was on hand, quite recovered from his gruesome wound. From there Willie hastened on home, landing in New York on June 12, 1894 — one day after his twenty-seventh birthday.

While it did not achieve all its goals, Chanler's expedition, the largest sent into East Africa up to that time, brought back a mass of scientific data and opened up a hitherto unexplored region that today forms an important part of Kenya. Honors were showered upon the intrepid adventurer. He was elected to membership in geographical societies in England and Austria. Harvard University took another look at its ex-sophomore and conferred a master of arts degree. Augustus Saint-Gaudens did Chanler's bust.

But from this time on, William Astor Chanler would nurse a prejudice against British colonial policy, and against the English and English "sportsmanship," that would grow steadily more pronounced as the years passed.

Between 1892 and 1894, while Willie was exploring Africa,
much had occurred in the family. The three girls, having hastened to England
for Bob's wedding, remained for the London season. Thanks again to Henry
White at the embassy, Alida was presented at court, and this time there was
no omission of the curtsey. Margaret Chanler declined presentation for
patriotic reasons. White House etiquette, she pointed out, made no provision
for curtseying to the President, and she would not pay greater deference to
any foreign sovereign.

Margaret did commission that expatriate American John Singer Sargent
to do a portrait of Elizabeth, and the painter was much taken with her
beauty: "the face of the Madonna and the eyes of the Child," he said.
Women with large, regular features were most admired at the time, but Bob
Chanler scoffed that Sargent "must have an eye of the old monks," and teased
Margaret with being "next in line for Madonna honors."

Alida had a thrilling taste of London society, and she enshrined herself
in family tradition by an encounter with the future Nicholas II of Russia, then
the tsarevitch, at a ball given by the Prince and Princess of Wales. According
to Lloyd Griscom, a private secretary of the American ambassador, the
story happened this way. The royal party opened the ball with a quadrille, followed by a waltz, during which a court chamberlain rapped his seven-foot staff
in front of Griscom and said, "His Royal Highness wishes you to dance."
Griscom spied Alida across the room, and as she was the only girl present he
knew, he hastily claimed her for a partner. They were making their turn of the
floor when the tsarevitch bumped into them and trod heavily on Alida's foot.
She tried to limp along, but a few moments later was petrified to see the
stocky, unsmiling Nicholas bearing down on them again. Griscom braced his

shoulder for the crash, and the tsarevitch was sent sprawling. Leading quickly to the far side of the room, Griscom held his breath, and his heart nearly stopped beating when a gold stick tapped his arm and said, "His Royal Highness wishes you to stop dancing." To his relief, however, he saw that the Prince of Wales merely wished to thin out the crowd.

Alida told a different story. She said she was escorted to the ball by Griscom. When the music struck up, they were approached by a chamberlain who "invited" them to open the ball. Despite their consternation, they could only comply, for the request was in fact a royal command. By this means Alida was placed opposite Nicholas, the guest of honor, it being the only method, under court protocol, by which she could dance with the future tsar. Had Nicholas spotted her in the crowd and arranged it? Under the "jealous glares of ugly duchesses," said Alida, she went through the quadrille with the future emperor. The family legend persisted that Nicholas was so deeply affected by her beauty that a year later he chose for his bride the celebrated beauty Princess Alix of Hesse-Darmstadt, who closely resembled Alida. It was a choice that contributed to the fall of the Romanov dynasty and the birth of the Soviet state.

Margaret sent long reports to Willie in Africa:

"Alida has been presented & much admired. . . . We give little dinners twice a week. . . . Elizabeth leaps from friend to friend the world over; she is rather like a humming bird . . . beautiful with the sunlight she reflects. Wintie has a 'black' [i.e., dark-haired] daughter to be called Hester Marion after the general's sister. . . . His being in business is splendid & he & Archie see each other every day & get on deliciously. The latter has 100 irons at fever heat & his wife [Amélie] under Weir Mitchell [the Philadelphia neurologist]. He travels from one interest to the other & looks well content with this state of things. He has made great good friends with the Stanford Whites, St. Gaudens & other men of their successful artistic calibre & you will see how good this is for him. He is much more what he was years ago than what he was two years ago. It has been splendid for Lewis. By going into the criminal courts he comes in contact with such a world of realities & crises & has his interest in people widened wonderfully. He is very good at it & we are proud of the position he has made for himself already. . . . The papers at home have left off explaining us as Amélie Rives' sisters-in-law. On her presentation they chronicled Alida as your sister."

She did not tell Willie about Elizabeth's horrible dream in which Willie appeared and told her he was dead. Elizabeth was so shaken when she awoke in the middle of the night that she recorded her experience on the spot, using scraps of paper taken from the waste basket.

But Willie managed to come home in good health and spirits. He then returned to Vienna to supervise the publication of von Höhnel's maps, the lieutenant having been recalled to naval duty.

Willie had not seen Bob since his marriage, but he frankly stated his misgivings about it to Margaret: "I am, of course, interested in all that concerns Robert & therefore look forward to meeting Julia. But I must confess that I cannot arouse any enthusiasm in a young man's choice. His notions are almost always wrong to begin with, and almost inevitably, particularly in independent people like ourselves, lead to regrets after a few years. The romantic marriages which turn out well are only in the eyes of the ignorant possessed of romance. There must be something else besides affection. In these days I should say particularly money. . . ."

The handsome young explorer was everywhere in demand. At Monte Carlo he ran into Henry M. Stanley, the explorer of the Congo, and was told that the king of the Belgians wanted to see Willie with regard to leading an expedition to open up a region in the Congo Free State. Stanley had been offered the job, but he had declined and recommended Chanler. Willie went to Brussels. King Leopold described the purposes of the expedition — to open up the territory to agriculture and industry — but Willie's suspicions were aroused because the terms were far too generous coming from a man so notoriously miserly and shifty in his dealings. Willie believed that if he succeeded, he would never collect his reward because he would not come back alive. He was fairly certain that the expedition would actually be a quest of gold and ivory. Another man did lead the expedition — which turned out to be a pillaging sweep through the back-country — and Willie was not surprised to learn the leader met a violent death on the return trip "by the accidental discharge of a rifle."

While in Paris, Chanler received a cablegram from von Höhnel saying his ship was to call at New York shortly, and hoping they might get together again. Dropping everything, Willie caught a fast liner and was at the dock when Höhnel's ship arrived. Whirling his friend ashore, Willie launched the two of them on three cyclonic weeks. Theodore Roosevelt invited von Höhnel to Oyster Bay. The Boone & Crockett Club gave him a dinner that led to Willie chanting Masai war cries. He went to Rokeby where he deduced that Willie's exuberance exasperated the three Chanler sisters at times. Both Elizabeth and Margaret had become converts to the cause of temperance, and they feared their brother would ruin himself through dissipation. Back in New York the Austrian watched Saint-Gaudens at work on Willie's portrait bust, then they sailed to Newport, where Daisy and Wintie entertained them. "With the best will in the world," von Höhnel said, "I could not give an adequate description of the many and varied experiences I lived through in those weeks."

Ten days after the explorer landed in New York in 1894, Alida Chanler came of age and at long last the family estate could be settled. This involved a division among the eight of them of property held in New York City, at Newport, and elsewhere, and specifically the disposition of Rokeby. What should be done with the old home? All the brothers except William were married, with households of their own, and Willie gave no indication of settling anywhere. To sell the property seemed out of the question. Instead, they decided to transfer the estate to the three sisters for their permanent home.

For Amélie Rives Chanler, the prior year had been propitious. In 1893 she was discharged from Weir Mitchell's care, her nerves presumably restored. In 1894 she went abroad again with Archie and in London repeated her social and literary triumphs. An incident occurred at this time that would later be recalled with an uncanny shiver by some members of the Chanler clan. At a crowded reception in London, Archie pointed out a tall, strikingly handsome young man on the opposite side of the room and said: "There is the man Amélie should marry."

At that very moment Oscar Wilde came up to Amélie, surrounded by her customary cloud of admirers, and said: "You are the most beautiful woman in this room, and I must present you to the most beautiful man in this room. You two must be seen together." He led her across the room to the man Archie had indicated and introduced her to Prince Pierre Troubetskoy, a half-Russian, half-American expatriate artist. Two years later, Troubetskoy was indeed the man Amélie married.

Archie returned to the United States alone, and again he and Wintie saw much of each other in connection with their joint business ventures. One major project was the establishment of a water power plant and cotton mill in North Carolina. The idea was Archie's, and both he and Wintie invested heavily in it. A town was created, called Roanoke Rapids, and Archie spent much time at the site, personally supervising the construction. Stanford White designed the building, with unhappy results. While attractive externally, the interior was unsuited to any utilitarian purpose, cotton mills being out of Stanford White's line. Many changes caused the costs to skyrocket and contributed to much ill temper.

In January 1895 Amélie had returned from Europe. The newspapers noted that she was not met by her husband, who was supposedly at The Merry Mills, the estate he had recently acquired in Virginia not far from Castle Hill. It was only in October of that year that the real news surfaced, that the previous spring Amélie quietly obtained a divorce in South Dakota. Uncontested, the decree had been granted on grounds of incompatibility. Amélie had asked for no alimony, but Chanler voluntarily settled upon her a lifetime income of $300 a month.

This was sensational news, for in 1895 a divorce was scandalous. The same year Alva Vanderbilt divorced William Vanderbilt in order to marry Oliver H. P. Belmont, becoming thereby the first woman of prominent social position to defy the wrath of public opinion. Even so, acceptance of divorce came about very slowly, and for years to come a divorcée would remain socially suspect, if not absolutely cast out.

Although the public was taken aback, insiders were hardly surprised when on February 18, 1896, Amélie married Prince Pierre Troubetskoy, in the same parlor at Castle Hill where she had wed John Armstrong Chanler nearly eight years before.

As Princess Troubetskoy Amélie ceased to exist socially for the Chanler sisters, although Alida did enjoy the titillation of being indirectly allied with such a shocking creature. Margaret regarded divorce as heinous, although she was willing to stretch a point in Archie's favor because she was so intensely annoyed by Amélie. The thing that Margaret could never condone was what she called "plural marriage," the remarriage of divorced persons while the first partner was still living. She regarded such remarriages as a blow against the sanctity of the family. Her firm adherence to this principle was to cause her much pain later in life. For the Chanler family generally, the relationship with Amélie was over. But to the end of his life, Archie Chanler would be identified by the public as "the former husband of Amélie Rives."

October 1896 brought two events of major importance. On October 8 Lewis surprised everyone by announcing his retirement from the practice of criminal law in New York County. He did so in the course of summing up the defense of a penniless client. He told the jurors that the systematic slights and prejudices to which he had been subjected by certain judges of the City's criminal courts had become intolerable, and he would never practice again in the courts of New York County.

But there were also private reasons for his action. Alice's health was again unsatisfactory, and a milder climate had been recommended. Lewis planned an extended sojourn abroad, preferably in England. A second child had been born to them, a daughter named Alida for her aunt, and the whole family would go abroad as soon as he could wind up the cases to which he was already committed. His retirement was widely discussed in legal circles and much sympathy was expressed for him. *The New York Tribune*, citing his painstaking work, commented that he would be missed in the Tombs.

But the true center of attention that month was twenty-three-year-old Alida's wedding at Rokeby on October 27. Her husband, Christopher Temple Emmet, was a young lawyer and sportsman, and one of the first graduates of Yale Forestry School. Temple Emmet came from a distinguished Irish family, which included Robert Emmet, the martyr to the cause of Irish freedom. Temple's direct ancestor, Thomas Addis Emmet, Robert's brother, had been implicated in the 1798 uprising and arrested, but was released when he consented to go into exile. Coming to New York, he had prospered as an attorney and political ally of DeWitt Clinton. To the Chanlers' relief, Temple Emmet adhered to the Protestant faith.

The engagement had been announced in September, and when word reached Margaret in Europe, she hastened home to make preparations, only to find that Stanford White had taken charge. There was to be a mighty gathering of the clan, of course, with only Daisy unable to attend. She had been called to Rome by the failing health of her mother, Louisa Terry.

Wintie kept Daisy abreast of developments. A special train was to bring the guests from the city, he wrote, and "the entire family, with the melancholy exception of you, will be assembled at Rokeby for the wedding. Just think of it! There is talk of Aunt Julia Howe, Aunt Tiny Griffin, and Aunt Betty White coming up for the night . . . Robert talks of coming over. . . . Archie says he will be 'drenched in calm' — ominous outlook!"

The festivities came up to every expectation. A special train brought 200 guests from New York and later returned them. The ceremony was held in Christ Church in Red Hook, presided over by the rector and the bishop.

Winthrop Chanler gave his sister away, and brothers Willie, Lewis, and Robert were ushers; the bridesmaids were all cousins of the bride except one; and the guests passed under an arch of autumn leaves and evergreens, erected by the country folk, as they left the church for the reception and breakfast at Rokeby.

Across the front of the house Stanford White had draped tapestries, and had hired Neapolitan minstrels strumming mandolins to stroll around the grounds among the guests. A canvas pavilion with a wooden floor had been set up for dancing, and a celebrated Hungarian orchestra provided music.

Only one sour note intruded: at the last minute Archie had telegraphed from Virginia that he was ill with pleurisy and could not attend. He sent his blessing and a present.

To the others his behavior was incomprehensible and inexcusable. "The man is daft!" Wintie exclaimed. As the head of the family, Archie's place was at his sister's side, even if in a wheelchair. His brothers agreed. Bob echoed Wintie's exclamation, saying Archie must be loony. Alida cried for hours upon receiving the telegram, sure that her brother was dying. Wintie filled the role meant to be performed by the absent head of the family, but the affront was not forgotten or forgiven.

Archie himself offered no excuses, and indeed, a short while later turned up at the Horse Show in Madison Square Garden, an annual event to which he was devoted. While in the city he attended meetings of the directors of his various companies, but soon hastened back to The Merry Mills. Then rumors began to filter north about strange doings at that estate. Archie was said to be shutting himself up for days, refusing to see visitors and conducting mysterious psychological experiments. His New York clubs rarely saw him, and after March 1897 they saw him not at all. To all inquiries the family intimated that Archie was in Europe.

The sensation was great, therefore, when in October 1897, one year after Alida's marriage, New York newspapers disclosed that John Armstrong Chanler was in Bloomingdale insane asylum at White Plains, north of New York City. The commitment papers under which he was held had been signed by his brothers, Winthrop and Lewis, and by a cousin, Arthur Carey, of Boston. Moreover, Archie had been in the asylum for seven months.99

PART III:

ARMS AND THE MEN

15 | OF LOVE AND LUNACY

Daisy Chanler had long been struck that although the Chanlers quarreled violently, they never quarreled over money or property rights. Instead, they tended to fight over moral or theological questions, or over issues concerning precedence and social propriety. So it would seem out of character for Wintie and Archie to have fallen out over business, but that is exactly what had happened.

Archie and Wintie were the principal stockholders in the Roanoke Rapids Power Company. In December 1896, two months after Alida's wedding, Archie called a meeting of the company's directors in the New York hotel where he stayed. A dispute over policy arose, and the brothers took opposite sides. Wintie was still incensed over Archie's failure to appear at Alida's wedding, and the Rokeby-style argument grew so heated that it almost led to blows.

The next day Wintie wrote Archie in a rage that he would henceforth communicate with his brother only in writing or through a third party. Archie replied just as heatedly, and added that he would be sending an auditor to look over the books of his father's estate, of which Wintie and Lewis Chanler were executors. Archie pointed out that there had been no accounting for five years, and he wished to satisfy himself that there had been no mismanagement of the estate. Although deeply affronted, Wintie replied that his brother could do as he pleased.

Meanwhile, another point of difference had arisen concerning the brothers' joint investment in a second company at Roanoke Rapids, the United Industrial Company, which had been formed to operate the mills. In this company Archie held stock with a book value of $175,000 and Wintie held

$50,000 worth. Elizabeth Chanler was a minor stockholder, as was Stanford White. In addition, Winthrop Chanler was the salaried president of this company, and both he and Armstrong were directors. Reflecting that it would be difficult to do business with a man who refused to speak to him, Archie relayed a suggestion that his brother resign as president and director of United Industrial. Wintie complied in a flash, and in January 1897 Archie reshuffled the board and elected himself president of the company.

A distressed witness of the brothers' estrangement was Stanford White. Archie had been talking about taking a vacation from business in order to carry out certain psychological experiments, so White proposed that Archie let him and their trusted friend, St. Gaudens, act for him. St. Gaudens declined the responsibility. But in January 1897 Archie gave White his power of attorney, reflecting that he could revoke it any time, and withdrew to The Merry Mills to focus on his experiments.

Archie had great intellectual curiosity, but his mind was not disciplined or orderly. His frustrating marriage to Amélie Rives had aggravated in him a tendency to solitariness and erratic behavior, and like all Chanlers, he was impatient.

During the end of 1896 and the beginning of 1897, Archie was exploring in himself a newfound faculty that William James would later call "mediumistic." His first intimation that he had such capacity came one evening while knocking the billiard balls around. He noticed that they had stopped in the pattern of the Great Dipper. He set up the balls, struck them, and again they came to rest in the same pattern. He tried a third time with the same result. Taking a pencil from his pocket, he started to make a note of the occurrence on the back of an envelope and was astonished to find his hand refusing to follow his thought but instead writing, "Get a planchette."

He procured a planchette, which is a sort of ouija board, and after a few tries found that coherent messages began to evolve under his manipulation. He rejected the thought that otherworldly forces were at work, but he was mystified as to what produced the messages. He had never even heard the word "subconscious," then just coming into use among psychologists, so he called the mysterious phenomenon his "X-faculty," X symbolizing an unknown quantity.

To test the validity of messages he received, Archie acted on one that was a tip on the stock market. He made a profit, but regarded the test as crude and did not repeat it. He also found his X-faculty was not always trustworthy, once causing him to burn himself painfully with live coals. Nevertheless, he kept practicing with automatic writing — though he preferred the term "graphic automatism" — and finally was able to write directly on a pad of paper with a lightly held pencil.

The most startling demonstration, however, came when his X-faculty made it possible for him to change the color of his eyes. Oculists who examined Archie's eyes after 1896 agreed unanimously that his eyes were then dark gray in color, while a highly qualified doctor who had known him before 1896 testified that they had then been light brown. And Amélie Rives Troubetzkoy swore in an affidavit that while married to Archie his eyes were light brown, just as she had described them in *The Quick or the Dead?*

Whatever actually happened, Archie became infatuated with his mysterious X-faculty, and he was most definitely in a credulous mood when it indicated that he was destined to carry out some lofty mission in life, the nature of which was not defined. His friends and relatives, however, were alarmed. Stanford White decided to look into his friend's condition personally and wrote to say he would visit The Merry Mills shortly. Archie replied by telegram that he was "too ill" to receive visitors. This increased White's uneasiness, and disregarding Archie's request arrived unannounced at the door of Archie's secluded home. With him he had brought a physician, Dr. Eugene Fuller.

Archie was initially annoyed when both visitors pushed rudely into the house. White introduced his companion without revealing that he was a doctor, and gradually thawed Archie's coolness. White urged Archie to abandon his hermit-like existence and plunge into the metropolitan whirl of New York for a few days. Archie was persuaded, and all three men took the train back together.

In New York, Archie checked into his usual hotel, the Kensington, where he received a clear communication — this time by means of "vocal automatism," or involuntary speech — saying that he should go into a "Napoleonic trance," during which he would "reenact the deathbed scene of Napoleon." How the trance would be induced the X-faculty promised to disclose when the moment arrived.

Shortly after this, Saint-Gaudens dropped in, and during their conversation Archie was given to understand by his X-faculty that the moment had come. He asked Saint-Gaudens whether he cared to observe the experiment, and the sculptor said he would. Archie stretched out on the bed, and taking a shaving mirror in both hands held it at arm's length above his head and stared fixedly at the reflection. After a few moments his mouth gaped, and he gasped for breath convulsively. This went on, Archie estimated, for perhaps ten minutes; then his hands slowly placed the mirror on the bed, his eyes closed, and the trance began. He retained consciousness and was aware that Saint-Gaudens, greatly affected, was pleading with him to break off the experiment. With perfect composure, Archie did, and Saint-Gaudens left, much upset and earnestly requesting that Chanler never repeat the performance in his presence.

The next day Stanford White and Dr. Fuller called at the Kensington. They expressed a wish to witness the Napoleon experiment themselves, and Archie consented to oblige. Everything passed off as before: Chanler lay entranced, with eyes closed, and while in that state he heard White whisper: "It is exactly like Napoleon's death mask! I have a photograph of it at home."

A couple of days after this, Dr. Fuller called again, saying he had brought a friend, an oculist, who was intensely interested in the change of the color of Chanler's eyes and wished to examine them. The three men had a long discussion about parapsychology, although the word had not been invented yet, in the course of which Archie expressed some unflattering opinions about the medical profession in general. The oculist examined Chanler's eyes and was full of questions.

The next evening, as Archie lay in bed reading, the door was pushed open without a knock by two rough-looking men and the alleged oculist of the day before. Brusquely he introduced himself as Dr. Moses Allen Starr, professor of nervous diseases at the College of Physicians and Surgeons in New York, president of the New York Neurological Society, and also president of the American Neurological Association. Informing Archie that he had a court order for his commitment on grounds of insanity, Starr ordered him to get up and come along quietly, warning that force would be employed if necessary.

Archie said that he told Dr. Starr " very quietly" that he declined to obey the doctor's command, and "finally succeeded in convincing him, without the slightest show of force, that he had not brought enough men with him to carry me off that night." Later Archie amplified the account to say that his subliminal self had warned him of imminent danger, and he had placed under his pillow the loaded revolver that he always carried when traveling. When Starr caught hold of Chanler's left wrist, Archie slid his right hand under the pillow, and pointing the gun "straight at the middle button of Dr. Starr's waist coat." Archie said he would not come, but would discuss the matter with the doctor if he promised not to try any rough tactics. But Starr said he would discuss it another time, and backed out of the room.

The next day two detectives from police headquarters appeared with a warrant for Archie's arrest as a dangerous lunatic exhibiting homicidal tendencies. The proprietor of the hotel, a personal friend of Archie's, examined the warrant, found it in order, and advised Chanler to submit. In the lobby the detectives displayed their warrant and said they had been told by Police Commissioner Theodore Roosevelt to show Chanler every consideration. A closed carriage was waiting. Archie got into it and with his captors was driven to Grand Central terminal, chatting amicably along the way.

Confident that he could soon rectify the mistake of the arrest, Archie felt no alarm. The twenty-mile ride to White Plains was brief, and late on the evening of March 13, 1897, John Armstrong Chanler passed through the gate of the asylum for the insane maintained by The New York Hospital, commonly called Bloomingdale.

The family was widely scattered: Lewis was in England, Willie was at sea, Bob was in France, and Elizabeth and Margaret were in India. Alida, although honeymooning at New Rochelle, was seldom consulted about family affairs, being considered too scatterbrained to grasp grave questions. Wintie alone was nearby.

Lewis, however, had been in New York recently, to meet with Wintie about Archie's announced intention to examine the books of their father's estate. Wintie laid before Lewis the whole story of Archie's growing "queerness," his erratic decisions, and those "crazy" experiments he was conducting. Stanford White added his own apprehensions, and the logical conclusion seemed to be that Archie had become deranged. For his own safety, they determined, he should be placed under restraint and medical care.

Lewis advised that word of Archie's condition be withheld from the press, and Wintie concurred. After all, with rest and total seclusion Archie might recover. On this basis Lewis consented to join Wintie in seeking their brother's commitment. Wintie also enlisted the cooperation of a cousin, Arthur Carey, who more than once had told Archie to his face that he was "cracked." Lewis took care of the legalities, and on March 10 Justice Henry A. Gildersleeve of the New York Supreme Court signed commitment papers, acting on the application of three next-of-kin, supported by the finding of Dr. Moses Allen Starr that John Armstrong Chanler was insane.

Word of Archie's confinement reached the other members of the family as a *fait accompli*, and they accepted the judgment of Wintie and Lewis as undoubtedly sound. Friends were told that Archie had gone abroad for an extended stay.

At the same time another emotional upheaval was causing the Chanlers distress, but at the moment it touched Elizabeth and Margaret alone. The Chanler sisters had formed a warm friendship with the John Jay Chapmans, a Boston couple living in New York. Minna Chapman was half-Italian, a woman of passionate temperament. She and Elizabeth had been strongly drawn to each other from their first meeting. John Jay Chapman came from a line of strongminded New England and New York reformers. Intellectually gifted, he was subject to psychic storms of a bizarre nature and overwhelming intensity. While courting Minna, he imagined that another young man had spoken of her slightingly, and had beaten him mercilessly. Then learning he was mistaken, Chapman had done penance by thrusting his left hand into a coal fire in his Harvard room and holding it there until it was so charred it had to be amputated. Yet these dark depths of Chapman's troubled nature were not obvious due to his witty urbanity and easy laughter. Chapman was passionately dedicated to the causes he espoused. As a lawyer and spokesman for the municipal reform movement in New York City, he had been a principal organizer of the Good Government Clubs that aimed at combating corruption and civic misrule.

When Margaret returned from abroad for Alida's wedding in the autumn of 1896, she took in the appalling situation at a glance: Elizabeth was desperately in love with the husband of her best friend. Margaret was horrified. The situation not only contained all the ingredients of heartbreak, but threatened to precipitate a horrific scandal: not only were the Chapmans congenially married, but they had two small sons, Victor and John Jay, Jr., and were expecting a third child any minute.

Margaret reacted energetically. Immediately after Alida's wedding, she snatched Elizabeth away for a long voyage to India and Japan, propinquity being one factor in the equation that she could eliminate. After a pause in England, the sisters traveled through the Mediterranean, the Suez Canal, and on eastward. In Ceylon the travelers were entertained officially, everywhere impressing their hosts by their dignity of bearing and the remarkable clarity of their diction. Crossing to the mainland they stopped at Madras, and then proceeded to Ootacamund, where the wife of the Resident proved to be a New York acquaintance. There they encountered a general who had marched to the relief of Kandahar in 1880, and he laid out an itinerary for them that took them clear to the Khyber Pass. Elizabeth applied herself to compiling a voluminous travel diary which she intended for Minna Chapman.

Then at Calcutta they received shocking news: ten days after the birth of her third child, Minna Chapman had died. The child, a boy, had been named Conrad. In a letter to Elizabeth, Chapman wrote that he did not want her to come home, but Elizabeth felt otherwise. Waving aside Margaret's objections, she resumed the ascendancy she normally exercised, and with all speed crossed to Bombay and there caught a fast steamer to Brindisi. From there the sisters traveled overland to France and sailed for New York on April 7.

On their landing, Wintie related the full story of Chapman's crushing blow and of Archie's no less crushing misfortune. Elizabeth promptly visited Archie in Bloomingdale, but found no reason to differ from Wintie's judgment. Her brother appeared rational to her on all subjects except one, but that one seemed preposterous to her. Archie claimed that his detention had resulted from a deliberate conspiracy by his brothers, who wanted to gain control and eventual possession of his inheritance. By their father's will, if Archie died without issue, his share of the estate would pass to his brothers and sisters in equal portions. What better way to ensure that he would not contract a second marriage and have children than by having him declared insane? Meanwhile, if the courts ruled him incompetent, his brothers and sisters would have the practical control of his property.

To Elizabeth the idea was fantastic. Chanlers never haggled over money, she pointed out, and she was certain her brothers' motives were honest. Pointing to the bars at his window, Archie said that they did not seem expressive of brotherly concern and pure motives. Elizabeth smiled and said the bars were there to keep him from running away. From the airy way she spoke, Archie began to suspect that "Queen Bess" was in the plot too. Visibly excited, he requested that Elizabeth not visit him again, for he had no need of her sympathy. Elizabeth did not call again.

The conditions under which Archie was held were strict but not unnecessarily onerous. Bloomingdale asylum was a private institution. Archie was assessed $100 a week for board, lodging, and medical care, plus the hire of two keepers, one of whom was always with him. He was forbidden to have any money, but ordered luxuries to be sent in at his expense. He could communicate with no one outside the asylum, whether by letter, telephone, or telegraph, except through the asylum authorities, who had full power to censor or suppress any communication at their discretion. He was allowed to have books and newspapers, and could take exercise inside the grounds, but always in the custody of a keeper.

Chanler found much to object to. He spurned the asylum food, terming it "badly cooked, adulterated, or decayed," and subsisted mainly on rations purchased from nearby grocery stores. Although a member of the medical staff visited him every day, the visits seemed mainly to get him to agree that he was demented, something he steadfastly refused to admit. This refusal was put down as confirmation of his insanity, because it indicated an inability to cope with reality.

Archie awoke to the gravity of his plight only when it was too late. His first reaction had been profound humiliation, and out of shame he had resigned from all his clubs. Next he cast about for a way to effect his release. He must, first of all, procure competent legal counsel. He was sure that the asylum authorities would never let past them any letter addressed to a lawyer who might "make trouble." And anyway, who would take the statements of a certified madman seriously? "Give a dog a bad name and hang him" was the adage that ran through his mind.

After several attempts at writing a completely convincing letter of appeal, Archie gave up in despair. He had no skill in writing and used to joke that the only thing he could write was a check. But he had kept up the practice of automatic writing, and one day the pencil spelled out the words, "I will write you a letter that will get you out of this hell-hole."

Gradually the letter took form. Running to several thousand words, it was a remarkable production. Dated July 3, 1897, it was addressed to Captain Micajah Woods, Commonwealth's attorney of Albemarle County, Virginia, who also practiced privately at Charlottesville. Archie knew Woods personally, and as a Virginia lawyer Woods might be presumed to be outside the range of Astor influence.

Archie explained his situation and the causes of his imprisonment. Chief among these he placed his long estrangement from the rest of the family, dating back to his marriage. The letter went on to describe his recent business quarrels with Wintie, and his giving Stanford White power of attorney so that he would be free to carry on the experiments in "esoteric Buddhism." He recounted how White appeared uninvited at The Merry Mills, how White tricked him into going to New York, how he had been examined by the false oculist, and how his eyes had changed color. This last was relevant, he stressed, because the commitment papers stated he was insane because he said his eyes had changed color.

Archie described how he lived "in solitary confinement in a two-roomed cell. A keeper sleeps in one of the rooms . . . and he is always with me. When I take exercise in the asylum grounds the keeper is always with me. . . . In the meantime, I am living in a madhouse. . . . Nothing prevents a patient from becoming homicidally insane at any time. In one of such fits of frenzy the lunatic might take it into his head to walk into my cell and attack me. . . . When you add to these 'surroundings' the active and sustained efforts of the resident doctors to talk me into becoming insane by declaring to my face that I am insane, and attempting to argue me into admitting that I am; when you consider this, you will, I think, conclude that I have my nerves and will-power under effective control in being able to remain sane."

Moreover, Archie contended that he had been illegally arrested and imprisoned. His address was given as the Hotel Kensington, New York City, when he was actually a bona fide resident of Virginia, and had never been registered at the Kensington except as a transient guest. He offered many proofs of this, including even the complaint sworn to by his brothers and cousin, which referred to him as having been "for several months at his home in Virginia." New York courts had, therefore, no jurisdiction in his case.

He pointed out many other irregularities and inconsistencies in the commitment papers and then took the doctors apart. Dr. Starr was especially excoriated, accused of deceit, moral turpitude, and medical ignorance. He had not, Archie said, limited himself "to a peculiar diet"; had not frequently gone into a "trancelike state . . . exposed myself to cold, neglected or injured myself . . . threatened other people . . . been confined in an institution for the insane in 'New Paris, France,'" and so on down a long list. He admitted that he had carried a revolver, but he denied that he could be described as "going armed." He admitted that he said the color of his eyes had changed from brown to gray, and so it had. He admitted that he had been in a trancelike state, but not "frequently," and confirmed that when in a trance he sometimes spoke French, as he sometimes did when not in a trance. He denied that he suffered from delusions.

Archie also denied the ruling that he was a maniac "with suicidal as well as homicidal tendencies." Here he cited his peaceable surrender to the arresting officers and his exemplary conduct since entering Bloomingdale. He conceded that he had, quite calmly, "frequently warned the authorities here that I would seek legal redress for the false imprisonment that I was undergoing, and that I would hold them legally responsible for their share in it." And as for why the doctors did not discharge him, Archie suggested that it was to their pecuniary advantage to keep him.

His summation was devastating: "The ground work of the commitment papers is an amalgam of avarice, malice, and mendacity. I was accused by persons who were not in a position to know whereof they — not merely spoke, but duly swore. These said accusers were all and severally on bad terms with me for years . . . [and] it was to the unmistakable interests of two of the said accusers, Messrs. Winthrop Astor Chanler and Lewis Stuyvesant Chanler [as executors of their father's estate], that I should be disfranchised, as an insane person, of my property as well as of my liberty. . . ."

Archie wanted Micajah Woods to bring, in cooperation with Senator Daniel, a habeas corpus action in a federal, not a New York State, court. The exact procedure he left to the attorneys, but he urged speed, stressed the need for secrecy, and apologized that because he was allowed no money, they would have to charge all expenses to his account.

And so the letter was written, but the problem remained of how to get it to Woods in Charlottesville. Months went by while Archie watched for an opportunity.

John Armstrong ("Archie") Chanler, man of the world, about the time of his marriage to Amélie Rives in 1888.

Amélie Rives Chanler at the height of her celebrity about 1893, not long before her divorce from Archie.

Winthrop Astor ("Wintie") Chanler, Harvard College, Class of 1885.

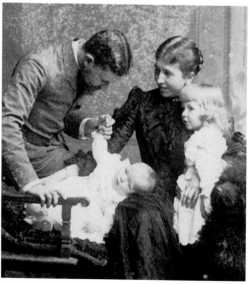

Wintie Chanler with his wife Margaret ("Daisy") Terry, and their first two children, John Winthrop (left) and Laura Astor Chanler. Photographed in Rome, ca. 1890.

Elizabeth Winthrop Chanler, a portrait by John Singer Sargent commissioned by her sister Margaret and painted in London in 1893. This family icon is now in the National Museum of American Art in Washington.

William Astor Chanler, Elizabeth Winthrop Chanler, and Margaret Livingston Chanler at the ruins at Taormina, Sicily, 1892.

Chanler Falls, in East Africa, discovered and named by Willie Chanler on the day after Christmas, 1892. This photograph was taken some thirty years later by another expedition.

Bivouac, East Africa. Seated from left: Willie Chanler, Lieutenant von Höhnel, and George Galvin; four Sudanese guards stand with Somali horses. The expedition, lasting eighteen grueling months, at the start comprised 160 men. Photo 1892.

Lieutenant Ludwig von Höhnel. A veteran of an
earlier East African expedition, von Höhnel was
cartographer and second-in-command of the Chanler
Expedition. He later resumed his career in the Austrian
Navy, retiring as a rear-admiral. Photo 1892.

George E. Galvin. A resourceful and intrepid local boy
from the Rokeby neighborhood, Galvin accompanied
Willie Chanler on his African and Cuban adventures
beginning at the age of 16. Later he ran his own travel
agency in New York City. Photo 1901.

A replica of the bronze bust of Willie Chanler by American sculptor Augustus Saint-Gaudens in 1895.

Willie Chanler (at far right) with other volunteers in Florida, chafing at the bit to drive the Spaniards from Cuba. Photo early 1898.

Lewis Stuyvesant Chanler at the start of his career as a defense attorney in New York City. Photo 1893.

Alice Chamberlain at about the time of her marriage to Lewis Chanler. Photo 1890.

Margaret Chanler. Within a year she would become the sole owner of Rokeby and the "Angel of Puerto Rico." Photo ca. 1898.

Miss Anna Bouligny (left), a professional nurse, and Margaret Chanler, at the military hospice they established in Ponce, Puerto Rico, in the summer of 1898. In 1939 Margaret received from the hand of FDR a Congressional medal honoring this service.

Robert Winthrop Chanler, mimicking the artiste, *in Paris about the time his daughter Dorothy was born. Photo ca. 1898.*

Julia Remington Chamberlain, younger sister of Alice Chanler, at about the time of her marriage to Bob Chanler. Photo ca. 1893.

Alida Beekman Chanler, in London in the dress worn at her presentation at Court.
Photo 1893.

Christopher Temple Emmet and his wife Alida Chanler at Tampa, Florida, eighteen months after their wedding. Before Temple Emmet could get to Cuba, Alida persuaded him to return with her to New York and safety. Photo 1898.

John Jay Chapman and Elizabeth Chanler Chapman with his three sons, from left; Victor, John Jay Jr., and Conrad, in Wells, England. Photo 1899.

Stanford White, his wife Bessie, and their only child Lawrence Grant White, in Egypt, about the time White finished remodeling Rokeby for the Chanler sisters. In 1916, Larry married Winthrop Chanler's oldest child, Laura. Photo ca. 1895.

16 | HOME RULE AND GUN-RUNNING

In England Lewis had been improving his time and talents at Cambridge University. There he studied international jurisprudence and participated in debates at the Cambridge Union. As Willie had often remarked, Lewis dearly loved to make a speech. Before long he was elected president of the prestigious Union, the first American so honored.

The English climate was proving beneficial to Lewis's wife, Alice. In fact, the whole English way of life suited her, and the family's contentment at Cambridge was completed by the birth of a second son, William Astor Chanler II. Lewis kept the family at home informed of his activities, including his interest in horses on and off the race track. And he badgered Margaret constantly for news of Rokeby — the farm, the "house people," and the affairs of Christ Church in Red Hook, of which he had become a trustee.

Sympathizing with the Irish Nationalists in their struggle to gain home rule, Lewis in 1897 campaigned for them under the sponsorship of John Redmond. A bellicose speech in Dublin, which the London press described as "breathing no end of threats against England," caused his Anglicized cousin, William Waldorf Astor, to deny testily that Chanler spoke for the Astors. Redmond offered Lewis a seat in parliament from an Irish constituency, but he declined, to Margaret's immense relief; she lived in dread that her brother would settle abroad permanently, becoming the sort of rootless exile whom she regarded with mingled pity and aversion. For his part, Lewis reminded Margaret, "You must not take life so hard; remember that you ought not to do the thinking for three [herself and her sisters] & a little self-indulgence is a good thing as a rest."

Willie Chanler was often at Tammany Hall during these days, and he reported that Lewis's stand for Ireland was warmly applauded there. Willie still had his eye upon a political career. Tammany's boss, Richard Croker, found a Chanler connection useful, and Willie enjoyed the roughhouse tactics by which Croker sometimes "persuaded" the votes to fall on the right side. Several Tammany district leaders became Chanler's firm friends, notably Tom Foley, leader of the Irish-Italian district east of City Hall.

Willie had also kept up a correspondence with Theodore Roosevelt, and toward the end of 1896, when Roosevelt was about to become Assistant Secretary of the Navy under President McKinley, Republican Teddy turned to Democrat Willie for practical help: "I know you are as strong in your views of foreign policy as Cabot [Lodge] and I are. It seems incredible that the Democratic party, the historic party of annexation, should be inclined to go against the annexation of Hawaii; but SO it is. . . . I think this is the time when you could use your influence in a way that would be invaluable to America. . . ."

Despite this junction of forces, the annexation treaty failed to pass at that time. The most explosive foreign policy issue was provided by Cuba, where insurgents were fighting a guerrilla war against the Spanish regime. The jingo press was broadcasting propaganda provided by a revolutionary junta, headed in New York by a refugee school teacher named Thomas Estrada Palma. Through the two largest newspapers in the country, William Randolph Hearst's *Journal* and Joseph Pulitzer's *World*, they were also whipping up interventionist sentiment in the United States. Estrada Palma and Willie Chanler had become very friendly.

The Cuban junta were also involved in smuggling war materiel to their comrades, compromising American neutrality and also drawing the nation involuntarily into war. The smugglers had to circumvent not only Spanish gunboats, but also the navies of the world whose governments were at peace with Spain. One American had already been sentenced to death by a Spanish court-martial, and only grudgingly reprieved when an uproar of indignation arose in the United States.

Willie sympathized with the Cuban revolutionaries and believed that the interest of his own country required the expulsion of Spain. In December 1897, Roosevelt had written to him confidentially saying that he believed: ". . . every European power should be driven out of America, and every foot of American soil, including the nearest islands in both the Pacific and the Atlantic, should be in the hands of independent American states, and so far as possible in the possession of the United States or under its protection." Nonetheless, the letter was completely unofficial. Secretary of State John Hay had in fact plainly told Willie, "If you get caught, we won't even know you."

Willie tried to enlist von Höhnel in his adventure, but the lieutenant was on sea duty, so Willie had joined forces with a daredevil known as "Dynamite Johnny" O'Brien. They procured two coastal steamers which they loaded with arms purchased secretly by the Cuban junta. To get the cargoes out of American ports required ingenuity and forged manifests. Willie's craft was the *Bermuda*. George Galvin wrote a farewell letter to von Höhnel from Willie's New York apartment which gave the details:

"I leave this morning for Philadelphia where I ship on a steamer as an A.B. [able-bodied seaman]. Our destination is the insurgent camp, Cuba. I sympathize deeply with them in their fight for liberty and only hope to be of some slight help to them in the field. I will go into a cavalry troop. Mr. C. [Willie] too will be on the same vessel but we will have to be as perfect strangers. It is a risky trip with little glory attached and very little chance of promotion, but there will be plenty of bad food, hard work, and a good chance of getting one's head blown off. However I don't care and only wish you too was with us. . . ."

Two months later, Willie, back from one successful trip, wrote to von Höhnel from a dingy hotel in Jersey City where he was lying low:

"I am afraid it will be impossible for you to understand my motives in undertaking this business. First I am, as you say, young & reckless. Second I sympathize with the Cubans in their gallant efforts in behalf of liberty, and third, I, being an American, feel it necessary to do what I can to separate entirely this continent from Europe. . . . It is no easy matter to get to Cuba I can tell you. We are chased from pillar to post by police, revenue cutters & warships. I have narrowly escaped capture twice but my old luck seems to stand by me. . . . Keep your heart up & dont picture me shot in the stomach, lamed, maimed, or hanged."

Willie's family saw nothing of him while he played at cat-and-mouse with the Spanish gunboats. One hair-raising escape story is impossible to verify independently, but it does authentically reflect Willie's resourcefulness.

Willie had several navy deserters in his crew, and to give them some diversion while waiting to make a secret landing on Cuba, he had a light naval gun mounted on the *Bermuda*'s forward deck under camouflage, which the deserters were allowed to use for target shooting.

On one trip the *Bermuda* at length received a signal to land its cargo in a little harbor on the Southern coast. As the ship boldly turned into the narrow entrance channel, directly ahead the crew saw a Spanish gunboat at anchor. The *Bermuda* had no space to turn around; she was trapped. Whether any command was given was never made clear, but off came the bow gun's housing and the gunners opened fire. With their first shot they struck the gunboat's magazine and blew the craft out of the water.

Frantically backing out of the cove, Willie considered what to do. Sinking a warship was an act of piracy, for which the *Bermuda* would be hunted down by every navy in the world. Filibustering was one thing, piracy was infinitely more dangerous; under international law, the fate of pirates was hanging.

Heading for the Florida coast, he called the crew together, explained their predicament, and warned that their necks would be in danger if they ever breathed a word about what had happened. To drive home the warning, he stopped at a lonely key and put ashore several of the toughest men, stripped to their shorts. All day he left them to the sun and mosquitoes. That, he told them when they were taken off in the evening, was only a taste of what would happen if they ever talked.

That night, off the Florida coast, the crew was put ashore and told to scatter. Then Willie scuttled the *Bermuda*, and with one seaman (presumably George Galvin) set out in an open boat for Cuba. He made the island safely and got into Havana without detection. There he took refuge in an elegant bordello, where he stayed until he believed the furor over the gunboat had sufficiently died down. Then he quietly made his way to New York.

Years afterward, one of Willie's sons read a fictionalized account of this episode in a pulp magazine. Knowing that his father had run guns to Cuba, the boy asked whether the story was true. Willie was startled, but confirmed that the account was essentially accurate, and that the ship in question was his own.

17 | DOMESTIC BREEZES BLOW HOT, BLOW COLD

Neither business altercations nor growing concern about Archie's mental stability seemed to dampen Wintie's high spirits for long. Dropping into the office of his friend Amos French early one morning in February 1897, he left this memo scribbled on the laggard banker's desk:

"My dear Amos,

I really want to remonstrate. Here it is after 9 o'clock and neither Mr. Waterbury, Mr. Kean nor Mr. French at his post. Shocking sloth, most dilatory dawdledom.

Yours in sorrow more than anger.

— W. CHANLER"

In September 1897, when Daisy's mother died, Wintie and the children moved to Rome with Daisy to stay with her father. The following month came word that the New York newspapers had found out that Archie was in Bloomingdale asylum.

Archie had been watching since July for a way to smuggle out his letter to Micajah Woods. Finally, on October 13, an opportunity had presented itself. A newspaper reporter taking the cure for morphine addiction was discharged. He volunteered to carry out Chanler's letter, but also, being a reporter, he took word of Chanler's whereabouts to the New York City newsrooms.

The next day *The New York Times* revealed the mental breakdown of "the former husband of Amélie Rives." His commitment had been procured by his "nearest relatives and friends," the *Times* said, "upon the advice of physicians, and after careful deliberation," because of an "alleged tendency to hallucinations and the manifestation of symptoms of nervous collapse. . . . He was taken to Bloomingdale quietly, and in order that his privacy there might not be intruded upon, the impression was allowed to obtain that he had gone abroad."

Both the *Tribune* and the *Times* interviewed Archie's law partner, Harry Van Ness Philip, who gave a mixed account:

"In the first place," Philip was quoted as saying, "let me say that I do not consider that Mr. Chanler is an insane person by any means. I saw him yesterday and he talked with me in a perfectly rational manner. Of course he realizes his condition and is sensible of the necessity of having absolute rest. . . . His mind became overtaxed, and some months ago his relatives and friends saw that he was getting into a bad way and needed the change and rest which only perfect seclusion could give."

Philip insisted that Chanler himself had wished to keep knowledge of his condition and whereabouts from the public, hence the reports that he had gone abroad.

This ostensibly candid account hardly squared with information that the *Times* gathered from other sources. To some of his friends, said the *Times*, Chanler had "evinced a disposition to object to his commitment to Bloomingdale asylum. Although manifesting no bitter feeling toward his relatives, whom he regards as being mistaken and ill-advised, he has expressed strong objection to his incarceration." The *Tribune* succeeded in reaching one member of the family, Willie, but he had little to offer: "My brother has been in the asylum for a few months, but is improving, and we hope for his complete recovery," Willie told reporters.

Willie had not been consulted about Archie's commitment, and while he was inclined to rely on the judgment of Wintie and Lewis, the inconsistencies brought out by the newspapers were disquieting. Willie had not spoken to Archie for a year because they had had their own argument, over a horse. Because of all the press attention, the extended family was getting very upset, so Willie urged Wintie to return and take care of the situation, which Wintie did in November.

In New York it took all of Wintie's diplomatic finesse to soothe the extensive Astor connection; the newspapers were constantly referring to Archie as "lawyer and clubman and great-grandson of John Jacob Astor." Moreover, the situation with regard to Archie himself had to be reviewed to make sure that there would be no fresh embarrassment. The press received assurances that the medical experts held little hope of Archie's early recovery and that concern for his welfare should preclude any further public inquiries. With his mission regarding Archie accomplished, in January 1898 Wintie sailed back to Rome and his wife and children.

The *Times*, cooperating with family desires, volunteered that friends who had heard Archie's own statement of his condition and wishes did not feel "called upon to interfere with the policy pursued by those responsible for his commitment." This proved to be the feeling of Micajah Woods after he had read Archie's appeal. The situation was one of extreme delicacy, and interference might be wholly unjustified. So Woods sent Archie a friendly but noncommittal acknowledgment of the letter and advised patience.

To the man in Bloomingdale, this was a bitter setback. "Give a dog a bad name and hang him" indeed. His brothers and sisters seemed determined to prove that he was demented, and the doctors now were diagnosing his malady as progressive paranoia. Yet he felt rational, and responded favorably to all the stimuli indicating sanity. But how could he establish the truth and regain his freedom? Who would accept his word? Where could he apply for help? Finding no immediate answer, he resigned himself to practice patience, as Woods recommended. But he would never, never admit that he was insane.

Since attaining her majority, Margaret had been elaborating her own life style. She did not contemplate marriage, but wished to live independently. With this end in view she persuaded her sisters to relinquish to her their shares in Rokeby. Then, with possession of Rokeby assured, Margaret cast about for a town house in New York. Under the guidance of Stanford White she purchased a dwelling on West 74 Street, just off Riverside Drive, on the upper West Side of Manhattan. It was agreed that the sisters should live with her in town, at least temporarily, and Margaret ordered an elevator installed for Elizabeth and a studio on the top floor for her painting. These changes had been completed when Margaret and Elizabeth returned from India, and the three sisters moved in, Alida to stay there with her husband until the house they were building in Portchester was ready.

On their return Elizabeth and Margaret found John Jay Chapman in a state of shock over his wife's death. Outwardly calm, he was actually near collapse. He had three small boys on his hands, the eldest only six; he was yoked to a profession that he disliked; he was burdened with debts; he was intellectually over-intense, and he had been cut adrift from his emotional moorings. During the summer of 1897 there was visiting back and forth in Newport, with the inevitable result that Jack and Elizabeth recognized that they were in love and came to an understanding that they would marry soon.

To contemplate marriage, and especially a marriage involving the heavy responsibilities of a ready-made family and an unstable husband, required some courage on Elizabeth's part. Her health was precarious, for she was periodically troubled by lameness. Chapman never had ridden on an even keel, but had spent his life asserting an identity that eluded him, striving to reform customs and institutions while his own nature was constantly bursting out of bounds. In the hope that her stability might bring repose to Jack, Elizabeth was willing to risk not only physical danger, but the possibility of a demoralizing failure. And Chapman responded.

Their courtship was quaintly subdued. They clung to their privacy and avoided being seen together, meeting surreptitiously in unlikely places where they were apt to encounter no acquaintance. These furtive meetings amused Chapman, for neither he nor Elizabeth was romantically young; he was thirty-six and she thirty-two, but he entered into the spirit of the adventure.

When Elizabeth informed her brothers of her proposed marriage, they were seriously alarmed. Chapman himself they welcomed; his background (he, too, had been a Porcellian at Harvard), his New York connections, his brilliant mind were all congenial, although his reformer zeal was not. It was for Elizabeth they feared, for they had accepted without question Mary Marshall's dictum that Elizabeth must never consider marriage. But their reluctance gave way before the serene determination of Queen Bess.

Bob Chanler's marriage with Julia had been skirting disaster for some time. The family did not know the full story, but they surmised much. The truth was that on his wedding night Bob discovered that the physical aspects of marriage filled Julia with a disgust that she could neither conceal nor overcome. She shrank, in addition, from the sheer vitality of her husband and his family. She was twenty, unversed in the world, and basically incurious. She craved orderliness, decorum, and security; the furious way the Chanlers hurled themselves upon their pleasures and objectives terrified her.

The first evening she and Robert spent at Rokeby, on their honeymoon visit, an argument had arisen at dinner, and the brothers soon were shouting at each other with such fierceness that Julia fled to her room. Bob found her packing to leave, declaring that she would not pass the night in a house where murder was likely to occur. Bob laughed and explained that it had been merely a discussion. The sort of thing that happened during an argument he showed her at breakfast the next morning, when he pointed out the knife gouges plainly visible in the mahogany dining table.

At a large reception given by the Winthrop Chanlers, Julia was pounced upon at the door, marched across the crowded, noisy room (those penetrating Chanler voices!), plumped down on a sofa, and given the hissed command: "Sit there! Don't move! Spread out your skirts! Willie is dead drunk underneath!"

Julia sensed her husband's artistic talent and wished to further it, but she recoiled from some of its manifestations. Bob's Bohemian ways and friends shocked her. She kept even wealthy Henry Clews at arm's distance, although he and Bob were the closest of friends, capable of discussing art and life at the Deux Magots for forty-eight hours straight.

When no child appeared, the Chanlers hinted at some deficiency in Julia. Willie scornfully believed she preferred fashionable gowns to children and put her down as heartless. Bob's inner rage and frustration finally drove him to the point of asserting his conjugal rights regularly on Sundays, and Julia would faint in anticipation of the ordeal.

In the autumn of 1897 Willie finally embarked on his political career. He won election to the New York legislature as the Tammany candidate in the Fifth Assembly District. During the winter session he entertained handsomely in the house he rented in Albany, his sister Margaret, her interest in political activity and social service spurred by the example and counsels of her great-aunt Julia Ward Howe, serving capably as her brother's hostess. Such was the family's situation in 1898, when public events suddenly eclipsed private considerations.

18 | NO PLACE FOR A MARRIED MAN

The nation's sensational press had been whipping up sentiment for armed intervention by the United States on behalf of the Cuban insurgents. The demand was for war, which President McKinley was resisting as best he could. Theodore Roosevelt, now Assistant Secretary of the Navy, fretted at Washington's inaction, and prayed for some event that would bring about the intervention which he believed inevitable. The Cuban rebels were reported to be in desperate straits, their forces threatened with collapse unless help came soon.

Whether accidentally or by premeditated act, on February 15, 1898, the battleship *Maine* blew up in Havana harbor, with the loss of hundreds of American lives. Although the cause was never conclusively established, Spanish treachery was popularly blamed and intervention called for.

The prospect of fighting came as a deliverance to Willie Chanler, bogged down in the humdrum preoccupations of the state legislature. Although he discharged his responsibilities loyally, he had little heart for them. Two bills he worked enthusiastically to pass concerned liberalizing the Sunday closing law for New York City's saloons and amending the code for regulating prize fights. The latter held personal interest for Willie because he owned jointly with several other sportsmen a stable of fighters and often worked out with them.

In February Willie paid a surprise visit to Bloomingdale asylum, for he wished to see Archie's condition for himself. Although Archie suspected he had come as a family spy, he greeted Willie cordially, and they talked for a couple of hours about Willie's political career, which Archie approved, and other matters. Finally, when Willie was leaving, Archie gave him a message for

Lewis and Wintie and Arthur Carey. Speaking with utmost earnestness, Archie said that the papers committing him to Bloomingdale bore "indisputable proof" of perjury, and much as he shrank from having "the brand of felony" placed upon his next-of-kin, the law must take its course. As a lawyer, Archie had only one piece of advice to offer, that "the said three gentlemen together with their wives and children emigrate without delay to the Argentine," where he understood that extradition did not run. Willie promised to transmit the message, but that was the only time Archie ever saw Willie at Bloomingdale.

Willie's attention now concentrated on war with Spain, in which he was determined to have a part. On March 11 he resigned from the Assembly, spurred by his eagerness to fight. First he needed to obtain reliable information about the government's intentions, so he turned to Teddy Roosevelt. But at the very same moment Roosevelt was looking to Chanler. On March 15 Roosevelt wrote glumly:

"Dear Willie:

"This is the first letter of yours that I have ever hated to receive, for I have been on the point of writing to you to know if you were going to raise a regiment, and to know if I could go along. I shall chafe my heart out if I am kept here instead of being at the front."

Willie answered that he intended to raise a regiment of volunteers, and on March 26 Roosevelt wrote back urgently: "Things look as though they are coming to a head. Now, can you start getting up that regiment when the time comes? Do you want me as lieutenant colonel?"

Winthrop Chanler, meanwhile, could not abide lying sluggishly in Rome. So despite his wife's misgivings, in March he crossed to New York again. On March 31 he reported to Daisy that the war talk was as "furious as ever." Off he went to Washington to consult Henry Cabot Lodge, all the while assuring Daisy that "I am not off to Cuba, my Honey, only going to Washington." Later, from Lodge's home, he relayed a second message stating that there was "no manner of doubt about [the *Maine*] having been blown up by a mine. . . ."

The President was preparing a message to Congress, but no one knew what it was going to say. On April 7 Roosevelt wrote to a friend, "if you are puzzled you can imagine the bitter wrath and humiliation which I feel at the absolute lack of plans. . . . If I were you I should get hold of Willie Chanler, who now intends to raise a two or three battalion regiment, to be commanded by a regular officer. With he and myself as lieutenant colonels, I am sure he would be delighted to have you as a major; and I should like to put Leonard Wood in as a major. We will have a jim-dandy regiment if we are allowed to go. . . ." Three days later McKinley called for intervention, and on April 20, 1898, he signed a declaration of war.

The next day an advertisement appeared in the New York newspapers:

A CALL IS HEREBY ISSUED FOR ALL ABLE-BODIED MEN

between the ages of eighteen and forty-five years who wish to enroll in an infantry regiment of United States volunteers in case of a war with Spain.

Recruiting office, 140-142 Sixth ave. Hours 9-12 and 5-7:30.

WM. ASTOR CHANLER.

The response to this recruiting ad was slow at first, but before evening a rush set in, and within a few days 1,550 men had signed up. Temple Emmet, as hot for action as any Chanler, helped in taking applications; he expected to be an officer in the regiment himself.

In the midst of this excitement, Margaret announced that she was going to the front as a Red Cross volunteer. She had been urging the men of her circle to enlist and thought she should follow her own advice and join up. She had no skills, but registered with the Red Cross for service in any capacity, meanwhile enrolling in a course of training in basic hospital routines. Because she spoke Spanish, she thought she might be useful as an interpreter, and she was prepared to fight the inevitable battles with bureaucratic red tape.

Margaret's decision cast Elizabeth's situation in a fresh light. Temple Emmet was heading for the war, and Alida had said that she would go at least as far as Florida with him, so Queen Bess would be left alone. Her immediate marriage to Chapman seemed advisable, "so that he can look after her when the others are away," as Wintie put it. A small family wedding was held on April 24 in the parlor at 317 West 74th Street.

Wintie wrote to Daisy that after the ceremony ". . . Margaret was literally at the end of the telephone wire waiting to sail for Key West with the Red Cross people. But the boat went without her for no women are allowed to go till the Army moves into Cuba. . . .

"Jack Astor [John Jacob Astor IV] has offered the government a battery of artillery equipped & furnished & the use of two of his railroads for transportation purposes in exchange for a staff appointment on some general's staff who is going to Cuba. . . .

"I am like the man who couldn't get into the Ark. . . ."

Willie was meeting with obstacles in regard to his regiment. The Chanlers were Democrats, and the Republicans were in control in Albany and Washington. Willie was told that neither the Army nor the State Militia could use his volunteers immediately. He appealed to McKinley, who was sympathetic, but pointed out that there was no provision in the Army's plans for volunteers.

Roosevelt was powerless to assist; then, somewhat lamely, he broke the news to Willie that Congress had authorized the raising of three regiments of volunteer cavalry (not infantry), and that Secretary of War Alger had offered Roosevelt the command of one. Considering himself unqualified, Roosevelt had declined, but had offered to serve under Leonard Wood. He thereupon was named the regiment's lieutenant colonel. As matters turned out, only this regiment — the First United States Volunteer Cavalry, the famous Rough Riders — was raised, and the command and subsequent glory remained in Republican hands.

Realizing that he had been checkmated, Willie reluctantly disbanded his regiment and made plans to join General Gomez's forces. Choosing a handful of adventurers on whose fighting qualities he could rely, he set out for Tampa, Florida, the staging ground for the war zone.

Left behind, Wintie fretted over his inactivity, but kept reminding himself that he was married and had numerous dependents. Of Roosevelt's good sense in throwing up an assistant secretaryship for a subordinate commission, Wintie had a poor opinion. He told Daisy: "Theodore has resigned . . . and goes to Cuba before long with a regiment of cow-boys from

Arizona & New Mexico. I really think he is going mad. The President has asked him twice as a personal favor to stay in the Navy Dept., but Theodore is wild to fight & hack & hew. It is really sad. Of course this ends his political career for good. Even Cabot says this."

Then casually, as if unaware of what he was saying, Wintie conveyed to his anxious wife the possibility that he might take some part in the show. Not in the actual fighting, of course, but in an observer role, out of danger. A week later he was in Tampa, and writing:

"We got here last night after a dreadful railway journey of 42 hours from New York. 'We' consisted of Willie, Temple Emmet & myself & 5 men whom Willie picked from his abandoned regiment . . . and who are to accompany him through the campaign. George Galvin was already here, having been sent on ahead to buy horses for Willie's party. What I wrote you at last I have decided to do. Nuñez [Gen. Emilio Nuñez] is here & will take me on his staff when he starts in a few days. . . . Cabot has got me passes which practically put the army & navy of the U.S. at my disposal, so that I can leave Cuba when I get tired of it or sick or anything. . . ."

In faraway Rome, where everyone thought that powerful Spain would quickly mop up the Americans, Daisy quaked at the transparent protests that no peril existed in the theater of war. But she kept up a brave front, praying and sending Wintie miraculous medals which she entreated him to wear. Wintie kept cheerily in touch.

"The plan," he wrote, "is to send about 5,000 U.S. troops as a base of supplies for the Cuban army under Gomez. . . . As soon as we land, we, that is Nuñez and his men will go straight to Gomez, who is waiting for us, with arms, food, & clothing. . . .

"Another man has joined Willy's party, a Dr. Abbott of Philadelphia, whom he [Willie] found camped at Taveta on Kilimanjaro, the first time he went to Africa."

Dr. Abbott, a collector, later curator, for the Smithsonian Institution, rode into Willie's camp unannounced one night after traveling halfway around the world to join the expedition, and was greeted with shouts of welcome. Other members, as portrayed by Wintie, included: "The Sergeant, a lovely 'tommy' who has ten years' service in the crack cavalry regiment of our army, the Sixth, and who left Buffalo Bill's Wild West Show and all his worldly goods to follow Willie to Cuba. . . . Grover Flint who was a trooper in the regular army for two or three years, another regular army boy, also resigned from Buffalo Bill's Show to join Willie . . . Geo. Galvin . . . then the

Kentucky grandson of Daniel Boone, fearful braggart and the worst (so far) of the party. Then Dr. Maximilian Lund, the hero of a thousand German duels, . . . then Temple, always cool, phlegmatic & very careful of tiny details . . . young Hood, son of the famous Confederate general of that ilk, a nice gentlemanly fellow . . . next to your Hubbie with a machete & revolver strapped to his little person. . .”

On May 11 Wintie reported: “Willie has been made a colonel in the Cuban army & has had an adjutant & interpreter & secretary given to him, one Captain Ramirez. Rumor has it that the Government (U.S.) has given Willie a Lieutenant's commission in the U.S. Volunteers, but he knows nothing authoritatively. . .”

The rumor was correct. In Washington a list of officer appointments had been released and included a commission as assistant adjutant general with rank of captain issued to John Jacob Astor IV (in return for his artillery and other favors), and a captain's commission issued to William Astor Chanler.

Wintie exclaimed at the news, and then went on to say that Willie had accepted his captain's commission and joined General Joseph E. Wheeler's staff in Tampa. But Willie did not wish just to abandon his men, so, as Wintie wrote Daisy, “I could do nothing but offer to take them in myself. This satisfied the Cubans and the men too. So here I am with 10 troopers at my back going in with Nuñez or Castillo as their personal escort. It is safe enough now. The Spaniards are all cooped up in Havana & the large towns. We shall have a bully time with flies & bugs & rain & the war will soon be over. . . . Theodore has got his band of rough riders all organized at San Antonio, Texas. If I get on the island first I shall be happy. Maybe I'll join my band to his. . . .”

But May turned into June, and nobody moved. In New York Margaret still awaited a call from the Red Cross, her patience quite exhausted. Alida, in Tampa looking after Temple, broke up the family's united front when it finally dawned on her that there were risks inherent in a soldier's life. The family version of this amazing realization, while possibly untrue in detail, had Alida driving into camp and beckoning Temple out of line: “You must come home, Temple,” she stated in her silvery, piercing Chanler voice. “I find that this war is dangerous.”

However it happened, Temple did return north with Alida, and Willie sailed with Gen. Wheeler to Cuba. At last, on June 14, Wintie could gleefully write that his group, too, had a boat, the steamer *Florida*, but it was yet another nine days before Wintie could finally write that he was on his way. His band of freebooters were all well, he reported, except Grover Flint, who had a broken leg. Then there was silence for three weeks.

What occurred during that time was later recounted by a seventeen-year-old Cuban participant named E. J. Connill. During the run down to Cuba and around the island to its southern side, the transports were escorted by the American gunboat *Peoria*. The first attempt to land was made at a point between the towns of Casilda and Trinidad, at the mouth of the San Juan River. A boat was sent in and was fired upon. Scouting parties revealed a strong enemy force, and the next day, June 30, the flotilla steamed sixty miles eastward and anchored west of Tunas, opposite a Spanish blockhouse defended by about a hundred Spanish regulars, well entrenched. General Nuñez ordered the blockhouse shelled by the *Peoria*, and then sent in two boats with Cubans and Chanler's irregulars. As the boats approached the beach, the Spaniards opened fire, and General Nuñez's brother Indalecio, who had charge of the Cuban boat, was killed, his boat sunk, and several of his men wounded. The rest, with Chanler's band, scrambled ashore, took cover where they could, and returned a vigorous fire.

Chanler soon was shot through the right elbow, and Abbott was wounded more seriously by a bullet through the shoulder. The command having devolved upon Wintie, he kept up the attack until dusk, then ordered the wounded evacuated. Wintie, Abbott, one Cuban, and Lund stayed on the beach.

Aboard the *Florida*, anxious watchers scanned the shore for some sign of life. At about eight o'clock a man was discerned swimming toward the ship with a knife clenched in his teeth. Hoisted aboard, he proved to be Lund, stark naked. He reported that Chanler and his companions had disappeared, and it seemed certain that they had perished. Lund told of fighting off sharks during his swim out to the ship, but the Cubans were scornful of the story, and despised him for having deserted his comrades. Lund insisted, however, that they had vanished, and there was no sign from shore.

General Nuñez waited several hours longer, then ordered the anchors weighed. But Grover Flint, who had stayed aboard the *Florida* because of his broken leg, begged permission to scout the beach one more time. Nuñez consented, and Flint was lifted over the side with his leg in the cast, and with two other Americans rowed stealthily toward the beach. Soon they were lost to the view of those on the *Florida*.

At four o'clock they returned, bringing with them Chanler, Abbott, and the Cuban. Flint said that as his boat slipped noiselessly along the shore, expecting at any minute to hear the crack of a Spanish rifle, instead he heard faint whistling — first "Yankee Doodle" and then "Pop Goes the Weasel." It was Chanler. Flint whistled back, and guided by the sound came up to the three men standing up to their necks in the water, where they had been driven by the ferocious mosquitoes. Only their faces were exposed, and these were so blotched and swollen that Wintie was recognizable only by his short golden beard. As he was hauled into the boat, he was heard to mutter, "This is no place for a married man."

Abbott had lost much blood and was weak, but the bullet that had passed through Chanler's arm had hit no artery and he suffered little. The next day Nuñez made a successful landing forty miles to the east, and General Gomez came down to the coast to meet them.

On July 10 the *Florida* steamed into Tampa Bay, and by July 15 Wintie was back in the Knickerbocker Club in New York, scrawling a lighthearted account of the adventure to Daisy. His arm was healing, he said, and as soon as it was normal again he proposed to rejoin his "brigands" in Cuba. "Willie is with General Wheeler at Santiago and has been recommended for promotion for gallantry. . . . Theodore is now Colonel of his regiment, and Wood is a Brigadier General."

The official report submitted by the senior American officer with the Nuñez expedition praised the bravery of Winthrop Chanler and his desperadoes, saying: "I cannot speak too highly of the gallantry of Mr. Chanler's men, who fought overwhelming numbers until dark, when they withdrew under cover of darkness, with the loss of one killed (Gen. Nuñez's brother) and seven wounded out of a party of twenty-eight men."

As Wintie regretfully sensed, the war had been won at El Caney and San Juan Hill, where Roosevelt and Willie Chanler played conspicuous roles. Willie had sent an account of the July 1 engagement to Elizabeth, honeymooning in the Catskills, writing directly from the "besieging lines around Santiago":

"By this time you must have heard of our 1st respectable engagement. . . . I was in the advance with Gen. Stunner and caught the fire heavily. We had to capture 3 forts by charging up hill under it a withering fire. The fight lasted from 6 A.M. till night when we finally established ourselves in the position we now occupy. You will be glad to hear that I did not receive a scratch. I had no idea that modern war was such a dreadful thing. I was really almost made sick by the sight of the men shattered by shot & shell. We lost in killed and wounded about 2,000 men. [The official count of American casualties was 1,572.] Many of my friends were killed. . . ."

But Willie's humor was also much in evidence during the battle. Much as he admired Theodore Roosevelt, Willie could not resist teasing his impetuous friend, even in the midst of a battle. Before the attack on San Juan Hill, Roosevelt rode to a hillock to get a better view of the ground ahead. Willie saw him sitting there, squinting into the distance (he was notoriously nearsighted), and as the bullets started to whip uncomfortably close and Roosevelt swung his horse to retire, Willie called out: "Don't move, Teddy! That's a bully place to be photographed!"

That day's fighting effectively terminated the war. Even as Wintie was announcing his safe return to Daisy, the Madrid government was suing for surrender terms, though the public did not know this yet. And in the meantime the Chanlers continued to rally. Lewis was on his way from Europe, intending to enlist, and Bob, at Newport with Julia, was considering how he might join in the action.

Elizabeth had hurried down from the Catskills to welcome Wintie back, and from New York she wrote to Mary Meroney at Rokeby, assuring the old nurse that "Mr. Winthrop's arm is nearly all right again." Margaret, she said, was still aboard the transport, perhaps due to be sent to Puerto Rico instead of landing in Cuba. And on August 4 she sent an urgent note to Mary Meroney: "Mr. Chapman has secured Mr. Wintie, Mr. Lewis, & Mr. Robert for a family gathering at Rokeby on Saturday the 6th, so buckle on your armor & get Lizzie Hartnett & any of the Mahoneys you can to help. It is short notice for you but Mr. Wintie may go very soon to Cuba. . . ."

But by the time the three brothers gathered, word was out that peace was at hand, and there was no question of Wintie's returning to Cuba. The war had ended for all the Chanlers except Margaret.

19 | MARGARET'S WAY

Twenty-seven-old Margaret was certainly behaving as no society-bred woman was expected to in 1898. Upon her arrival at Tampa, she had found no provision made for the twenty Red Cross nurses she accompanied. And the reports coming in from Cuba simply angered her: "The number of wounded on both sides compared to the nurses makes modern neglect seem more outrageously cruel than anything in the helpless Middle Ages," she wrote home furiously.

By bullying the officers in charge, some of whom opposed the whole idea of permitting women near the front, she managed to get her band aboard a converted passenger steamer, the *Lampasus*, and headed for Key West. From there on progress was slow, inasmuch as the ship was towing a barge loaded with pontoons for the army engineers. At Guantanamo the nurses were denied permission to go ashore because of an epidemic in the port. The captain of the *Lampasus* tried to get the whole group shipped back to New York, but Margaret spiked that scheme.

Next the *Lampasus* steamed for an undisclosed destination that turned out to be Ponce, Puerto Rico, where a task force under General Nelson A. Miles had just occupied the island. Here the Red Cross contingent was requested to accept a dangerous assignment; on board the general's transports were hundreds of men ill with typhoid and other diseases; could the nurses improvise a hospital on the *Lampasus*? They agreed to do so if the patients would lie on mattresses spread on the decks instead of in the berths, which would be impossible to keep clean.

This was agreed on, but immediately a series of crises set in. The cooks deserted at the sight of the tottering skeletons coming aboard the *Lampasus*.

Fortunately Margaret had brought a spirit lamp, which was used to boil milk and prepare broths. It was kept burning around the clock.

Patients died, and the corpses were stowed in the lifeboats until dark, when they were carried out to sea and disposed of secretively to prevent a panic. Margaret took charge of the laundry; she hunted up a huge pot and set a stowaway to work boiling sheets and clothing. The officers on the transports kept their distance; whenever one was compelled to come aboard on official business, he would stiffen with horror at encountering delirious fever patients wandering about.

The naval authorities did not like having a "pest ship" in the harbor. They were convinced that the plague was raging aboard the *Lampasus*, and they kept its decks under constant surveillance through field glasses. Now and then at night potshots were taken at the liner; one morning Margaret found a bullet embedded in her window frame. When the navy thought they spotted a plague victim on deck — actually the man was suffering from boils — they sent a naval officer aboard to hoist a yellow quarantine flag, the sight of which threw the patients into acute alarm. Margaret ordered the flag hauled down as often as it was raised by a visiting officer, a contest that kept up for a week, while friends of Margaret's brothers aboard other ships in the port laid bets on the outcome. Meanwhile, the burials at night went on, and the army sent new patients to replace those who died or recovered.

The deadlock was broken when orders came for the *Lampasus* and its Red Cross nurses to proceed to Fort Monroe, in Virginia. But this did not suit Margaret. Since she was not under official orders, she quietly went ashore, determined to find some place of usefulness there. With her went a volunteer professionally trained nurse from New Orleans, Anna Bouligny. Of the twenty nurses who went north on the *Lampasus*, eight contracted typhoid and died.

On shore, Margaret by diligent inquiry learned of an "American hospital," a place which proved to be a one-room schoolhouse with a dirt floor. It was crowded with enlisted men, most of them fever patients. There were only two medical orderlies and a few apathetic Puerto Rican women, languidly fanning the patients to keep off the flies.

Although Margaret had no official standing, she sent for an American doctor, then nailed up a poster hand-lettered in Spanish announcing that the wretched building was an American hospital where only relatives could visit patients — that got rid of the fan-wavers. She sent Anna Bouligny to buy food for light and liquid diets. After several days the women obtained authorization to serve with troops in the field, so the schoolhouse was closed and its patients transferred to the general hospital on the hill.

To Margaret's surprise, whereas sick or wounded enlisted men were assigned to specific hospital quarters, officers could select their own. As a consequence, many officers lay seriously ill in wholly unsuitable surroundings. Margaret immediately rented the largest vacant house she could find to serve as an officers' hospital. She was assigned a couple of medical orderlies, and Anna Bouligny took charge of the kitchen and provisioning. Margaret served as nurse from 6:30 in the morning until 8:30 at night. She was strict in her schedule, and wasted no energy in romanticizing her work. Implacably practical, she knocked off work at the stated time every evening, and allowed nothing to interfere with her getting a good night's rest. For relaxation she would drive into the hills in the evening with Miss Bouligny, who sang French opera arias.

Margaret had left New York with $200 in her purse, and in Puerto Rico she was obliged to stretch her credit amazingly. Checks were cashed and requisitions filled by means known only to herself, but mainly by simply refusing to accept otherwise. Not one patient died while in her care, although some did succumb later. When one of the officers died after being taken to the general hospital, his brother asked Margaret not only to attend the funeral, but to read the service. The New York press reported on her devotion, embellishing her story to include tales of her contracting diseases or suffering combat wounds. Indeed, word of her good work spread so far that a friend of the Chanlers heard about it in Tehran, where he was stationed at the British embassy.

After five weeks, professional Red Cross nurses came to relieve her, and so Margaret and Anna Bouligny moved on to Cuamo Springs and later to San Juan, where they continued their volunteer service. On October 18 Margaret watched with satisfaction as the last soldiers of Spain marched to the embarkation dock, boarded their transports, and steamed away. The war was over and her task was finished.

Soon after that, she and Anna Bouligny returned to New York. By then Margaret was known to the readers of the Hearst and Pulitzer papers as "The Angel of Puerto Rico."

With peace in sight, Wintie set out for his own hearthside, his ebullience unquenched. On the eve of sailing he cheerfully informed Cabot Lodge:

"I am off tomorrow on the *Normandie* for Havre. The bad repute of the French line will result in making me much more comfortable than I would be on the other lines as there is scarcely a soul going over on her. I shall take a large revolver; and on the first sign of shipwreck proceed to massacre the crew and then man a life boat myself."

Lewis Chanler had already returned to Monaco, but announced that he intended to settle in the United States shortly with his family. Bob and Julia had gone abroad again, Rokeby continuing to oppress and frighten Julia. On October 3 Willie Chanler was honorably discharged with a citation for bravery. Elizabeth and Alida were happy that the strife had ended, and Margaret got back to Rokeby in time for Christmas. To her Wintie wrote from Rome:

"Lord! How we wish we could be with you! That's out of the question, however, so we won't waste time over it. Thanks very much for your long & most entertaining letter from Porto Rico. . . . You did good work down there, my dear. You did better than any of us by a long chalk. I suppose Clara Barton trembles on her throne. . . . They tell me you are to have some kind of a monument. I hope it is a husband. Some nice attractive patriot with only one leg & glad to take not only 4 meals a day but even your name if you so insist."

20 | A CANTER IN POLITICS AND A PERMANENT COMMITMENT

Willie Chanler returned from Cuba an authentic war hero. Reports of his exploits had appeared sporadically in the newspapers, and added to his laurels as a sportsman and explorer, they made him a highly eligible political prospect. He was young, handsome, energetic, rich, dashing, and socially impeccable; he was equally at home in his clubs and at Tammany Hall; he had received academic honors; and he was even the author of a book recounting his adventures in Africa, entitled *Through Jungle and Desert.*

In the fall of 1898 the Democratic organization of New York offered to run Willie for the House of Representatives from the Fourteenth Manhattan District — solidly Republican territory. An unwieldy territory with a polyglot population, both rich and poor, it contained many Irish and Italians, as well as some of Willie's wealthy friends. His opponent, the incumbent congressman, Lemuel Ely Quigg, had captured the district from the Democrats two years before. Quigg was the Manhattan deputy of the Republican state boss, Tom Platt, and he had the endorsement of Theodore Roosevelt, who was running as the Republican candidate for governor of New York. Quigg appeared unbeatable. Liking the odds, Willie accepted the nomination.

He threw himself into the campaign as though he were plunging into Africa again. He spoke at street rallies and presided at beer busts, keeping the speeches short and the beer flowing. What little he had to say he said with engaging candor, all the while whipping up enthusiasm with bands, street banners, posters, circulars, letters to the press, fireworks. Both sides spent a lot, but Willie managed to outspend Quigg by $6,444.85 to $5,998.45.

The press gave the contest good coverage, the Republican *Tribune* sneering at the stress Chanler's camp was placing on his aristocratic background, and the independent *Herald* commending Willie's democratic modesty and earnestness. At election time Quigg held the edge in the betting, and Willie's friends were not confident.

But when the returns were in, Chanler was the winner by a landslide plurality of 6,060 votes. It was a resounding victory, and the press sang his praises. Said the *Herald*: "Captain William Astor Chanler . . . went through Quigg's bailiwick like a tropical tornado. He saw everybody and everybody liked the looks of the young explorer and soldier. He was full of blood and enthusiasm. He did not pretend to know anything of the political game, but . . . he whipped the Republican county chairman by sheer force of personality."

Quigg was stunned by the result, and the size of his plurality surprised Willie himself. He celebrated by joining two organizations seldom fused in one individual — the Friendly Sons of St. Patrick (qualifying through his Armstrong ancestors, who came from Ireland) and that most blue-blooded of New York's honorary military units, the Old Guard. Tammany rewarded him by electing him a sachem, as his father had been before him.

Roosevelt, who had won his own race for the governorship, was delighted by Willie's victory: "I am awfully glad he is in Congress," Teddy wrote to Wintie in Rome. "I do not like his party associates at all, but on the great questions of foreign policy and the army and the navy, he is just the man to do good work in Washington."

Lewis and Alice Chanler were about to return home. Alice's health had improved steadily, and Lewis was hankering for law practice again. Also, Alice had begun to think about a political career for her husband. Certainly Lewis had every outward requisite: tall and graceful, with open, boyish features, a resonant voice of singular carrying power, a polished speaker, high-minded, interested in public affairs, and endowed with abundant energy. Moreover, Alice felt that she was the ideal sort of wife for a man in public life — she was a shrewd judge of character, a clever hostess, as well as brainy and ambitious. There was general satisfaction in the family when the Lewis Chanlers headed toward New York.

At the same moment Elizabeth, her husband, and the three Chapman boys headed toward Europe. Chapman had suffered a traumatic political shock, for he believed that Theodore Roosevelt had sold out to the Republican bosses in order to be selected as the Republican candidate for governor. So bitter was the falling-out that he and Roosevelt did not speak to each other for nearly twenty years. Jack Chapman wrote off T.R. as a "muddle-headed

and at the same time pigheaded young man," while Roosevelt coined his celebrated phrase, "on the lunatic fringe," to describe Chapman's place in
political life and thought.

But even in England, Elizabeth could not keep Chapman out of political agitation. The Boer War was on, and he took the side — hardly popular
in London — of the Boers. Supper conversations threatened to become acri-
monious, with Chapman exclaiming that both England and America seemed
to be "mad just now over bloodshed, commercial interests, and jingoism," so
in the summer of 1899 Elizabeth moved the family to the tranquil cathedral
town of Wells.

Representative "Wm. Astor Chanler" moved to Washington, where he
was joined by Margaret, who once again came to act as her brother's
housekeeper and hostess. Chanler performed his congressional tasks unspec-
tacularly. He was chagrined that he could not run off to fight with the
Boers in South Africa, so in compensation he outfitted a volunteer as his sub-
stitute and paid his passage to the front. Life in sedentary Washington went
against the grain. Willie would dash up to New York on weekends to watch
his horses run, and during the week he would blow off steam by mad gallops
through the Maryland or Virginia countryside.

Margaret was creating a reputation of her own in Washington. Her work
in Puerto Rico during the war was widely known, and a resolution was
introduced in Congress to award her a medal expressing the nation's gratitude. But she curtly observed that other women deserved just as much
honor, so the resolution was shelved.

As her brother's hostess, Margaret fulfilled all the requirements, but she
considered most of social observances to be sheer nonsense and a waste of
valuable time. Time and energy could be saved, she pointed out to a senator's
wife, if groups of congressional wives held a joint reception once a month,
rather than their weekly "at homes." This revolutionary proposal found its
way to a society reporter, and Miss Chanler's daring originality provided grist
for newspaper commentary for weeks thereafter.

Meanwhile, the confusion into which Archie's affairs had been thrown
by his confinement in Bloomingdale asylum had snarled the affairs of other
members of the family, with their interlocking interests and sharing of
income from certain properties held in trust. Henry Lewis Morris, the
family lawyer to whom, for the most part, the Chanlers delegated fiscal

administration, had been pressing for a precise definition of Archie's rights and position under the law.

Theoretically Archie was in charge of his own affairs, inasmuch as he had not been declared incompetent by any court. Actually, however, he had no control over his estate whatever. Stanford White still held Archie's power of attorney for business transactions, but this still left a large area not covered. In midsummer of 1898 Lewis Chanler and Morris tried to persuade White that Archie should be ruled legally incompetent. But White declined to be a party to such a step. In 1899, however, Wintie and Lewis Chanler took action on their own responsibility, overriding White's objections.

The procedure called for the hearing of testimony by a sheriff's jury. If Archie was judged incapable of administering his affairs, the court would be petitioned to appoint "a committee for the person and estate" to manage his estate for him.

People had several times suggested to Archie himself that he go before a sheriff's jury as the most expeditious way of vindicating his sanity, but Archie had refused. First, he feared a trap by his relatives, and second, he had lost confidence in the justice dispensed by New York courts, especially when it involved Astor interests. Archie believed that the correct way to obtain his release was to petition the federal court for habeas corpus protection.

On June 13, 1899, New York newspapers published an account of the hearing, held the day before. Archie had not appeared nor had he been represented by counsel. Three medical witnesses had testified.

Dr. Samuel P. Lyon, the director of Bloomingdale asylum, testified first. He said that Chanler had been notified of the hearing, but had declined to attend, because of a chronic backache he claimed to have acquired in Bloomingdale. Dr. Lyon believed that while Chanler did feel pain, and really had a backache, it was not extreme enough to incapacitate him. Chanler's disease, he said, was clearly paranoia, and there was no hope of a cure. Citing the delusions which he said Chanler harbored, Dr. Lyon said Chanler imagined himself to be a magnet and his stomach a Leyden jar; that at times he believed himself to be Napoleon, and at other times imagined himself to be a greater man than Napoleon. The doctor swore that several times Chanler had evinced a desire to kill him, and that he believed people were trying to poison him and hence would not eat the institution's food. Dr. Lyon noted that before the war with Spain, Chanler had been preparing to bring his case before the public, saying the people of Virginia would come to his rescue as soon as they learned of his unlawful detention; but after the start of the war he had changed his mind, saying he did not wish to add to the nation's anxieties. Chanler had compiled a statement of his case so voluminous, said the doctor, it "filled a book more than three inches thick." He was also writing a book of poems, mostly sonnets, of a satirical and enigmatic nature.

Dr. Carlos F. McDonald, an eminent alienist, gave corroborative testimony, stating positively that Chanler's malady was incurable. He, too, dwelt upon Chanler's alleged delusions. He said Chanler's case presented "the most striking case of paranoia that I have ever seen in my life." Some years later, Dr. McDonald testified that he could identify a paranoiac at a distance of several feet by the shape of his head, but nonetheless, his was considered expert testimony.

Then Dr. Austin Flint, a celebrated neurologist, added the weight of his authority. Yes, he swore, John Armstrong Chanler was suffering from progressive paranoia, and his disease was incurable.

The jury made no attempt to examine Chanler, either by fetching him from Bloomingdale or by interviewing him there. On the contrary, since the hour was late and the jurors were impatient to get away, a verdict of insanity and incompetency was quickly returned.

Press reports identified John Armstrong Chanler as "formerly the husband of Amélie Rives," and mentioned that he was thirty-six years old. They did not mention that he had already been in Bloomingdale more than two years; nor did they point out that the verdict of the sheriff's jury was in effect a sentence of life imprisonment without hope of reprieve.

Lewis and Wintie, as executors of their father's estate, promptly applied for appointment of a "committee for the person and estate" to administer Archie's affairs, and the case was marked closed.

21 | A NEW CENTURY BEGINS

One subject upon which Margaret felt qualified to speak was the nursing of soldiers in the field. Except for male nurses, who really were only medical orderlies, the Army had relied upon Red Cross volunteers, but a bill before Congress would create a corps of Army nurses. Margaret was heartily in favor of the bill, not only for itself, but because she enthusiastically approved any action that increased equal opportunity for women.

The bill was encountering stiff opposition, from the surgeon general, among others, who thought the admission of women into the Army revolutionary and uncalled for. Margaret joined forces with other like-minded women to organize a lobbying campaign on behalf of the bill, but soon realized that its passage was being further endangered by rumors coming from the Philippines regarding the allegedly frivolous conduct of Red Cross nurses assigned to the army there. When her co-workers became alarmed, Margaret undertook to go to Manila and find out the truth.

On May 24, 1900, she set out from New York for San Francisco, to embark there on an Army transport. She was equipped with letters of introduction to Army commanders in the Far East and intended to make a thorough inspection of the army hospitals there. The trip was to last six months and would take her not only to the Philippines, but to Japan and China as well.

From Manila she wrote directly to Secretary of War Elihu Root that the rumors about the Red Cross nurses were groundless. They had been studiously circumspect and efficient, and the doctors were singing their praises. On the subject of the need for a corps of nurses, "the fear of the Surgeon General" was keeping the military noncommittal, she reported, and she noticed many inadequacies in the hospitals, particularly regarding necessary supplies like bed sheets.

As her transport had arrived at Manila Bay, others had been steaming out, carrying troops to China to relieve the Peking legations besieged by the Boxers, xenophobic rural insurgents encouraged by the empress. Margaret debated whether to follow them, and when a fair chance arose, she did sail for Nagasaki. There she found no facilities for receiving the wounded coming from China, and on her own initiative she rented and fitted up a house as a depot hospital, with beds for thirty patients. Great was her indignation when the first transport bringing casualties declined her hospitality, and sailed directly for San Francisco. "Fear of the Surgeon General" again, she surmised; and she was not surprised to hear later that every one of the patients, denied a brief rest at Nagasaki, had died during the long voyage.

Margaret made her way to China, where the Boxers had finally been defeated. Visiting battered Peking, she toured the imperial palace and saw its treasures strewn about just as the fleeing dowager empress and her court had left them. She noted the sandbags that the women of the British legation had sewn for a breastworks during the siege; at the start these had been made of coarse cloth, but later sumptuous brocades, woven for the imperial use, had been pressed into service. A British officer snipped swatches of these priceless brocades for Margaret to add to her collection of souvenirs. A small centuries-old iron cannon was also dispatched to Rokeby.

Having seen and done all she had come for, Root's unofficial inspector in the Far East sailed for home. She reached Washington in late November and found a storm raging over her confidential report. Somehow her letter had leaked to the press, and she was being berated for "meddlesome interference" with military concerns. Root lectured her, saying she should have known that "there is no such thing as a private letter to a public official," and the nurses corps bill was defeated. The cause was saved, however, for Root embodied the Women's Army Nursing Corps in his general reorganization of the Army a short time later, marking the first time women were integrated into the uniformed armed services on a regular basis.

Watching this turmoil from the sidelines was John Jay Chapman, home from Europe with Elizabeth and his sons. To Chapman, his wife's family was a constant source of astonishment and entertainment: "There is always one Chanler in the newspapers," he observed. "The Chanler theme dies in the bassoons and is dropped in the pathetic drum solo — but hark the flute!"

Lewis and Alice Chanler had settled in New York City, where Lewis had picked up his law practice without difficulty; he told Margaret with satisfaction that "within 26 hours of landing from England I had a criminal case on my hands & have been very busy ever since."

Alida's new baby girl, named Margaret, joining her two-year-old sister, Elizabeth, was not the only recent addition to the family. Daisy Chanler had given birth to a third son while Wintie was hunting chamois in the Austrian Tyrol. The boy was christened Hubert, after the patron saint of hunters.

Wintie was in tip-top trim. "In hard training all summer," he told his friend Amos French. "Chamois shooting and mountain climbing; and . . . never a time to drink." He had inaugurated the new century by a hunting expedition in Asia Minor, as the guest of his cousin and former guardian, Rutherfurd Stuyvesant. The hunt had been organized at Alexandretta, and Wintie enjoyed himself thoroughly, bagging plenty of game and poking through the rubble of centuries that littered the landscape. Wintie had sold his Tuxedo Park house for $60,000, and this windfall had temporarily lifted him out of his habitual money doldrums.

Margaret had persistently begged Wintie to settle in America. Daisy's father had died at a ripe eighty-seven, and there was nothing further to hold them at Rome. The notion of digging in permanently was inviting, but Wintie was not quite yet decided.

Willie, too, was proving a disappointment to Margaret, for he was abandoning politics. The life was simply too tame: he required action, combative action, as he confessed to his friend von Höhnel, now serving as naval aide to the Emperor Franz Josef. The gerrymandering of his congressional district gave him a plausible pretext for not accepting renomination in 1900. He was impatient to get away.

Christmas found him with the family at Rokeby, helping to launch the old house on the new century. Rokeby hummed and clattered with grownups and children. Around the table on Christmas Day of 1900 were ranged the Chapmans and his three sons; the Lewis Chanlers with their three children; and Alida and Temple Emmet with their two. Their hostess, Margaret, radiantly returned from the Orient, gave the toast that ever afterwards was drunk at ceremonious Rokeby gatherings:

"To all who have been here; to all who are here; to all who would like to be here."

Willie took fire as the dinner progressed, and held the group entranced by tales of adventure that glistened like jeweled tapestries. Jack Chapman, new to the performance, with his knack for impromptu versifying, fixed the scene in a rhyme entitled "The Snake Charmer." The stanzas ran:

The tide of victuals was running slack
(My interest failed at the canvasback),
And still the waiters circulate
With wine on wine and plate on plate;
And the glasses yellow and red and green
On the distracted board are seen,
Like an autumn garden, stalk on stalk,
When Willie Chanler began to talk.

What he said I'll not repeat. . . .
For could a mortal understand
How he reached his sacred heat,
Or what the meaning of his hand
As he raised it, and the eyes of all
Followed its movements magical?

He talked of Egypt — how he slew
In an afternoon ten thousand men,
And half a thousand women too!
(The last to frozen rivers grew,
For they looked too long on his eyes of flame,
And returned to their consorts never again!)

And next a lion he did tame,
And with the skin old Kruger smote,
Till the mane grew fast to Kruger's throat,
And Cecil Rhodes gave up the game!
Now touching lightly on the Czar —
And the Duchess of the Alcazar —
And what he won from the Shah in a fight
And lost at faro in a night.

And ever the visitors craned their necks,
And the waiters listened behind the door
To catch but a word if they could no more
Of that marvelous stream that might perplex
The brain of a Plato to unravel,
Of history, legend, intrigue, travel.

Now a whisper about doth go,
"Does he believe it — is it so?
We don't know and he don't know!"
And still the continuous stream doth flow.
"Is it opium? Is it wine
That makes his glassy eye to shine,
And tinctures yours and dazzles mine,
Until the decanters seem to dance
In tune with the flashing of his glance?"

He is telling the laws of the Boogla-Goo,
The secret clique that rules Bombay;
He himself was the chief, they say,
The very Pyjam of the How-do-you-do,
That poisoned the Princess of Cathay
And won the bride and turned the tide
Of the Mongols in Baffin's Bay.

One at a time they came up the pass,
One on an elephant, one on an ass,
While he with sorceries manifold —
A handful of silver, a pound of gold
And the hair that the witch of Atlas gave
When Genghis Khan came out of the grave —
Did frighten them all away!

He talked till the brain of the men that night,
Like absinthe mixed with dynamite,
Gave off blue sparks, and the lamps burned low,
And still the murmur about doth go:
"Did he do it and is it so?
We don't know and he don't know
If it be false or if it be true."

Nobody living ever knew,
Or in eternity can find out —
We only obey his call;
He is merely weaving his charms about —
Till the snakes crawl in, and the lights go out —
The charmer has charmed them all.

There was need of Willie's verbal hashish on that Christmas night of 1900, for the minds of the Chanlers gathered around that festive board were not at ease. Three brothers were absent from the circle. Wintie once more was shooting in Sardinia. Bob was in Paris, from where he sent brave but homesick greetings. And Archie?

The fact — at first discreetly hushed but now trumpeted by newspapers to all the world — was that on Thanksgiving eve John Armstrong Chanler had disappeared from Bloomingdale asylum, and the most diligent search had failed to turn up a single clue to his whereabouts or fate. Had he perished? Many people believed he had. Or was he at large? And if so, where?

That his disappearance was voluntary seemed indicated by a note found in his room. Addressed to Dr. Samuel P. Lyon, the medical superintendent of Bloomingdale, it read:

"My dear Doctor:

"You have always said that I am insane. You have always said that I believe I am the reincarnation of Napoleon Bonaparte. As a learned and sincere man, you, therefore, will not be surprised that I take French leave.

Yours, with regret that we must part,

J. A. CHANLER"

PART IV:

THE ART OF MATURITY

22 | TWO LATITUDES OF LUNACY

Dr. Lyon was chagrined, so chagrined that he informed no one of Archie's disappearance for twenty-four hours. He thought he understood Chanler, but quite obviously he did not.

Back in 1897, when Archie had failed to enlist the help of Micajah Woods, he had resigned himself to waiting for some new development. Meanwhile, he took care to commit no action that might be construed as irrational, to conform to every rule and cause no trouble. He became a perfect example of sweet reasonableness, with one exception: he would not admit that he was insane. Otherwise, this model inmate had only once seriously annoyed Dr. Lyon.

In conversations with the doctor, Archie liked to remind him that Archie's conservators were paying Bloomingdale $5,000 a year for his keep. One day Archie read in an account in a newspaper of a parrot that had prevented a robbery by shrieking "Stop thief!" at the intruder. He begged Dr. Lyon to obtain the bird for him because there were times, he said, when he felt "as lonesome as Robinson Crusoe on his desert island." But Dr Lyon, not relishing the prospect of being greeted by a parrot screeching "Stop thief!" every time he entered Archie's cell, angrily denied the request, and it was several weeks before harmonious relations were resumed.

When he was declared permanently insane, Archie's "X-faculty" apparently went on leave, except to suggest that he begin a systematic reading of the Bible, and this he did. Then abruptly, to Archie's amazement, his "X-faculty" began to rhyme in couplets. The couplets came in a stream, then a flood. Next Archie found himself writing sonnets, particularly in response to newspaper items that irritated him: Germany's saber-rattling emperor

Wilhelm II was castigated and yellow journalism's most aggressive vulgarian, William Randolph Hearst, was taken apart as "a tin-horn gambler from the vasty West." Archie composed a whole sequence of sonnets praising the cockroaches of Bloomingdale for guarding him from the predatory bedbugs. And another sonnet, titled "Destiny," looked forward to the day when:

> Once I have got to Court and had my say,
> Once Law hath rescued me from this foul tomb
> Till then my lawyers strong will toil amain
> Until the links they break of this Hell-chain.

Early in June 1899 Archie obtained permission to walk outside the asylum grounds without a keeper. His conduct had been exemplary, and he was granted the privilege on his simple promise not to try to escape. At first the exercise aggravated a backache which he had acquired since entering the asylum, and so he stopped. But late in the year, his health improved and he resumed his walks.

He now had a plan. Gradually he increased the distance that he could cover until he managed twelve miles easily, six out and six back. In a town six miles away, he rented a post box, using an assumed name and small sums of cash which he managed to borrow from visitors. Then he wrote again to Micajah Woods in Charlottesville, directing Woods to reply to his postal box.

No answer came. Archie tried a second time in February 1900. A month later he received a friendly reply in which Woods pleaded unfamiliarity with New York procedures and suggested that Archie contact a certain New York lawyer. Archie immediately did so, and the lawyer responded positively. When prodded about what was happening, he appeared to be considering the case and asking for additional opinions. By October it became apparent to Archie that nobody was going to risk interfering between a crazy man and his rich and powerful relatives. If he was ever going to get out of Bloomingdale, he must accomplish it himself.

Still, he made one final appeal. He asked one of his own law partners to come see him, which the partner did. Archie begged him to undertake the case, but this attorney also sidestepped involvement. As he was leaving, Archie asked him for $10.

The next afternoon, the day before Thanksgiving, Archie sauntered through the asylum gate, waving to the guard, and headed eastward toward Mamaroneck, where he caught a train to New York. At Grand Central

Terminal he sent a telegram to Dr. J. Madison Taylor, the Philadelphia neurologist under whose care Amélie has been placed some years back. During visits to Amélie at that time, Archie had become quite friendly with Taylor. The telegram announced that one "John Childe" was coming to Philadelphia and would call on Taylor in regard to a client whom he represented.

Thus far Archie had been lucky, but in New York it seemed likely that he would encounter someone who knew him. He quickly hailed a cab and was jolted across town to the Jersey City ferry, all the way holding a handkerchief to his face as though suffering from a nosebleed. Across the Hudson he boarded a train for Philadelphia, where he went directly to Dr. Taylor's office.

At first the doctor did not recognize his caller, but as Archie began to describe his "client's" case, Taylor became struck with the resemblance between Mr. Childe and his old friend Armstrong Chanler. When he remarked upon it, Archie confessed his identity, and asked Taylor's help.

His situation was perilous. Although convinced that he was sane, legally he was demented. He possessed no civil rights. He could not appear in court, testify on his own behalf, incur debts, dispose of his property, or choose where he would live. As a fugitive from a mental institution, he could be arrested on sight and returned to the asylum. What he desired, Archie said, was for Taylor to observe him for several months, in order to test his sanity. After some hesitation Taylor agreed, and that night Archie entered Dr. Taylor's private sanitarium under the name John Childe.

Archie had spent three years and eights months in Bloomingdale, during which he had received two visits from the brothers and sisters who had put him there, either by their action or by passive assent.

Lewis was the first member of the family to hear of his brother's disappearance. Asylum guards were scouring the surrounding countryside, but had found no trace. There was the note that Archie had left for Dr. Lyon, saying he was taking "French leave," but Dr. Lyon had not divulged that yet. Lewis hastened to White Plains but gleaned no helpful information, and the next day he instituted a police search.

The newspapers sensationalized the story, the *Tribune* reporting that the missing man was "well provided with money," quite harmless, and capable of taking care of himself under normal conditions. Rumors and false leads abounded. The missing man was reported in New Jersey, Philadelphia, Washington, Virginia, and Europe. The impression spread that he had either fled abroad, or was dead; perhaps he drowned in one of the small lakes near Bloomingdale. Several ponds were dredged, to no avail.

The family believed Archie was hiding with friends, and the longer he stayed out of sight, the better it would be for all concerned. When Wintie received the news, he wrote to Willie: "Where is Archie? The fact that nothing has been heard of him is a good sign. He is with friends who take care of him. I consider that apart from our total ignorance of his whereabouts, his escape is a good thing for him & all of us. His money is rolling up for him. His affairs will be straightened out, so that when he turns up, as he is sure to do, there will be enough to keep him well wherever he wants to be. Poor old boy! There are lots of madder men than he at large. . . ."

In Philadelphia, Dr. Taylor was coming to the same conclusion, for he could find no evidence that Archie was insane or had ever been insane. He brought in professional consultants as well, including Joseph Jastrow, of the University of Wisconsin; Dr. Horatio Curtis Wood, professor of clinical diseases at the University of Pennsylvania; Dr. Allen McLane Hamilton, president of the medical college of Cornell University; Thompson Jay Hudson, author of *The Law of Psychic Phenomena*; and William James, professor of psychology at Harvard University.

When Dr. Taylor closed his private sanitarium six months later, he transferred Archie to a private hospital in Concordville, Pennsylvania. There Archie opened a bank account under the name John Childe, and wrote checks and kept the balance correctly.

In the interim, he had engaged counsel: in Virginia, Micajah Woods and State Senator John W. Daniel; in New York, Augustus Van Wyck, a former New York judge. In July 1901 Archie was moved again, this time to Lynchburg, Virginia, under the name John Clinton. He stayed in Lynchburg six weeks, maintaining a checking account at a Lynchburg bank and conducting himself in a manner that invited no invidious attention. On September 20, 1901, nearly a year after fleeing Bloomingdale, Archie alighted from a train at Charlottesville, Virginia, was recognized, admitted his identity, and announced that he had come to vindicate his sanity in court.

The story again was sensational, North and South. Here was an escaped lunatic, a man thought to be dead, walking the streets of Charlottesville, greeting old acquaintances, welcomed by them. A prepared statement was put out by Chanler's counsel, outlining the salient facts of their client's confinement and escape, and revealing for the first time his whereabouts and activity during the intervening months. His counsel unanimously vouched for their client's "sound condition of mind and body . . . as disclosed by personal contact and through frequent correspondence."

In White Plains, Dr. Samuel Lyon was seriously annoyed: Archie, he felt, had let him down. "He pledged his word that he would not escape," said Lyon plaintively. "He is as insane as when he was committed to this asylum. He is absolutely incurable."

The stage was set carefully for the climactic scene of this drama. Archie went to stay at a friend's estate and for several weeks he rode around the countryside, mingling with people and resuming his place in the life of the community. Everywhere he was well received. Then a neighbor, Cary Ruffin Randolph, petitioned the Albemarle County court to examine into the medical condition of John Armstrong Chanler, suspected of being insane and at present a fugitive from an asylum for the insane in another state. Randolph prayed the court to determine whether a "committee of the person and estate" of the said Chanler should be appointed.

A hearing was set for mid-October, but delayed when Archie received a request from Lewis to hold the proceedings until Wintie got back from Europe and Willie from Mexico. At last, on November 6, 1901, the hearing opened in Charlottesville. The courtroom was filled, but while a lawyer was on hand to represent the interests of Archie's "committee" in New York, no member of the family was present.

Archie took the stand and recounted the history of his case, culminating in his escape and his subsequent activities. Then Dr. Taylor related his association with Chanler, and described the strict conditions under which Chanler had lived in Philadelphia. He said he regarded Chanler as perfectly sane and capable of managing his own affairs. The head of the Concordville sanitarium agreed. More than a score of witnesses — neighbors, tradesmen, business associates living in the region and in North Carolina — testified to the same effect. Finally, expert written opinions were offered in evidence which bore out, in technical terms, the conclusions already presented; no evidence had been submitted to them, they reported unanimously, indicating that Chanler was insane or incapable of managing his affairs. Several praised Archie's dogged probing into the little understood phenomena of ESP — automatism, telepathy, trance, the whole field of perception. William James stated that for his readiness to incur grave risks in exploring the forces latent in himself, Chanler deserved "nothing but praise."

No testimony contrary to this being presented, the court ruled that "said J. A. Chanler is a sane man, capable of taking care of his person and of managing his estate . . . Petition is dismissed." A cheer went up at the verdict, but Archie searched in vain for one representative of the family to make his amnesty complete. For him the triumph of the day was streaked with bitterness.

Outside Virginia, Chanler's plucky fight to re-establish his rights and reputation had attracted wide and often admiring attention. Newspapers commented upon the strange case, and its still stranger outcome, for Archie was still a legal outcast in New York State. *The Brooklyn Daily Eagle* observed that the Virginia court's decision held grave importance for everyone. "If Chanler," the paper said, had "never been insane or incompetent, his liberties have been scandalously invaded . . . Let us hope that satisfactory proof that he was insane when he was committed to Bloomingdale may be produced. There is no doubt that capable physicians and disinterested physicians decided that it was best for him that he be deprived of his liberty. But were they mistaken?"

To Archie the next step was clear: he must regain his rights and control of his property in New York State, where the bulk of his wealth lay. Meanwhile, he had at last attained national renown for something besides being "the former husband of Amélie Rives"; now he was known as the man who was legally a lunatic in New York, and legally sane in Virginia.

23 | SUNSHINE AND TRAGEDY

Bob had neither advocated nor opposed Archie's commitment, but during Archie's years in Bloomingdale, no communication had taken place between them. Bob had been preoccupied with his own problems. Pushed or guided by designing elders into a loveless marriage, he was also torn by his still undisciplined impulse to paint. He strove erratically for domestic fulfillment and serenity, but he remained at odds with Julia, frustrated in his desire for children, and never accepted as a lover. It was not altogether surprising, therefore, that this period of his life was marked by Bohemian excesses and reckless behavior.

Nor was Julia in much better case. She had her mother's love of neatness, regularity, good manners, smart dress, fashionable friends, and a well-run household, but she lacked her mother's ruthless determination and cool calculation. Nor did she receive any maternal support. Once Mrs. Chamberlain had arranged a socially advantageous marriage, she believed her duty discharged. Like Bob, Julia learned that society regarded younger children as expendable, and that her mother thought her not quite up to standard.

Bob and Julia visited the United States several times, but received no encouragement to settle there. Neither Daisy Chanler nor Elizabeth Chapman nor Alida Emmet, the reigning Chanler hostesses, looked favorably upon the establishment of a competing household. Nor, even more decidedly, did her own sister, Alice Chanler. After each visit, therefore, Bob and Julia retreated to Europe where Bob pursued his art studies, and Julia resumed the more congenial European rhythms which she had known most of her life.

The outlook did seem to change in 1898. After five barren years, Julia became pregnant, and this proof of Bob's virility, of his effectiveness as a man, gave him confidence in his artistic hopes as well. Julia was forced to endure long conversations between her husband and Henry Clews, as they strode up and down beside her bed, shouting and smoking cigars, debating theories of art.

On November 24, 1898, their daughter Dorothy was born, but her malformed left arm was shrunken and withered. At first the shock threw Bob into despair, and his brother Willie never forgave Julia, for he believed her tight lacing during pregnancy had caused the deformity.

Then Bob took action. He set about obtaining corrective treatment for the baby, who was carried from clinic to clinic across Europe. The case achieved medical notoriety because it resembled Kaiser Wilhelm's disfigurement, and the kaiser ordered medical consultants to follow Dorothy's treatments minutely, reporting directly to the emperor; but nothing proved successful. Bob fought against giving up hope, and lavished love on this child who was both a joy and a reproach.

The misfortune seemed to postpone indefinitely the idea of going home. Bob was embarrassed, although he tried to hide the hopelessness of the situation from Rokeby retainers like Mary Meroney. On December 19, 1900, he wrote to her: "Don't you think that we are never coming home. Some day we will. You see we have a lot to do over here for Dorothy, & to get her arm into shape before we leave. She is getting on fine, & is the prettiest little thing you have ever seen & as gay as a cricket. . . . She has a very nice English nurse almost as nice as you are. . . . I would not be surprised to see a brother in a few years just to share her father's joy. . . ."

The hint of another child was pure bravado. Julia's pregnancy and its sorry outcome had intensified her aversion to every manifestation of physical passion. Retreating to her daintiness, she would freeze her husband's advances with a shudder of loathing.

Wintie, meanwhile, had been on the verge of leaving Rome and going home "to occupy the Newport house forever & amen." But in January of 1900 he was laid low by serious injuries. "My first fall in all the years I've hunted in this country," he told his friend Amos French. "I was riding a nice filly I had just bought and was a little too bold with her. The result was that she gave me a bad toss over a flight of rails too big for her and fell on me twice. The ground was hard as stone and in getting clear she kicked me in the right collar bone, breaking it in two places. But that's nothing of course. The worst was the squeezing I got in the groin and thigh muscles of both legs & a bad bruise deep up my —. Shut off my water works for five or six days . . . I'm all right, battered but still in the ring. . . . I see there is a great boom in Wall Street.

I made a hundred francs a month ago playing écarté — the only raise I have made this year. . . . But then — I never had any business head. Write soon & don't lecture me. . . ."

Apart from inherited money, Wintie's main source of spending money for many years came from accident claims. More than one insurance company had given way under the strain of his perverse persistence in tumbling off horses. Once, fearing to appear crudely repetitious, Wintie based a claim on grounds other than fox hunting: he said he had been injured "in a balloon ascension." The company settled the claim but cancelled his policy, whereupon Wintie threw his business to Lloyd's of London, famed for its willingness to insure anything.

Word of Wintie's accident reached Theodore Roosevelt, who had just been inaugurated as Vice President: "They talk of my leading a 'strenuous life,'" he wrote. "Good Heavens, I would not face the risks you continually run for a good deal! My days of chamois hunting and fox hunting are over."

Wintie wrote his sister Margaret: "For Heaven's sake, don't tell Elizabeth or Alida! They might turn the mental or Christian Scientists on me & rile me all up." Alluding to Alida's increasingly numerous progeny, he inquired when she expected "(what number is it?) I can't keep track of her rapid fire propensities."

The sedentary interval of recovery, so unusual for him, turned Wintie's thoughts toward home, and he told Margaret that he and the family would be sailing for Boston in September; Cliff Lawn was ready for them at Newport. To Amos French, he confessed: "I am going to settle down at Newport for good & all, and never wander more."

His wife, Daisy, however, was thinking of realities that Wintie ignored. In a letter to Margaret, she made it clear that she did not wish to bias her husband's decision, "we seem to be very hard up & it is certainly easier to economize over here. When I tell you that since the first of June Mr. Morris has not sent us a cent & we have lived entirely on what Aunt Laura gave me, you will realize that Wintie's income is in a bad way. . . . I want him to do what is best, but if we go home he must be kept out of business as all his financial ventures seem to have been disastrous."

Margaret was constantly angling to get the family all back home, with Rokeby the focal point; also, she was perturbed by stories she heard about Daisy's supposed attempts to take Wintie into the fold of Rome.

In August Wintie's family caravan made an intermediate stop in London, where Daisy wrote distractedly imploring Margaret to please find a suitable maid "to stay with me till I find some one to fill the place permanently. The good German one I took to replace Cecilia would not go to America & the Italian who came to me this spring is such an idiot that I send her back tomorrow."

They made the crossing with a mountain of luggage — packing cases containing pictures and furniture and "old Roman belongings." Cabot Lodge had given them a letter that smoothed their way through customs, and on September 6, 1901, they landed at Boston. Aboard the train for Newport that day, word reached them that President McKinley had been shot at Buffalo.

Wintie's thoughts immediately went out to Roosevelt. He wrote at once to his cherished companion, and on September 14, the new President replied on stationery carrying the engraved heading: "Executive Mansion, Washington":

"Buffalo, N.Y., September 14, 1901

"Dear Winty:
"Your note of the 12th just received. I have about as heavy and painful a task put upon me as can fall to the lot of any man in a civilized country. But it is a real pleasure to know that you and Mrs. Winty are back on this side. We shall very soon want to see you down at Washington.

Ever yours,
THEODORE ROOSEVELT"

From Newport, Wintie wrote to Cabot Lodge: ". . . Dear old Theodore, he is there after all. It is a dreadful thing to get what you want in such a way. He is too good a man to win on a foul, but there he is & thank God for it. He seems to have the confidence, good will & sympathy of the whole country. He has said very little & that little was dignified & proper. I got a line from him the morning poor McKinley died, but when I shall see him I do not know. Yesterday, I went to the Memorial Service at Trinity Church here. The place was overflowing, scarce standing room. All the churches the same. Senator Wetmore says he could hardly get into the Cathedral in New York. All is still draped in black, & the newspapers in mourning, very gloomy. Poor Mrs. Theodore! I am afraid she is heart-sick with fear for him. Of course he refuses escorts & behaves as one expects him to behave, but she must suffer. Still she had a taste of it while he was in Cuba, and after the first few weeks she will get used to the strain . . ."

Besides the national tragedy, the Chanlers had been visited by a private grief. In a tower room at Rokeby, closed to even a ray of sunlight, lay Elizabeth's brilliant husband, John Jay Chapman, who had suffered a complete mental and physical collapse.

24 | THE ORDEAL
OF "QUEEN BESS"

Elizabeth had gladly accepted all the risks of marriage, but this was truly put to the test when, late in 1899, she gave birth to a little girl who died almost at once. Her brothers and sisters, who had been anxious throughout her pregnancy because they feared she would not survive childbirth, feared more the emotional shock of her first child's death. Elizabeth, however, gave way to no grief, and late in 1900 the family learned that she was pregnant again. Although others trembled for the outcome, Elizabeth was serene. She yearned to find fulfillment in motherhood.

Her husband, Jack, however, was nearing the point of exhaustion. Anxiety over his wife compounded the stresses of his many other activities — law, lecturing, writing, agitating. "Politics takes physique, and being odious takes physique," he jotted in a memorandum to himself. "I feel like Atlas lifting the entire universe. . . ." During the winter of 1900-1901 he came to sense that something was amiss: his mind would go off on a tangent and he would be unable to follow a thought through. The symptoms were not sufficiently severe to cause alarm, however, and in March Elizabeth went to Washington to visit friends; she was expecting her child in a few weeks.

While she was gone, the crash came. Jack was in the midst of a lecture out of town. He seemed to lose the thread of his thought; then sounds became blurred, and although he could hear the audience asking questions and then somebody saying, "He doesn't understand," he was unable to answer coherently.

Somehow he managed to get back to his hotel, and the next day, feeling better, he returned to New York. Although the condition had eased, he was frightened. Reasoning that he needed exercise, he went for a long walk, during which he had the odd sensation of feeling "something break in the inner part of my left leg near the thigh." He realized that this was serious, but since the leg continued to function, he walked home and went to bed.

Elizabeth, summoned from Washington, found her husband too weak to stand and rambling in his speech. As she had before their marriage, Margaret again assumed command. Jack must be given quiet, intensive care at Rokeby. Brusquely she alerted Mary Meroney: "Mr. Chapman will go up on Wednesday morning reaching Rhinecliff at 1 o'clock. . . . He will have a trained nurse with him just to pacify Mrs. Chapman. Put him in the tower room and put her in the parrot room, . . . I shall be up in a day or two. . . . Mrs. Chapman is better but I don't think much of married life. . . ."

Elizabeth remained in New York while Margaret supervised Jack's care at Rokeby. On April 26, Elizabeth gave birth to a son. As soon as she could travel, she hastened with the baby to Rokeby, where she found her husband apparently demented.

To the Chanlers, the welcome word of Elizabeth's safe delivery took precedence over the reports of Jack's condition. From Rome Wintie wrote to Margaret that her "cable announcing the successful arrival of the Elizabethan prodigy gave us all great relief joy & pride & was duly answered. . . ."

And with characteristic obliviousness about Jack's condition, Bob wrote an effusive letter to Chapman:

". . . I heard God knows how that Bet [Elizabeth] was with child & I trembled with dread, for you see I saw her two years on her back etc., & have a baby malformed. So I have not written, but now dear Jack between you & me without sentimentality — I have the joy that Christians of old had when shouting Christ is risen, Christ is risen. There is only one answer to skepticism & vice & that is birth, child, reproduction. There is only one sad & melancholy being & that is a virgin who dies barren. I hope you will pardon my writing so freely but I feel very strongly about it. Bet is now a woman, she has overcome her blight in youth & is a magnificent reproductive woman, that makes men work & life worth living. . . ."

The baby was christened Chanler Armstrong Chapman, the ceremony taking place at Rokeby. Jack was brought down to witness the occasion, but his condition could hardly have been worse. Day after day he lay in bed with his knees drawn up to his chin, under the delusion that he had lost the power of walking, and he was tormented by hallucinations. He had to be fed, bathed, clothed, and constantly watched. He could not bear daylight; even a ray coming in through a slit at the top of the drawn blind causing excruciating pain. His intellect seemed eclipsed.

Temple Emmet, who was very fond of Jack, came to stay with him. When the family considered placing Chapman in a mental hospital, Emmet objected and won the argument. Jack remained bedfast nearly a year and then at first he had could only crawl on all fours.

Patiently, Elizabeth persevered in encouraging his return to rationality. When Jack was able to endure the sunlight, she had him carried into the garden, where they would sit for hours, holding hands. A long course of massage helped straighten out his legs, and eventually he was able to hobble about on crutches. His mind slowly recovered its vigor, and his humor returned. Nearly a year and a half after he was stricken he wrote to Margaret: "Conrad [his son, aged five, from his first marriage] informed me the other day that the name of the mule I drive is Clara Barton. I rather doubted your naming the mule in this way, but Annie Galvin says that George Galvin told her that this is the name the mule bore in Cuba. At any rate it is a wonderfully intelligent animal. I never knew how superior they were to horses, especially when they look around at you and ask you if you intend to go home from this point in the road."

By October 1902 Jack seemed sufficiently strong to travel, and Elizabeth took him to Europe. With the four boys — Chapman's sons, Victor, John Jay, and Conrad, and the baby — a tutor, a nurse, and maids, they sailed for Italy. In the spring they traveled to Austria for bathing. The tutor and Victor and Jay bicycled to a watering place on the river Sann, ninety miles away. Nine-year-old Jay ventured into a deep part of the bathing pool, was caught in the swift river current, and swept into an outlet. Three days later his body was recovered more than a mile downstream.

The shock affected Chapman curiously. Although Jack admired all his sons, calling them "king's children, and I am a stepfather to them!" Jay was perhaps his favorite. Nevertheless the boy's death seemed to seal over all the previous wounds. Announcing that he had thrown away his crutches, Jack told Elizabeth calmly, "Now we can go home."

They sailed directly. The ordeal had changed him deeply; even his appearance was altered, for during his illness he had grown a beard that would characterize him thereafter. His hair, once dark and glossy, and his beard, were now gray.

The next two winters Jack and Elizabeth lived in Edgewater, a old house down the hill from Rokeby. Solitude, rest, and mental exercise worked their alchemy, and in time Chapman regained both physical vigor and his mental tone. But he completely changed the pattern of his life. He left the law behind, and never again engaged for long in reform agitation. He wrote — improvisations, critical biographies, essays, literary exegesis, poems, children's plays, and enchanting letters — but the audience these personal and unorthodox works attracted grew smaller and smaller as they improved in quality.

The Chapmans resumed their rather stately entertaining in their town house on West 82nd Street, and to the designs of Charles A. Platt they built a country home, Sylvania, on the hillside above Edgewater, adjacent to Rokeby. There the troubled spirit of John Jay Chapman, sustained by Elizabeth, would find some measure of peace.

25 | GRADUS AD PARNASSUM

In a manner only slightly less dramatic than Chapman's recovery, Bob also began providing surprises. In 1901 he came to stay with Margaret at Rokeby. Julia had come with him, but returned very shortly to their Paris home, recoiling from American life in general and the rusticity of Rokeby in particular.

Bob was still striving to find his niche. In Europe he had been hypnotized in turn by Gothic art, the Renaissance masters, by ceramics, by tapestry; but the discovery in a Paris shop of a Chinese screen proved to be the crucial catalyst. In the screen he found a form offering infinite variability. Originality, brilliant coloring, and superb style were at its base, and he evolved a philosophy of the screen as a symbol. A screen was not static or stationary; it could be placed in different lights and perspectives and settings. And there was always a hidden side. The visible side satisfied the aesthetic sense, while its invisible side was an enigma — beauty might be there — or hideousness — or nothing! The surface of a screen offered a foundation for rich, closely viewed effects that were too startling for murals. At the same time, however formal in design, a screen was, after all, a domestic article of furniture, intended to be enjoyed in intimate surroundings. It was in this medium that Bob achieved some of his most novel work.

Prompting him to return to America had been an instinctive understanding that he was bound to prove himself in the midst of his own heritage. He must live by his own standards, but within the orbit of his family and fortune. He was and would remain ineradicably a Chanler, although perhaps the least typical of them all. He was also driven by a need to equal his brothers.

Bob soon obtained commissions to decorate the Fifth Avenue homes of several wealthy friends, and at Rokeby he flung himself into the farm work, going into the fields with the hands, fishing and drinking cider with them, just as he had done as a boy. The men liked him, but to them he was always "Mr. Robert," the social gap having widened with time. He also brought his art to Rokeby, decorating the walls of a bedroom in the back of the house — it is said in a single night of intense activity — with painted scenes of crows, poppies, and Catskills. There followed a joint portrait of Julia and Josiah House, pensioners living in the gatehouse who had recently observed their seventy-fifth wedding anniversary. To help in his commissioned artistic work, he brought from Paris a talented assistant, François Ladigeois, who stayed in New York, carrying out Chanler's designs, which called for the painstaking application of such exotic materials as gold leaf, aluminum, and glass.

Margaret was baffled by her brother's artistic urge, but welcomed his return to Rokeby. Lewis also approved of Bob's new conduct, for he had always considered Bob's lifestyle dissolute. It was Margaret who first guessed that politics might provide a safety valve for Bob's excessive energy. John Sullivan, the head gardener at Rokeby, one day broached the subject with Bob: "Mr. Robert," he asked, "will you run for the Assembly?"

"Sure!" Bob obliged, "What is it?"

Duly informed, he embarked on a campaign highlighted by scattering dollar bills throughout the county. Lewis, who was running for town supervisor in the same election, strongly disapproved and largely because of Bob's horseplay both brothers were beaten.

Willie, the Tammany sachem, lectured Bob on such amateurism, and suggested he try again. This time Bob made a more serious effort. He sponsored baseball teams in four towns, supplying the uniforms and equipment. He also underwrote four brass bands. A Poughkeepsie lawyer-banker, Edward E. Perkins, observed the popularity that Bob was attracting by these tactics and offered to manage his campaign, if Lewis also would run again for supervisor.

Lewis often spoke at length, making a good impression with his height, his pleasant earnestness, and boyishly appealing face. Bob made no speeches, but stepped up his own style of vote-seeking. He bought a farm in Red Hook, a mile east of Rokeby, and offered thirty acres to the town for a baseball park and picnic grounds, where he staged harness races and beer parties. His master stroke was importing a prize bull. For years the farmers of Delaware County had been cornering the cattle prizes at the state fair, much to the disgust of their Dutchess County competitors. Bob invited his neighbors to make free use of his pedigreed bull, and in a couple of years the Dutchess farmers began capturing prizes. The grateful rural voters sent Bob to the Assembly and made Lewis town supervisor and member of the County Board of Supervisors.

Whatever services Bob performed as Assemblyman have not been recorded, but his artistic progress during this time was not curtailed by political enthusiasm. And happily for his financial situation, the death of his Great-Aunt Laura Delano in 1902 nearly doubled his income and that of each of his siblings. The last surviving daughter of William B. Astor died childless in Geneva, leaving the bulk of her very considerable wealth in trust to her relatives, principally the Chanlers.

This new inheritance led Bob to make a generous financial provision for his wife, whereby Julia would receive $20,000 annually "off the top" of his income. Morris, the family lawyer, tried to restrain Bob's impetuosity until they knew just how much his share in the estate would come to, but Bob had his way. But even as he was dealing openhandedly with Julia, he was ignoring petty debts. He built a house on his Red Hook farm from designs by Warren & Wetmore, the architects who some years later were to complete the Grand Central Terminal, but at the same time though, he neglected to pay his artistic workmen. Ladigeois wrote plaintively that "the work progresses [but] I should be happy if you would think of me a little bit because the dollars fly away and disappear!"

In 1904 Julia was expecting another child, and the prospect triggered an explosion of creative energy in Bob. He threw himself into the painting of an enormous panel, showing life-size giraffes browsing in a forest. It was a Gothic conceit, fantastic and symbolic and original — real figures in an unreal setting — the graceful animals reaching into the delicate canopy of leaves for the fruit hanging there and standing amid the straight, silvery trunks of the trees. The trees were not tropical, but cool white birches; and the fruit which the giraffes would be plucking daintily would be red-gold oranges.

Bob painted like a demon, and in February 1905 wrote to Margaret:

"Julia is very well & is nearing her goal. We expect the birth this week and it may not come for two. . . . With the care Julia is taking of herself, she should have an 11 lbs. child. She walks every morning & eats & sleeps well. Dorothy is a great big strong girl very pretty talkative & gay, with a streak of Chanler nerves & quickness.

"I am painting very hard with Ladigeois. We are doing a decoration for the Salon 5 yards high & 5 yards wide. It will probably be turned down, but never mind. I shall be satisfied if I like it myself. Perhaps you may see me established yet as a decorator in New York with my farm & my politics. I am also studying socialism & feel very interested in it. . . ."

The painting, "Giraffes," was exhibited at the Salon d'Automne in 1905, and eventually was acquired by the French government.

On March 25 the baby was born — a girl — and christened Barbara, although nicknamed Julia, for her mother. Bob got very drunk and was very wild for some time after the happy event.

26 | WIDE-AWAKE WILLIE

Immediately after the war in Cuba Willie had wangled a mining concession from the new government that included both iron deposits in Pinar del Rio province and the El Cobre copper mines near Santiago. The iron deposits he left unworked while he threw his energies into developing the Cobre workings. In the shifting political struggles in liberated Cuba, Willie had worked with the faction behind Secretary of State Orestes Ferrera and had masterminded at least one governmental upset. The winners expressed their gratitude quite concretely. Writing to Margaret on December 1, 1902, Willie reported:

"We have found the [El Cobre] mines in splendid order & one & all are satisfied that we have a huge fortune in sight. I left my friends in Santiago & came here to play politics & business combined. Was in during the strike & turned it to my great advantage. *Entre nous*, I am floating the Government loan of $35,000,000. . . ."

At the mining town Willie learned to quench his thirst with a local rum concoction. Bringing the recipe back to his New York clubs, he introduced the daiquiri cocktail to America.

The profits from the loan proved to be illusory, but Willie was not discouraged about Latin America's potential. He promoted a resort hotel in Puerto Rico, and in Mexico successfully walked off with a concession to equip the city of Tampico with a new sewage and water supply system. Accounts of the Mexican episode were typical Willie legends.

The story went that President Teddy Roosevelt was concerned about European capitalists' apparent takeover of Mexico's economy. He proposed, unofficially of course, that Willie should look into the situation; ostensibly he would be dealing in Mexican turquoises. Willie agreed, and quickly satisfied himself that American capital was indeed being frozen out.

To test his belief, he submitted a bid for the Tampico concession, but a European competitor won the contract. When he paid his farewell call on President Porfirio Diaz, Willie said that he believed he had been shut out by collusion and that he would report to President Roosevelt that the Mexican government was pursuing a discriminatory policy against citizens of the United States. Diaz requested that Chanler delay his departure and come back the next day.

Upon entering the president's office this time, Willie saw three bids on the Tampico project spread out on Diaz's desk: one from an English syndicate, one from a French, and the third from a consortium of Dutch bankers. Diaz urged Chanler to examine them; he found them identical. Then Diaz asked whether Chanler might not wish to resubmit his bid. Willie took the hint, undercut the estimates of his competition, and won the concession, which carried a contract for $2,187,000.

Another version of the story tells how Willie used a negotiating trick he learned from Cecil Rhodes. If Rhodes encountered an opponent who resisted all persuasion, he would reach into his vest pocket and produce several large diamonds. While continuing to talk, he would play with them, roll them like dice across the table, and toy with them absently. Nearly always, Rhodes said, the antagonist would be mesmerized by the gems, and where money had failed to talk, diamonds did. When Willie found Diaz stubborn, it was said, he wired to New York for the largest diamond in Tiffany's and tossed it on the dictator's desk with an allusion to his known taste in precious stones. And, the story went, diamonds won again.

However the concession was won, Willie left his Latin American agent, Horatio S. Rubens, to iron out the details and hastened back to New York, crowing to Margaret: "Rubens has settled my Mexican matters & I am a big winner — the first of this generation so far financially."

There was, however, a sequel to the story. Willie needed capital to carry out the contract, but found Wall Street cold to the project. One day he was visited by an emissary of the Dutch consortium who told him that they and their European associates were responsible for his inability to raise working capital. The embargo could be lifted, the man said, if Willie would agree to help them in Venezuela. That country's exceedingly venal dictator-president, Cipriano Castro, was trying to float another international loan, and an American syndicate was prepared to underwrite an issue of bonds, at an extortionate premium; the first installment had actually been paid.

The Venezuelan government was nearly bankrupt already, staggering under outstanding bond issues held mainly by European investors. Reports of the new loan were causing these bonds to plummet on the European exchanges, and to complicate the situation, German bankers were intriguing with Castro to get a foothold in the country. As bait they had sold him two Krupp cannon, with which Castro hoped to overcome his rivals.

The Dutch investors were not opposed to the American loan, but they wished to save their own investments and turn back the threatened German takeover. To do this they were ready to back an insurrection against Castro. The revolutionaries were pro-American and pro-Dutch, but they needed help. Perhaps Chanler might raise a body of irregulars — soldiers of fortune who could come to the aid of the insurgents at the critical moment.

The prospect of a revolution was an irresistible lure. Long before, his closest friend, Ludwig von Höhnel, had perceived that "war and revolution are the fields in which [Willie's] vivid imagination loves to roam," and in view of the chronic chaos afflicting many Latin American nations at the time, everything he was told sounded plausible. The element of danger was the final attraction.

From this point forward in the story, Willie himself left a fictionalized account of the uprising. Through his connections with dubious characters in the Far West, he recruited several hundred desperadoes and soldiers of fortune — cow punchers and cattle rustlers, bank robbers and gunmen, gamblers and Indian scouts, ex-lawmen and "wanted" fugitives. All were hard riders, expert with weapons and spoiling for a fight. The freebooters, thinly disguised as colonists, were transported to a point on the Venezuelan border. They were well armed and mounted and provided with logistic support. At a signal from the insurgents, they marched inland, overcame opposition in some spirited fighting, captured the Krupp cannon intended for Castro, and appeared on the verge of overthrowing the dictator when suddenly the revolution was called off. Only then did Willie discover that the uprising had never been intended to succeed; it was merely meant to force Castro to break with the Germans and come to terms with his European bondholders.

Although furious at this betrayal, Willie was compelled to disperse his men. Venezuelan bonds rallied, and Willie found his credit good in Wall Street. Backed by adequate capital, he carried out the job at Tampico, although the profit turned out to be smaller than he had estimated; but to the Chanlers, money was always a secondary reward.

To facilitate his trips between New York and the Caribbean, Chanler acquired a seagoing houseboat, the *Sanibel*, and kept it in commission constantly. The craft provided privacy for Willie's secret consultations, and many a conspiratorial figure became a guest aboard. Sun Yat-sen, then living in exile, sought help for his projected overthrow of the Manchu dynasty, as did the so-called Young Turks, looking to rejuvenate the decrepit Ottoman Empire.

Political conniving did not distract Willie from his racing stable. He was a pillar of the Jockey Club and continued to display his silks at the racetracks. He also liked musical shows, and in 1903 he genuinely startled the family by announcing his engagement to a musical comedy star, Minnie Ashley.

Born Beatrice Ashley in Charlottesville, Virginia, she had grown up in Massachusetts and had been on the stage for ten years when Willie met her. De Wolfe Hopper had first engaged her for John Philip Sousa's comic opera, "El Capitan." After two years she joined Augustin Daly's company — he named her Minnie — and scored her first hit in "The Greek Slave." In "I'm a Naughty Girl," she outshone the star, and in "San Toy" in 1901, she had the town whistling, "Rhoda, Rhoda, ran a pagoda, She sold tea and ices and soda."

In 1903 she was headlined in "The Country Girl," and during its long run Willie was seen in the audience nearly every night he was in New York. When news of an engagement was conveyed to the Chanlers, there was a real flurry, but Willie's choice was quickly accepted, for he mandated it with a gay imperiousness there was no withstanding.

His sisters pouted for a while. An actress . . . The stage! . . . Qualms were overcome partly by Willie's insistence, and partly by Minnie's own charm and demure air of good breeding. Alida wept as usual, though she could not disapprove of her brother's marrying for love. A decade earlier Willie had decried romantic marriages ("there must be something else besides affection; in these days I should say particularly money"), but at thirty-six he was happily of another mind.

It was the press that raised an issue not before published: the bride, it seemed, was divorced. The Episcopal Church frowned on divorce and forbade church weddings for divorced persons, but the officiating minister saw no problem, and the wedding took place on December 4, 1903. Wintie served as best man. Also present were Lewis and his wife, Alice, Margaret, Elizabeth and Jack Chapman, Alida's husband, Temple Emmet, the bride's widowed mother, Horatio Rubens, Willie's Latin American liaison man, Jack Follansbee, partner of many a carouse; and George Galvin.

How the situation fitted in with Margaret's well-known refusal to countenance "plural marriage" was never explained. Margaret in many ways closely resembled Willie, both being people of action, pragmatic and decisive in their reaction to events. Margaret gloried in Willie's go-ahead individualism; it matched her notion of how a Chanler should live. She had gladly served as Willie's political hostess and was sharply disappointed when he abandoned politics. Margaret's affection for Lewis, her "twin" from nursery days, was deeper, warmer, more personal, but Willie's achievements satisfied her pride of family, and for him she overlooked much.

Minnie resumed her real name, Beatrice, and settled smoothly into the role of society matron. Beatrice proved a thorough success. With his Mexican winnings, and advised by Stanford White, Willie bought a country home at Sands Point, on Long Island, and he also took a house in town. There and aboard the *Sanibel* Beatrice entertained gracefully. There was never any question of her returning to the theater, and Margaret subsequently put down to her credit that Beatrice never mentioned that phase of her life again — in Margaret's presence. Actually Beatrice retained many of her theatrical friends and kept up her interest in the theater for years to come. But her tact was remarkable, and she came to be cited as one of the few actresses who had made the transition into society flawlessly.

Beatrice's first child, a son, was christened William Astor Chanler, Jr., although Lewis Chanler's younger son, already nine years old, was named William Astor Chanler II. To avoid confusion, Willie was granted prior claim on his own name, and Lewis's son became William Chamberlain Chanler.

Willie was happy, no doubt about it, and shortly before the birth of Willie Jr. he wrote a letter full of contentment to his explorer comrade, von Höhnel, inviting him to visit. Von Höhnel was unable to obtain the necessary leave, but three years later, he was able to spend two weekends at Sands Point and also to renew his comradeship with George Galvin, who was prospering under Willie's guidance.

In 1905, at age thirty-three, Galvin married Helen Goldner and they had seven children. During the early part of the century, he managed Willie's horse breeding stables in Virginia, and later Willie set George up as a travel agent at the Vanderbilt Hotel in New York, of which Chanler and Alfred G. Vanderbilt were part owners. From that time on, Galvin made all the Chanlers' travel arrangements.

Von Höhnel found the Sands Point ménage charming and peaceful, but not quite the right setting for his explorer friend. He suspected that Willie had not been tamed by marriage, "his mind being just as unconcerned and sprightly as ever, full of enterprise and exploit, as if there were neither wife nor kin for him in this world."

27 | A FUGUE IN DRUMS AND PICCOLO

With Theodore Roosevelt President, Wintie and Daisy Chanler had become fixtures of the innermost circle at the White House. The President's special intimates were Henry Cabot Lodge, Elihu Root, Gifford Pinchot, William Howard Taft, Leonard Wood, Owen Wister, and Jules Jusserand, the French ambassador; but in Wister's opinion, Wintie was the closest of all to Roosevelt. He sought no office and wanted none. When urged to put Wintie's talents to work, the President would roar: "I don't want Wintie to work! I want him to play with!"

In 1902 Wintie first experienced what for him was the heavenly ecstasy of riding to hounds in Ireland. On the steamer across he became disgusted with the novels Willie had handed him — "that dreadful Maxim Gorky" — and in desperation began to read the Irish train timetables. The station names bewitched him. "There is one station called Knockeroghery," he wrote to Daisy with glee; "it must be the original starting place of all Irish housemaids. . . ."

All during November 1902 letters of sheer ecstasy streamed back: "My first day with these famous hounds. Why, O why, haven't we been here for the last 10 years? . . . . You never saw such horses in your life — perfectly beautiful monsters of strength & grace, & moreover in a state of condition we never see at home . . . And the girls! Lawks! What pretty, quiet eyes, with down-drooping lids, rose & ivory complexions, and voices soft as velvet. They all ride like angels with wings, or devils incarnate. . . . The lovely, soft-voiced girls have no other topic of conversation. Without lots of books I would go mad here or become a sort of centaur. . . ."

He repeated visits to Ireland annually thereafter, but he also finally established a permanent home in the best approximation of the Irish paradise he had yet found. In the spring of 1904 he and Daisy moved to

Geneseo, in western New York state, and purchased Sweet Briar Farm, where he hunted happily with the Wadsworth pack.

Like Daisy, Winty devoured books: "While in Dublin I went a-mousing in book shops & got a new play by Yeats which I bring to you," he informed Daisy, "all about Cuchulain and Concobar et al. Very Yeatsish & charming. . . . I am half minded to get a wise man to read Gaelic with me at tea & dinner. It really fascinates me, all this misty, dim eld. For it is older than time & they seem so much better men than the Greeks. . . ."

In a long affectionate letter to his wife, Wintie recalled their youth and 1884, ". . . when I first came to Rome. Do you remember, old lady mine? . . . Ah — dear — Rome has changed since then, has it not. No more music of fountains in old palace courtyards, no more interminable stairs to climb, no more nice simple people with pleasant easy ways, asking little, enjoying much. . . . And you a little frail white vision in black bombazine [mourning for Sam Ward], or was it alpaca? I can see you there with the light in your eyes dimming the stars, and me 'all overish' with a sort of boy's bubbling joy & love mixed, & he didn't know what it all meant or where it was taking him. . . ."

During the early 1900s Lewis had been making headlines. He had a bone to pick with the city's criminal courts. In a speech before the Women's Municipal League, a group of civic-minded women organized and headed by his sister Margaret, Lewis said that justice was not the objective sought in these courts, but convictions, right or wrong.

"I am not blaming anyone," Lewis told his audience, "and I consider the situation much better than it was a dozen years ago, but these are facts. Our whole machinery is geared to secure convictions because all the persons connected with it want to justify their existence. The policeman is judged by his arrests, even if the persons arrested are afterwards acquitted. The judge wants to secure convictions because he knows that if he does not, the district attorney's office will not give him any cases to try, or only small ones. And the prosecuting attorney wants to secure convictions because he knows that is the path of advancement. The result is that the counsel for the defense enters the court with the case practically prejudged against his client. The counsel is plainly told that he is only taking up the time of the court uselessly. I have had judges intimate to me that they intended to give me very short shrift, and I got short shrift."

This speech and similar criticisms aroused the rancor of certain judges, and Chanler was, indeed, made to feel it. The consequence was to quicken his interest in a political career. Bob, too, had retained an interest in politics. In 1906, when Bob returned from France, Tammany sachem Willie discussed the matter with both his brothers. The Dutchess County Democratic leaders agreeing, the brothers decided to try the 1906 state election. Willie sought a major nomination for Lewis, and thought Bob should run for county sheriff. Because Dutchess had been a Republican stronghold since the Civil War, a concentrated assault would be needed to topple it.

Margaret prepared to throw her abundant energy into a campaign. Despite the fact that she had half a dozen irons in the fire — municipal reform, suffrage, social welfare, and operating a model dairy farm — Rokeby could be used as campaign headquarters, from which the entire county could be reached.

Luck played into the Democrats' hands when irregularities were uncovered in the office of the incumbent Republican sheriff, and Lewis Chanler had prosecuted the case, opening the way for Bob to enter the race. In anticipation, Bob resumed his public-spirited activities at Red Hook. In August he staged a clambake that eclipsed anything the county had ever seen. More than three thousand men, women, and children showed up. The Chanler Brass Band was there, the Chanler Baseball Team, the Chanler Drum Corps, and the Chanler Hook & Ladder Company. The Chanler ball team beat the team from Chatham, and in the Chanler stable the famous prize bull and blooded stallion were on display. But the largest attraction was the food.

Tables were set up to accommodate five hundred people at a sitting, and there were six sittings. The Chanler Women's Auxiliary, under Margaret's command, served the food — 65,000 clams, 2,200 pounds of bluefish, 1,800 lobsters, 30 barrels of sweet potatoes, 1,200 chickens, 6,000 ears of corn, 3,000 bottles of soda pop, 3,000 bottles of beer, and 5,000 cigars. Bob kept urging people to eat more. After this Gargantuan feast, it came as no surprise when Robert Chanler announced his candidacy for sheriff.

Lewis's turn came next. In a complicated party fight, William Randolph Hearst's Independence League, acting as a separate party, nominated Lewis for lieutenant governor, Hearst himself having accepted his party's nomination for governor. This independent nomination carried little hope of winning, but Hearst managed, by bitter infighting, to capture the Democratic nomination as well and take with him the entire Independence League slate. Tammany Hall was furious and the campaign promised to be stormy.

Willie managed both his brothers' campaigns. Lewis accepted his nomination from the porch at Rokeby at length and fluently. Bob did so in a few down-to-earth remarks. The county organization deployed a battalion of party orators on the Chanlers' behalf, and Lewis attracted attention by canvassing in an automobile, the first ever used in that area for political campaigning. Margaret energetically marshaled the women in support of her brothers, for although women could not vote, they did influence their men folks.

Amid all this activity thirty-six-year-old Margaret provided a momentary distraction by getting married on October 3, 1906 — a colorful occasion whose splendor outdid even Alida's wedding and surprised most of her family and perhaps even herself. Margaret's husband was Richard Aldrich, music critic of *The New York Times*. Aldrich was forty-three, a man of erudition, charm, and reputation in his field, but he had no wealth. He came of a Rhode Island family, had been a classmate of Wintie's at Harvard, and had studied music in Europe. On his return he became music critic for the *New York Tribune*, soon transferring to the *Times*. Retiring and conservative, he occupied a position of influence in the music world. However, it was the disparity in the couple's wealth that had interested the public most. That an Astor heiress should bestow her hand upon "a man of no means but possessed of brains" was interpreted as a sign of the growing independence of women.

Three hundred guests arrived for the wedding by special train from New York, with more coming by motorcar. Mr. and Mrs. John Jacob Astor IV were delayed when their automobile broke down. The ceremony was held in the Red Hook church; Wintie gave the bride away, and Lewis, William, and Robert were on hand, with their wives and children. The whole countryside took a holiday, the houses displaying flags and flowers at the windows, and the children staring open-eyed at the long line of vehicles filled with people bearing famous names.

There was no honeymoon trip, the bride being far too busy electioneering.

As the campaign progressed, Bob Chanler supplied the comic opera touch by galloping about the countryside in Western sheriff's garb, complete with six-shooter, drumming up votes. Riding with him was his chief deputy, in chaps, spurs, and sombrero — Richard Harding Davis, the era's much-idolized adventurer-reporter. Right down to the wire the extravagance continued, and when the votes were counted, artist Bob had been swept into office by a majority of 2,787. Lewis carried the county by the slimmer margin of 569 votes, but the Democrats succeeded in electing their entire county ticket for the first time in half a century, a stunning victory.

The real anomaly of the election, however, was the result of the statewide voting. In the contest for governor, Charles Evans Hughes, the Republican nominee, defeated Hearst, but the entire rest of the Democratic ticket was elected, so that Lewis and his party colleagues were to serve as the official cabinet of a Republican governor.

Once the gaudy excitement subsided, the Chanlers had a chance to take cognizance of two events that had occurred during those high-tension days. On June 25, 1906 — just as the political pot had begun to bubble — Stanford White, cherished friend of the Chanlers, had been shot and killed in Madison Square Garden. And in the midst of the October crescendo of oratory and blaring bands, Archie Chanler had published a book in which he publicly accused his brothers and sisters of heinous crimes.

28 | "WE FEW, WE HAPPY FEW, WE BAND OF BROTHERS"

Since escaping from Bloomingdale, Archie had not been entirely silent. After establishing his sanity in Virginia, he had required time to adjust to unrestricted freedom of movement. The failure of his family to make any conciliatory gesture shocked him, and in simple disbelief he had put off taking legal steps to recover control of his property in New York. His sole liquid assets in Virginia had been a $1300 bank deposit, and he had been obliged to sue to get possession of that. Thereafter he obtained loans and mortgages on his real estate in Virginia and North Carolina in order to meet living expenses.

Archie resumed his former social life in Richmond, where he was elected a member of the Westmoreland Club and to the board of governors of the Albemarle Hunt Club. He was a vestryman of his church, although his habit of profanity raised some eyebrows. He spent much time in North Carolina in connection with Roanoke Rapids, and actually designated that state as his legal residence. He also obtained a certification of sanity from a North Carolina court. North of the Virginia line, however, he continued to remain in jeopardy of arrest.

Between 1901 to 1904 Archie appeared as either defendant or plaintiff in several actions against Wintie having to do with the conduct and disposal of the North Carolina properties. In every legal encounter, Archie emerged the winner. His chief preoccupation during these years, however, was the restitution of his fortune and erasure of the stigma of insanity from his name.

He encountered difficulty in securing counsel who would conduct the suit along the lines he laid down. The lawyers he consulted favored a direct petition in the New York courts to vacate the commitment order and the ruling of incompetence, but that would have required Archie to enter the jurisdiction of the New York courts, a move that he was convinced would result in his being locked up again. What he wished to do was to expose the iniquity of New York's sanity laws: he wished to challenge the legality of his commitment on the grounds that the statutes were unconstitutional. Attorneys were reluctant to undertake so formidable a cause, especially since their client could pay them only if they won the suit.

Finally, Archie set to work on the brief himself. For two years he corresponded with lawyers in each of the state capitals, collecting data and assembling what he termed "an array of authority of the highest class that would appall an intelligent and learned adversary to overthrow, or rather, to undertake to overthrow." His incentive was the conviction that he, John Armstrong Chanler, had been chosen by Providence to unmask the "foul ordure masquerading as law in the state of New York." He regretted the necessity of appearing as his own counsel, but preferred to fight rather than submit.

In August 1904, the suit was filed — *Chanler v. Sherman* (the lawyer in charge of Archie's "committee") — in the United States Circuit Court for the Southern District of New York (New York City). Archie charged that the order committing him to Bloomingdale had been illegal and therefore of no effect; that the order had been procured by perjured testimony; that the 1899 hearing to determine his competence had infringed his constitutional rights because he had been denied an opportunity to cross-examine witnesses "hired and produced to swear falsely" against him; and finally, that the appointment of both a committee of his person and estate had been illegal. He therefore petitioned the court to restore his civil rights and liberties.

The press treated the suit gingerly. As Archie had always maintained, his family were powerful in New York. The suit also ran into determined opposition, nominally by Sherman, but expressing the will of the Chanlers. The family winced under the publicity, of course, but they also declined to retreat from their contention that Archie was mad. Nor would they voluntarily surrender the indirect control they exercised over his wealth.

The action passed into the torturous channels of depositions, demurrers, and replications, and the public soon found it dull. Better stuff for gossip came from Archie's life in Virginia. Naturally self-assertive and extraordinarily independent, Archie displayed behavior that could only be called eccentric. Never rid of the fear of arrest, he developed suspicions of some of his neighbors, and swore out warrants accusing them of wishing to murder him. He continued the habit, formed in the asylum, of sleeping most of the day and staying up all night. But most strikingly, he undertook a stern crusade to halt the invasion of Virginia roads by that newfangled nuisance, the motorcar.

Archie was not alone in his loathing of automobiles. Several states enacted laws to curb the menace, and the Virginia Code required the driver of a motorcar to maintain a careful lookout for approaching horses. If signaled to do so, the driver had to stop, get out, and lead the horse past the stationary machine. Archie took pleasure in enforcing this provision to the letter. On horseback, he patrolled the roads around The Merry Mills. To his saddle he had riveted a large green umbrella; from the pommel hung a Klaxon horn, and a loaded forty-four. At night he attached red and green running lights to his stirrups, and from the belly girth hung a lantern. Wrapped in an Inverness cape, Archie presented a frightening embodiment of law enforcement, especially when he loomed out of the mist on a dark night.

At the Westmoreland Club Archie spread dismay among some of the elderly members. He ate alone, at noon or midnight, usually on a dozen baked apples and a quart of vanilla ice cream. He ate a fish by picking it up whole and chewing along one side and then the other as if he were playing a mouth organ. When he talked, Archie was apt to pour out a staccato stream of uninterrupted and uninterruptible wordage; once he backed a waiter into a corner and lectured him on his "X-faculty" from half-past eight until half-past eleven.

Such behavior was obviously eccentric, but there was logic behind much of his oddness. People everywhere were deploring the "outrages" committed by automobilists. Archie did something concrete and effective. He ate what he liked when he liked. He liked privacy and allowed nobody, servant or guest, to remain overnight at The Merry Mills: even Grady, his valet, was dismissed soon after sunset, the shutters were closed, and Archie's personally devised "burglar alarm" was put into operation. This consisted of two ferocious-looking dogs chained to an overhead trolley wire running around the house; all night the dogs would circle the building, a deterrent to prowlers.

In 1906 Archie altered his tactics when he discovered that Wintie and a handful of minority stockholders were plotting to freeze him out of control of the Roanoke Rapids Power Company by an assessment on the outstanding stock. Stockholders who refused or were unable to pay the assessment would be squeezed out. Archie's assessment came to $17,000, and he desired to pay it and so protect his investment and majority position;

but the court-appointed referee declined to allow Sherman to make the payment on Archie's behalf. Archie inferred that the referee was acting under Wintie's influence.

Archie thereupon boldly decided to place his predicament before the public. He published his exhaustive, nearly 500-page brief in October 1906 under his own imprint, Palmetto Press, of Roanoke Rapids, North Carolina. Entitled *Four Years Behind the Bars of 'Bloomingdale', or The Bankruptcy of Law in New York*, the book was launched with a speech that Archie made in Roanoke Rapids on October 15. To an audience of townspeople, he outlined his situation and stated his desire to acquire a clean record mentally. He also derided the "mysterious hocus-pocus" by which the referee appointed to sit on the stock assessment matter was preventing him from paying his assessment. The speech lasted two hours, and to the audience the speaker appeared as sane as any of them.

The book did draw press attention. Tracing the history of his misfortunes since 1897, Archie unfolded a crazy-quilt of evidence and assumption, coupled with a lushness of invective that made sensitive readers' hair stand on end. He portrayed the peril in which every person stood — especially people with money — from the application of the sanity laws prevailing in 40 percent of the states of the union. Someday, he promised, he would bring out a textbook on sanity legislation in the United States which would shock the nation and bring about urgently needed reforms. He kept this promise in a later book, which was widely praised in the law journals.

His arraignment of his brothers and sisters was unsparing. He held them responsible for having him declared insane, because they wished to control his property now and inherit it later. He marshaled a vast array of argument to demonstrate the incompetence, mendacity, and venality of the renowned medical experts who had certified him a paranoiac. In spite of its many flaws and invective, the book told a spine-chilling story and was shot through with a throbbing sense of outrage.

"No man could regret more than the plaintiff," Chanler apologized, "the dire, the grim necessity of washing so much family linen in a court of law . . . But what, let us ask the great American public, is a party to do when his family accuse him, under oath, and drive the oath home with an action of law, which, illegally, but none the less surely and swiftly drives said party into a madhouse cell in which he lingers nearly four years. . . .

"One would think that the least brothers who had had the heartlessness to have plaintiff confined for life as a hopeless lunatic and incompetent without a hearing or an opportunity to be heard, that the least brothers worthy of the name could do, upon hearing of plaintiff's escape from gaol and approaching trial to test plaintiff's said sanity and competency in Virginia, would be to be present at said trial, and thereafter, provided that plaintiff was therein proved sane and competent, present plaintiff with the glad hand of brotherhood and propose to plaintiff to let bye-gones be bye-gones — and let it go at that. No such thing.

". . . After totally ignoring said Virginia proceedings, by which plaintiff's sanity and competency were triumphantly vindicated . . . Mr. Winthrop Astor Chanler has the face to swear, in an affidavit as recent as a year ago, the sixth of last June, as follows: 'The plaintiff is still incompetent to manage himself or his affairs.'"

But despite his hopes, public interest was torpid at best. Although he mailed review copies to newspapers throughout the nation, only two dailies in New York City paid it any attention, and the apathy elsewhere was comparable. The *New York World* commented guardedly that "one may search fiction high and low for a case like this in real life. It is one of the most remarkable stories of modern times." And the *Richmond Evening Journal* pointed out that all the documents were put into evidence with absolute candor, so their authenticity could not be questioned. But bookstores, frightened of libel actions, would not handle it.

Archie's suit against Sherman ("T. Tittlebat Sherman") dragged on, and although there was no direct communication between him and his brothers and sisters, messages did pass back and forth through friends or "neutral" members of the family, like Beatrice, Willie's wife. Archie liked Beatrice; he was sure that she was not in the conspiracy against him. Through these intermediaries, the Chanlers urged Archie to abandon his federal court action and appeal directly to the New York Supreme Court, which had found him insane, to set that decision aside. But Archie simply suspected that the family wished to entice him back to New York where they could railroad him back into an asylum.

There were two concrete developments. First, the New York court authorized Sherman to pay Archie an allowance of $17,000 from his annual income, estimated at upwards of $60,000. This enabled Archie to preserve The Merry Mills from seizure for debt, and gave hope that he might eventually pay his lawyers. And second, in June 1908 the Superior Court of North Carolina granted Archie's application to change his name from Chanler to Chaloner (actually the original spelling of the name). From that time forward, Archie referred to his siblings as "ex-brothers" and "ex-sisters."

29 | POLITICS AND A SHOOTING

In January 1907 one ex-brother, Lewis, took the oath of office as lieutenant governor of New York State at Rokeby, while ex-brother Bob was sworn in as sheriff of Dutchess County.

In Albany, Lewis presided over the Senate and worked amicably with Governor Hughes to secure passage of some reform bills. Lewis was popular with the legislators and in demand as a speaker. Alice proved an effective hostess, who formed her own shrewd judgments on political matters. The couple established their permanent home in Tuxedo Park, where Alice was a devoted gardener. Lewis preferred to talk, play tennis, and take long walks around the lake.

His two-year term as lieutenant governor passed quickly, and in 1908 he seemed his party's the most likely choice for governor. But the city bosses felt he had shown too much independence in office, and too much readiness to cooperate with Hughes. Alice detected this hostility and urged Lewis to wait until the situation looked more favorable. He pooh-poohed her suspicions; whereupon Alice warned that he would rue the day.

One of Hughes's reforms had been to outlaw racetrack betting. Lewis had rather favored the bill even though he kept a racing stable himself. At their convention the Democrats adopted a platform calling for repeal of the ban on betting, and then they nominated Lewis for governor. Thus Lewis found himself apparently catering to his own, personal interest. Willie, his campaign manager, scented the danger. The whole platform was bound to be unpopular, Willie predicted, and he advised Lewis to make no speeches at all. Instead, Willie would plaster Lewis's picture all over the state and make the appeal on his brother's open honest features.

But silence was inconceivable to Lewis. He stumped the state, speaking often, well, and interminably. Worse, he endorsed the party platform and defended it against all critics. Alice, too, vainly warned against this, but the flow of words kept on, and ten days before the voting, the tide was definitely running in Lewis's favor.

Hughes had been drafted to speak for Republicans outside the state, so did not campaign in New York in earnest until just before the election. Then, in a whirlwind tour, he confronted Lewis with ten questions, demanding a yes or no answer. The questions all aimed at bringing out Lewis's real feeling regarding the party platform. Although Lewis gave the best answers he could, they were not convincing, and Hughes was re-elected.

The returns were received at Rokeby on election night, and as the extent of the disaster became clear, Alice kept her eyes fixed on her husband. Although she said nothing, her bitterness was plain. Not even Bob's exuberance could dispel the gloom.

As sheriff, he had been a success, the scourge of the county's chicken thieves. He had just about emptied the jail at Poughkeepsie; such tenants as obstinately refused to submit to eviction reportedly were treated with the tenderest solicitude — good cooking, cigars, and periodic leaves of absence. Politics with Sheriff Bob was fun.

But Bob's wife was not amused. In the fall of 1906, just before Bob's election, Julia had returned to Europe for good. A year later she obtained a divorce in Paris. The annual provision of $20,000 which he had made for her was changed to $10,000 for her, and $5,000 for each of the daughters.

In 1909, at the urging of the county Democratic leader, Lewis ran for the Assembly and was elected in another countywide sweep for the Democrats. Not only was Lewis sent to the Assembly, he was also re-elected as supervisor for Red Hook.

When 1910 came around, Lewis decided to retire from political office altogether. He notified the county chairman, who informed him about a young man a few miles south of Red Hook who wanted to run for the legislature, but who would need Lewis's help. When Lewis asked who this young hopeful might be, he was told, "Why, young Franklin Roosevelt. He thinks he would like to get into politics."

On the basis that he could help his distant cousin to win by running himself, Lewis consented to seek his Assembly seat again. But it turned out that Roosevelt wanted to run from Lewis's district because the Chanlers had built up a strong Democratic following. Lewis balked at this; let Roosevelt take his chances on the state Senate, he said, for the Senate district took in both Dutchess and Columbia Counties. He'd help Roosevelt carry

Dutchess, but "if he can't pick up enough votes in Columbia to win, to hell with him."

Lewis ran and Franklin Delano Roosevelt ran, adopting Lewis's method of campaigning in an automobile, and both men won. It was the only election in Roosevelt's long political career in which he carried his home county, but Roosevelt bore Lewis a lasting grudge for not allowing him to run for the Assembly,

In the legislature Lewis thought Roosevelt was conceited, cocksure, and shifty. A fight developed at the start of the session over the election of a United States senator. The Tammany boss wanted "Blue-eyed Billie" Sheehan, a traction magnate, but the traction interests were in bad odor with the public, and there was much opposition to Sheehan. The Democrats caucused on the nomination. Lewis brought word of the caucus call to Roosevelt, and checked to make sure that he understood how a caucus operated — that once a decision was taken in caucus, it would bind every member of the party.

At the caucus, Lewis spoke vigorously against Sheehan, but was outvoted. He nevertheless accepted the mandate of the caucus and supported the nomination. Roosevelt defied the caucus and joined the Republicans in opposing Sheehan. This action received widespread publicity and earned Roosevelt a reputation for independence, but it ruined him with party regulars. It so disgusted Lewis that years afterward, Lewis refused to vote for FDR as governor of New York.

As the political fortunes of the Chanlers waned, another sensational headline came to plague the family. This time John Armstrong Chaloner — Archie — had killed a man.

The event occurred in the midst of the sensationalism surrounding the murder of Stanford White by Harry K. Thaw. White had been an intimate friend of the Chanlers, closest of all to Archie until his commitment to Bloomingdale. White had remodeled Rokeby in 1894-95, had supervised Alida's wedding in 1896, and had been on the friendliest terms with Wintie and the three sisters. A few years later his only child, Lawrence Grant White, was to marry Wintie's oldest daughter, Laura. Thaw's trial had unloosed journalistic coverage so unbridled that the district attorney protested in court against the baseless vilification of the dead man. The cloud of accusation was so dense as to envelop all White's acquaintance; he was depicted as a monster of depravity, a systematic despoiler of virgins. Any evidence that might expose the falsity of the accusations was excluded by the tactics of

Thaw's counsel. White's social and business friends were universally afraid to speak out and defend him, with the single courageous exception of Richard Harding Davis.

Since he was in no way connected with the scandal, Wintie did not feel called upon to say anything, although he assured his wife that the gossip could not possibly be true. Margaret never faltered in her loyalty, placing in the hall at Rokeby a simple marble tablet inscribed with austere affection, noting the year of his Rokeby project:

Stanford White
Architect and Friend
MDCCCXCV

Thaw's trial opened in January 1907, and after three months of lurid sensationalism ended in a hung jury. In January 1908, he was again placed on trial, his defense now being insanity, and on February 1 he was judged guilty but insane and committed to Matteawan prison for the criminally insane. The state prison was in Dutchess County, and the county sheriff was normally responsible for certain aspects of its operation. Thus it was that *Thaw v. Chanler* was docketed when Thaw's lawyers sued to obtain improved living conditions for their millionaire client. Bob's personal reaction, as county sheriff, is not on record.

Thaw's chief counsel had invented the phrases "dementia Americana" and "brainstorm" to account for the killing, and discussions of such terms were still fresh in the public mind when newspapers blossomed with headlines that "Amélie Rives' divorced husband," John Armstrong Chaloner, had shot and killed a man in his country house, The Merry Mills.

A factory mechanic named John Gillard, who lived about two miles from The Merry Mills, had become notorious in the neighborhood for beating and threatening to kill his wife and children. She had appealed to Archie, and he had told her to run to his house for protection if she was attacked. Meanwhile, since Gillard was out of work, Archie subsidized the family.

On March 15, Archie was conferring in his bedroom with his farm manager, Ernle Money, when he heard a commotion downstairs. He went to investigate, carrying in the pocket of his dressing gown a small revolver that he always had with him. As he reached the foot of the stairs, he saw Gillard's son, a boy of fourteen, run out of the dining room, crying, with a red welt on his forehead. Darting into the dining room, with Money right behind him, Archie saw Mrs. Gillard crouching behind the table with a baby in her arms, her hair loose, her clothing torn, and Gillard trying to strike her with the fire tongs.

Archie leaped for Gillard, who turned and struck him twice with the heavy tongs. The second blow knocked Archie down and partially stunned him. Money grappled with Gillard and threw him down, at which point Archie sent Grady, his valet, to fetch a rope. Gillard struggled to his feet and again lunged for his terrified wife, whereupon Archie drew his pistol. Gillard grabbed Archie's hand and in the struggle that followed, there was a shot, and Gillard fell dead with a bullet through the temple.

Word of the shooting reached Richmond in the early hours of the morning, and reporters scurried out to The Merry Mills. There they found Archie breakfasting on roast duck and ice cream, while beside him lay the corpse. Nothing had been disturbed — the overturned furniture, the bent and blood-stained fire tongs, Mrs. Gillard's hat and hairpins scattered around, and the drying pool of blood around the dead man's head right beside Archie's chair.

A coroner's jury absolved Archie of any guilt after hearing the evidence. Mrs. Gillard testified to her mistreatment over a long period of time, and showed her scars. Money and the valet added their testimony. Archie described the struggle and maintained that he had simply done his duty as a Christian and a gentleman. The magistrate agreed heartily. Archie paid for the funeral and also the expense of sending the widow and her children back to England where they had relatives. Archie had contemplated inscribing this epitaph on Gillard's gravestone: "He Died Game."

The exploit brought a stream of visitors to The Merry Mills, so to avoid endlessly repeating his account of the affair, Archie pasted a newspaper clipping on the dining room wall and had embedded in the floor, marking the spot where the corpse's head had lain, a copper star inside a circle — it is there to this day, covered by a carpet.

The Chanlers bore the appalling publicity with what fortitude they could muster. Bob sent a note of approval, but Wintie was furious, and the episode did stiffen the opposition to Archie's fight to regain control of his New York property.

30 | A DREAM OF LOVE
AND ALL THAT

In his later days Bob would assert that his family had pushed him into politics to get him away from art, and that he contracted his second marriage to get away from his family. Neither effort was an unqualified success.

In 1906 a prima donna of striking loveliness appeared on the New York scene. Her name was Natalina Cavalieri, and she moved in a cloud of legendary triumphs scored in European capitals from St. Petersburg to Madrid. The Metropolitan Opera, in the midst of its rivalry with Oscar Hammerstein's Manhattan Opera House, had offered the new soprano $1,200 a performance, a fee which put her in a class with the likes of Caruso, Scotti, and Eames.

Cavalieri made her New York debut in the American premiere of *Fedora*, Giordano's tale of "blood, murder, and wicked passion." She sang the title role, supported by Scotti and Caruso. She received a rapturous reception, although *The New York Times* music critic Richard Aldrich expressed reservations. Her voice, he judged, was "a light lyric soprano, very pretty in quality but not rich or vibrant," marked by "a good deal of tremolo" and a tendency to run to "unpleasant shrillness." But he agreed that "her figure is exquisite, and her face is a delight to see."

Two weeks later Cavalieri sang in the title role of Puccini's *Manon Lescaut*, and this time she scored an unquestionable triumph. Puccini had landed from Italy just in time to attend, and the audience gave him eight curtain calls after the second act. The superb cast — Cavalieri teamed again with Caruso and Scotti — outsang themselves. This time Richard Aldrich glowed in his encomiums, although he was not normally given to raptures.

During the 1909–10 season Cavalieri went over to the rival Manhattan Opera House, where she became the magnet that drew Bob to the performances. Whenever she sang, the former sheriff was present, all but smothering her with bouquets. Offstage the pair were seen at the theater, at Delmonico's, Sherry's, the art galleries, Tiffany's — all the smart places. It was plain that Bob was infatuated, and Bob's brothers and sisters did not like it at all. Winds of scandal whistled around the lovely Lina. Had she not danced naked at the "Folies Bergère" in Paris? Had she not been thrown out of Russia? Did she not concede that she had come up from the gutter in her native Rome?

Bob cared not a bit. Soon rumors of marriage appeared in the newspapers, and Lina encouraged these without committing herself positively. Yes, Bob had asked her to marry him, she said, but she had not accepted him yet: "It is so pleasant the way it is," she explained curtly. "Mr. Chanler is very nice, very kind, very good. I like him as much as any man I know. He is very rich, too, and that is a nice thing. The money a man has is a part of him, *n'est-ce pas?* . . . Why can he not be always glad to care for me and not for marriage? Bah! It is an ugly word! And it is so stupid to marry and spend all the time and money getting a divorce, when you need not have been married!"

Avowals like this produced no rejoicing at Rokeby. Wintie was disgusted by the vulgarity; Margaret was repelled; Elizabeth grieved; Lewis deplored, and Alida wept. Only Willie had nothing to say, but only because he was deep in the Sahara desert.

Bob was warned he would risk a serious break with his relatives if he persisted in his infatuation, but he shrugged, and gave the press his own view of marriage: "Lina has had her affairs — why not?" he said tolerantly, "So have I. So has every man you know, and many women. I don't know why I should expect a woman to have lived an absolutely perfect life when I haven't."

Lina promised to give Bob a definite decision by April 15, and on that day from Paris she cabled saying: "I will accept your proposition of marriage on my return to New York next season. Much friendship and love. Answer by cable."

Bob cabled back: "I accept your proposition. It is a long wait but wise," and caught the next ship for France. On rejoining his "darling Lina," Bob pressed for an immediate wedding, and on June 18, 1910, Lina and he were united in wedlock. No member of the Chanler family attended, although Lina's brother, Oreste Cavalieri, did. No congratulatory messages came from America.

As the summer progressed, Bob's friends observed a change in him. He seemed to be chronically short of cash. He painted and sold small canvases for trifling sums, and grew nervous, downcast, and depressed. Then in September, he disappeared, and on September 5, the Paris correspondent of Hearst's *New York American* cabled an account of Chanler's recent behavior, with disclosures about his marriage that started a story which engrossed newspaper readers for weeks.

Bob, this account ran, was believed to be on his way back to America without his wife. A few days previously, Lina had checked out of the Neuilly hospital, where she had undergone an appendicitis operation, and was met at the hospital door by Prince Paul Dolgorouki, a Russian nobleman well known in Parisian night life. Lina had taken the train to a seaside resort, and the prince was believed to have followed her.

Two days after publication of this dispatch, Lina returned to Paris and indignantly denied any estrangement from her husband. But two days later, the World published what it stated were the sensational facts of the situation:

"Robert Winthrop Chanler, who last June was a millionaire, is now a pensioner on $20 a month allowed him by his wife, Lina Cavalieri. His dream of love has been shattered. . . . Cavalieri has Chanler's entire fortune, and he is in America, penniless."

In the World's account, Cavalieri had played Bob along, all the while accepting attentions from Prince Dolgorouki, whose fortune made Chanler's look "like pocket money." But if the Prince married without the czar's consent, he would forfeit his fortune, and the consent was not forthcoming. Lina had, therefore, finally sent the cablegram accepting Chanler.

Before the wedding a Paris notary and an English solicitor joined the cast. These two, the World report said, had examined Bob regarding his means of support, and he told them frankly that his property was in trust, and after paying his former wife and children $20,000 a year, he had an income of roughly $30,000 for himself. The legal gentlemen thanked him and went away.

Then, four days before the wedding, Lina told Bob the unexpurgated, unvarnished story of her life. Recounted the World:

"She related all the experiences of her childhood; how as her girlish prettiness developed into womanly beauty she became the pet of certain men of the great world of Paris, the leader of the demi-monde, disputing the title with Cleo de Merode and La Belle Otero. She told of her life in the Paris half-world, of the attractive bachelors, the dashing married men and aristocrats who had wined and dined her and loaded her with jewels, fine gowns, costly hats, expensive lingerie. . . . Chanler heard all of this, but he was so filled with a desire to possess Cavalieri that it did not disturb him."

Finally, three days before the wedding, "while Chanler was being caressed and petted by the beautiful prima donna, the English solicitor and the French notary reappeared with formidable legal documents. . . . Taking the documents from the solicitor, Cavalieri ran up to Chanler, threw her arms around his neck and said he must sign them before she could marry him — that by signing them he would be transferring all his money to her, but she would take excellent care of him, managing his income and relieving him of all the annoyances and cares of business, leaving him free to paint pictures and to love her to his fullest desire.

"Chanler signed the documents, and transferred everything he possessed, even his interest in the alimony payments to his first wife, to the prima donna."

A couple of mornings after the wedding, over coffee and croissants, Lina notified Bob that she would board and lodge him gratis and give him $20 a week for spending money. Should he require more than that, he could earn it by painting.

And Bob did make a half-hearted attempt to follow this program, the *World* recounted. He daubed street scenes and sold them to friends for $25 or less. But his humiliation was completed when Dolgorouki showed up in Paris and paid marked attention to Bob's bride. When Lina entered the hospital, the prince was assiduous in his calls, and when Bob visited his wife after the operation, he had found Dolgorouki seated on her bed, chatting cozily. To avoid a scene, Bob had said nothing; but when Lina left the hospital and went to the shore, Bob took his troubles to Willie, who had just come back from the Sahara. Willie urged Bob to go home, which he did.

The story was out at last, and the Chanlers were outraged. Wintie forbade Daisy to see or communicate with his brother, and the rest of the family shunned him in New York. But not Archie. From The Merry Mills the family's only certified lunatic wired his brother merrily: "Who's looney now?"

The phrase became the catchword of the decade. Comedians flattened straight-men with it, street urchins yelled it, cab drivers growled it, lawyers, preachers, statesmen intoned it with varying inflections, newspapers editorialized about it, called it the most widely heard three-word ejaculation since "*Et tu, Brute?*" The phrase was set to music, and "Who's looney now?" became better known than the national anthem. It inspired a comic strip. For the rest of his life Bob would never get entirely clear of its corrosive irony.

Bob's attorney had nothing to say. The Chanler family had supposedly washed their hands of him. Lewis explained curtly that Robert's property was in trust and he doubted that it could be signed away. In Paris, Lina was expressing indignation at reports that she was avaricious; she had not received one cent from Chanler, she declared. Oreste Cavalieri, her brother, had turned up in New York and began dealing out interviews charging Chanler with deceit.

The lawyers, of course, were busy on both sides of the ocean. In New York, Lina's attorneys placed the prenuptial contract on record, and it proved to be everything it had been reported to be, one clause giving Cavalieri irrevocable power of attorney to collect Bob's income. Bob's lawyer dryly remarked that irrevocable in Paris was one thing, and irrevocable in New York another. Lina, he said, would be old and ugly before she ever collected. Then help for Bob came from two widely different sources: from Julia, his divorced wife, and from his Fifth Avenue tailor.

The tailor sued over an unpaid bill, and he asked for a judgment and appointment of a receiver for Chanler's estate. This, of course, would tie up everything until all claims were satisfied. Julia, meanwhile, petitioned the court to set aside the prenuptial agreement because it deprived Bob of the power to pay her alimony or child support.

The tailor obtained his judgment, and Bob's assets were frozen pending a general settlement. The tussle then went on behind the scenes, with Oreste Cavalieri bargaining for his sister, and Willie Chanler arguing for Bob. Bob himself was reported to have told Margaret that he never wanted to see Lina again.

In Paris, Lina grew outspokenly more disdainful of her mate as the haggling dragged out. Society women in Boston voted to boycott her performances, and her engagement to sing there was canceled. Her scheduled season in Paris was curtailed because, she said, of recurrent attacks of "lassitude." She even claimed that Bob had married her because he wanted advertising, because prior to their marriage, no one had ever heard of him as a painter.

As usual, the lawyers had the last word. Six months after the initial blowup, a settlement was reached by which Chanler was to pay Cavalieri $80,000 and she would tear up the prenuptial contract. At the same time she applied for a divorce in Paris and in due course received the decree.

Bob raised the cash that Lina insisted on by mortgaging most of his New York City property, with the consent and even cooperation of his family. Gradually the Chanlers had become reconciled with him, although Archie had stood up for his "ex-brother" and the family honor from the start. It was Prince Dolgorouki who became the greatest object of Archie's contempt. Buying the biggest Berkshire boar he could find, Archie named it for the prince and put it in a sty beside the railroad tracks with a sign reading:

HOME OF PRINCE DOLGOROUKI
BIGGEST BOAR IN CAPTIVITY.

31 | HELL AND THE SLOPES
         OF HELICON

The winter of 1908–09 Wintie spent with his family in Rome. When, on December 28, a disastrous earthquake destroyed Messina, in Sicily, killing 60,000 people, Wintie threw himself into the relief effort with zeal. In gratitude the Italian government conferred upon him the order of the Crown of Italy. Then in the spring of 1909, having missed the hullabaloo over Archie's shooting of Gillard, he returned home to Geneseo.

Even financial reverses resulting from the panic of 1907 failed to quench his amiability. Writing to Amos French, he joked, "'Easy come, easy go' as Ned Potter says when his children marry in spite of him. As for me, I look upon the loss of my profits as an escape — Mr. Morris would have grabbed & buried them probably."

Mr. Morris, the family lawyer, was often sorely tried by the casualness of his clients. At any moment he might be saddled with some outlandish commission, like the time when Wintie decided to send his children a real live donkey to ride. Without forewarning he consigned it to Morris. During the crossing the beast foaled, and the unwinding of this bureaucratic complication — the invoice said one donkey — took days. Meanwhile, both animals were kept in a customs shed, where Morris had to provide for their care until he could finally forward them to Sweet Briar Farm at Geneseo.

The 1907 depression affected all the Chanlers as property values shrank, but their standard of living was not visibly lowered. Margaret even paid off the mortgage on her West 74th street house with her inheritance from Great-Aunt Laura Delano. This city home became the focus of a circle that included both social figures and people with brains.

Before her marriage Margaret's musical interest had been that of an informed amateur. She tried to make the transition to her husband's level of professionalism, but with only partial success. For six months she attended all the concerts and opera performances that Aldrich was obliged to review, but the saturation finally produced a sensation of "hearing a symphony in one ear and an opera in the other," and her doctor prescribed a sparser musical diet. Nevertheless, the house on 74th Street remained open at all times to the great of the musical world.

One of Margaret's other frequent visitors was her adored great-aunt, Julia Ward Howe, who had helped inspire much of her interest in politics, reform, and nursing. When the old lady could no longer go up and down stairs in her modest house in Boston's Back Bay, her niece installed an elevator for her. Margaret immensely admired her great-aunt, the family member whom she most closely resembled, even though Margaret had none of the spirit of mischief that Julia never lost. Margaret also liked to read Great-Aunt Julia her poems, which seemed to please the older woman because the verses recalled to her the verses of her brother, Sam Ward, who was Margaret's grandfather.

Committing rhymes to paper was a weakness of the Chanler-Ward family. Julia Ward Howe had scandalized Boston, and her husband, in 1853 by publishing a book of verses titled *Passion-Flowers*, and Sam Ward's *Lyrical Recreations* had appeared in three editions, all privately subsidized. In 1907 the fit seized Alida, who brought out a privately printed volume of blameless verses titled *The Hidden Places and Other Poems*. This led to a second volume *Psyche Sleeps*, also privately issued, three years later. Margaret followed suit the same year with *Sonnets for Choice* and then *The Horns of Chance*.

John Jay Chapman, who wrote sonnets himself, insisted that the act was unnatural — "like an Englishman trying to say his prayers in French" — and Archie was piqued by the sudden attention being paid to his sisters' verses, when he had been producing sonnets wholesale for years. His efforts, after all, reached back to his days in Bloomingdale. To demonstrate his long familiarity with the lyric muse he published, in 1908, at his own expense, a volume of sonnets, entitled *Scorpio*. Its purple cover was embellished with a seven-strand knout, the strings dripping with blood. To avoid repercussions that might adversely affect his litigation, Archie issued his book in England. His aim, he said, was to combine "the strength of Juvenal, the keenness of Voltaire, the fierceness of Swift, and the form of Byron."

Archie's book did not pass unnoticed. Lord Alfred Douglas, the cause of such trouble for Oscar Wilde, reviewed it for *The Academy*, observing that the author plainly preferred "whips, scorpions and the knockout blow" to tender lays of love.

Archie's attention was roughly diverted from sonneteering when Judge George C. Holt, of the United States Circuit Court at New York, threw out his long-standing suit against his "committee," Thomas T. Sherman. Holt ruled that the court that had ruled the petitioner incompetent, the New York Supreme Court, was the tribunal to rescind that ruling. Archie swiftly appealed Holt's ruling and sent to every member of the House of Representatives, by special delivery mail, a fifty-four page notification and demand that Judge Holt be impeached.

At the same time he made even more clear the gulf that divided him from his brothers and sisters by registering a new will, leaving his entire estate to schools and charities. Beneficiaries included Columbia University, the Paris Prize Fund, and the town of Roanoke Rapids, which received $10,000 to be applied "to the annual purchase of a Christmas tree for the public school children and a present for each child."

The house and grounds of The Merry Mills he deeded to the public, with the stipulation that its swimming pool and twin bathhouses, named "Neptune" and "Diana," remain open to "the gentry, persons distinguished by birth or position in the neighborhood," without charge. The control and income of all the properties Archie reserved to himself during life.

Under his own imprint, The Palmetto Press of Roanoke Rapids, North Carolina, Archie reissued *Scorpio*, now called *Scorpio No. 1*, for American readers, promising to make it the first in a series of "poetic quarterlies." Archie felt he could maintain a steady schedule because his "normal monthly output" of sonnets was about fifty, and he had a stockpile of five hundred to draw from.

Coincidentally, his interest in graphic automatism, dormant during his preoccupation with legal forays, revived and produced nothing less spectacular than a communication from Hell with a splendid description of that region and a defense of its ruler, Satan.

To make known this authentic glimpse of the hereafter, Archie invited reporters from Washington and Richmond to a hotel in Alexandria, on the Virginia side of the Potomac River, of course. Seating himself comfortably, Archie assured his audience that he didn't believe a word of the document he was about to read. This out of the way, he explained that the document was an almost verbatim record of a conversation he had with a deceased friend, former Confederate general and New York clubman, Thomas Jefferson Miller, while Archie himself lay in a "Napoleonic trance" at The Merry Mills.

Archie then proceeded to read the alleged interview, which took two hours and twenty minutes to complete. After some opening chat, Archie's informant, Miller, announced that he was now in the Hall of Audience of Hell, "standing against the wall on the right side of the hall looking towards the fiery throne. Upon said throne sits Satan."

The hall was "so huge as to be practically incomprehensible to mortal ideas of architecture . . . miles long, miles wide, and miles high." It was constructed of pigeon-blood rubies as big as bricks, set in diamonds of the purest water. To enhance the dazzling effect, the diamonds were interspersed, every few feet, with sapphires "as blue as the Mediterranean." The floor of the chamber was spotless white marble that took on the hue of whatever passed over it. If seraphim flew over it, the pavement blushed red, whereas if cherubim crossed, it gleamed cerulean blue. The roof of the hall was of crystal "so pure the eye can pierce it."

Contrary to what some preachers were saying, Miller stressed, Hell and Purgatory were real places, and after death every mortal had to undergo torment in reparation for his misdeeds upon earth. Miller said he had just emerged from his own ordeal — in fact, his head was still bandaged — but he felt wonderfully purified and uplifted by the experience. He suspected that he had been let off rather lightly because he had already experienced his share of Hell on earth as "a New Yorker with social standing, and no money."

After passing through the cleansing initiation, each person could select his or her own place of permanent abode — Heaven or the Kingdom of Sin, both annexes of Hell — or could choose annihilation. Hell itself was really quite fascinating. Contrary to rumor, its temperature was mild, its climate ideal. Satan, Miller described as being as in every feature like Napoleon Bonaparte "at the apex of his power." Satan was not a bad sort at all, although as Jehovah's prosecuting attorney he was forced by the rules to assume a harsh and forbidding aspect; in reality, he was a prince and a gentleman, "a hero and noble creature, maligned as no other being has been maligned since the beginning of time. . . ."

When he finished, Archie repeated his utter disbelief that it had been Miller talking, or that anybody, himself included, could communicate with the dead. As a strict and believing Episcopalian, he rejected the whole theory of spiritualism absolutely, and he was placing the communication purporting to come from Thomas Jefferson Miller before the world in his capacity of an "O.K. medium," so certified and accepted by William James.

Archie's revelations had a thundering publicity success from coast to coast. In San Francisco, the *Chronicle* thought the color-changing pavement of Satan's audience hall would be "worth going far to see," and that the credibility of Archie's spirit informant could be vouched for, since, "having been on the opposite side to General Sherman in the late war, he ought to know what Hell is, and as a New York clubman it is reasonable to assume that his present address is the correct one."

In Chicago, the *Tribune* also was impressed by Miller's veracity, but for a different reason, namely, because "Hell would have no terrors for a man who had been broke in New York."

The Fort Wayne, Indiana, *Gazette* remarked that "John Armstrong Chaloner claims to have received a message direct from a friend in Hell. It's a wise man who knows the habitat of his friends."

The *Albany Press* and the *Boston Globe* pointed out that Miller's delineation of Satan as the exact image of Napoleon was going to necessitate "changing all the labels on deviled ham."

And so it went, with ripples of merriment spreading across the nation at this latest vagary of the "former husband of Amélie Rives" and "author of that celebrated phrase, 'Who's looney now?'"

Meanwhile, Archie petitioned the New York Supreme Court to increase his annual allowance of $17,000 to $33,000. He gave several reasons. First, he wished to disseminate his writings more widely, and submitted samples of his books for scrutiny by the court. The publications included *Four Years Behind the Bars of Bloomingdale*; *Lunacy Laws of the World*, a compendium and analysis of the laws on insanity, to which he appended a sheaf of favorable notices from law journals; *Scorpio No. 1*; and a pamphlet entitled simply *Hell*. These books, he contended, were weapons in the crusade to which he intended to devote the rest of his life, namely, bringing about reforms in the unjust and vicious lunacy laws of the world.

He had other pressing needs, such as paying the heirs of some of the lawyers who had died holding his IOUs and the support and expansion of the weekly lectures he was giving in Richmond to arouse public sentiment against the outrages being committed upon young girls in the back seats of automobiles on Virginia's rural lanes. Finally, he requested a sufficient stipend to enable him to live out the rest of his days surrounded by the comforts to which he was accustomed.

Although the income from Archie's estate the previous year had totaled $40,000, the court declined to approve the increase. Undaunted, Archie reviewed his application, lowering the sum requested to $24,000, and this time the court granted the raise.

Archie's poems received a degree of attention nationally that his sisters' had not inspired. Shock, incredulity, and indignation were registered by most reviewers of *Scorpio No. 1*, with here and there a gamey word of praise. The "hostiles" Archie took on in prose and verse.

The range of Archie's muse was certainly wide. He metaphorically cuddled up to kittens ("Cats little lions be"), and thundered righteously against that lascivious dance, the Turkey Trot ("Vulgarity, debauchery, hand in hand / Now whirl their way down Gotham's gilded halls"). In one sonnet he addressed William Waldorf Astor, the cousin who was buying his way to an English peerage, as "The future Duke of Asteroid," and in four other sonnets he took his relatives to task in lines running from "My kind family imprison'd me 'for fair'" through "My million and a half quite turned their brain," to the full indictment in "They Are Seven":

> With seven brothers and sisters I am curst.
> My jurors, they, and all are fair to see.
> In them doth beauty make of mask the worst
> That e'er in noble guise hid treachery.
> The women charming as the men are brave —
> With charm which the beholder soft doth lave
> As cooling unguents o'er a burning scar.
> Yea these lovely ladies left me to dry-rot,
> Linger and perish in noisome cell;
> And yet these warlike brothers blood forgot,
> And doomed me untried to a living Hell!
> Three ladies and four gentlemen's the roll,
> Their record's knell do I now slowly toll.

But self-revelations merely gave the press opportunity to ridicule the author of "Who's looney now?" The "Bard of Bloomingdale" and the "Roaring Rhapsodist of Roanoke Rapids, N.C.," were epithets tossed at him, although Edgar Saltus, in *Vanity Fair*, found Archie's poems "like anchovy paste on the buttered toast of our literature," and wished there were more lunatics like him.

Despite the rough going, Archie followed *Scorpio No. 1* with *Scorpio No. 2* about six weeks later. This collection contained sonnets newly coined and mint-fresh, interspersed with a few taken from the stockpile. Targets blasted in this new broadside included the Social Register; flat-chested members of the Women's Christian Temperance Union; faith healers; certain judges ("male prostitutes"); Bernard Shaw ("Bogus Bashaw of Letters"); New York's "400," and the slit skirt ("This fashion is a nasty, sluttish trick"). There was praise for George Washington, Walt Whitman, Robert Emmet, and three Carthaginian commanders — Hamilcar, Hannibal, and Hasdrubal.

The second installment of Chaloneriana drew somewhat less ribald commentary than the first batch, but it also marked the demise of the poetic quarterly, although by no means did Archie retire from the literary field. More than once he would live up to a *Baltimore Sun* headline: "IN TORRID VERSE — CHALONER BREAKS OUT AGAIN."

32 | WARS FOREIGN AND DOMESTIC

In his personal affairs Lewis seemed to have started a long decline. At the end of his second Assembly term, he retired from politics, fatally increasing the tension between him and his wife. Alice resented his failure in politics, and reproached him for it so constantly that even their children tried to make her desist. Lewis craved domestic warmth and tranquillity, but these Alice could no longer provide. During Lewis's last term in the Assembly the two had become almost totally estranged. Lewis spent more and more time at his club, in town, and busying himself with his law practice.

For Bob, the Cavalieri episode suddenly matured him. The emotional shock of his disillusionment threw him into his artistic work with new intensity and a new sense of power. His work became bolder, more innovative; he felt that at last he had crossed over the threshold into creative and personal independence.

Elizabeth had always been religious, and her travail during her husband's breakdown, together with her responsibilities as mother and stepmother to young sons, only deepened and broadened her faith.

At the nadir of Chapman's descent into delusional irrationality, she had called in a Christian Science healer named Mrs. Hopkins. Elizabeth engaged her under a promise that in addition to her salary and expenses, she would be receive an income for life if she succeeded in bringing about Chapman's recovery. Under a seemingly placid exterior, Mrs. Hopkins concealed a personality of great force. She was unprepossessing in appearance — short, with red hair, dressed always in black satin, with a black hat or veil. Her manner was precise and businesslike, and she brooked no disobedience to her commands. Chapman did recover, and Mrs. Hopkins did receive the promised annuity.

Her place was then taken in the Chapman household by a woman who had been trained in Christian Science but had left that connection. This healer, Mrs. Edith A. Martin, was a large, heavyset woman, with a commonsense outlook and easy ways. She was comfortable to have about the house the Chapman children felt.

Once Elizabeth had both Mrs. Martin and Mrs. Hopkins as house guests, a risky encounter which passed off smoothly, to the immense surprise of the Aldriches at Rokeby. Richard Aldrich, out riding, would encounter Chapman driving with one or the other of his practitioners, and would report back to Margaret: "Saw Jack out driving with the Thin Mystic." Or, "Saw Jack driving with the Fat Mystic."

Neither Chapman became a Christian Scientist, but both had a consuming belief in the power of prayer. Every morning Elizabeth set aside half an hour for prayer and meditation; as the years advanced, her habitual attitude, except at moments of great stress, became one of unshakable inward serenity and sureness of faith. And this only strengthened the authority she wielded, by force of character, over her relatives.

Jack Chapman's intensity of religious feeling had been noticeable even when he was a boy at St. Paul's School. He would make devotional gestures before imaginary shrines, and when called to bat at cricket, he would kneel and pray silently, while the game stood still. This had been too much even for that hotbed of religiosity, and he had been invited to leave.

When staying at Sylvania the Chapmans attended the family's church in Red Hook and sat in the back pew, arriving just as the service started. In this way they were also the first to leave, preceding the Aldriches, who occupied a front pew. Sitting in the extreme rear was also helpful because Chapman was apt to become lost in his private devotions and remain standing after others were seated, or upon his knees after the rest of the congregation had risen.

In 1909 Margaret gave birth to a son, named Richard Chanler Aldrich. To his mother, his appearance meant that the Rokeby heritage would be preserved. A year later a daughter was born, named Margaret Astor Chanler Aldrich, later known in the family as "Second Maddie."

Time, marriage, and motherhood in no way diminished Margaret Aldrich's prejudice against religious conversion (especially abandonment of Protestantism for Roman Catholicism), temperance prejudice against strong drink, feminist prejudice against male domineering, and moral prejudice against what she called "plural marriage," remarriage when a former partner was still living. Divorce she deplored, but under certain circumstance she might tolerate it. Her ambivalence tempered her attitude toward both Archie and Bob after their marital breakups, but her increasing aversion to "plural marriage" frequently led to embarrassment. At a reception in Wintie's home she refused to take the hand of Anne Harriman Sands Vanderbilt, who had been divorced twice and whose current husband had been divorced. Wintie tramped all the way from midtown to West 74th Street, in vile weather, to read his sister a lesson in courtesy. But Margaret was not to be won over. She continued to close doors as her principles demanded, willing to suffer the loss of friends and the narrowing of her own horizon as time went on.

Her antagonism to Catholicism was to the institution and doctrine, not individuals, and she drew a distinction between those who were born into the faith and those who defected from hereditary Protestantism. The latter she could not forgive.

In the family, sunny Alida, the youngest, was referred to good-naturedly as "stupid." She was thought too scatterbrained to understand complicated matters. Alida was indeed sentimental and generally happy; she loved company, chatter, singing. But she was more complex than the others gave her credit for, and she was certainly more subtly strong-minded. Unlike her brothers and sisters, she did not remember her childhood at Rokeby fondly, and sought in adulthood to create the kind of magical family which she had so sorely missed.

When she married Temple Emmet, the young forestry graduate, he wanted nothing more than to disappear into the woods to pursue his profession. Alida supposedly put a stop to that by saying, "I'm going to have twelve children, and I certainly don't intend to do all that way out in the woods." In 1905 she commissioned a house to be designed by Charles A. Platt, the architect of Sylvania, with barns by Stanford White, and built in Stony Brook, Long Island, high on a bluff overlooking Long Island Sound, and there the growing Emmet family — eventually there were nine children, but again an Egerton died in infancy — led a charmed and charming existence on the fluctuating income from Alida's inheritance. Discouraged from work as either a lawyer or a forester, Temple turned his energies to sports and the production of organic foods to satisfy his eccentric food fads. In his idiosyncratic eating habits, he bore a striking resemblance to several of his Chanler in-laws.

Alida had been drawn toward Catholicism by the example of Wintie's wife, Daisy. Daisy had a convert's zeal and insisted upon ritual observances of every feast and festival; and she grew enthusiastic when telling of the comfort her faith gave her. A frequent guest at Wintie's Sweet Briar Farm was Father Sigourney Fay, a jolly Irish priest; for long stretches he acted as domestic chaplain to Daisy's household, more than half of whom, the girls, were being reared as Catholics. Meanwhile the boys also were being "persuaded" by every subtle means their mother could devise.

This attempted contamination of her nephews disturbed Margaret extremely; the barrier between her and Daisy, while tacitly ignored, had remained impenetrable from the time of Wintie's marriage. By now, however, Daisy was firmly established and enjoyed a heavy superiority in numbers. Margaret fretted and grieved, for she felt that Daisy would never rest until she had gathered her entire flock into her fold, including Wintie himself.

Of this there seemed to be little chance, religion being a matter that Wintie Chanler could take or leave with happy indifference. He was not averse to the Roman church, and he certainly had no feeling against its members, providing they were well bred. He even joked that he might embrace the faith were it not for "bothersome details" like eating fish on Friday, going to mass, and so forth. He could never make that sacrifice, he said; but he might — in fact he would gladly — become a Catholic when his head was "six inches off the ground in my last fall off a horse."

When Margaret and her husband sailed for Europe in the early summer of 1910, Alida was teetering on the verge of conversion, although Margaret was not without hope. Margaret was expecting her second child, and for the sake of country air and quiet, took up quarters with her husband in a remote village in Wales. Aldrich hated missing "the best musical season London had seen in a decade," and to make matters worse, he received a letter from Alida "announcing very contritely that she has converted to Rome and that in view of Margaret's condition, would I please break the news to her at the most appropriate moment." Deciding that "it is dangerous to have an excess of steam confined in a small vessel," he awaited their return to London to inform his wife.

Eventually, regardless of Aldrich's reluctance to bear the blast of his wife's reaction, the message had to be delivered. The initial thunderclap reverberated through Margaret's entire social connection, and then settled into the form of an absolute refusal to speak to her sister Alida, or to have any commerce with her except upon unavoidable occasions such as funerals and weddings. Indeed, she did not speak to Alida for the next forty years, although Alida was constantly in her thoughts. Margaret simply mourned Alida as one dead.

The loss was doubly hard to bear because from the time her second child was born, Margaret had embarked on a determined campaign to make Rokeby a happy meeting place for the entire family, with herself the center. There were nieces and nephews in growing numbers, and cousins and young friends, all of whom must be made welcome at Rokeby. Margaret was an effective hostess. In summer the place was alive with youngsters, Margaret's religious and social prejudices not carrying over to the next generation. Children ran in the halls, romped in the fields, or camped on the stairs, lost in some book. The whole house hummed. Margaret organized barn dances, outings, picnics; she played cards and read aloud; there was music and free-for-all discussion with everyone. And of course there were horses and dogs and other pets.

In 1912 Daisy stirred Margaret again to righteous fury by building a chapel on the grounds of Sweet Briar Farm. Only by roundabout report did the news finally reach Rokeby that the chapel had been consecrated with a special blessing from the Vatican and the gift of a relic, a "fully authenticated piece of the True Cross." Margaret's indignation exploded, and she penned a letter so furious it skipped syntax and was less legible even than most of her writing.

"Dear Daisy,"

"Words fail me yet I must speak. One day in October I learned the appalling fact that in gratifying sectarian self-indulgence on your part the extreme of denominationalism had been reached at Sweet Briar Farm — that a chapel had been reared by you who know more fully than I do that Wintie is no longer master within his own gates. . . . To this extreme which makes Wintie the laughing stock of his community is apparently a mere bagatelle, for you have sent me the tokens of relationship in Christmas gifts, as have also your daughters, who I am told were all present at the ceremony which marked the entry of Ecclesiastical rulings and the end of their father's supreme authority in regard to all that transpires upon his country seat. . . . The Christmas gifts lie unwrapped, first fruits of your curious undertaking, as foreign to American marriage as was the trick with the ring [kissing the officiating prelate's ring] by which the Sacrament of your wedding ceremony was polluted.

In your direction all is dark. Here love lies bleeding.

MARGARET"

The reaction at Geneseo was one of defiant ridicule, but from that day the door between Daisy and Margaret closed forever. Daisy never entered Rokeby again, and although Wintie kept in touch, it was at decreasingly frequent intervals.

Wintie's restlessness pressed in on him steadily, and in 1912 he went to England to hunt with the Melton Mowbray and Belvoir hounds. Although he assured his friend French that "I feel like a fighting cock," his health was not satisfactory. X-rays disclosed a kidney stone, and on July 31, 1913, his badly diseased kidney was removed in a Buffalo hospital. For weeks he lay at the point of death.

That winter he was taken to Washington, where he reported himself "fat and sassy," although his head was given to dizziness, and his memory was poor. He dined with the Franklin Roosevelts, Franklin being then Assistant Secretary of the Navy in President Wilson's administration; but Wintie's thoughts turned irresistibly to a time when Theodore Roosevelt had occupied the same position and the evening was very restrained.

In the summer of 1914 Wintie returned to Sweet Briar Farm. His mood was nostalgic; he was growing old, he thought. Theodore Roosevelt wrote to their mutual friend Spring Rice: ". . . I received a very pathetic letter from Winty Chanler the other day. Winty is such a delightful person and such a real faun that I hate to think of the misfortune of our common humanity falling on him — you and I are eminently human and it is all right we should have misfortunes; but Winty ought by rights to enjoy himself to the very last."

The struggle seemed lost when Wintie suffered a relapse. But a Harvard classmate, Dr. William Thayer, head of the medical department at Johns Hopkins, took over where the surgeons had failed and pulled Wintie through the crisis. Within a short time he was able to announce the engagement of his daughter Hester to Edward M. Pickman, a Bostonian, whom Wintie rated "the perfect pick."

The marriage was celebrated in January 1915; and a year later his daughter Laura became the bride of Lawrence Grant White, son of Stanford White. This event was followed shortly by the birth of the first Chanler grandchild — a son, to the Pickmans, whom they named Anthony Patrick.

When the baby was five months old, Wintie addressed a personal letter to him, at 700 Acre Island in Maine, where the Pickmans were summering:

"My dear Tony Pat:

"Thank you so much for your dutiful letter which pleased me greatly. I can quite understand your remarks about the loneliness of life on an island & the almost total lack of male society. You have my entire sympathy, for I suffer greatly at home here on account of the absence of male companionship. My boys are of course very nice, & pleasant fellows enough, but there are no men about. . . . Your mother is an excellent soul, but then so is your grandmother — my wife. A man is what you need. So I have made up my mind to pay you a visit at 'rugged Ithaca' or whatever your damned island is called & we shall have a good time 'among the rocks — the lonely rocks.' I am bringing some excellent tobacco & a noggin of old rum, . . . Kindly impress upon your too careless father the importance of having a sufficiency of food & drink laid in for me, appropriate to my very strict diet, . . . I have no hesitation in placing these instructions upon your young but sturdy shoulders feeling sure, as I do, of your complete responsibility. . .

"With my best love to your Ma & Pa, I am,

My dear chap,
Your affectionate Grandfather
WINTHROP CHANLER"

It was the summer of 1916. A postscript to the letter touched on matters about which Wintie had ever spoken sparingly: "It is clear that the Germans are laughing at us. I hope Wilson will sever diplomatic relations at once and recall Gerard [United States ambassador at Berlin], send Bernstorff [German ambassador] home & talk turkey to the Kaiser."

Reality was pressing in on Wintie, who all his life had side-stepped it laughingly. Had he not once quoted, to console a bereaved friend, a saying: "A man is born crying and those who welcome him to the world laugh. Let him so live that when he dies he laughs, and those who bid him farewell weep."

"You remember Hugh Fraser?" he queried Amos French. "He was killed in action on August 5th — a Captain in the Royal Scots Fusiliers attached to the VIth Brigade in Flanders. A glorious end to a rather useless and ineffective life."

Glory — that was what he must taste. The United States was drawing nearer to involvement in the war raging in Europe; perhaps he might play a part in that yet. The thought put vigor into his pain-racked bones, and although now only a shadow of his former bounding self, Wintie Chanler eagerly accepted the urge to move on again.

33 | WHAT MAY GO ON
UNDER A BURNOOSE

When Willie took not only his family but his racing stable to France, it seemed to indicate that he expected the change of domicile to be permanent. His wife, Beatrice, took to the place and the people at once; the French she found particularly congenial, but her tastes differed widely from those of her adventure-seeking husband. She liked elegance and the arts. Willie, she had learned, could be exciting, even breath-taking at times, but he defied domestication. Willie's drinking was another problem. All these tendencies culminated, about 1909, in a dawning suspicion that separation might be salutary for both.

When Willie began talking about making a trip deep into the Sahara Desert, Beatrice reminded him sharply that he had a wife and two dependent children, Willie, Jr., five, and Ashley, two. Willie met this reminder with a characteristic grand gesture: he made over the better part of his estate to his wife and sons in trust, reserving to himself only a sum sufficient to meet his personal needs and those of his thoroughbreds. Then on the friendliest of terms, he and Beatrice said goodbye in the autumn of 1909, and she sailed for home with the boys, while Willie remained in Paris. There was no formal separation, and the future of their relationship was left vague.

Willie's penchant for intrigue and revolution had drawn his attention to the faltering Ottoman Empire. In 1909, in an attempt to revitalize the Turkish hegemony, the Young Turks — a party of progressive liberalism — deposed the reactionary Sultan Abdul Hamid and installed Mohammed V in his stead. To Willie the aims of the Young Turks were sympathetic. At the same time he was intrigued by reports coming from North Africa about the growing power of the Senussi, a secret sect of Arab fanatics who were not only

Archie Chanler several years after his escape from Bloomingdale Asylum and about the time he changed his name legally to John Armstrong Chaloner. Photo ca. 1906.

Robbery Under Law

OR

The Battle of the Millionaires

A PLAY

IN THREE ACTS AND THREE SCENES

TIME, 1887

TREATING OF THE ADVENTURES OF

THE AUTHOR OF

"WHO'S LOONEY NOW?"

BY

JOHN ARMSTRONG CHALONER

AUTHOR OF

SCORPIO

———

SUNDAY'S COMPLIMENTS TO SOCIETY WOMEN.

"We're always hearing about poor girls who go wrong, and sell themselves to the Devil, and tempt men into sin. If you believe what some folks say, you'd think it was only the six-dollar-a-week factory girl that filled the joints, and wrecked the homes, and lured away mothers' darlings. As a matter of fact, some of the most dangerous women, some of the most unprincipled sirens, are to be found among the daughters of the rich; women who will lie for money, steal for money, wear the scarlet letter for money—murder for money."—William Sunday.

———

SECOND EDITION

———

PALMETTO PRESS
Roanoke Rapids, North Carolina
NINETEEN HUNDRED AND FIFTEEN.
TWO DOLLARS

The title page of a 304-page, privately printed volume, bound in brilliant purple cloth with gold and crimson lettering, from the Bard of the Merry Mills.

Winthrop and Daisy Chanler, at rear of photograph, on the terrace at Sweet Briar Farm, Geneseo, New York, with their seven surviving children. From left: Hester, Marion, Hubert (in front), Theodore, Beatrice, Laura, and Gabrielle. Photo ca. 1914.

Sylvania, the west elevation, facing the Hudson River. Designed for the Chapmans by Charles A. Platt and built in 1904 on land immediately adjoining Rokeby to the north. Sylvania continued to be the principal residence of the Chapman family for nearly eighty years.

Elizabeth Chapman with her son Chanler Armstrong Chapman shortly after his birth in 1901, when John Jay Chapman was recovering at Rokeby from a complete physical and mental breakdown.

John Jay Chapman with his sister-in-law Beatrice Chanler, wife of Willie Chanler, on the west portico at Sylvania. The empty sleeve is a reminder of his missing left hand, burned off in an act of penance. Photo ca. 1915.

Victor Emmanuel Chapman, several days before his death in June 1916, when he was shot down in a dogfight. Chapman's valorous death became an inspiration to Americans nine months before the U.S. entered World War I.

Willie Chanler sailing in Florida during his honeymoon, 1904.

"Minnie Ashley": her success in musical plays made her a toast of Broadway, but she left the stage when she became Willie's wife, resuming her given name, Beatrice. Photo ca. 1903.

William Astor Chanler, a signed portrait photograph by his fellow carouser and clubman James L. Breese. Photo ca. 1906.

Beatrice Chanler with her children, Sidney Ashley Chanler (left) and William Astor Chanler, Jr. By this time she and her husband were living apart. Photo ca. 1913.

Lewis and Alice Chanler and their three children. From left: Alice Chanler, Lewis Stuyvesant Chanler, Jr., Lewis Chanler, William Chamberlain Chanler, and Alida Chanler. Photograph taken at their home in Tuxedo Park, New York, at the time of Lewis's campaign for governor in 1908.

Lt. Gov. Lewis Chanler speaking from the front porch at Rokeby, accepting the Democratic nomination for governor of New York, in 1908. He was narrowly defeated by the incumbent, Charles Evans Hughes.

Chanler campaign pins: from left, Willie's 1898 Manhattan Congressional contest, Bob's 1906 Dutchess County race, and Lewis's gubernatorial race in 1908. Only Lewis lost.

The three politician brothers talk strategy on the west lawn at Rokeby, as Lewis (at left) gears up for the 1908 campaign. Willie is in the middle, Sheriff Bob at the right.

Margaret Chanler, who in 1906 married Richard Aldrich, with her children Margaret ("Maddie") at left, and Richard ("Dickie") Chanler Aldrich at 317 West 74th Street, the day news was received of the Titanic *disaster. Photo April 1912.*

Margaret Aldrich and Lewis Chanler, closest of siblings, in the octagonal library at Rokeby during the 1908 campaign. The circular radiators were installed by Stanford White in 1894.

Richard Aldrich on Crusader, with Dickie and Maddie Aldrich in front of Rokeby. Photo ca. 1919.

A detail from "Giraffes," an early large-panel painting by Bob Chanler that won admiring notice in the Paris Salon in 1905 and was exhibited in the Luxembourg Museum.

Natalina ("Lina") Cavalieri, the beautiful diva who was briefly, and expensively Bob Chanler's wife, eliciting from Archie the celebrated cable, "Who's looney now?" Photo ca. 1905.

Bob Chanler with his daughters Julia (left) and Dorothy. Photo ca. 1919.

Alida Emmet at Rokeby with her two oldest children, Elizabeth ("Lybba") at left, and Margaret. Photo ca. 1900.

Alida Emmet, a detail from a portrait by Wilfrid de Glehn, a follower of John Singer Sargent and the husband of Temple Emmet's sister Jane. Photo ca. 1912.

Temple Emmet, in a signed portrait photograph by James L. Breese. In 1905 the Emmets moved into "The Mallows," a house designed for them by Charles A. Platt and situated on a bluff overlooking Long Island Sound at Stony Brook. Photo ca. 1906.

hostile to their Turkish overlords, but lived for the day when all Christian infidels would be driven out of the territories of Islam.

Just who the Senussi were, and what they might be up to, was a matter of debate, but several European governments were deeply concerned over their activities. This period saw the high tide of colonial expansion, with France, Britain, Italy, and Germany all scheming to annex further chunks of Africa, including territory held by the Turks. In the west, the French were moving irresistibly into Morocco, where in 1912 they would establish their protectorate, detaching that nation from Turkey. In the east, the British, having swallowed up Egypt and the Sudan, were gazing covetously upon the bordering Sahara regions. In the southeast, Britain and Italy were disputing Somaliland, while along the Mediterranean, France, having long since incorporated Algeria, was nervously watching Italy's designs upon Tripoli (modern Libya), which the Turks still held. Along the sidelines strutted Germany's martial Kaiser Wilhelm II.

Stretching southward from the Mediterranean coast deep into Equatorial Africa lay the vast Sahara Desert, a prize waiting to be seized. But the Arabs, it appeared, were becoming increasingly bold in their determination that neither Turk nor infidel should remain in possession of Muslim lands, and the Senussi were understood to hold the key to the region's fate.

No European was known to have seen the leader of the Senussi, or to have successfully infiltrated their ranks. Of the few rash adventurers or spies who had tried to penetrate their secrets, most had not returned alive. But well-founded rumors described the Senussi as a strictly organized, militant religious sect, under the leadership of a mystery-shrouded holy man called The Senussi. The brotherhood was believed to muster a well-armed fighting force, the main detachment of which was said to be a camel corps of 5,000 men. Great quantities of arms and munitions were said to be stockpiled deep in the desert, while a modern gun factory was believed to be operating under Senussi control in the Kufra oasis, a thousand miles from any seaport. The Senussi himself was said to move about constantly, preaching hatred of infidels and usurpers, and his followers were sworn to obey him to the death. He was said to be served by couriers mounted on racing camels, who linked some 300 training centers where recruits were indoctrinated and those showing promise of leadership were marked for special service.

Willie proposed to solve the mystery. He went about his preparations with his customary thoroughness. First, he would make an exploratory trip into the Sahara in order to gain experience in desert travel, study the terrain, and sound out the temper of both Arabs and Turks. On this venture he would go as a simple tourist, traveling for pleasure. He was well posted on the plans being nursed by the European powers and knew how ignorant they all were of the exact situation. He asked von Höhnel to come along, but the Austrian was pinned down by naval duties; nevertheless, he managed to assist Willie in numerous sensitive ways.

Willie set out soon after New Year's, 1910. In early February he wrote von Höhnel from Tripoli that he was living with the US consul, William Coffin, and was trying to get permission from the pasha to go to Murzuk. Willie was in his element. Murzuk, his objective, lay 600 miles south of Tripoli, in the heart of the district known as Fezzan — by caravan, a month's hard journey.

The pasha was agreeable, even promising to furnish Willie with an armed seven-man escort. In addition Willie planned to take an interpreter, a cook, two camel men, fifteen camels, and two horses. He soon learned, however, that in Tripoli "*inshallah*" served the same purpose as "*mañana*" in Spanish countries. Finally, three weeks later, he was ready to depart. Letters to von Höhnel followed from halts along the route, as opportunities occurred to send them by northward-wending caravans.

From 100 miles south of Tripoli came word that the journey was prospering and that Willie was taking many photographs of Roman ruins. There had been no trouble with desert brigands, but the nights were bitter cold.

On March 25 Willie wrote that the Arabs were suspicious of him, but that he was thriving under the hardships. He also reported: "The influence of the Senussi is apparent everywhere & most of the population are his devoted adherents. The people are unwilling to talk of him, but I hope to get information from Sami Bey the Mutasareff of Fezzan who is at Murzuk. . . ."

Willie went on to detail French activity south of Murzuk and the advice he was giving the Turks on how to protect the caravan routes from the Sudan to Tripoli. "As you see," Willie confided to his associate, "I am throwing my lot in with the Turks & in case I make further travels this will be of immense advantage to me. Of course say nothing of this as my home is at present in Paris & I should not be popular there were this known. . . ."

He reached Murzuk at last. Sami Bey he found compatible; indeed, he liked all the Turks he had met. He also admired the Tuaregs — "a finer race than the Somali, better looking & much more dignified. They never beg & in shaking hands only touch the tips of their fingers. They cover their faces & leave bare the crown of their head. They have beautiful hands & feet & tall slender figures." The Tebbons, too, Chanler approved of; they were very war-like and used riding camels.

Already Willie was forming plans that he did not commit to paper. Leaving Murzuk on April 24, he got back to Tripoli on May 24, but was immediately incapacitated for ten days by a painful return of his "rheumatics." Early in June, however, he got back to Paris, and there his family rejoined him.

Bronzed, hardened, uncharacteristically slim, Willie was invested with new glamour, and for a while Beatrice and he were reconciled. But the reunion did not last for long. Actually Willie's health was uncertain, and his carousing in Paris not only brought on the rheumatism again, it also exacerbated his sometimes rampaging temper. In the fall Beatrice sailed back to New York with the boys, and Willie stayed behind in Paris, nursing a throbbing foot and cheering on his horses.

In January 1911 he returned briefly himself to New York to help in the negotiations over Bob's settlement with Lina Cavalieri. Indeed, it was Willie who actually carried the settlement cash to Lina in Paris — and he made certain that she signed the release before she got her money.

Back in Algiers in February 1911, Willie's eye was focused on the mounting tension in North Africa, where the Arabs were becoming openly belligerent, while the competing European powers drifted toward a show-down. As he had stated a year before, he would cast his lot with the Turks — a decision that would, if known, render him suspect in both France and Italy.

In mid-August 1911 Willie wrote von Höhnel from Paris: ". . . You have probably read in the papers the excitement here in France over the Turkish occupation of Tibesti and Borku [districts on the southern edge of the Sahara] . . . The Turks are right in claiming all they can & I am sure they can make good their claim & hold the territory as France is too far from its base in the Sahara to take the aggression, & England will never interfere having troubles enough of her own in Egypt."

Then he added a personal note: "I am in robust health now that I have had my tonsils removed, & firmly believe that most of my alleged gout & rheumatism came from poisoning from my tonsils. Being in such good health my mind turns to travel & adventure. It is possible I shall go to Constantinople the end of October . . . Strictly *entre nous* it is possible I may be allowed to travel again in Tripoli; in which case I should order 15 Mauser pistols & 5000 rounds of ammunition from Junghaus. Could you get him to quote a price on these delivered in Tripoli (without mentioning my name) through that gentleman [Basil Zaharoff, an international arms broker] we met in Vienna . . . ?"

Chanler did visit Constantinople, carrying letters of recommendation from Turkish officials in Africa, and in the Turkish capital he discussed with government leaders a plan to blunt the threat of Arab nationalism in the Sahara. It was an open secret that Italy was only awaiting the strategic moment to invade Tripoli, and there were reports of a secret accord having been reached between the French and the Italians, in which France would allow Italy a free hand in Tripoli in return for Italian sanction of the French penetration of Morocco. Tripoli was conceded to be virtually defenseless against an Italian attack, but Willie proposed to rally the desert tribes to Turkey's support by appealing to Pan-Islamic fervor. The Turks listened, approved, and authorized Chanler to undertake the mission in his own way. To strengthen his hand, they commissioned him a colonel of auxiliaries, and as a mark of honor the sultan presented him with 500,000 Turkish pounds.

Disguising himself as an Arab holy man — wearing a burnoose and dying his face and hands — Willie wandered the Sahara, stirring up the Arabs to resist the expected Italian invasion. Much as they hated Turkish rule, the Tuaregs and other warlike tribes responded to Willie's warnings that rule by the Italians would be harsh, whereas Turkish rule was mild, and at least the Turks were followers of the Prophet. Aware that his Arabic was imperfect, he represented himself as coming from a district notorious for its slovenly speech. Going from oasis to oasis, he preached resistance to the infidel, and with the help of the knowledge gained on his previous journey, formed contacts with influential members of the Senussi sect, and finally met The Senussi himself.

The audience took place at an oasis deep in the desert. Willie was ushered into a dark room lit only by a thin shaft of sunlight coming through a hole in the ceiling. Under it sat The Senussi, with only the crown of his head visible. Willie deduced that the setting was designed to awe The Senussi's followers, for he observed that as the beam of sunlight moved, the leader shifted position so as to remain directly in the light.

Willie managed to recruit a fighting force of several thousand desert Arabs, well mounted and armed. Through agents Willie was landing weapons and supplies at isolated spots along the coast and stockpiling them for ready availability. The Turkish authorities looked the other way as Willie's warriors drilled, and when in 1911, the Italians made their first invasion landing, the Arabs were ready.

In that brief war only one real battle was fought, and that was a triumph for Willie's irregulars. Italian warships landed marines and soldiers on an apparently deserted coast, but the Arabs were waiting for them, hidden in a ravine. Willie sent out a decoy caravan that moved slowly toward the invaders, then swerved and headed back into the desert. The Italians jubilantly pursued, whereupon the tribesmen swooped down on them from ambush. The Italians threw away their arms and ran toward their ships; casualties were heavy, and abandoned equipment littered the course of their panic-stricken flight. Disdaining to come within range of the offshore guns, the victorious Arabs melted back into the desert. Willie's family, meanwhile, were enjoying themselves in a rented Venetian palazzo.

After recovering from the shock of this unexpected reception, the Italians revised their plans, made landings in force, and pushed their conquest easily against crumbling Turkish defenses. But by then Willie had left the conflict.

One morning he had found outside his tent a friendly offering of fresh camel's milk, which he drank without thinking; such gifts were common. But immediately he realized that the milk had been poisoned. By resorting to heroic antidotes, the poison was thrown off, but Chanler was left so weakened that he could no longer direct his auxiliaries, and by the time he had recovered fully, the Turkish cause in Tripoli had been lost.

Although his grand design had failed, Willie was not finished with intrigue in Africa. In 1912 he served for a while as military advisor to the "Mad Mullah" of Somaliland, who was resisting both British and Italian encroachments. Before disappearing into the hinterland on this adventure, however, Willie conceived a vast irrigation scheme which he contended would restore fertility to a large area of the desert where the ruins of ancient cities showed that at one time a numerous population had flourished. The plan centered on a pipeline that would carry water across a range of mountains, windmills being employed for pumping power.

In Egypt he unfolded this scheme to his cousin John Jacob Astor IV, honeymooning there with his second wife. Jack became enthusiastic and undertook to provide all the capital required. Astor headed back to the United States to start the project going, while Willie vanished for the time being into Somaliland. When he re-emerged, he learned that Astor had perished in the sinking of the Titanic. The irrigation plans sank with him.

Returning to Paris, Chanler occupied himself ostensibly with his racing stable, although a mysterious flow of furtive callers passed through the flat he had taken at 19 rue de la Tremoille. Arabs, Turks, Chinese, emissaries from the Balkans came and went secretively. plotting to ends that only Willie knew.

The separation from Beatrice had become permanent, although there was no formal action and they remained friendly. She had her own apartment on the left bank; Willie's was on the right bank. Usually Beatrice had the two boys with her, but they saw a great deal of their father as well.

Willie had struck roots in France. He had acquired business interests there — two stone quarries and an ochre mine — that he managed personally, and twice a year he returned to New York to look after his investments there.

It was in Paris, in December 1913, that Willie's carousing caught up with him. One morning he showed up at the American hospital in Neuilly with a badly fractured right leg. Splinters of bone were embedded around the kneecap, necessitating a series of operations. The wound had to be reopened repeatedly, and three months after entering the hospital Willie was described by the correspondent of *The New York Times* as a "shadow of his former self . . . his physique shattered. He still suffers pain so intense that at times his life has been despaired of." Eight months after the accident, Wintie wrote to Amos French that "Willie may have to get his leg amputated, poor lad. He writes gaily about it & does not seem to mind at all. He and Sarah Bernhardt can get together now." And Willie's leg finally was taken off, after protracted delays.

But in August 1916 he was back in New York, fretting over his inability to get into the war in Europe, already two years under way. Wintie noted that his brother ("now known as General Joffre") was on hand "with a jointed wooden leg [and] tales of glory. He is to get a nice new aluminum one with many joints and resume his many activities before long."

34 | A ONE-LEGGED WAR

The early years of the twentieth century brimmed with pleasant activity for the Aldriches. Winter and summer, West 74th Street and Rokeby were centers of constant coming and going. Aldrich's friends included the leading musical figures of the period — the Paderewskis, Marcella Sembrich, Albert Spaulding, Enesco, Percy Grainger, Gustav Mahler, the Ernest Schellings, Walter Damrosch, Granado and his wife. Margaret found these hard-working musicians easier to get along with than the painters or writers who leavened the throng. She thought musicians were better talkers, too, and conversation was life blood for a Chanler.

Aldrich stood at the top of his profession. He was publishing books as well, including guides to Wagner's *Ring* cycle and *Parsifal*. Sometimes his critical duties placed him in delicate situations, as in the spring of 1913, when Lina Cavalieri returned to the United States for a concert tour. She announced that she would herald her return by singing from the steps of City Hall; but the mayor forbade this, so instead she appeared with Lucien Muratore, leading tenor of the Paris Opera, in the city's largest theater. Aldrich reported the concert of his former sister-in-law judiciously, stating that she was "quite as beautiful as her most youthful pictures would have us believe" and noting that she seemed "very nervous" and "perhaps she did not do herself justice as a singer." The audience, he commented, "was large and friendly."

When war came in 1914, the Aldriches were unreservedly sympathetic with the Allies. Margaret organized the West Side branch of the Red Cross in New York City and recruited women to roll bandages and prepare surgical dressings for shipment to England and France. This "war relief" did not deflect her from the cause of suffrage, however; instead, she pressed for the vote harder than ever. In caustic letters to the newspapers she pointed to the mess that the statesmen had got the world into and proposed that the women be given a chance.

In January 1917, Aldrich was summoned to Washington and taken into the Army's intelligence service with the rank of captain. Margaret remained in New York, but in April, shortly after America entered the war, she moved to Rokeby, intending to keep that place open as a refuge for family members whose arrangements were being dislocated by the war. This mainly meant the children, her own and various nieces and nephews.

In her public character, Margaret could be imperious, abrupt, and persistent; but in the domestic circle she was warmly affectionate, adept at the skills of hospitality and homemaking. Writing from Rokeby to her news-hungry husband, she conveyed the scene in a leisurely chat covering many pages:

"Dearest : On the lawn under the pine tree Hester [Emmet], Maddie and I; Dickie busy with his bicycle appearing and reappearing. Here is Mademoiselle with a tin pan calling both children to find rabbit feed. . . . The safe will not open for me. I sat in front of it as though I were in church, and turned in vain, like the Ash Wednesday penitential office. . . ." Then came some Red Cross talk, and a discussion of a new music teacher for Maddie and Dick, a bit about luncheon after church, and a pat for the good work being done by Franklin Roosevelt as Assistant Secretary of the Navy. She wrote of Jack and Elizabeth being in town to pick up their son, and said that she "had a word with McVeigh [Morris's successor as family lawyer]; he has a lease on hand for me which should increase income a thousand." Next came a long meditation on which of the three cars to get rid of, especially considering that gas rationing was likely. Local gossip followed, with Margaret admitting that "I should be a little livelier about returning hospitality."

Niece Hester Pickman's husband, a lieutenant in the Naval Reserve, had been called up for dangerous convoy service just before the birth of their second child. And Lewis had enrolled in the officers training course at Plattsburgh, New York, although he was well past military age. He plodded through the rugged training doggedly, and returned to New York exhausted. He was in the midst of a celebrated trial (the Tanzer case) when pneumonia struck, and for weeks he lay near death. Recovery was slow, and the doctors insisted that he must abstain from all taxing activity during convalescence. This break in effect marked Lewis's retirement from law practice.

There was more behind his breakdown than physical strain: for some time he had been deeply attached to Julie Olin Benkard, a lively young matron at Tuxedo Park and a Livingston descendant who had grown up in Rhinebeck, a few miles south of Rokeby. Alice reacted violently, and the quarrel had become so bitter that Lewis had moved into his club.

The romance dated back to before Lewis's election as lieutenant governor. One day Julie's husband had remarked that Lewis was stuck at home alone and suggested that Julie invite him to dinner. Julie had never met Chanler before. He came, and shone in the table talk so brilliantly that the dinner was repeated at his own house, with the same guests, and then repeated again. Lewis was completely taken by Julie; he found her a pretty woman who endorsed his enthusiasms, admired his style, and was an ideal foil for his exuberance.

Lewis requested a divorce, but Alice refused. Devoted to his children, Lewis longed to hold their affection, but for the most part they sided with their mother. To his older son, Stuyvesant, Lewis wrote that he had hoped to discuss the situation frankly with him, but Stuyve had provided no opportunity.

"I see that you have no understanding of the situation," the heartsick letter went on. "I am not going to write about it and there may be no use in talking about it save to give you an understanding of my point of view; . . . It is all very sad," he summed up, "but it has been going on since before the house was built and I simply cannot stand it any longer — for it gets worse instead of better, and this is quite apart from family bickerings at table."

The Chanlers watched the disaster unfold and said nothing publicly. Margaret was despondent, for Lewis's unhappiness struck home to her especially. But she was also distracted by the tragic death of Jack Chapman's oldest son, Victor.

When the war broke out, the Chapmans had been visiting in Germany, and they barely succeeded in reaching London. Victor was with them. Both Elizabeth and her husband had been shocked by their brief glimpse of war, and Jack's mind groped for some justification of this reversion to brute force. He concluded that the war could be justified only if it were waged as a crusade to end wars, to be followed by universal disarmament.

The vision was bold, but Chapman believed that the unique hour had arrived when it could be attained. Roughing out a "Memorandum on Compulsory Disarmament," he spent August laying the proposal before leading British statesmen, including Arthur Balfour, Lord Haldane, and Sir Edward Grey, the Foreign Secretary. All reacted favorably, but there was a hitch. What Chapman strove to elicit was a declaration by the government defining its policy in advance as one of no territorial gains, after Germany had been defeated, and of enforced disarmament of all nations, backed "by gunboats" if need be. Such a declaration Chapman believed to be the key to the success of the entire program. But none of the statesmen with whom Chapman talked could be brought to make such an announcement, although Chapman pleaded that without such a statement the war would degenerate into senseless slaughter. His view was strongly endorsed by notable Americans then in London, including the three Henrys — Henry James, Henry Cabot Lodge, and the aged Henry Adams. But his effort bogged down in talk.

Meanwhile his son Victor, fired by idealism, announced that he wanted to join the Foreign Legion and fight for France. Jack asked whether his son's impulse might not be the product of restlessness, or simply a desire to get out on his own. Victor slunk out of the room so dejected and crestfallen that Elizabeth remonstrated. She said she would rather see Victor dead on the battlefield than that look on his face again. Jack yielded. On August 8, 1914, Victor caught the train for Paris with his father's blessing.

In Paris Willie was beside himself: here was a war, and he not in it! He was still in the hospital, with the doctors debating whether to amputate his gangrenous leg.

For the Chapmans, the Allied cause had become their cause, without reservation, because of Victor. He was in the Legion, and had found a virtual comrade-in-arms in his Uncle Willie. If only he had two good legs, Willie grumbled, he would be in action side by side with Victor, in spite of his age (he was nearing fifty). In more ways than one, Willie was proving a model for his nephew. When Victor volunteered for a machine gun detail, an assignment considered almost suicidal, he explained his choice with a remark of Willie's — "because it is the most dangerous!"

But trench warfare soon palled, and Victor longed to transfer to aviation. It was well nigh impossible to pry an enlisted man away from the Foreign Legion, but a unit of American fliers was being formed, and Victor applied to join it. With Willie's help, his transfer came through. The change of duty transformed Victor. But secretly, his father had a premonition that Victor was doomed. Elizabeth heard him mutter, as he roamed from room to room, "the boy will not get through."

After completing flight training, Victor was moved to the Verdun front and quickly gained a reputation for daring. In numerous air duels he escaped unscathed until June 17, 1916, when he was wounded. But he succeeded in bringing his crippled plane down, and laughed at his wound, a deep head gash.

Willie, hobbling into the Travellers Club on a still awkward artificial leg, heard of Victor's escape, and using all his influence wangled a permit to visit the front, a rare privilege. Victor proudly exhibited his plane to his uncle, and described his battles in the air. Both men thoroughly enjoyed the visit.

A week later, on June 23, with his head still bandaged, Victor took off on a routine flight to bring some oranges to a wounded comrade in a hospital several miles away. Unexpectedly he ran into a dogfight between three American planes and five Germans. Without hesitation he plunged in, and although the three Americans got away cleanly, he was shot down behind German lines.

Chapman was at Sylvania, out driving, when the news reached Barrytown. A farmer took the message, and a few minutes later handed it to Chapman as he drove by. To the farmer's astonishment, Chapman glanced at the telegram, nodded, and said quietly, "That's good." Going to the house, Chapman walked into the library, where Elizabeth was reading, and stood in the doorway. One glance at his face told her everything. "Victor is dead," he said, and she bowed her head in silence.

As the first American aviator killed in the war, Victor Emmanuel Chapman became a symbol of American chivalry and idealism, a rallying point for a growing number of Americans who wished to go to the Allies' aid. The French government honored the young flier with posthumous awards of the Médaille Militaire and the Croix de Guerre with two palms. Impressive memorial services were held in Paris and New York. Victor's parents became curiously identified with his tragic heroism, and mourning for their son became almost a cult over which they presided. Lewis and Bob hastened to Sylvania only to find the Chapmans in a strange state of exaltation, as though uplifted and purified by their sacrifice.

When finally America did enter the war, Chapman's last living son from his first marriage, Conrad, volunteered in the Navy and was assigned to Atlantic convoy duty; later he was transferred to the Pacific. His father and stepmother made no attempt to hold him back, but they did refuse to let Elizabeth's seventeen-year-old son, Chanler, go to war.

After Victor was killed, Willie withdrew for a while to a Swiss convalescence clinic, and then in August took off for America. He had investments at home that required periodic checking, and the war was complicating these. His income now depended on earnings in business, one of which was the Vanderbilt Hotel at 33rd Street and Park Avenue. The hotel had been a joint venture of Willie and his friend, Alfred G. Vanderbilt. After Vanderbilt died in the sinking of the Lusitania, Willie bought his shares, thereby gaining majority control. Beatrice, who had turned her energies to sculpture, executed with the help of her instructor a 400-foot-long frieze for the hotel's ground floor, and every effort was being made to place the Vanderbilt on a par socially with the Waldorf-Astoria, two blocks away on Fifth Avenue. George Galvin was placed in an executive position on the Vanderbilt staff.

During the early days of the war Beatrice had been taken up with a variety of interests, including the Stage Society, of which she was president. But at the outbreak of hostilities, she had launched a relief project, called the Lafayette Heroes Fund, that gradually came to absorb her entirely. Its first activity was to provide so-called Komfort Kits for the troops in the field. Later the fund undertook to acquire the Chateau de Chavaniac, Lafayette's birthplace, and equip it as a center for the sons of French army officers.

Beatrice was deeply moved by the sufferings of the French people, and dedicated herself passionately to their cause. As a fundraising device she staged a pageant at the Century Theater in New York, in which more than two hundred children, most of them descendants of Revolutionary figures, took part. Part of the pageant, a playlet written by John Jay Chapman, "Washington and Lafayette," saw three Chanler cousins portraying Washington, Lafayette, and Hamilton, and Ashley Chanler, aged six, Beatrice's younger son, spoke the epilogue, written by Richard Harding Davis. Theodore Roosevelt addressed the children, telling them ringingly to "never be neutral between right and wrong."

While checking his own concerns, Willie also at this time came to an understanding with American naval intelligence, by which his privately supported network of communications in Europe and North Africa would be put to counterespionage uses.

In January 1917, both Beatrice and Willie returned to France, leaving their sons in New York in the care of a governess. Willie wrote this loyal young woman of his pride in Beatrice's activities: "... I am proud of her. She is the only one of this family keeping up its end of this war — my lameness makes me pretty useless. Her presence here is for a few weeks more absolutely necessary. I will then try to find an absolutely safe route for her and she will go home. Just now there is no safe route and her life is worth too much to be risked." The danger was, of course, from German submarines. Beatrice got back to New York in June and threw herself into propagandizing for France. America had just entered the war, and she found an eager audience for her eye-witness accounts of the destruction she had seen in the French countryside, the pitiable plight of homeless thousands, and the heroic endurance of the fighting men. Wishing a permanent base in the city, she purchased a house at 141 East 19th Street, in what was known as "the block beautiful." Bob had acquired a house and studio a few doors away, next to that of Henry Clews, his sculptor society friend.

Willie met repeated rebuffs in his attempts to force his way into the shooting. He divulged his frustration in a letter to Jack Chapman on July 1, 1917:

"On the anniversary of Victor's death I took the liberty of presenting, in your name, one thousand francs to be equally divided among the mechanos of the Escadrille Lafayette. In due time you will get acknowledgments signed by these men. You know the life of an aviator depends largely on the condition of his apparatus which is in entire charge of the mechano, who never by chance gets the slightest recognition officially & only such small presents as the none too rich pilots may be able to afford. The idea pleased the aviators immensely & I fancy they will write you a letter too if their scatter brains can settle down for a moment.

"I am having myself patched up in the hope of getting in the air as a mitrailleur or observer or something. . . ."

To Elizabeth, Willie wrote a week later saying that Bley, Victor's mechano, "comes to see me whenever he has leave which is often," but "his untutored mind" seems unable to grasp the idea of dividing money, and apparently he had felt that he should have the entire thousand francs that Willie had presented to Bley's group in Chapman's name.

It was April 1918 before Beatrice got back to Paris. She found Willie fuming over his failure to crash into action. Although she did not know it then, he also was in a high state of irritation because he was struggling to break his dependence on the painkilling drugs given him for his amputated leg. He succeeded, but at the cost of days of agony, which left him depleted and tense. In this condition he flew into one of his sudden tempers when Beatrice reported that she was deep in debt, and the governess was actually awaiting funds.

Willie's anger passed, and the couple continued to live in friendly association, on good terms. The Lafayette Heroes Fund absorbed Beatrice's energies, and for her war work she had been made a chevalier of the Legion of Honor. Willie was getting about on the only artificial leg he had found even faintly satisfactory — a plain pegleg, like that of his ancestor Peter Stuyvesant. And with the war's conclusion in November 1918, Willie again found himself in his element as he tangled in the skeins of intrigue at the Paris peace conference.

35 | "THE MOSQUITO BLOWS HIS OWN HORN…"

In 1914 Wintie had lain in Johns Hopkins Hospital and heard eminent surgeons state positively that he had at most a few more months to live. Then Dr. Thayer had somehow worked a miracle, patching Wintie together sufficiently to give him a new grip on life.

It seemed incredible, nevertheless, that immediately after the United States entered the war, Wintie began to pull strings to join in the fun. As luck would have it, General John Pershing, appointed to command the American Expeditionary Force, had requested that his friend General William M. Wright, find two men of experience who knew the French language and were familiar with the European scene, who could serve as interpreters and aides. Wright nominated Wintie and William Corcoran Eustis, a hunting companion of Wintie's.

Wintie shamelessly campaigned to get confirmed. He appealed to Senator Lodge to obtain commissions for Eustis and himself and listed as his own qualifications: ". . . mentioned for gallantry in the 2nd Florida Expedition to Gen. Gomez and was wounded . . . the silver medal for distinguished service from the Red Cross (Pres. Taft, in the Messina earthquake 1909) . . . two medals from the Italian government and a decoration from the present king of Italy in recognition for my services in Messina and Reggio di Calabria at that time . . . special work for our ambassador to Italy, Lloyd C. Griscom, during the earthquake trouble . . ."

Wintie wanted that job as he had wanted few things in life, and in spite of his fifty-three years and shaky physical condition he got it. A panel of doctors certified him to be "hunting sound," his numerous disabilities being disguised in terms so obscure the military was baffled. On May 18, 1917, Eustis and he were inducted into the army at Governors Island, New York, with temporary rank of privates. Their commissions, they were assured, were "in the works."

Wintie jauntily paraded his private's tunic at Delmonico's and the Knickerbocker Club, and early in June sailed in Pershing's party for Europe. Already, he had informed Daisy, he felt years younger.

Dilemmas arose in England because of the interpreters' lack of rank in the midst of high brass. Wintie gaily recounted in letters home that the British government had assigned "The Savoy [hotel] for Officers, the Imperial in Russell Square for clerks, typewriters, and interpreters, and the Tower of London for enlisted men." As a special favor, Eustis and he were allowed to put themselves up at Brown's Hotel, and since their services would not be required in England, they were permitted to occupy themselves as they pleased. Their first calls were on their tailors and bootmakers.

At Nancy Astor's, her diplomacy was put to the test when Wintie dined with her and a group of British officers. When the English saw Wintie's private's uniform, they whispered to their hostess that their regulations forbade their sitting with an enlisted man. Without blinking, Nancy assured them that Chanler was no soldier, he was a Boy Scout! The dinner passed off charmingly.

Paris was next, and there Wintie was placed in charge of interpreters. "I feel like a Roman Centurion & ready to bully my subordinates!" he told his wife. "I have just been paid my first cheque by Uncle Sam 'for the month of May — $36.67.' I shall have it photographed & framed & then squander the princely sum! 'Wine, women & song!' So look out, old wife, and pray the Saint's to make me thrifty!"

Willie wrote to Elizabeth that he had met Wintie and found him "very happy and very busy. Some Cubist barber has trimmed his whiskers till he is a perfect 'Uncle Sam.' He is very well & taking good care of himself. I am really proud of the old boy. He is the only one of our generation in the family who is doing anything near the front." The note of envy was plain.

At American headquarters at Chaumont, Wintie was kept busy as a sort of trouble-shooter, showing distinguished visitors around. The failure of his commission to materialize did not dampen his spirits. By a stroke of luck he was assigned as "guide, philosopher, and interpreter" to an American military mission sent to inspect Italian artillery. And in his next letter to Daisy, written from the Grand Hotel in Rome, Wintie grew lyrical in a rush of nostalgia: "O Roma Nobilis! Here I am, my bestest — once more in the busted old cow camp you like so much! Well — I like it too . . ."

In Rome, on October 13, one day before his fifty-fourth birthday, his commission came through. Spruce in a "spotless tunic, stinking of benzine, my old well cut down breeches, beautiful boots & leggings, a Sam Brown belt & a commission as Captain of Cavalry in the National Army in my pocket," he strode into the dining room of the Grand Hotel "like old Heliogabalus himself. I had a grand feed."

The visit to Italy was devoted mainly to inspecting munitions factories, and after several weeks Wintie returned to France. There he put in a hard winter behind the lines, shepherding bigwigs, cheerfully enduring cold and short rations, and reporting gleefully that he had "not a pain or an ache in my body except when I fall down stairs & crack a rib, & even then I do not miss a day on the job." One of the doctors who had condemned him to an early grave chanced to meet the spry interpreter and growled in disgust that Winthrop Astor Chanler was "the greatest joke Providence ever played on the medical profession."

At home, that winter was bitter, and Wintie's lightheartedness was a boon. Daisy moved to Boston to be with Hester and her babies, and she accepted the wartime hardships courageously. When forced to stand in line to get a coal ration she did not complain. But sometimes she was shaken by the defeatist sentiment she heard expressed constantly among her intellectual acquaintance. Brooks Adams, brother of Henry, would lecture dinner tables on the criminal folly of America's getting into the war and spilling the blood of its young men to no useful end, because France had been beaten from the outset. And Dr. William Sturgis Bigelow, the Japanese enthusiast, assured his friends that if the Germans, after crushing France, should come over and conquer the United States, things would not be so very bad after all. Clean streets, splendid museums and hospitals, an efficient police — these were prevalent in Germany, and Americans could do with more along those lines, he felt. Time and again Daisy leaned on her husband's confidence and exuberance to keep up her own spirits.

In February, Wintie suffered a sharp personal grief when Cecil Spring-Rice died. "This hits me harder than anything in a long while," he admitted. He was perfectly aware of the bitter facts, and he grimly counseled his son Hubert, who was preparing to enter the Naval Academy at Annapolis:

"The Boches are as formidable on the sea as ever they were in regard to submarines. On land their late drive into Italy shows how hard they still are to beat. They are the most terrible, strong & able fighters the world has yet seen, & may win yet in spite of all that foolish people say about them."

Fortune sent Wintie back to Italy with a special mission which involved contacts at the highest government and military levels, calling for familiarity with etiquette, protocol, and the ways of Italians from royalty down. He also took his first airplane ride, over Padua, and he was thrilled. The pilot circled and looped and barrel-rolled over the city, and Wintie described the sensation to Daisy as "air-swimming."

A fresh complication arose when several British officers inquired of the general in charge of Wintie's mission regarding "an old Etonian" who they heard was a member of his staff. The general turned to Wintie for enlightenment — what was an Etonian? When duly informed, the general was enormously impressed — and then "tonight he discovered that I was a grand-nephew of Julia Ward Howe & he nearly choked," Wintie reported. "He learns about me by accident & that impresses him enormously. He said yesterday, 'Why in Hell didn't you stay in Washington & tell of your Cuban service etc. etc.? They would have made you a major at least and you would have deserved it!' I said, 'General, a mosquito blows his own horn more than any of God's creatures and is hated therefor!' He laughed & said no more."

When fighting erupted along the Alpine front, Wintie snatched the opportunity to see action at the front. As an observer he carried no sidearms, his only weapons being "a thundering big stick, a knife, and a bitter tongue trained to curse in 4 languages, English, French, Italian, and Boche." He was permitted to witness a counterattack at night against an Austrian battery, in which the commanding colonel was closely followed by an orderly carrying a basket of bread, fruit, cheese, and wine. Nonetheless, the warrior proved as lion-hearted as he was well fed, and earned extravagant praise from his commanding general. To Wintie's surprise, he and another American officer who had briefly come under fire were recommended for the Medal of Valor.

The sense of family was strong in Wintie these days. Chancing to be in Genoa, he begged a day's leave to visit the grave of the grandfather whose sunny spirit he had inherited — Sam Ward. Sam had died at Pegli, a few miles beyond Genoa, and lay buried there, far from all his kindred. Sam had been Daisy's uncle as well as Wintie's grandfather. She had loved him devotedly and had been with him when he died. Wintie wrote her a simple, moving account of his trip to the grave.

"I secured the services of a ragamuffin who knew where Campo Santo dei Inglesi was," he said. "So up the hill we trudged & at the gate met a priest who told the lad where he could find the guardino. He left & soon returned with the man. Of course he knew nothing of the grave or anything else, but somehow — probably the old man's spirit whispered to me — I found it at once, to the right of the entrance gate. You remember — a cross with a little ivy on it? You & I gave the man money to plant roses, my dear! The whole cross & place is covered with one huge rose bush in full bloom, save on the top of the cross which has a great bunch of ivy . . . Do you remember how we poured wine on his grave? The keeper would not believe me when I told him to pull aside the vines & roses & he would find the name of 'Samuel Ward, born 1814, died 1884' — and on the other side . . . 'erected in loving memory by Archibald Primrose, Earl of Rosebery, and F. Marion Crawford.' We had to use the crook handle of my cane to pull the growth away — for I wouldn't let him cut or destroy. I gave him 5 francs to trim the roses later on so they would have better growth and said I would be back in the fall to see how he had done his work. . . ."

A big push by the Americans along the French front was expected, and Wintie itched to get in on the show. In Padua he lit a candle ("the 3.50 lire kind") to Saint Anthony, telling the saint frankly that he was a rotter, but had a pious wife and children, and to put in a good word for him. Upon returning to his mess, he found that Saint Anthony was prompt indeed, for awaiting were the Italian campaign ribbon and a promotion — to quartermaster, a bookkeeping job that Wintie loathed. Venturing another candle, he implored the saint for something better. And "Hooroosh! I went over to the office & the officers there said, 'How do you like your new job?' I said, 'What's that?' 'Why, aide-de-camp to General Wright. He telegraphed asking for you.'"

Thereafter Wintie became prodigal of candles to the accommodating saint, and he also confided to Daisy that he thought he might turn Catholic, because he liked color and movement and incense — or "perhaps I shall become Presbyterian, for I like simplicity, too."

Back in France, Wright's division began to move up and Wintie warned that "from now on my letters will probably be dull reading," since most of the "amusing stories" were about "battle, murder, & sudden death." At this juncture he was shaken by the death of Theodore Roosevelt's son, Quentin. Summoning his courage, he wrote to Teddy, telling him about having met

Quentin at the front. In reply he received a letter from Roosevelt that awakened echoes of memory:

"Dear Winty: . . . You feel exactly as I do about these young fellows dying, while you and I, who have warmed both hands before the fire of life, and whose blood has now begun to run thin and cold, still live. Yet if all our sons should be killed, their mother and I feel that, even altho we were crushed by the blow, we would rather have it that way than not to have had them go. Moreover, you are absolutely right . . . it is the woman who pays in a case like this. It is the mothers and wives who feel most deeply. The men have to go ahead and do their business in the world anyhow; and that is an immense safety and comfort. Thank you. Ever affectionately yrs . . ."

In a few weeks Roosevelt himself died.

In September Wintie's communications were filled with broken phrases: "Excuse this dirty sheet of paper but we are not in a dainty place . . ."

"That night I slept in the motor — in my clothes — as I did the night before in case of counterattack . . ."

"Boche planes drone over us constantly & every night they drop bombs . . ."

"The rattle of artillery goes on but one pays no attention to it . . ."

"All night the airplanes dropped bombs around us. Now as I write at 1:45 A.M. the bombs explode continuously in the neighborhood . . ."

On November 1 his division went into battle against the retreating Germans, and the letters became disjointed. Then — "Peace is on the table" . . . "Italy has given Austria the *coup de grace*. The war is soon over . . ."

"Dear God! How I hope for it!" he confessed. "To be clean, to sleep in a bed with sheets, to talk with educated people who speak one's language, to see quiet pleasant countrysides and never speak of war. And yet, God forgive me! I like it all tremendously & shall feel utterly let down & denatured after a few weeks of peaceful existence. I understand why soldiers take to drink in peace times. Poor devils! How tame it all is to them . . ."

Four days later: "I heard the last shots fired. Crossed the Meuse with our troops at Pouilly-en-Argonne above Stenay. Heard the last shot at 10:50 A.M."

A week later he was in Paris at the Crillon and was eventually mustered out with the rank of major. How good the feeling was that he had taken an honest part in a great communal experience. The ordeal had been grueling, but at no time had it snuffed out his impish delight in living. In the bleakest days, his humor had found nourishment in the contemplation of a mad world and its denizens, including himself.

But then from blazing battlefronts to home and the mundane monotony of New York — how tame it seemed. Wintie found his family in a rented house on East 35th Street, and there was a homecoming celebration, of course. During the night, groping in the dark along the unfamiliar hall, Captain Winthrop Chanler tumbled down the back stairs, opening the new era of peace with sulfurous curses that petrified his entire family.

36 | RIP VAN WINKLE REVISITS HIS VILLAGE

The outbreak of the war in Europe stirred Archie's "X-faculty" into prophesying the outcome of the conflict. In a letter to the *New York Herald* on August 4, 1914, he transmitted this remarkable forecast of the outcome of the struggle just begun:

1 - The war would last more nearly three years than three months;

2 - The German fleet would be captured or sunk;

3 - Austria-Hungary would be dismembered;

4 - Hungary would be made a separate nation under a king of its own;

5 - Alsace and Lorraine would be restored to France;

6 - The Slavic provinces seized by Austria would be made a separate kingdom unless they chose to merge with Serbia;

7 - After the war, France and Great Britain would form "the police force of Europe" and would compel disarmament and enforce peace;

8 - France's armies would "reverse the verdict of 1870" and hurl back their German enemies.

The *Herald* printed Archie's communication in part and forgot about it. It would be remembered five years later.

Archie's sympathies were totally — even violently — with the Allies, and he fired salvos of ferocious sonnets at the Germans. When newspapers hesitated to publish them, Archie published them in a book entitled *Pieces of Eight*. All in all, where Archie stood in respect to the war overseas was made abundantly clear. And he made just as clear where he stood in regard to insanity laws in general and his own predicament in particular.

The public was reminded of Archie's puzzling status by the developments in the Harry Thaw case. Stanford White's killer had been convicted of murder while insane, and had been confined in Matteawan asylum. Escaping from there, he had carried on a long, costly fight to have the verdict annulled, and he was finally adjudged sane by the New York Supreme Court. While an appeal was pending, Thaw slipped out of the state, and was at once termed a fugitive from justice by the New York authorities. Some newspapers thought this put Thaw in the same boat with Chaloner — both free men everywhere except in crazy New York.

But Archie would not have it that way: he occupied a category of his own, being sane in some areas on the map and a looney in others. Thaw, on the other hand, had been declared sane in New York, where previously he had been insane, and therefore he had become "sane all over."

Having embarked upon a literary career, Archie produced volume after volume from his Palmetto Press, each odder than the last. They dealt indiscriminately with topics of high moment and with trivialities. *Jupiter Tonans*, a collection of war sonnets, led off, closely followed by plays and tragedies "in blank and other verse" and in prose. These were followed by *Hell*, an amplification of his earlier revelations. "The Hazard of the Die" and "Robbery Under the Law, or the Battle of the Millionaires" were dramas on widely divergent themes.

All the plays contained novelties. The final scene of "The Hazard of the Die," a drama about Cataline's conspiracy, was one long stage direction. "Robbery under the Law" was a thinly disguised retelling of Archie's consignment to Bloomingdale and his escape. Archie announced that he would perform in it all over the country, playing in tents, as part of his campaign against "the vicious lunacy legislation obtaining in 40 per cent. of the States of the United States." After each performance, he said, he would address the audience "for ten minutes exactly" on the "black and foul stigma now staining the fair name of law, justice and liberty in these United States in the name of lunacy law."

In 1915 Archie abandoned his long-sustained war against the motor car and purchased one himself, although he asserted it was to be used in a jitney service. The next year his defenses crumbled completely, and he petitioned the New York court to grant him a special allotment of $1,700 from his unexpended income to buy a car for his own use. He needed one for his monthly trips to Richmond, since the spinal affliction he had acquired in Bloomingdale made it painful for him to maintain a sitting position longer than an hour. He proposed to have a couch installed in his car, he said. The court granted the request.

The car — a seven-passenger Pierce-Arrow limousine — was ordered, with bed built in, according to Archie's specifications. The body was painted in blue and white stripes; and to make certain of getting the right color and pattern, he tore the tail off a favorite shirt and forwarded it as a model to the coachmakers. Later he added a field kitchen to the interior.

Archie had appealed to the United States Supreme Court against the lower court's rejection of his suit to compel restitution of his property rights in New York, and he was suing seven newspapers for libel in connection with their reporting of the Gillard affair. Under protection of a court order prohibiting his molestation by any state authority, he entered Washington and testified in the action against the *Washington Post*, regaling the jurors with a blow-by-blow account of the fatal encounter. He also threw in his religious beliefs, observations on the difficulty of keeping workers on the farm, and explanations as to why he slept by day and worked by night. His book, *Four Years Behind the Bars of Bloomingdale*, he told the jury, was really "the story of the Four Hundred from inside."

The jury found for him and awarded him damages of one cent. This he said was entirely satisfactory to him, since he had proved his point.

In January 1917, the Supreme Court rejected his appeal, indicating that his recourse lay in the New York courts where the order of incompetency had originated. Archie set to work preparing a second frontal assault, in the form of an application to the New York Supreme Court for the discharge of Sherman and his "committee" with a ruling that he was competent to manage his interests. After spirited hearings, Justice Tierney denied the application on the technical grounds that his relatives, who had initiated the proceedings in which he had been declared incompetent, should have been made parties to the suit.

This brought into the open a nice point, for had Archie's brothers and sisters at any time since his commitment approved the restoration of his liberty and property, all opposition to his plea would have ceased. In effect, his own family had been responsible for those long years of humiliation and disability in the eyes of society and the New York courts.

"If the petitioner has become competent to manage himself or his affairs," ruled Justice Tierney, "he is entitled to an order discharging the committee, and requiring the former committee to restore to him his property."

Archie was advised to renew the application, citing all his heirs and next of kin so that they might approve or oppose the petition openly.

One person who had sanctioned Archie's commitment in 1897 had long since gone on record as believing that Archie had suffered enough, and probably suffered unjustly. In 1915 Arthur Carey, Archie's cousin, objected to the transfer of the Chaloner Prize Fund's moneys to a philanthropic corporation on the grounds that Archie had not been consulted in the matter. "I am one of the defendants in this suit in my capacity of a subscriber to the Fund," Carey had written, "and I do not wish to associate myself with an effort . . . in any way that would put a slight upon Chaloner. He has suffered a great deal, and the fact that he has lived as a sane and competent citizen in Virginia for fourteen years raises a serious doubt in my mind of the moral justice of treating him as an insane person in New York."

Seeing hope in Justice Tierney's ruling, Archie set about trying once more. All the while he had been pushing his libel suit against the *New York Evening Post* for its one-line sarcasm on the Gillard affair that "the latest prominent assassin" had taken the precaution "to have himself declared insane before he shot his man." Archie was asking $100,000 damages.

On June 7, 1918, Henry Astor died. Henry's existence had been all but expunged from the memories of New Yorkers for a generation, and they were therefore startled when reminded that his death severed the last direct link with the founder of the Astor fortune. Henry had received his share of the family wealth straight from his grandfather, the original John Jacob. The property, mostly midtown Manhattan real estate in the Times Square area, had been placed in trust, and Henry had been precluded from disposing of it by will; under the terms of the trust, it passed to the children and other descendants of his brothers and sisters, among whom the Chanlers were the largest group. The value of the estate could only be guessed, though appraisers were confident that it would come to not less than $20,000,000.

Willie, acting for all the heirs, immediately applied for a partition, and in the subsequent settlement each of the Chanlers came into a substantial sum. This windfall Wintie gaily called "the last cookie in the jar," and Margaret shared her good fortune with the Rokeby staff, some of whom received one thousand dollars cash. For Archie, the inheritance raised the total value of the property over which he was denied control to more than a million and a half dollars.

The *Post*, of course, had thrown all possible obstacles in the way of Chaloner's damage suit, but at long last a trial date was set, in May 1919. United States Judge Augustus Hand granted Archie a writ of prohibition enjoining the New York police from seizing him as an escaped lunatic so that he might appear and testify in his own behalf. Archie practically caught the next train for New York. He had not seen the city of his birth since 1897, except for that one furtive ride across Manhattan on his flight from Bloomingdale in 1900.

The metropolitan press prepared to receive him like a modern-day Rip Van Winkle, emerging from a twenty-year sleep. Reporters met him at the train and rode with him to the Hotel Brevoort, where he was pleased to find that at least that old-fashioned place had hardly changed at all from the way he remembered it.

In his suite he gave reporters a general interview. He apologized for taking the most comfortable chair and propping his feet upon another, explaining that his back ailment forced him to sit so. The reporters thought he looked old-fashioned: he wore his hair long, in the style of the Nineties, and his light tan overcoat was of a cut in vogue twenty years before. But his figure was slim and his movements were easy, his features lively and expressive, and his eyes had the brilliant intensity that had been noticeable in his photographs. He answered questions frankly and courteously. During the interview he gestured frequently with his walking stick — the famous malacca with a silver bear's head and the motto "Leave Me Alone." Although his hair had begun to thin and was streaked with gray, newsmen thought he would easily pass for ten years younger than his age, which he said was fifty-seven.

Asked whether there was any possibility that he might meet his estranged relatives, he replied tartly that he had only "former relatives," and "Hell will be frozen tight and I'll be skating figure eights on it before I'll have anything to do with a single one of them."

The next morning the "modern Rip" set out to view his altered home town. Upon emerging from the hotel he glanced up and down Fifth Avenue and in astonishment exclaimed, "Where are all the horses?" There was not a horse in sight, nothing but automobiles.

Stepping into a waiting automobile, he was driven slowly up the Avenue. In his eagerness to see everything he kept turning and twisting in his seat, now and then poking his head out of the window to see better, excited as a child. In the loft district he cried:

"Look at the foreign names! Where do they come from? All this used to be devoted to residences when I lived in New York."

The sight of Madison Square caused him to bubble with enthusiasm. He admired the temporary Victory Arch that had been erected there to welcome the troops coming back from France, and the Metropolitan Life tower, new to him.

"That tower! That's glorious!" he cried. "And — what do you call it — the Flatiron? Fine! Fine! I'm proud — happy and proud — to think that I'm a New Yorker when I see these things. I've read about them, but this is like the realization of a dream. Old Rip never had such a fine awakening as I'm having! This Avenue beats anything Paris, Berlin, Petrograd, or any other capital possesses. It's much finer than the Paris thoroughfares."

The car moved on, and Archie nodded toward Stanford White's Madison Square Garden, with its Giralda tower, as to an old friend. At 29th Street he spotted a former residence in which he had lived while cramming to enter Columbia College; the building had hardly changed; and the Waldorf-Astoria at 34th Street also was familiar.

"Oh, I know that place," he said. "All the Four Hundred used to go there." And he voiced a poor opinion of New York's socially elite — "commonplace, artificial, conceited, and damnably dull — and that includes my former brothers — I've blackballed them all."

The current women's fashions he disliked. "This straight-up-and-down — dreadful! Don't women want the world to know they have waists and busts? They look like perambulating washboards!"

The Public Library at 42nd Street left him almost speechless with admiration; he recalled the ugly stone walls of the old reservoir that had occupied the site. And the changed aspect of 42nd Street, as the car turned westward toward Broadway, astounded him.

"Last time I saw this Street it was covered with little two-story cheap shops, there wasn't a decent thing to look at. This is wonderful!"

A halt was made to let him inspect the Hippodrome, at Sixth Avenue ("better than the Coliseum in Rome," he called it), and next came Broadway and Longacre Square, where the recently opened Automat restaurant fascinated him. He followed patrons about, watching them drop nickels into slots and taking out everything from soup to coffee.

"Like a miracle of the Arabian Nights!" he marveled. "They rubbed a lamp and got what they wanted. Here you slip nickels in and get what you wish. Extraordinary!"

Archie confessed that he was bewildered when he tried to sum up his impressions. The last time he had seen the city, he finally said, it had been at the awkward stage of growing up — gangling and unsure of itself. "Now it has flowered into perfection, the belle and queen of the world's cities, and I am stupefied with admiration."

Naturally, after this publicity buildup for Archie, Judge Hand's courtroom was packed when Archie's trial began on Friday, May 16. The first day was devoted to bringing out the essential facts of the Gillard shooting. Grady told of his part in the fracas, as also did Ernle G. Money. When the trial resumed after the weekend recess, Archie took the witness stand himself.

He spent two days recounting his personal history, from birth to the moment he began grappling with the enraged Gillard for the pistol. At one point in describing the death struggle Archie said that they were "leaning against the sideboard — a Sheraton sideboard — S-h-e-r-a-t-o-n," he spelled the name for the stenographer. He denied categorically that he had ever intended to shoot Gillard; he only wanted to save the man's wife from injury and get Gillard out of the house.

Going further afield, Archie told about his "X-faculty's" predicting the outcome of the war correctly; about his experiments with automatic writing and mediumship, about his commitment to Bloomingdale, his escape, his voluntary submission to prolonged psychiatric study, and about being pronounced sane by eminent authorities including William James. He concluded with a brief account of his life in Virginia for the last twenty years, his position in the community there, his social connections, and his varied activities.

The second day of Archie's testimony proved to be a battle of wits between the witness and counsel for the *Post*, William Wherry, Jr. This contest Archie won hands down. Wherry's questions were aimed at indicating that Archie was crazy. He probed so deeply into certain psychological factors that Archie complimented him:

"You have been mighty well coached in this case, Brother Wherry," he said with a flourish of his cane. "I ought to give you a fee myself. You are quoting words from my brief in the Sherman case."

Wherry was tripped when he asked sarcastically whether Chaloner really believed his "unconscious" mind had written whole books. The witness replied that he had never written an unconscious word in his life, that the proper word was "subconscious." As for what his "X-faculty" could do in the way of literature, he pointed to half a dozen books stacked at his elbow and said, "There's the result."

Wherry brought up Archie's claim that he was "the best authority on lunacy in forty-eight states and Great Britain," and Archie referred him to his four-year course of study in Bloomingdale, backed by years of postgraduate research.

Wherry was curious about that copper marker in the floor of the dining room at The Merry Mills, and Archie explained it had been placed there so that he would not be continually annoyed by the questions of visitors. "I did it to save myself trouble. I didn't want to go constantly into details about the tragedy, and I conceived this as a medium to explain things."

Archie caught the drift of Wherry's questions quickly, and seized every chance to score a point in his favor, or counter a damaging innuendo. Frequently he got in his answer before his own counsel could object; and when he unwittingly infringed the rules of evidence, he apologized to the Court; thereafter he invariably turned and requested the judge's opinion before giving an answer that might be out of order. Repeatedly he returned to his understanding of the nature of his "X-faculty" or subliminal self.

"I am not a spiritualist," he insisted. "I don't believe in it. But I do believe that I have succeeded in doing what Samuel Taylor Coleridge almost did. I am able to reproduce in literary work the labor of the 'dream faculty' out of which Coleridge said he got his wonderful 'Kubla Khan.' Coleridge produced ninety-six lines of his poem, and they were perfect beyond comparison, as you know. I can produce everything that my 'X-faculty' produces when I set it to work, and I can comment on it and correct it."

In summing up, Wherry made attack after attack upon Archie's credibility ("Who can believe a crazy man?") while Archie listened with unruffled courtesy. When the oration was finished, he handed his legal adversary a sonnet he had composed while the eloquence was flowing entitled "Gladiator versus Retarius." In it, Wherry, as Gladiator, bit the dust.

In charging the jury, Judge Hand instructed that the language of the *Post*'s comment was libelous *per se*, since it called Chaloner a murderer; but that since the evidence regarding the shooting rested almost wholly upon Chaloner's testimony, the jury must form its own opinion of his mental state — whether he could be believed or not — in arriving at a verdict. Their decision, therefore, would in effect be their verdict on his sanity or insanity.

The jurors deliberated fifty minutes and returned with a verdict for Archie, awarding him $30,000 damages. The jurors indicated that they had no doubt about his perfect lucidity, the amount of damages being the only matter in debate. Archie was not in court at the end; he had hurried off to work with a stenographer on the other lawsuits he had pending. A reporter brought him the news.

"Fine! Fine! Fine!" Archie shouted, thumping the reporter and the stenographer on the back. "You know, before I left Virginia my 'X-faculty' told me I would get $40,000. I guess $30,000 is about as close as it could come in round numbers."

The next day Judge Hand ruled the award excessive and reduced it to $17,500. But that did not faze Archie, and that same day he assigned the entire sum to his creditors. The Merry Mills, he divulged, was mortgaged to the hilt.

Successful at last, Archie prepared for another go at regaining control of his New York property by filing a fresh action in the New York Supreme Court. And in this action he heeded the injunction given previously and named all his heirs and next of kin as parties to the suit.

For Archie's brothers and sisters the situation was critical. For two decades they had sanctioned the resistance offered to Archie's fight for rehabilitation. Now the verdict of the libel jury rendered virtually certain that the New York Court would follow suit. Adopting the only tenable course, Archie's brothers and sisters capitulated. It was unconditional surrender.

Beatrice, who had taken no side in the argument and consequently had remained friendly with all, took the initiative in approaching Elizabeth, and the result was a letter to Archie, signed by Elizabeth but concurred in by all, making their abandonment of opposition clear. The momentous document, dated at Sylvania, Barrytown-on-Hudson, on June 9, 1919, read:

"Dearest Archie:
"I know I speak for all your brothers and sisters when I tell you that they will do nothing to obstruct any steps you may take to recover complete control of your rights and property, nor do anything to interfere with your personal freedom. Indeed, it has been for many years their wish that you should be reestablished in your personal freedom and property rights.
Your affectionate sister,
ELIZABETH"

Entered into the record, the capitulation became official on June 19, and Archie told the press:

"This means, of course, that Othello's occupation's gone, and that the further retention by Mr. Thomas T. Sherman of the post of committee of my personal property would be a work of supererogation. But if he does not step down and out gracefully and it becomes a showdown, I feel safe in saying that I can 'deliver the vote' — the solid vote of the entire delegation of the Chanler family, male and female, against him."

On July 12 Justice Ford heard arguments on Archie's petition. Sherman neither opposed nor favored it, and the judge stated that he felt capable of delivering judgment then and there, declaring Archie competent; but the respect due to the ethics of the bench required him at least to look over the papers before ruling.

The decision came two weeks later, on July 26, 1919, and Justice Ford made it emphatic. He noted that Chaloner had been declared sane in Virginia and North Carolina; that he was a member of the New York bar in good standing; that he had "taken an active part in litigation in which he has been involved"; that he had "managed his properties in the Southern states successfully and methodically"; that he was a graduate of Columbia College with degrees of bachelor of arts and master of arts; and that he had studied in three institutions of learning in France.

Justice Ford concluded: ". . . for upwards of seventeen years since he was judicially declared competent in a sister state we find the petitioner living a sane and well ordered life in the enjoyment of social, religious, and public esteem and honor outside of New York. What more proof is needed of his competency to manage himself and his affairs in this state also? What need is there for referees, experts, or juries? Why should he be subjected to further harassment? . . . I declare the petitioner to be sane and competent to manage himself, his property, and his affairs, and to go forth and mingle with his fellow men, freed from the incubus which he has borne these many years. The prayer of the petitioner is granted."

Except for Archie, not a Chanler was in court to hear this ringing vindication. But in his hour of triumph, Archie showed himself magnanimous and unpredictable. As soon as the decision was handed down, he sent a telegram of congratulations to each member of his family, indicating his desire to let bygones be bygones; and that evening he called on his sister Elizabeth at her West 82nd Street home. They had not seen each other for half a generation.

The next morning, in the exercise of his newly restored prerogatives as a free man and responsible citizen, he summoned reporters to his hotel and distributed a typed manifesto declaring that he intended to devote the next seven years of his life to waging war on the "lunacy trust" in the United States and Europe. Also included in the message were Archie's considered opinions of the manners of New Yorkers (much improved over those of twenty years before, "except of course in the subway"), the Manhattan street car service (greatly inferior to that of Richmond), and the telephone service ("the worst out of Hell").

All of this the newspapers printed under Archie's unresolvable riddle: "Who's looney now?"

PART V:

DEATH OF THE WHITE HART

37 | HALF A CENTURY AND
THE NEW GENERATION

When Wintie Chanler fell down the stairs on his first night home, a familiar cycle was started over again — an insurance claim for physical wear and tear, an argument with an adjuster, and a debonair settlement. Wintie contended that he had sustained a head injury, resulting in damage to the brain. How much was his brain damaged, he was asked. Prohibition was coming in and Wintie's wine cellar was depleted; for about $800, he guessed, he could restock it sufficiently to last him through the long drought. The insurance company paid with such alacrity that the rest of Wintie's family cried in anguish over his failure to have demanded more. But Wintie was satisfied with his claret.

Discharged from the Army on January 7, 1919, Wintie found his plan for living changed fundamentally: there was no longer any Genesee Valley Hunt, and without hunting, Sweet Briar Farm lost its chief attraction for Wintie. When he bought a farm in New Jersey with an active pack in the neighborhood, Daisy was dismayed. She could not bear to give up Sweet Briar, and Wintie couldn't live without hunting. Financial retrenchment was imperative, so in December 1920, Wintie, Daisy, and their youngest daughter, Gabrielle, sailed for Rome.

When she returned several months later, Daisy solved their dilemma by reorganizing the Geneseo pack as a subscription hunt with Wintie Master of Fox Hounds. This changed the picture entirely: Wintie took up his new activity with relish, and supplemented the season at Geneseo with hunting at Pau, in France. Winters in Paris provided a pleasant contrast, and his letters ceased to grumble. Writing to Amos French from Pau, Wintie recalled how sick he'd been, and commented jubilantly: "But now while I am a young active gent of near 59 I really prefer galloping about with horses & hounds. . . . It is very easy & has done my liver & rheumatism no end of good. . . . So far I've had no faults — nearly everyone else has. . . ."

The luck did not last. After celebrating Christmas in Paris, he returned to Pau and promptly fell, his mount turning a complete somersault and landing on him, fracturing the collarbone "for the third or fourth time. I felt the bone go." But he expected to be back in the saddle in three weeks, when he would go to Ireland for the hunting there, then back to Pau. He was free to do as he liked, because Daisy was at Hyères on the Riviera, enjoying a "thoro'ly happy & comfortable & interesting visit at Edith Wharton's charming chateau there."

At the end of the war Elizabeth began worrying about the threat of socialism, so in the summer of 1919 Jack took her abroad. Only the week before Archie had been rehabilitated by the New York Court, and in a public demonstration of the family's reconciliation he had escorted his sister to the pier.

In France the Chapmans visited the scenes of Victor Chapman's last days and laid flowers upon his grave in the cemetery at Thiancourt. In Paris Chapman found Willie in his element, pulling strings contentedly amid the turmoil of the peace conference and the remaking of the map of Europe.

During the conference Willie had taken a hand in the backstairs bargaining, relaying information gleaned from confidential sources, and acting as intermediary in delicate negotiations. Ambassador Henry White, who had been almost a "second guardian" to the Chanlers since their first introduction to Europe, was constantly in touch. For communicating with correspondents during the conference Willie employed a simple code for the leading statesmen at the council table: Lloyd George was "Scott," President Wilson was "Caine," Clemenceau "Smith," Foch "Campbell," and Petain "Dodds." The French, Italian, and British governments were "Box," "Cox," and "Sox," while Italy's Premier Orlando and Foreign Minister Sonino were "Tox" and "Wox."

Newcomers to Willie's apartment were startled by the walls of the outer room, festooned with the realistic-looking artificial legs that Willie had bought and discarded or had set aside for occasional use. He never found one that stayed comfortable long, and as he constantly shifted from one to another he hung the collection along the walls to have them handy. When a stranger entered the flat, his first horrified impression was that he had blundered into a dissecting room.

Racing helped to use up his throbbing energy. At the outbreak of the war, he had moved his thoroughbreds to the south of France, and with the return of peace he resumed his activity at the Paris tracks. Nearly every racing day he might be glimpsed speeding to the track in his custom-built Hotchkiss. During his gun-running days, Chanler had been a good customer of the Hotchkiss arms makers, and the goodwill continued: every three years the tonneau of his car would be transferred to a new chassis. Willie's horses had their share of successes, and although he would not go to England to see them run, he occasionally shipped a likely contender to compete there. Willie's dislike of England and the English had become so venomous that he refused to cross the Channel for any reason except to be fitted with some improved type of leg.

Willie's relations with Beatrice had settled into a pattern of "separate but equal" amiability; they remained solicitous of each other, but preferred to live apart. The boys stayed with their mother or aunts when not in school, although on Willie's visits to New York, or during summer vacations, they saw much of their father, too, and he was constantly watchful of their education.

In 1921 Willie published a novel based on the revolution he had masterminded in Venezuela. Filled with derring-do fighting, it also contained an elaborate description of Willie's methods and experience. Entitled *A Man's Game*, the book was issued under the pseudonym John Brent.

Wintie was amused that Willie had lifted the title from a book by a Civil War cousin of theirs, but what bothered Willie was that the publishers had cut his manuscript drastically: "They have left in only the bare story — a rapid — far too rapid — recital of incidents & so have made a short cheap cinema-like tale instead of the novel with character development & important side matters showing how real revolutions are made & the steps taken to make them. . . . This irritates me greatly & is a sickening lesson against the future."

In the summer of 1922 Margaret and Richard Aldrich took their son and daughter to Europe, planning from then on to give the children the educational benefit of spending every third summer abroad. When she sought Willie's advice about her problem with deafness, he was probably the only family member who would have dared to suggest that she might try Lourdes. "Although," Willie notes, "as you know, a devout Christian, I have been helped a great deal by the Islamic faith; and lately I have been massaged by a Hindu Yoghi much to my benefit. I am so open-minded that I would, once at least, even listen to a tip from a Voo-doo worshipper, a Mormon, or even a Holy Roller — but one religion I do bar, and that is the Hebrew."

The eight Astor orphans by now were at or beyond the half-century mark. In 1923 Wintie Chanler was sixty, Archie a year older, and Alida the "baby," was turning fifty. A handicap for them in dealing with their children was the lack of any extensive parental memories in their own experience. As orphans they had been molded by influences other than parental — influences coming from the servants, governesses, and guardians. They had no pattern to follow, or to avoid, in bringing up their own children. Wintie, inclined to sidestep disagreeable or bothersome responsibilities, had left the rearing of his children mainly to their mother. And since Daisy had grown up in a well-regulated household with definite ideas of propriety and responsibility, she had succeeded in transmitting to her children suitable ideas of deportment, conventionality, and contentment in marriage.

But the childcare practiced by Alida, Elizabeth, and Margaret was arrived at more haphazardly. Alida set a pattern of rather careless affection, and her home at Stony Brook was a sunny place, lively with young people actively enjoying themselves. There was singing, painting, group amusements and games. After Alida's conversion, she proselytized zealously to bring her children into the fold. Children and guests learned to protect themselves from her rampaging religiosity by subterfuge, such as by keeping an extra pillow concealed to be whisked out after the first had been doused with holy water. Grief was accepted in her household with the same direct simplicity: when her own Egerton died, the dead infant was kept in the sitting room for several days because everybody found him too beautiful to part with.

Alida's gaffes provided numberless anecdotes in the family. In Paris she was once overheard admonishing a tableful of children, "Speak French so the servants won't understand you." She was beautiful and irradiated her setting, and managed to have her children grow up somewhat like her — charming, individualistic, earnest, fey.

Elizabeth and Margaret worked out rules of child conduct on the basis of reason and affection, and although the rules were well intended, the rigor with which they were applied, combined with their parents' dominating personalities, produced rebellion as often as compliance, and misunderstanding more often than compatibility. Neither Margaret nor Elizabeth had been young when their children were born, and that increased the difficulty of establishing an affinity between the generations.

Elizabeth's loss of her infant daughter had aroused Margaret's enduring sympathy, and she tried to make up for it by sharing her own daughter.
In town, young Maddie was regularly sent to spend Sundays with the
Chapmans, whose arid intellectuality bored and repelled the child. Elizabeth,
a semi-invalid, entertained her niece by quiet conversation from her bed, or
by reading to her ("Shakespeare and such stuff"). When Maddie objected to
her mother, Margaret would allow her to say what she wished, with perfect
liberty of expression, and then would go on as before. Some of the rising generation came to look upon their elders as out of step with the times.

Willie was ambitious for his sons, but it would have been hard for
anyone to duplicate his far-ranging vitality. An outcropping of wild oats in a
young man Willie looked upon as harmless, even commendatory. When
Chanler Chapman, Elizabeth's son, took off on adventures, Willie felt no
alarm, although his sister did. But when Chanler showed signs of settling
down, and became engaged to Olivia James, a great-niece of Henry and
William, Willie wished him well.

But the generations were also divided by darker traits that were rooted
in the older Chanlers' eighteenth-century atavism. In Willie this took the form
of hardening his deep-seated, irrational anti-Semitism. He accepted as
authentic that widely recognized forgery, *The Protocols of the Elders of Zion*,
and by the mid-1920s he had convinced himself that already the French government, probably the British, and certainly the Vatican were under the
sinister domination of Jewish interests, who exercised their control in occult
ways not open to the naked vision. To counteract this supposed worldwide
conspiracy became a large part of Willie's "business," in the course of which
he financed agents all over the globe, employing them to compile dossiers on
Jewish public figures in Western Europe, China, South America, and the Near
East, as well as the United States.

Meanwhile his brother-in-law, Jack Chapman, though acting on a
higher intellectual level, stirred up a hornets' nest by publicly combating what
he saw as a growing Catholic infiltration of American politics and education.

The darkening effects of prejudice were also showing in Margaret, in
spite of the mellowing influences of her domestic harmony and personal
achievements. Indeed, the very stability of her marriage increased her resistance to the triple abominations that she believed struck at the basis of family life: divorce, "plural marriage," and defection of born-and-bred Protestants
to the banner of Rome. The times were changing, but not Margaret. Each

fresh loss of a friend to divorce or remarriage brought another pang, for she was intensely loyal, and closing the door of Rokeby to a relative who had erred in any of these ways inflicted a cruel wound upon her spirit. But she would not modify her defense of the family as an institution, no matter what bitterness her action might impose upon herself.

This growing bigotry mystified Richard Aldrich. He had no part in it and could only guess at its intensity, for to him his wife's prejudices appeared to be irrational. Certainly they were for him inexplicable. He disapproved of them, deplored their increasing manifestation, and protested their application, but found himself helpless to change them.

Already Daisy had been virtually excluded from Margaret's presence, and the antipathy on Daisy's part was perhaps equally strong. Wintie appeared at Rokeby less and less frequently. Alida and Margaret had maintained no direct communication after Alida converted, although messages passed back and forth between Rokeby and Stony Brook through the medium of uncorrupted members of the family who were welcome at both houses. At long intervals the sisters met unavoidably, at a family wedding or funeral, but they would pass each other without a nod. Both loyal and both tenacious, each mourned her unhappiness, but neither had any intention of giving in.

Then Lewis Chanler tangled the network of family relationships outrageously.

38 | "THESE THINGS WERE
NOT DONE IN MY DAY"

Lewis had settled into a routine of living that suited him well enough, but did not suit the conventionalities, because Alice would not agree to a divorce that would allow him to marry Julie Benkard. Lewis lived at his club or followed Julie as she moved from fashionable New York in winter to fashionable Newport in summer, with periodic stays at Paris, Monte Carlo, Cannes, or the health spas most in vogue. Lewis's children were torn in their loyalties, resenting the equivocal position in which their father was placed, sympathetic to their mother yet privately thinking she was acting rather shabbily in the matter. Their daughter Alida was distressed, because she was about to be married; and Stuyvesant, the elder son, was even more upset. Married himself since 1920, Stuyvesant and his wife, Leslie, had gone to London to live, where he had entered upon a banking career.

Stuyvesant had graduated from Harvard in the class of 1914 and served as an artillery officer in the World War before starting his career. Shortly after taking up residence in London, he was startled to hear that his mother, in an abrupt reversal of policy, had consented to give Lewis his divorce.

Alice announced her decision with a typical lack of finesse while driving with her younger son, William, through Scotland. One day in the car she suddenly announced: "Your father has been cutting down my allowance, and I have decided to give him a divorce if he will guarantee me $25,000 for life." Having been asked by her husband to run an errand to his London tailor, she informed Lewis in a cablegram that read: "I have ordered your suits and you may have your divorce."

Lewis himself was taken aback by this sudden change and concluded that she probably wished to marry again. He was happy to accommodate her, however, and after notifying Julie, he sailed for Paris to oversee the legalities. For her part, Julie also sailed for France to get a divorce, taking with her teenaged daughter, Elsie; an older daughter, Phyllis, was left in boarding school.

The news of Lewis's pending divorce took his relatives by surprise, and the realization that he intended immediately to marry Julie Benkard created a sensation in some quarters. Nothing quite like this situation had arisen in the family before; even Bob's notorious marriage to Lina Cavalieri had not been the culmination of a prolonged and widely known liaison. For Margaret, her favorite brother, her childhood "twin," was preparing to cast himself into the pit of "plural marriage." She had never truly regarded either Archie or Bob as fully responsible for their situations, but Lewis was solidly respectable and knew the difference between right and wrong. For Margaret, the very hold that Lewis had on her heartstrings forbade the slightest wavering in this case above all others. Duty must prevail.

Lewis's sons refused to meet their mother's successor. Young Willie wrote a scathing letter to his brother Stuyve, in which he poured out his youthful objections. He also wrote a cool though correct letter to his father, but inadvertently he posted the letters in the wrong envelopes, so that the scorcher reached Lewis in Paris. This blast was forwarded on to Stuyve in London, with a note saying, "I see this letter is intended for your eyes."

Stuyve wrote back that he hoped his father would excuse Willie's intemperate language on grounds of youth and went on to explain his own distress. This letter threw Lewis into a rare rage, not only because he was offended by the suggestion that he must have read a letter not intended for himself, but also because he construed it as impudent interference. The more he thought about it, the madder Lewis got, appending first one, then a second angry addition to the letter.

A week later, in response to word of the birth of his first grandchild — a daughter, to Stuyvesant and Leslie in London — he wrote again, sending minimal congratulations and then continuing: "As to the 'unpleasant fact' as you put it I quite understand what you meant by reconciliation and it was with that understanding that I wrote as I did.

"The lady in question has a most deep rooted objection to being forced to know any of my family, and she made a special condition in particular as to my children, insisting absolutely that any move must come from them. Had I made any attempt against her wish you might then have acted in accordance with your judgment, but to write as you did giving me notice was the most impertinent act a son could commit and unforgiveable."

It was in this cheerful atmosphere that Julie and Lewis were married in Paris, in a civil ceremony, on May 23, 1921. In the autumn they returned to New York, where they soon acquired a house at 132 East 65th Street. There Julie, a tiny person who barely came up to the shoulder of her tall, slim husband, soon gathered a circle of congenial friends quite outside the Chanler acquaintance. But for Lewis the situation remained trying.

Alice lived in New York, and naturally the children took her feelings into account while they strove to establish some relationship with their father again. Lewis was forced to meet his daughter without her mother's knowledge, in public places, and he only glimpsed her baby at a rendezvous in a railway station.

The agitated family conferences went on. At his wife's insistence, Stuyvesant wrote his father a conciliatory letter, which his brother Willie thought unnecessary. Willie was oddly realistic: "Of course it will be very unpleasant meeting her [Julie]; I don't know what would happen, as she knows our attitude only too well; and we have been far from polite to her in the past."

In mid-winter that year young Willie informed his brother that he had seen their father again and "he looked well and cheerful, but he doesn't seem to be seeing much of his old friends. . . I think he will never try to have any of us meet her, anyway, and I'm very glad that you have made it up with him again. I'm afraid he's not going to be very happy. . . ."

Willie was wrong. On the whole, the next few years were ones of great happiness for both Lewis and Julie. Their life followed a regular pattern — summers in Paris and winters in New York. Julie had discovered Bahaism, and became an enthusiastic convert to that amalgam of ethics and mysticism drawn from several religions. Lewis indulged her fervor tolerantly. Although admitting the good points of Bahaism, Lewis remained a detached observer and devoted Episcopalian.

In Paris Lewis revived his racing stable and ran his horses on the tracks around Paris. There he and his brother Willie were able to renew the rivalry of their Rokeby days. Both backed their own horses heavily, and gloated when they won. Willie's star, named Mansour, won the Prix du Président de la République, one of the most important stakes in France. Another thoroughbred carrying his silks was Seguridab, winner of the Omnium Stakes. Nearly every racing day during the 1920s the brothers might be seen heading for the tracks, Willie in his sleek Hotchkiss, Lewis in his sedate Rolls-Royce.

Willie was delighted to meet Julie as his brother's wife. As a token of his esteem, he even gave her a ring made up for him at Cartier's — platinum with the signs of the zodiac enameled in black. Julie ordinarily cared little for rings, but this one pleased her and she wore it constantly on her little finger.

Lewis was fond of his stepdaughter, Elsie, while she admired his elegance, his deference, and his aristocratic bearing. Once, however, she became the innocent cause of a breach between Julie and him. Julie had a way of quoting Elsie's views in support of her own during an argument, until one day Lewis's patience snapped: "To hell with Elsie!" he roared. "I don't care what she thinks!"

Julie recoiled. She and her child had been cursed, she told herself, and it was unthinkable that they should stay one hour longer under the same roof with their reviler. Gathering up Elsie, she dashed for the railway station and got aboard a train about to depart for Calais and London. While they were waiting for the train to start, Lewis strolled up, poked his head through the window of their compartment, and calmly asked whether they had enough money. Julie snapped that they did, but Lewis insisted on looking into her purse. When he saw the pitiful amount she was carrying, he stuffed a wad of English banknotes into her handbag. Then raising his hat politely he strolled away.

Julie and Elsie enjoyed their vacation for several days, but then Julie began to worry. Not a word came from Lewis: might he be ill? Seized by foreboding, she dashed for the next train back to Paris. After an all-night ride, she arrived grimy and exhausted at dawn. Flying to the apartment, she burst into the bedroom and found Lewis peacefully sleeping. Aroused from his slumber, he eyed his wife severely and said: "I think you should know that all the time you were away your dog was miserable."

In New York, Lewis found that not all of his family had ostracized him; in fact, only Margaret remained absolutely implacable, although the Winthrop Chanlers omitted to call, and Alida politely looked the other way. Bob, however, was on the friendliest terms with both Julie and his brother; he had no difficulty in understanding the fascination that occult mysticism held for Julie, while she sensed in Bob a nature that intuitively grasped recondite truths without having to reach them through slow reasoning. The Chapmans entertained Lewis and Julie at a dinner where Julie enjoyed her first experience of several Chanler voices at the same time. When Bob, Elizabeth, and Lewis all talked at once it seemed to Julie that the walls shook. She shuddered to imagine what eight Chanlers would sound like.

One day Lewis received a telegram from Archie in Virginia, saying that he was coming to New York for a few days and would like to dine with Lewis and his wife in their home. In view of the harsh things that Archie had said about Lewis during the long estrangement, the latter was rather taken aback, but he prepared to make Archie welcome. In his telegram Archie had prescribed the menu he wished to have served to him personally; it included several dozen oysters and a steak weighing at least two pounds, together with an assortment of asides. He was not to be spoken to while eating, because he was taking only three or four meals a week and must not be distracted. He came, devoured his meal in silence, then leaned back and talked delightfully, describing his life at The Merry Mills, where he presided as a sort of benevolent godfather for the whole countryside. Julie was won by his finely chiseled features, his beautifully clear enunciation, and his distinguished manners. He was dressed in excellent taste, quite conventionally, except for one detail — he wore no socks. This, he explained, was in order to avoid ostentation.

Elsie Benkard was entranced by a large opal ring that Archie wore; it seemed out of keeping with his otherwise subdued attire. He told her it was magical, and could perform all sorts of wonders; for instance, if caught in a traffic snarl, all he need do was rub it, and immediately the jam would open up. He demonstrated for her how it worked during a drive in his new automobile, a Pierce Arrow touring car, painted bright red, with a grizzly bear's head on the side.

Some time after this visit Archie made a munificent gift freighted with consequences. During a stay at Rokeby, Archie had nearly collided with a car driven by Lewis's son Stuyvesant. Archie read occult significance into the event, especially since Stuyvesant had remarked that it was a pity that the Chanler name seemed likely to disappear from the roll of landed proprietors along that stretch of the Hudson. Archie owned Ore Lot, a 300-acre riverfront farm a mile south of Rokeby, but had never paid much attention to it because he was firmly rooted in Virginia. He proposed to give Ore Lot to Lewis, with reversion to Lewis's eldest son and so on down through the generations, in this way perpetuating the Chanler name on the river. At the same time he gave Margaret 120 acres of woodland he owned that adjoined Rokeby.

But Lewis had no desire to live upriver. When Lewis declined the gift, Archie made Ore Lot over to Stuyvesant Chanler, thus accomplishing his purpose. News of the transfer came shortly before Thanksgiving 1923, and it produced an emotional upheaval at Rokeby. With Stuyvesant in possession of a neighboring estate, Lewis would probably visit from time to time. While Margaret would welcome Stuyvesant and Leslie and their children at Rokeby, for Lewis the edict of banishment stood. The crisis became especially tense when Elizabeth made it clear that she and Chapman would receive Lewis and Julie at Sylvania, just north of Rokeby, just as they had received them in New York.

On New Year's Day 1924, Margaret sat down to write one final appeal to her sister to abstain from a betrayal of principle: "The last thirty years have contributed to society the successive or plural marriage," she pronounced gloomily. "This is neither intrigue nor life-marriage; it is a third state in form and substance. . . . Can marriage be regarded as a temporary contract subject to good behavior of both parties? Responsibilities cannot be assumed and then wiped out because a woman is a shrew or a man has a double standard. Plural or successive marriage leads to undermining of responsibility, to the replacing of principle by personal wishes, and is therefore a menace to character, a bad example, and cruelty to children. . . ."

The plea was a Parthian shot. Elizabeth, the rock against which family opposition shattered quietly disposed of it in one of her "Queen Bess" pronouncements. She replied to Margaret: "Darling: There is one point of comfort that I seem not to have given you quite clearly, & as it is bad to have any misunderstanding between us I shall put it plainly now.

"I sympathize too deeply with those who share my views on plural marriages — I may say my horror of them — to allow my house to be a spring-board whence any of my family who are plurally married may invade the society of this or any other neighborhood.

"I well remember how, years ago, I sympathized with those who felt that old Mrs. Richard Hunt had a perfect right to receive her son Dick and his divorcée wife in her own family, as any mother naturally would, that she was wrong to entertain at large for them. She would have seemed to me to be an unnatural mother if she had refused to receive her son & his wife into her house. When she tried to re-instate them socially, she seemed to me to be a menace to monogamy. . . .

"P.S. I think I ought to tell you, too, that if you or any other neighbor or member of my family received harlots or pro-Germans or any other undesirable group of people into their house in a private & personal manner, I should not consider it my business. The receiving of 'sinners' & eating with them may become a duty in any life at any moment."

So the situation held, nobody retreating. Between Ore Lot and Sylvania ran a bridle path through the woods, across Rokeby land; but this convenient access was closed to Lewis. In any event, as no house was built on the Ore Lot land until the year of Lewis's death, the latter stayed at Sylvania and had no particular need for the path. He never challenged his sister's action in excluding him, and when hints were relayed to him that he as a family member would still be accepted at Rokeby, but his wife of course would not, he studiously and proudly ignored these timid overtures.

39 | FANTASIAS AND FORESHADOWINGS

In 1919 Archie's disposable wealth increased enormously. In the final accounting rendered by his discharged "committee," Archie's estate was valued at $1,636,195, with a spendable income of some $112,000 a year. This handsome sum he set about dispersing in ways both prodigal and pleasing to himself.

His Paris Prize foundation had been a discerning contribution to art education, and he was delighted when the prize was reactivated under trustees (having passed out of his hands during his declared incompetency) and another award was made in 1920. His ideas regarding the possibilities of visual education by means of motion pictures were radically progressive, and shortly after his rehabilitation he undertook a coast-to-coast tour to promote the idea among state educational authorities. He went about this promotion, of course, in his own peculiar way.

The tour was made in his hearse-like automobile with its built-in sleeping berth and field kitchen. When his chauffeur objected to going because his parents were feeble and he doubted they would survive until he got back, Archie had him bring them along.

They stopped along the way to sell visual education to school boards and legislatures, leaving a $5,000 donation in some states to get a program started. When he reached Los Angeles in July 1920, he informed the newspapers that he would give them "a hell of a break" if they sent reporters to his hotel. The presence in their city of "Who's Looney Now?" (as Archie had taken to calling himself) proved a sufficient magnet. He told them he was completing arrangements to produce a motion picture based upon his life in Bloomingdale asylum. The film would be called *Within the Law*, and he would star. It would be a major blow in the war he was waging against the "lunacy trust." For an encore he favored the reporters with a demonstration of his "X-faculty" in action, taking down by graphic automatism messages purporting to come from Abraham Lincoln, George Washington, and Quentin Roosevelt. The Los Angeles press found these revelations less pertinent than the amazing fact that John Armstrong Chaloner, besides being the author of the phrase, "Who's looney now?" was "the multimillionaire great-grandson of John Jacob Astor."

Arriving safely home again (his film project having come to nought), Archie continued making educational gifts. Many were made anonymously, and almost any educational enterprise of merit could be assured of a check for $1,000 or more by merely asking for it. Only after his death, for instance, did it become known that he had been sending $3,000 annually to a school for girls in upstate New York. He did not even keep a record of all his gifts.

The Chaloner bounty covered the local scene as well. At one time Archie had 250 people on the estate payroll. He was the first line of help for anyone in trouble, paying for medical expenses, groceries, taxes, schooling, and vacations for children. He spent so freely that by December 1920, he was compelled to appeal to his family for temporary assistance when he lost a suit brought by an unpaid attorney to whom the jury awarded $12,000. To tide himself over the crisis, Archie asked his brothers and sisters for a loan of $30,000, amply secured by his share of the revenues from their properties held in trust. The request was debated among the family, and when some reluctance was manifested, Archie offered, through his attorney, to promise, as a condition of the loan, that he would never ask for another. This suggestion grated harshly upon Margaret, and the loan was granted, without accepting the proffered pledge.

Archie now turned to the lecture platform to acquaint the public more widely with the nature of the subconscious mind. He first appeared in the assembly rooms of Christ Church, on upper Broadway, the church of which the Chapmans and the Aldriches were members and whose rector was a family friend. His audience consisted mainly of newspaper reporters. Archie recounted how he had discovered he had mediumistic powers and offered his practical revision of the Golden Rule as a means of helping weak and fallible humans to cultivate righteous conduct. The injunction, he contended, should be, "Do not do unto others what you would not they should do unto you."

The response of the press was extensive enough to encourage Archie. He next hired the Cort Theater and lectured three more times in the next few months before larger audiences in his exposure of the iniquity of the lunacy statutes. Since he had been certified mad and locked up because of his experiments with the subconscious mind, he felt qualified to discuss the subject and to show the public how rational this "X-faculty" was.

Leaning gracefully on a piano in the yellow glow of a single lamp on the darkened stage, Archie spoke occultly, he explained, his address being composed by his subconscious as he went along. At the start he took down the dictation, but as his subconscious warmed up, he allowed a stenographer to take over.

In his second lecture at the Cort, Archie's subconscious held an extended colloquy with his famous great-aunt, Julia Ward Howe. She began by describing to Archie her consternation upon finding herself, immediately after her demise, standing before Satan in Hell, stark naked. But instantly her modesty was relieved by the discovery that in the twinkling of an eye she had grown an amazing head of hair "like Lady Godiva's" which covered her quite adequately. She was relieved to hear that inasmuch as she had no earthly imperfections to be purged away, her arraignment in the court of judgment was only a formality, to comply with the law, and she was dismissed.

The most popular part of the universe, Mrs. Howe reported, was called The Kingdom of Sin, and it was frightfully overcrowded. Fortunately it was also extremely large, and God in His tact, having realized that its inhabitants would dislike being identified as Sinners, had endowed the kingdom with the euphonious alternative name, Philistia.

She next surprised her nephew by announcing that the human race had shown itself incapable of self-government — quite an about-face for the woman who had spent much of her existence on earth ardently campaigning to give women the vote. She also predicted the coming of the millennium within five years, when "retribution will stalk red-handed and Bolsheviki will get their desserts."

In his third lecture Archie read two new scenes in "Hamlet," dictated through Archie's "X-faculty" by the spirit of William Shakespeare himself. After reading the interpolated passages to an incredulous audience, Archie expounded the intention of the new scenes, which was to confound the blockheads who contended that Hamlet was mad. There were other changes in the play, too: Ophelia did not go mad, there was no grave-digger scene, and at the end — after the king had been stabbed, the queen poisoned, Laertes poisoned, Hamlet stabbed — then the fatally wounded Hamlet gallantly placed a cushion for the fair Ophelia, she drained the dregs of the queen's poisoned wine, and the lovers expired in each other's arms, mouthing verse that to the audience sounded very blank indeed.

Even at home in Virginia, where Archie's eccentricities were no novelty, he was sometimes mistaken for what he was not. Several times a week he drove to Richmond, eighty miles away, to pick up his mail and attend the movies. An avid fan, he thought nothing of seeing four or five pictures in a day. His nocturnal trips at high speed through the sleeping countryside aroused the suspicions of a Warrenton constable, who guessed that he must be a bootlegger. The constable flagged the car down, and found in it the pistol that Archie always carried out of doors. Archie was hauled before a justice of the peace, and explained that he kept the weapon handy because of threats against his life. The magistrate nodded sympathetically and released him.

Archie busied himself with numerous improvement schemes. He worked out a plan for importing Chinese coolies to replace black field hands, but found the cost prohibitive. In 1923 he took issue with the trustees of the Paris Art Prize when the young woman who had won the award was disqualified on the grounds of plagiarism: the painting she submitted was a copy of another artist's painting, a photograph of which had appeared in an art magazine several years before. The jury of artists who made the award defended their choice by contending that the girl had improved upon the original composition, while she denied ever having seen the other painting. The business men trustees, however, revoked the prize and ordered another competition, from which the offender was barred.

Archie had been delighted when a woman won the prize — and was doubly delighted when another woman won the second competition. But excluding the first winner from a fresh chance to prove her talent he regarded as unfair; so he awarded her a matching prize from his own pocket, after writing abusive letters to the trustees.

In 1923 Archie returned to the lecture platform briefly to set the public straight about Emile Coué, the apostle of auto-suggestion, whose formula, "Every day in every way I am getting better and better," had become an international rage. Coué was correct up to a point, Archie conceded, but he was dead wrong when he said that the subconscious mind was a slave to continuous suggestion. On the contrary, Archie testified, his subconscious was a mean and tricky tyrant, always trying to trip him up or catch him off guard and do him an injury. When going up stairs, for example, his subconscious would cause him to stub his toe and take a tumble. Or when alighting from a moving streetcar, his unconscious would induce him to get off backwards and go sprawling.

In the same lecture Archie also gave a demonstration of telekinesis in which sixteen small ivory balls were supposed to reassemble into constellations. The reporters looked but saw no stars.

Religion came more and more to preoccupy Archie's fertile brain, and in 1924 he published a book devoted wholly to doctrinal exegesis. It had the longest title of all of Archie's published works:

A BRIEF FOR THE DEFENCE
of
The Unequivocal Divinity
of
The Founder of Christianity
as
The Son of Jehova
In the Legal Sense that the Legitimate
Only Son of A king
is
Heir Apparent and of the Blood Royal

———

Inspired in Spots

———

by
JOHN ARMSTRONG CHALONER
Member of the Bar of New York
Author of
"Chaloner on Lunacy"

In a prepublication statement the author said that the book was aimed at confuting "modernists" and "Biblical revisionists" — "Clerical Parasites, barren of anything most remotely resembling truthfulness of character, with an eye single to the 'loaves and fishes' . . . A Brief for the Defence is an attempt at purging the Sheepfold of the Lord of these Clerical Ticks."

In 1924 Archie made a new will, which expressly declared that "the prolonged misunderstanding between my brothers and sisters and myself has been entirely [and] happily removed." Blame for the "said misunderstanding" was placed squarely upon the alienists who had pronounced Archie insane, the "charitable view" being taken that they had acted out of professional ignorance.

Twenty-seven individual bequests were made to friends, relatives, and employees. These ranged from clergymen and Archie's valet (left $1,000 apiece) and his New York barber (left $2,500), to a "Blind Editorial Writer of the Portland, Oregon Journal" ($1,000) and handymen at The Merry Mills (from $250 to $500 each). The rest of his property, without exception, was to be turned over to a New York corporation, to be formed under the name "The Chaloner Estate, Inc.," and shares in which were to be allotted according to an intricate schedule of percentages. Sixty-five percent of the shares were to be held in varying amounts by charitable institutions or individuals, including his brothers and sisters, Amélie Rives Troubetskoy, and St. Margaret's Home for orphan girls at Red Hook. The remaining shares were to be divided between the Universities of Virginia and North Carolina, to provide student scholarships. These were to be known as "Raleigh Scholarships," in honor of Sir Walter Raleigh. Few restrictions were placed upon the awards, save that they must be competitive and apply to the entire university curriculum, including the postgraduate. They were to be repaid by the beneficiaries, without interest, when these were earning sufficient income to do so "without burdening him or her, or her children;" and "if never able to do so, no nagging or dunning of said winner by lawyers or university authorities is to be tolerated." And the scholarships must be of sufficient amount "to enable the winner to live in comfort and also buy what books are necessary."

Archie shunned all actions that were petty.

In many ways the Chanlers were representative of their social class — wealthy, family-conscious, cosmopolitan, rooted in historic American ideals — but in other respects they diverged strikingly from the norm. They did not follow the normal pursuits of their time and environment. No Chanler man applied himself seriously and systematically to earning money; they didn't go on Wall Street, or become industrialists or bankers or merchants. All were out of step with the dynamic materialism of their age. They had come into maturity at the precise moment when the new rich were competing in the luxurious display, building marble palaces ostentatiously called "cottages" at Newport, putting servants in livery, maintaining enormous yachts. None of these excesses touched the Chanlers, though they lived in the midst of them. None ever had liveried servants; at Rokeby the housemaids were giggling country girls who wore checked gingham frocks. The contrast between the Chanlers and their surroundings became even more striking in the 1920s, the era of jazz and bootleg gin, of the "lost generation" and the raucousness and vulgarity that went hand in hand with an uprushing sense of release from constricting social fetters.

The life that Margaret led at Rokeby was anachronistic in many ways. She derived her notions of place and duty from two interlocking sources — patrician ancestry, with its code of responsibility to the community and inferiors, and intimate association with servants during childhood. As a consequence, she had adopted domestic simplicity and orderliness on the one hand, and public service through social welfare and civic reforms on the other.

Intellectual Elizabeth and her husband had little empathy with the spirit of postwar times. As early as 1920, Chapman was assuring his friends that "it's a horrible world, no matter how you put it . . . any endeavor in letters, art, intellect, or morality seems always to be in a skiff awash and wallowing and about to be submerged." Six years later he deplored the "general vulgarization of everything due to the increase in the world's population and the outcomes of science." Poems and prose of high quality flowed from his pen, but they found little or no acceptance publicly. Elizabeth, often ailing, was serenely detached, occupying herself with music and meditation, the creation of a rock garden at Sylvania, or with small handicrafts, such as composing decorative panels by embedding in plaster seashells she gathered during winter stays in Florida.

None of the Chanler sisters exhibited the ruthlessness and desire to attain the topmost rung on the social ladder that had animated their formidable Aunt Caroline Astor. They accepted and moved freely in society, but they did not submit to it.

The Winthrop Chanlers intermittently made a splash socially, but as birds of passage they remained outsiders abroad. In their social views, the Winties fell between aristocratic practice and plebeian theory. As Americans they were devoted to the egalitarian principle that all men are born equal, but by temperament they leaned toward European elitism. Daisy definitely responded to rank. The one place where they remained long enough to put down roots was Geneseo; yet their life there was in part an anomaly — riding to hounds is not typical of America.

Willie was a throwback to swashbuckler days. He might have accompanied Clive into India as a gentleman freebooter; he was chivalrous within his code and enamored of conquest for its own sake, not for profit. After losing his leg, he was forced to conduct his wars at second hand, by correspondence and conspiracy, but this he attempted without cease.

Lewis, the most conventional of the brothers, still had not hesitated to flout the prejudices of his social peers with regard to his personal life, and Archie, of course, was a story unto himself.

The one member of the clan who succeeded in creating a world absolutely his own, was Bob. His struggle against the oppressive restraints of exalted ancestry, family prominence, and enervating wealth had been long and tumultuous. But finally, in the riotous milieu he created for himself in New York, he succeeded in working free.

Bob had been born an artist, with an artist's sense of values, but nobody realized it for years. When, after painful fumbling and false starts, he finally began to comprehend his talents and his needs, he shocked and baffled his family and friends. In their world, "artist" suggested all sorts of socially undesirable things — a vagabond, a "Bohemian," a person of loose morals, unprincipled, undisciplined, a rebellious idler, and so forth. Painters did not make money; their work became valuable, if ever, only after their death.

Daisy was an exception because of her upbringing in Italy, where artists were normal, respectable beings, and to a lesser degree Archie also had some grasp of artistic endeavor. Jack Chapman expressed the feelings of the rest of the clan in a rare burst of candor when he wrote to Beatrice, Willie's wife, to warn her against the dangers of promiscuous society. Beatrice was reported to be entertaining writers and artists, people such as Arturo Toscanini and the Barrymores, and Chapman was concerned.

"My dear Beatrice," he wrote, "I wish I had your unshocked, ingenuous, young nature. How can you keep it up? Don't you know that all Russians are immoral, and have no standards of conduct? . . . A woman in your position, and without the guidance & protection of a strong wise man, cannot be too careful in the choice of her associates & friends. There is the especial class whose propensities toward evil are so well known that I should not mention them but that some tendencies in your conduct have given me concern, quiet but deep, thoughtful concern, to use no stronger word, as to your future. The class I refer to is the class of Artists. They are invariably corrupt and irregular in their private lives & in their ideas. . . . I would seriously urge you to have few acquaintances among artists — and especially to draw back your skirts from sculptors and sculptresses. Most of them are foreigners — need I say — Italians, Frenchmen and Russians and you know what foreigners are. They don't speak the truth, or pay their bills, or keep the sabbath."

Shortly after his divorce from Cavalieri, Bob hid his humiliation for several months in the Arizona desert, living among the Moqui and Navajo Indians, studying their ways and making countless sketches of their ceremonials and life-ways. He returned east with a profound sympathy for them and anger at their betrayal by their conquerors. He also came back convinced that he was and would always be fundamentally American, and that therefore his career lay in his own country. The crassness of American life, its constraints and jejuneness in matters of art and ideas, repelled him.

During his political period, Bob had tried in effect to live on two levels — the artistic and the Philistine, but the experiment had not worked. To the electorate of Dutchess County his dabbling in art had been amusing but inexplicable; to those who esteemed him as an artist, his political shenanigans had been amusing but regrettable. The shock administered by Cavalieri at last made him choose consciously to apply himself exclusively to art and his social liberation.

He had learned that his imagination required broad expanses; his flamboyant compositions gushed over walls and ceilings. He belonged to no group or school; he was neither realist nor symbolist, neither an abstract artist nor representational one, but all of these at times. No sooner was a label fastened to him than he defied it; his designs were too complex, too eclectic, too individual to fall into any set category.

Essentially he was a painter of ideas, of moods and feelings. The Chinese screen which he had happened upon in Paris had opened the door of self-knowledge to him. Its creator was not concerned with mere delineation of an object, but with rendering the idea of that object, the essential quality which it shares with all similar objects. This was Bob's instinctive approach. A Chinese critic was to say of his work: "He knows the souls of his mediums better than he knows their bodies. He knows anatomy, but it does not interest him. Psychology is for him everything."

Bob also painted the world of the subconscious — a disturbing world that exists but is visible only in dreams. And his painting was always dynamic, kinetic, never static. Bob painted the way he lived — headlong, extravagantly, on a scale larger than life, flinging himself into sensations and experiences with limitless abandon.

Guy Pêne du Bois described him in 1921 as "a giant over six feet tall and built in proportion — not merely structurally in proportion, he has a proportionate voice and gesture and appetite. He lives in a world peopled by pygmies. His table is set with enormous goblets. He is cramped for space in two large houses in East 19th Street.... His whisper is a rumble of thunder. His stairways creak as he climbs them. But he is feared only by those who do not know him. He happens to be, like a great many romanticists, a great child. He has the innocence of children, their enthusiasms, their extravagance, their willingness to be amazed, and their gullibility...."

Behind all the sensuousness which du Bois perceived in Bob's paintings, he felt he also had a knowledge of the history of art shared by few American painters. And he thought no one a more voracious reader.

Bob constantly produced the unexpected. He could be gentle in speech or burst into Rabelaisian earthiness. His scorn for whatever he did not like was brutal; he was indifferent to reputation or social standing, and he never hesitated to offend his friends.

Early in the century Bob had begun to exhibit in New York, although he received few commissions for the massive works he specialized in. For the Hudson-Fulton celebration he painted a panel that he later destroyed. He contributed the largest exhibit shown at the revolutionary Armory Show in 1913, a panel entitled "Brooklyn Bridge," which evoked the tremendous arch of the bridge's pier, with the towers of Manhattan behind it and the river shipping in the foreground, the whole enclosed in an ornamental border of fishes, crabs, and seahorses. As he began to get commissions from wealthy friends to decorate their homes, he utilized his Moqui sketches to fill rooms with buffalo hunts. On a screen he reproduced — spiritually as much as physically, it was said — the Hopis' snake dance.

But it was Bob's spectacular style of living that caught the public attention. His home at East 19th Street was actually two houses thrown together to provide rooms big enough for a man of his dimensions. The top floor was one enormous studio; the basement was a playroom and gymnasium. In-between were a drawing room, dining room, and bedroom.

He decorated the house himself. On the entrance hall walls, strange birds and beasts browsed and flew about, monkeys swinging from the branches while elephants and hippopotami lumbered along the ground. As one went up the stairs one passed all manner of beasts of earth and sea and fowl of the air incongruously intermingled — cheetahs and buffaloes, badgers and crocodiles, beavers and fiddler crabs, boa constrictors and flamingos, llamas and porcupines, zebras and birds of paradise.

The walls of the dining room were living — behind lighted glass panels swam rare Japanese gold and silver fish. On perches around the room were bright-plumaged birds. The bedroom was a triumph of inventive fancy — walls and ceiling a mass of exotic foliage, from amid which peered detached eyes, while interspersed blobs of color represented souls. The bed was twelve feet by fourteen — large enough for four persons of average size to lie at the head, while three more reposed across the foot. The bed stood twelve inches off the floor — easy to fall into, and practically impossible to fall out of. Along the sides, within handy reach, were drawers stocked with every restorative and hangover antidote known. Bob christened his home the "House of Fantasy," and as such it became one of the era's landmarks.

It was the frenetic Twenties, the "splendid drunken Twenties," to quote one of Bob's neighbors, Carl Van Vechten. With his actress wife Fania Marinoff, Van Vechten lived next door to the House of Fantasy. George Bellows lived across the street, and Elinor Wylie's home was in the same block. Among this freshly liberated generation of talents, the promoting and pursuit of drunken parties was the pivot upon which their lives turned. Morals were unshackled and blear-eyed stupor or screaming frenzy were mistaken for catharsis of the soul. And of all the parties staged, those at the House of Fantasy were the most notorious. Bob's hospitality was as wide-open and as accessible as his bed. Little was expected of the guests except that they be clever and amusing; otherwise, all taboos were lifted.

One never knew on arriving for the first time at 147 East 19th Street whether one would be clasped to Bob's bosom, or thrown down the stairs. Once accepted, however, one was always welcome; the front door had a trick lock, so that those in the know could walk in at any time. On most days there were half a dozen guests for luncheon, and the table talk might grow Hogarthian, but it was never stupidly obscene or trite or platitudinous. Wit was encouraged, but not the smug, shallow wisecrack of Broadway.

It was a mystery to his friends where Bob had picked up his education, since he had received almost none as a boy, and had never studied formally anywhere. Yet he was widely read and always abreast of current ideas and political developments. The fact was, of course, that once he began to read, he had become enamored of books and read omnivorously, retaining what he read.

Bob flung himself into his painting with ardor, painting at any hour of the day or night. He would often leave a party in full swing at 2 a.m. and go up to the studio to work, while the revelers downstairs snake-danced through the rooms. His wealth enabled him to experiment with bizarre materials and styles: he painted on canvas, wood, plaster, silk, glass, metal, velvet, and drawing board; he used gold lavishly, sometimes in high relief, sometimes as an underlay or overlay. He gave his screens a patina by applying successive coats of lacquer or paint, rubbing each one down laboriously, although he also employed workmen to perform these time- and energy-consuming tasks.

He might have a half dozen decorative folding screens in process at one time. He would outline the design, designate the treatment, and supervise the craftsmen as they carried out his intentions, touching up a detail, improving a line, tempering a hue, so that the finished screen always bore his unmistakable imprint. Daisy deplored this assembly-line practice, feeling that it cheapened his work, but Bob did not agree.

By the time of World War I, Bob was already becoming a legend in New York. Early in the conflict he turned 147 East 19th Street into a center for war relief, and used it as a recruiting station for the Lafayette Escadrille. When his brother Willie was about to lose his leg, Bob went to Paris to stand by. Ironically, soon after his return, he suffered a similar misfortune when a car in which he was riding crashed into a tree in Central Park. Bob's right leg was broken in several places, and he was in the hospital for eighty-one days while the surgeons strove to avoid amputation. They succeeded, but the leg was shortened, and from then on Bob walked with a cane. Denied daily exercise, he put on weight and acquired that air of an Oriental sage that would dominate the image of him thence forward.

Bob went out sparingly; he brought people to him. He was a rich man, and he lived on the scale he had always known, with servants, a secretary, a valet, and assistants to relieve him of minor chores in the studio. He welcomed young artists, and almost every newcomer was taken to the House of Fantasy to be looked over; those who Bob believed had talent he aided indirectly by buying their works through third parties. But he did not haunt Greenwich Village, and some of his contemporaries resented his careless affluence and denigrated his talent.

The carouses in the House of Fantasy grew wilder as the 1920s progressed. Parties lasted for days, and the uproar was terrific. Bob liked to invite thirty or forty people to drop in after the theater, and at such times anything might happen. Bellows was forbidden by his wife to attend these blowouts, but nearly everybody else of prominence in arts and letters, the stage, politics, or the more tolerant wing of society, did come there, and many went away shocked. Ethel Barrymore was quoted as saying: "I entered that house in the evening a young girl, and came away early the next morning an old woman."

Bob's sisters, of course, deplored these revels, but left the door open to redemption by blaming not Bob himself, but the influence of his evil companions. His style of living did not interrupt his relations with his family. His nephews might be forbidden by their parents to enter the House of Fantasy, but they did, and Bob watched over their morals. He would not allow shocking behavior before the young people, and if the going got rough, he would order his nephews out. His nieces came only when he entertained decorously, as he did now and then.

Marriage was not for Bob after two sour experiences, but celibacy was not for him either. Eventually he became involved with two charming redheads. One was a good-natured, buxom, kind-hearted Irish woman, named

Clemence Randolph; the other was small and fiery and generally reputed ugly — a dyed redhead named Louise Hellstrom. They functioned alternately as hostess at the House of Fantasy, both living on stipends paid regularly by Morris & McVeigh, the Chanler family lawyers.

During the 1920s Bob's two daughters were in New York, and with the consent of their aunts they were allowed to frequent their father's studio, so long as they left the house by midnight. Just before their arrival, Clemence Randolph, who had been living in the house, moved to an apartment. Bob allowed his daughters to listen to the conversation, but they could not join in. At no time did they ever overhear anything objectionable; the talk was free, sometimes extremely so, but it was neither coarse nor scandalous, and Bob saw that the guests did not pay the girls too marked attention.

One day that curious creature, Sadikichi Hartmann — poet, art critic, essayist, and moocher — arrived for luncheon and found the daughters in the studio. Hartmann knew nothing about Bob's family, and when the girls introduced themselves as Bob's daughters, he broke into a grin.

"Daughters! Hah!" he exclaimed. "How charming! What a nice way of putting it! How delightfully new!"

He was grabbed and pitched down the stairs, Bob roaring after him: "They are my daughters, damn you."

Bob's attitude toward his daughters was fatherly but frank. That he thought of himself as a family man was indicated by the portraits of his first wife and the girls that hung in the dining room. And he impressed upon his daughters that they should pay attention to their aunts' instructions.

"Learn everything your aunts tell you," he told Julia, the younger daughter, who was seventeen. "Do everything they say, and when you are thirty, if that is not for you, go your own way. If you want to have a baby," he added with a twinkle, "have one, and I will bring it up in a basket in the studio."

Two topics never discussed in the House of Fantasy were Bob's illustrious ancestry and his fortune. His secretary had a standing order to send all bills to the lawyers, and any caller who tried to talk about Beekmans, Stuyvesants, Astors, or other branches of Bob's pedigree were shut up bluntly.

His behavior was at times baffling. At luncheon one day he became annoyed by a mewing kitten. Snatching it up in one hand, he grabbed a steak knife in the other and blurted, "I'll kill it!" The guests held their breath. But after a minute of scowling he said, "Hungry?" and, tucking the kitten into the pocket of his coveralls, started feeding it bits of chicken off his plate.

When the ceiling of the new Grand Central Terminal developed leaks and the paint peeled off, Chanler was invited to submit an estimate for redecorating. The ceiling had been painted to show stars in their places, and Bob sketched a new grouping of constellations, based not on astronomy but upon his own notions of fitness. But the directors moved so slowly, he lost interest, and when finally asked to state precisely what he proposed to put on the ceiling, he glanced around the circle of directors and replied gravely: "Chorus girls and guinea pigs, gentlemen."

Stage people liked Bob. At a performance of "No, No, Nanette" Bob was sitting in the orchestra, but he fell asleep leaning on his cane. At the song "I Want to Be Happy" he woke up, and clapped and clapped.

"You like it, Bob?" the leading lady called down to him.

"Fine! Fine!" Bob boomed back.

"All right, let's do it over again for Bob Chanler!"

The song was repeated, and at the close Bob stood up, said "Thank you," bowed, and left the theater.

41 | "THE HORNS OF ELFLAND
FAINTLY BLOWING"

In 1919 Archie lost no time reintegrating himself in Chanler family life. As far as he was concerned, his brothers and sisters had ceased to be "ex," even though he received no formal word of repentance on their part. Many of his nieces and nephews he had never seen, and some had never heard of their extraordinary uncle.

Immediately after winning his legal liberty in New York, Archie had taken an apartment in the city, from which vantage point he began to renew his relations with his family. So speedily did this proceed that peace was established with Wintie — against whom Archie had hurled his most outrageous accusations — during the Christmas holidays of 1919.

During the summer of 1920 Archie visited Geneseo, and Daisy found him a difficult guest. Years of living alone had nourished Archie's oddities. He remained in his room all day with the shades drawn and the shutters closed, sitting under a lamp with a red shade; at no time could he be disturbed. After nightfall he and his chauffeur would take long drives through the countryside alone. Archie ate dinner only once in every three days, but then wolfed down three days' rations in one sitting. His chauffeur drove Daisy's French maid literally out of her wits; and it was necessary to send her to a rest home for a while to recover. Nevertheless, Archie's conversation was delightful, his courtesy unfailing, and his opinions on many topics clear, logical, though often original. He approved of the country life preferred by his brother's family, and since Wintie was not one to harbor rancor long, the reconciliation seemed complete. Archie paid further visits to Sweet Briar, coming twice in 1922. His extraordinary eating habits now included salads of fresh-cut lawn grass.

Sweet Briar was the scene of elaborate wedding festivities in October 1922, when Wintie's daughter Beatrice married Pierre Francis Allegaert. The wedding occurred during the hunting season, so after the nuptial mass, the bridal party joined in a hunt breakfast during which the huntsman and whips brought the hounds around. Toasts were drunk, the signal to mount was given, and the entire party — hosts, guests, and bridal couple — galloped off to the music of the hunting horn.

During the hunting season Wintie had plenty of congenial employment, but at other times he was always on the edge of boredom. In his sixtieth year, he wrote to Amos French "I've rarely been in better condition. This last Sat. & Mon. I was 5 & 6 hours in the saddle galloping & jumping . . . without fatigue or ill effect."

That winter the Winties made their ritual pilgrimage to Paris, and when Daisy's health seemed poor, he packed her off to Hyères to visit Edith Wharton and invited his son Theodore, who was preparing to enter Oxford in the spring, to join him. His youngest child, Teddy was a namesake and godson of Theodore Roosevelt.

The summer of 1923 Wintie's youngest daughter, Gabrielle, was married to Porter Ralph Chandler in Geneseo. The couple had known each other since they were children, and as youngsters had both passed through Wintie's stern course on horsemanship. He used a mean-spirited pony which excelled at tossing its riders for the children's training. The rule was to get right back up again after a fall, and it was strictly enforced. Young Porter was bucked off so hard he was knocked senseless, to his mother's expressed indignation. She felt that Chanlers, with all their children, might afford to lose one or two, but Porter was her only son.

Then it was off to Europe again, the Winties lunching with Edith Wharton at Hyères, listening to their son Teddy tell about his friend Scott Fitzgerald, and then on to Rome. Meanwhile the days brought steady news of the death of friends, causing Wintie to write French that "you & I must get used to this sort of hopeless catastrophe. The apples drop when they are ripe."

In 1926 Edith Wharton invited the Chanlers on a cruise through the Aegean islands on a chartered yacht, the *Osprey*. Wintie insisted that Daisy accept — Daisy and Edith were intensely compatible — but Edith was too intellectual for his taste, so he would go hiking with an English friend in Crete.

The *Osprey* sailed on the last day of March. In Paris Willie thought his brother looked frail and in no condition to tackle Crete. He was upset that Daisy should be so nonchalant, but Wintie laughed at his brother's concern and sailed for Crete. There he and his companion trudged across the island on foot, carrying rucksacks and sleeping in the verminous inns, subsisting on bad food and the acrid, belly-scouring Cretan wine. The adventure exhausted the sixty-two-year-old, although he enjoyed it. But when Willie saw him on his way home, he was shocked at how bad his brother looked.

Wintie landed back in New York on June 20; Daisy was due in another week. Lewis Morris, the Chanler attorney, met him at the pier and was so alarmed that he telephoned to Amos French. French went at once to the club, where he found Wintie looking "very badly," and persuaded him to come to his house in Tuxedo Park pending Daisy's arrival. When Wintie arrived the next day, the conductor had to help him off the train, and the Frenches immediately put the sick man to bed.

On Friday, June 25, Wintie insisted on returning to New York, where the following Monday he met Daisy when she landed. The next day they traveled to Long Island, to see their daughter Laura and the grandchildren, and to visit Alida's brood. Laura's husband had just bought a yawl, and Wintie volunteered to sail as crew. It had done him a world of good, Wintie told French on July 2, just before heading home to Geneseo.

The Fourth passed quietly at Sweet Briar Farm. In a joyful bulletin to French, Wintie announced: "I am no longer on the water waggon, thank Bacchus!" But Daisy noted that his moods seemed muted; he had become very gentle. Frequently he rode out to savor the velvety summer countryside. On one ride with Daisy he suggested they have a little canter. She told him to set the pace and let him take the lead. But his horse had gone only a few paces when she saw that the reins were slack and his knees had lost their grip, and before she could reach his side he swayed and slid to the ground. Throwing herself off her mount, Daisy cradled his head in her arms, but he was unconscious.

He had suffered a massive stroke. For days he hovered, now and then delirious, but mostly in a coma, while his wife wrestled with a dilemma of conscience. Wintie had said, either facetiously or not, that he would become a Catholic when his head was "six inches from the ground" in his last fall off a horse. The doctors held out no hope of recovery. To bring her husband into her faith had been an object of Daisy's prayers ever since their marriage. A family council was held, and they appealed to Porter Chandler, who was both a Protestant and a lawyer. He advised that the dying man was entitled to the benefit of the doubt, and that what Wintie had said should be accepted as his true wish in default of any known retraction or denial. Accordingly, Winthrop

Astor Chanler, while in coma, was taken into the church *sub conditione* and received the last sacraments. Without regaining consciousness, on August 24, 1926, he died.

The month-long agony had prepared Wintie's relatives for his death, but they were not prepared for his baptism while he lay helpless either to consent or object. To Margaret and some others this high-handed procedure resembled a spiritual rape, committed in contempt of their brother and themselves. Margaret was stunned into temporary silence; but Daisy's next step provoked an explosion of wrath and indignation at both Rokeby and Sylvania.

Wintie's widow assumed that he should be laid to rest with his parents in the Chanler vault in Trinity Cemetery in New York, and she automatically requested the family lawyer to procure from the Episcopal authorities permission for a Catholic priest to conduct a Catholic consecration and committal rites at the tomb. The permit was granted, and Morris, the lawyer, apprised the various members of the family of the arrangements.

Elizabeth, the "conscience" of the Chanlers, placed her interdict upon Daisy's plan. The idea of allowing Roman Catholic rites to be performed upon ground consecrated by her own church and hallowed by family tradition — a Protestant tradition — revolted Elizabeth, and she telegraphed peremptorily to her sister-in-law at Geneseo: "I am against having the Roman Catholic branch of the family use our family vault. My parents were both strongly opposed to the Roman Catholic church. They built their vault and lie in it. No Roman Catholic priest must officiate there. I feel sure that this is the opinion of my brothers William, Lewis, and Robert, and of Mrs. Aldrich. There will be trouble if the Catholic minority in the family oppose the views of the majority."

Lest Daisy fail to grasp exactly what was meant, this telegram was confirmed the same day by a letter reading:

"Dear Daisy:
"My telegram this afternoon was sent after hearing from Lewis Morris that he had procured a permit from Trinity Church for a Roman Catholic service in Trinity Cemetery. This in no way affects my own feeling in the matter. Trinity Church feels that its ground is not desecrated by another form of Christian burial. But this is not a question of desecrating the ground of Trinity Cemetery. It is a question of flying in the face of Protestant views held by the founders of that family vault and by six of their seven surviving children.

"We do not want to have a Roman Catholic ceremony there & we refuse our consent to it. I have cabled Willy & Lewis and have telegraphed Bob, and I know what their answers will be.

"I hate to be taking strong action against your wishes at a time like this, but some instincts run deeper than mere affection, as you well know, and such is my instinct to preserve the vault for what it was intended to be, — a Protestant burial place.

Your loving ELIZABETH"

At Geneseo the reaction was one of injured amazement. Back came a telegram from Hester Pickman: "I don't think you have any idea dear Aunt Elizabeth how shockingly you distress us. We do not dare show Mama your telegram. The long strain has been very hard on her. What you suggest means a future scattering of the family remains. I feel sure you would reconsider your request if you realized how we feel."

Reconsideration was not in Elizabeth Chapman's mind, nor was it in Daisy's. Throughout the next two days the messages flew.

Willie cabled from Paris: "Indifferent to dogma. Hope the dear old boy will rest with family."

Archie, who somehow had not been included in his sister's roundup of family opinion, sent a three-page night letter from Virginia urging moderation, but not giving his formal consent to Daisy's proposal.

Bob was distressed, but sided with Elizabeth, at the same time sympathizing with Daisy. And John Jay Chapman, although backing his wife, strove frantically to avert a public scandal. In a letter dispatched to Daisy the day after Wintie died, Chapman put some hard questions, including:

"Do you have very strong feelings about the Chanler family vault in Trinity Church cemetery? I can hardly believe it. Would you have brought Wintie's body back from Europe out of piety toward this Episcopal cemetery? Wouldn't you rather have him lie in a Roman Catholic cemetery anyway? This would be logical. And to bury him at Geneseo would be natural and I should think that you & all his children would like to have his grave in the place where he has lived & where you & they still live.

"Now it happens that this is a matter that will, so far as I can see, make years of acrimony — serious, deep — things to be avoided if they can be avoided without injury to religion. Will it operate as an injury to the Roman Catholic Church to have Wintie buried in a Roman Catholic cemetery in Geneseo? This family vault is not a chapel, but in the minds of a Protestant family who have attended the funerals of their parents there and heard prayers there it is their private chapel, sacred to their inner feelings and filled with memories and family tradition. To them a Roman Catholic service seems not only a horrid idea in itself but an affront to the dead . . .

"We were getting along very nicely on the religious matter & I was looking forward to good feeling and the right sort of union. . . . It does seem to me that the venom & stroke of the thing will have come from your side if you push the project through — which I don't believe you will."

But Daisy would not budge. That Winthrop Chanler had a legal right to be buried in the family vault was incontestable, and she telegraphed that the interment would take place as scheduled "within three days."

Elizabeth Chapman thereupon served notice that she would take legal steps to have her brother's body removed from the vault. Her husband at the same time drew up a petition to the courts to order delay of burial, and drafted an appeal to Dr. William Manning, Protestant Episcopal bishop of New York, requesting him to use his good offices to procure a discreet abandonment of the permit by the Catholic authorities, to prevent the issue from reaching the courts and inflaming religious passions among the public.

Laura White came forward with a compromise solution: let both a Catholic priest and a Protestant clergyman be present at the committal and conduct their respective services. Elizabeth rejected all proposals.

At Rokeby the atmosphere was snapping with tension. Richard Aldrich was appalled by the fierceness of the conflict, but he saw that he could deflect neither his wife nor his embattled sister-in-law. He wrote a heartsick letter to Daisy, privately conveying his grief at the death of "my old friend, my classmate, my brother-in-law," and his distress that he had not been able to "come to you at the last moment. I suppose I needn't tell you why I couldn't. The reason is one that remains as inexplicable to me as ever after all these years: and one which I must only consider a kind of mania or madness: a cruel one to wage at such a time as this. I assure you there was too much at stake for me to risk running counter to it. . . ."

For two days the deadlock held, neither woman giving way, Elizabeth was prostrated by the struggle, but it was finally Daisy who yielded. The funeral, she announced, would be held in the chapel at Sweet Briar on the 28th, and burial would be in St. Mary's Catholic cemetery in Geneseo. So Chapman set aside his appeal to Bishop Manning and relatives and friends assembled at Sweet Briar. The mass was celebrated by several assisting priests, and during the service Wintie's hunting cap, horn, and whip lay upon his coffin. Neither Elizabeth Chapman nor Margaret Aldrich was present.

Once it was over, characteristic messages of understanding poured in. Bob wrote from New York: "Now that Wintie is gone and the whole thing is over, we should pick up our threads, as our rope is broken.

"It seems very right that he should have died a Catholic so that you and he and your children may all be buried together, for you know that according to the laws of your Church there is anathema against the Protestants . . .

"I am very glad Wintie was not buried in our cemetery in Trinity Church, as every time one of your family would be buried there, the Church would have to reconsecrate the ground, which to me would be very distasteful . . . I think the spot you placed Wintie in is very beautiful, and I am sure he will hear the hounds singing like the Indians in the happy hunting grounds. God bless you!"

From Virginia Archie wrote:

"Good old Daisy:

"Thanks for the note ending with the beautiful words: 'He passed in his sleep to where beyond these voices there is peace.' As I wrote: 'Wintie died the death he would have wanted — IN THE FIELD.'

Affect'y yours

J.A.C.

"P.S. Years ago Wintie told me . . . about going over to the 'R.C.' Church: 'I'm not going over except on my deathbed. Then I'll do it to please my wife.' Proffetic was it not! I said: 'That's ALL RIGHT.'"

Willie paid his sister-in-law the highest compliment of which he was capable — a tribute to her bravery. His short note read:

"Dear Daisy,

"The cable telling me of dearest Wintie's death has just come & my heart goes out to you in grief. He was the nearest & dearest of my brothers & you can guess what a terrible blow his death is to me. I do not need to tell a brave woman like you to be brave; but I write this to express my grief and deep sympathy.

Much love,

WILLIE"

The epitaph that Daisy chose for Wintie's gravestone came from a letter of Madame de Sevigny to her daughter:

"*Tout en fait souvenir, et rien ne lui ressemble.*"

Some thought that Wintie might have preferred the epitaph he had suggested for himself:

"Here lies one who laughed in many lands."

42 | ROKEBY REVISITED

With the first real break in the circle — Wintie's death — Margaret reaffirmed her determination to sink the family roots deep at Rokeby. There she intended to keep the Chanler banner flying in defiance of temporary and personal disagreements; there family would prevail, if not absolutely in her own generation, then through the younger set.

During the 1920s Rokeby was a lively place — a big, rambling house, with floors branching off at odd levels, set amid woods and farmland, noisy with children running up and down the stairs, bolting out the doors — a place of singing and companionship, of ample food, sound sleep, and out of doors a world to roam in adventurously. The rooms spelled tradition: each had some link with this or that ancestor, this or that occurrence. Margaret insisted that, regardless of her relations with their elders, the nieces and nephews and their friends should make Rokeby their home at intervals. She invited them all by turns, saw that they came to know each other and were taught the ways of family. Daisy had ceased to visit, but her children were welcome, and Alida, though shut out from direct communication by her apostasy, relayed messages to Rokeby through her children, who were frequent guests. Though Lewis was forbidden his boyhood home, his sons and daughter were included in Rokeby's hospitality without reserve.

The elder Chanlers abounded in vitality. They seemed to some of their offspring uncomfortably grandiose, over-possessive and over-mastering. The sheer weight of their personalities could be disturbing. They went their ways without doubt or expectation of successful refutation. Their creed was simple but set: 1) certain fixed rules governed society; 2) they had learned those rules; 3) as long as one observed the rules, one was secure. Yet with all their self-sufficiency, they were not hidebound, and they were never trapped into accepting mere conformity as the true coin of propriety and worth.

The differences between the Chanler sisters and their sisters-in-law were plainly perceived by their second-generation critics. It was Daisy and Beatrice who entertained with a lavishness appropriate to the times, as did Alice and Julia, Bob's former wife. They ran their households efficiently, kept excellent servants, and provided the best of food and conversation and diversion through borrowed talents. The Chanler sisters felt no need to display talents of others to make themselves felt. One sensed that they were great ladies, in their quiet, old-fashioned, sometimes quaint ways.

Of course there were wide contrasts in their personalities, which even showed in their dress. Behold Margaret at Rokeby, crisp in white piqué skirt, great blouse, black cotton stockings, a large white hat with daisies on it, and cotton gloves. A watch attached to a heavy chain would be tucked in her waistband. In sunny weather she carried a parasol; on rainy days she resolutely "walked her mile" on Rokeby's porch. Elizabeth, puttering in her rock garden at Sylvania, tended toward heavy silks, blandly rich but faintly dowdy to her nieces' eyes. And at Stony Brook, Aunt Alida reveled in frothy negligees, exquisite lingerie, and the lightest, brightest, gayest styles, very up-to-date.

Sundays at Rokeby were maintained in the tradition of Cousin Mary Marshall — church-going, meditation, reading, music. The Aldriches for a while read Molière aloud together every Sunday afternoon in the library; it was supposed to help Richard with his stammer. Bob's daughter Julia was often corralled for these sessions, French being her native tongue; but if she fled for relief to Sylvania, her Uncle Jack Chapman would pounce on her to read aloud to him.

Hammer-and-tongs arguments still flourished at Rokeby. For Margaret this hangover from her childhood was a necessity; she required it to blow off excess energy. Her husband, Richard, was not argumentative, but Margaret found that young Julia could hold up her end of a dispute with entire credit. Margaret tried to avoid arguing with Julia on either her own property, or on her niece's home grounds, the Red Hook farm, so disputes took place while tramping up and down some neutral field.

Now and then the younger set — who were divided between admiration of their elders and astonishment at their occasional preposterousness — were given a glimpse of the sort of legendary rows their parents had carried on as children. At the time of Beatrice Chanler's wedding at Geneseo the clan had gathered in force, and one evening at the dinner table there were

Daisy, Wintie, Bob, Jack Chapman, and Aldrich, with a niece and a nephew. Suddenly a fight erupted among the elders, during which they shouted and acted in a way that scandalized the young people. His own daughter thought that Bob behaved like an outrageous child, and the other men more like boys than adults. But the young people had to admit that Bob had been screamingly funny.

With her nieces Margaret had educational ends in view at all times. The ethic underlying her actions had to be passed along to the new generation, not by preaching, but by doing. The fundamental theme was the responsibility imposed by wealth, social position, and leisure upon those enjoying these gifts to employ them for the benefit of others. Margaret inducted her nieces into the sort of chores which were incumbent upon herself, as chatelaine of the manor, assigning the girls to sweep out the church at Red Hook, supply the altar with flowers, sell tickets for the church bazaar (and then attend and patronize the booths), entertain the rector at tea, help organize the annual party for the orphans at St. Margaret's Home, appear at village funerals, trim the Rokeby Christmas tree, and organize barn dances for all the retainers and neighbors. Only through loyalty to God, church, home, and country, could the Chanler inheritance be justified.

Also unspoken but impressed upon those destined to succeed were the rules of conduct. Some seemed ludicrously out of harmony with the cynical Twenties, harking back as they did to the eighteenth century. It was axiomatic, for example, that the prejudices of one's social inferiors should be scrupulously respected; to offend them would show ill-breeding. Margaret required her nieces to wear hats on Sunday when out walking on the chance that they "might meet one of the farmers."

There was an etiquette of gloves and the correct use of calling cards, even though the custom might be outdated. One must never be smart, or strive for social prominence in any vulgar or outré manner. Men and women were governed by different standards: men might err, drink to excess, and dissipate, but they could be saved by the piety and good works of their women. Social and religious patterns were so interwoven that they seemed inseparable, which is why embracing an alien faith caused Margaret such extreme distress.

In 1920, the summer following Archie's restoration to legal liberty, he made his first return to Rokeby. Margaret's children, Maddie and Dick, now eleven and twelve, were fairly jumping with excitement after being told for the first time they had an Uncle Archie. Margaret had kept them in the dark because she had simply blocked him from her consciousness, as she did any information, events, and ideas that threatened to upset her mental or emotional equilibrium. At first, Margaret was terrified when her brother announced that he was descending on Rokeby. There was something psychic about Archie, she sensed, and she disliked psychic manifestations. Nevertheless, she prepared to make him welcome.

Archie came and remained for a week. To the children he appeared extremely handsome; he was slightly built and thin, and had aristocratic features and piercing eyes. He wore a monocle, and his manners were charming. Like many solitaries, he could maintain silence for hours; but when he did speak, the words streamed out. His eating habits were bizarre. Although he appeared regularly for lunch, he dined only twice during the week he visited. One day squabs were served to the twelve people at the table. As the platter was passed several helped themselves, but when it reached Archie, he nonchalantly scooped all the remaining birds onto his plate and attacked them hungrily. After frantic signaling between Margaret and the maid, scrambled eggs were placed before the five unfortunates who were left without squab. Archie paid no attention.

On the whole Archie's Rokeby visit was a success, and he repeated it at subsequent family reunions. The Aldriches kept up the Christmas tradition — a huge tree, the house filled with guests, excited children, presents for the servants, drinking Christmas toasts, and the rest. At one of these festivities Archie brought dozens of boxes of chocolate creams of a kind he said were exceptionally good, and handed them out liberally. And year after year he would send great quantities of these chocolate creams to Rokeby, until everybody finally grew sick of them.

A practical firmness marked all Margaret's dealings. The villagers felt that "Miss Margaret" would be strict in her accounts with them, but always fair. St. Margaret's Home was in her special care, as it was in Archie's, and much correspondence passed between Rokeby and The Merry Mills regarding its maintenance. But whereas Archie was careless in his benefactions, Margaret was even-handed and vigilant.

To the younger set the Chanlers' great times seem to have been in the past; the show seemed to fade as it progressed: the first act splendid, the second act bitter, the third act faltering. What would the final act be? The oncoming generation had not, of course, been molded by the forces that had shaped their parents, who in a very special sense continued to be nourished by a group spirit that in their children was diluted. The personalities of the elder Chanlers, while sharply distinctive and contrasting in many ways, were not wholly separate; each in some measure drew strength from, and shared the limitations of, all the others. Their voices, uniform in timbre and tonality, were an outward manifestation of their close kinship; and they drew sustenance from a mutual "feedback," a kind of telepathy, which their successors could only imperfectly receive.

43 | PATTERN FOR PARADISE

In addition to his massive murals and screens, Bob had also turned to portrait painting, although he deprecated his accomplishments in the field. But he had no lack of sitters, for besides friends many social and financial figures were flattered to have their likenesses taken by "a great-grandson of John Jacob Astor." Some were rudely shaken by the results, however; bankers found themselves depicted as wolves, with dripping jaws, or as hideously bloated serpents. They recoiled from the enameled eyes and slavering lips they had been given, and dowagers fled sobbing from portraits that likened them to bejeweled pigs. Bob's well-wishers protested against these gratuitous affronts, but he shrugged and said that was the way his sitters looked to him.

Not all his subjects received this grotesque treatment, of course, and an exhibition of his work in the late Twenties included portraits of Leopold Stokowski, Mercedes de Acosta, Emily Vanderbilt, Alfred Lunt, and Avery Hopwood, to mention only a few. Van Vechten wrote a foreword to the catalogue for this exhibition, in which he said that being painted by Bob Chanler was "a career, a social experience, and an education." No wonder, for Bob liked to do his portraits in the midst of a crowd carrying on helter skelter.

Commissions for the murals he preferred doing were scarce. Architects were wary of his independence, and he quarreled with patrons. Rather than alter a line of his design, Bob would walk out on a $25,000 job. While the demand for his screens kept the workshop busy, dealers remonstrated in vain against his custom of duplicating his screens over and over, doing only a portion of the work himself.

But Bob continued to act as the spirit moved him. He would not succumb to flattery any more than to denunciation. The man was a bundle of contradictory impulses, consistent only in his urge to portray the beauty and terror of life in forms strange but never chilling. He could veer from the most delicate sensitivity to Rabelaisian coarseness in a moment. Proud to be of his family, he rebelled against its constriction; inescapably a member of his social class, he reviled it; rich, he disdained wealth yet never offered to do without it. When his brother Archie crowed "who's looney now?" about Bob and his marriage to Lina Cavalieri, the label stuck; Bob could not shake it, nor did he try. To the world much of his conduct was crazy, in a gusty, boisterous, good-natured manner, and the notoriety of his conduct prevented any just perception of his stature as an iconoclastic artist of both originality and profundity.

His many nieces and nephews were naturally intensely curious about their fabulous Uncle Bob. Most of them were forbidden during their early years to enter the House of Fantasy. Margaret thought it a den of iniquity into the exact nature of which it was better not to pry. But there was always time, she consoled herself, for Bob to repent, reform, and be redeemed.

Once Alida, badgered by her brood, sent word to Bob that she was bringing all her children for luncheon. Bob was watching from the window when the file appeared, Alida in the lead, followed by her troop in order of ages and sizes. To Bob the line seemed to stretch clear back to Third Avenue, and flinging open the window, he shouted: "Go away, Alida! I haven't food or room in the house for them! Blessing on them! Take them back to Temple!"

For a while Bob operated his own distillery and brewery in the basement of 147, where he made applejack and beer. The applejack he distilled out of Dutchess County hard cider, which he had shipped down the river in dozen barrel lots. He would personally pick up the shipments at the dock and ride back to the studio perched in triumph on top of the load. Why he was never molested by the law his friends never understood, for when the still was working the fumes filled the street. Perhaps it was the family's Tammany connection, or perhaps it was Bob's generosity with the cops on the beat. Bob drank what he brewed and served it to his guests, to their horror.

Whenever Bob visited his farm at Red Hook, he liked to brag about his prowess as a farmer, although the farmers thought his expertise largely imaginary. One hot day during corn planting, he whipped off his shirt, seized the reins of a horse-drawn planter, and set off down the row in a blazing sun, laughing and joking with the men at work all the while. Each time at the end of the row he halted for a swig at the cider jug. Between the heat, the exercise, the cider, and the frequency of swigs, Bob's rows grew more and more zigzag. Never mind, he said, the corn would grow just as well in crooked rows as in straight.

Four times a year Bob paid calls of courtesy at the farmhouses on the estates, sometimes taking his daughters along. The girls were impressed by the warmth and affection with which their father was received on these visits. There was nothing strained or artificial in the welcome extended: Bob was genuinely liked.

By 1924 Bob's corrosive drinking was bringing about a general deterioration of both his health and temper and reinforcing the misanthropy that underlay much of his surface turbulence. In May of that year he announced he was going abroad to stay indefinitely. From France his postcard messages home suggested that he had found a haven of respectability, intellectual integrity, and moral honesty in an oddly named "bachelor's quarters" in a posh Paris brothel. But by the summer of 1926 he was back in New York, much affected by his brother Wintie's death.

Bob had bought an old mill in the artist colony of Woodstock in the Catskills west of Rokeby to serve as his summer studio. When he was flooded out, he moved into a house he had given Clemence nearby.

He continued to support his two mistresses. The small and fiery Louise dabbled in poetry and painting when in New York and dabbled in gardening and dramatics at her house in Woodstock. Buxom, good-hearted Clemence had an overwhelming urge for a child. Bob endorsed her wish, but not to the extent of becoming the child's father. In 1927, when Clemence discovered that she was going to fulfill her objective, Bob was pleased for her sake. The father not being part of the picture, Bob offered to underwrite all the expenses in connection with the baby's birth, and Clemmy thereupon sailed for France, where in due time the child was born.

Bob followed Clem to France, but headed at once for the Riviera, where he was said to have chartered a yacht aboard which he staged flamboyant parties. One of his most assiduous guests was Isadora Duncan. Her vogue on the wane, Isadora was clutching at her fame, and in September 1927, newspapers reported that Isadora and Bob Chanler were engaged to be married. The rumor later was passed off as a joke or a publicity ploy on Isadora's part, with Bob's drunken connivance; and less than a week after the rumor was printed, Isadora was dead, strangled when her scarf became entangled in a wheel of a speeding sportscar.

Not long thereafter, Bob was taken to a hospital in Paris, suffering from acute uremia; his whole system giving way. His daughter Julia was in Paris at the time, as was Bob's secretary, Suzanne Tirlet. Willie and Lewis were also in close touch, and Willie tried to talk his brother into some moderation of living, without success.

In the spring of 1928 Bob suffered a general collapse. Clemence managed to get him to a hospital and sent telegrams to the family. Julia, who was traveling in Spain, received a stream of messages from relatives urging her to hurry back; then came one from her father. It read: "Have a good time."

The illness was grave; but gradually Bob pulled back to health, or a semblance of it, and by mid-August he was able to write to sister Elizabeth: "Clem found my quarters, the doctor, etc. Brought me here alone a sick man, staid 9 days & then left to take care of her splendid baby & sent for Tirlet who has held the fort & is going strong. Tirlet says Clem saved my life. She almost carried me on her back to the doctor. I could not walk, suffocating, but she pulled me, carried me in & did the trick. Anyway it is all over now & I'll see you in October."

Recovery was slower than Bob had anticipated. When Willie visited the hospital, he confidentially reported to Elizabeth that Bob was in a bad way: "His internal economy almost demolished. His life might be prolonged if he would drop his hard-drinking associates, live quietly, and amuse himself with his painting."

But for Bob Chanler living quietly was not living at all. Before the end of 1928 he came back to New York, and so he was not in Paris when his daughter Julia was married to George Beach, a pianist and composer, in January 1929. Uncle Willie did the honors for the family, complaining loudly of a toothache and showing off his wooden leg rather too grandly to please his niece.

Bob resumed his accustomed ways, and in the summer of 1929 he predictably suffered a heart attack. He was taken from Woodstock, where he was stricken, to a hospital in nearby Kingston. Bob admitted that he was "scared," but he reassured Margaret that he was recovering, although "a bad liver is a foolish plaything . . . A weak heart does not matter as one does not get excited . . . *Piano va sano* [live quietly, live healthy] is good for a weary heart."

The promised improvement came about, but slowly. Since July, he noted sadly in a letter to Julia, he had painted nothing but three portraits. One of these provoked an argument with his brother Willie. The portrait was of Willie, Jr., and Beatrice had it on loan. Knowing that Bob was often strapped for cash, Willie cabled an offer to buy the painting for $500. Back came a scornful rejection: never did a portrait for less that $1,000, said Bob. This amused Willie, who replied:

"Dear Old Boy:

"Glad to get your cable which shows you are taking an interest in things & have 'a good appetite.' As I cabled & wrote you I want that picture you made of Willie — but I cannot pay $1,000 for it, as I have not that sum & don't expect to have 'a loose grand' to spend even on a portrait done by someone I love. . . . I am sure that the portrait is a fine one & doubtless worth even more than what you ask; but facts are facts & I cannot, to my great regret, pay $1,000 for it . . . I am more than happy that you are at last taking really good care of yourself & feel sure you will live long & be happy in doing fine work.

Your loving brother,
WILLIE"

The outcome was predictable. Writing to Willie shortly afterward, Bob's secretary acknowledged "the check covering half the price of the portrait of your son William, came in two days after Mr. Chanler made me cable you; and he thanks you very much for sending the instructions to Mr. Morris so rapidly."

As had so often happened, Bob's lawyers had informed him that his account was nearly $8,500 overdrawn. His daughter Julia was finding it impossible to make ends meet on her allowance and appealed for an increase, saying that otherwise her husband would have to abandon hope of a concert career and find employment, perhaps as a clerk in some bank. Bob was sympathetic and replied that of course Julia's husband was "not supposed to be a bread-winner." He increased Julia's allowance.

At the same time he was being pressed for money by Clemence Randolph. She was pregnant again (by the same married man), and late in November 1929, she sailed for France again to await the birth of the child. Once more Bob paid all expenses. Clem's letters teemed with the sort of chatter that reflected her happy-go-lucky, improvident self, but her demands for money drove Bob's secretary frantic. She tried explaining that times were hard, in view of the stock market crash, and lectured Clem on the absolute necessity of living within her $400 monthly allowance. Clem accepted the scoldings contritely and continued her feckless prodigality.

Bob spent the winter of 1929-30 in Bermuda, but the vacation did him little good. From the mainland his other inamorata, Louise Hellstrom, pelted him with attentions, such as cabling angrily:

"TIRLET TOLD ME SHE WOULD ARRANGE WITH UNION CLUB FOR ME TO CHARGE THEATER TICKETS UNION CLUB SAYS ACCOUNT CLOSED AM PERFECTLY FURIOUS WHAT A SHABBY TRICK REGARDS LOUISE."

Bob replied that he had ordered the account closed because he couldn't afford the club — "drinks too high." Whereupon Louise wired to the secretary:

"HEAR BOB IS DRINKING AGAIN CABLE ANSWER IMMEDIATELY."

And this was followed by:

"ICY COLD SAILING SATURDAY MEET ME LOVE LOUISE."

She came, found life in Bermuda dull, fought with the hotel management, smashed furniture, and sailed back to New York in a huff. Bob paid her no heed. He was drinking heavily again, putting on weight, and was feeling disgusted with existence generally.

In the spring Bob returned to New York still half invalided. He tried a change of doctors and got one who imposed a strict regime. He mustered strength to paint a screen for Alida, but this spurt of work brought on another crisis. Climbing the stairs to the studio had become too great an exertion, and shortly after receiving a cable from Clem announcing the birth of her son and asking for $200, he moved back to Woodstock for the summer, attended by a valet and a nurse. Most of the time he spent in bed, brooding.

His relations with Louise were more an exacerbation than a satisfaction, although she was in her way attached to him. Her incessant appeals for money, however, moved Bob's secretary to protest that he was too sick to be bothering about anyone's budget problems.

That summer brought a searing heat wave, through which Bob struggled to survive. His heart specialist was summoned from New York, but could provide little relief. Alida contributed her bit by sending Bob a medal of St. Theresa: "Pin it on your undershirt, and don't lose it or give it away. I have worn it myself over a month & I have included you in my prayers (or requests) to her. Her prayers are very powerful & they say she is particularly interested in helping men."

In the midst of all, the lawyers warned that Bob's overdraft had jumped to nearly $15,000 and retrenchment was imperative: "You will realize that it is impossible for me to keep on paying bills at this office and at the same time send the same amount each week," Lewis Morris wrote. But instead of retrenchment, fresh expense was incurred by engaging a night nurse.

Because of the suffocating heat, Bob had his cot moved into the garden. Around him throbbed the summer gaiety of which he had been a part for many seasons — picnics, theaters, moonlight bathing, applejack, dances, bonfires, lovemaking, thrills. The names of the smart set and the Bohemian world studded the reports forwarded to Clem. Bob lay through it all and endured. Finally the heat wave broke, and he debated sailing for Europe. The doctor, however, advised against this and suggested a warm climate. Charleston, the cradle of the Chanlers in America, was decided upon. Arrangements were made to go south by ship — Bob, his secretary, his daughter Dorothy, his nephew Ashley (Willie's younger son), a valet, a nurse, and a Chrysler touring car.

In October 1930 a messenger from the family lawyers' office brought to Woodstock Bob's revised will, with minute instructions as to how it should be signed and witnessed. This formality concluded, the preparations for departure south were speeded up, but amid turmoil. Suzanne Tirlet described it all confidentially to a friend:

"Our life has become so complicated that I have to take my typewriter into the woods to be able to use it. *Le Père est bien malade depuis 5 semaines.* He is worried and scared. Walter and Jean came here for a weekend, which ended in great disaster, as we had to get them both arrested after the second day to get them out of Woodstock. Walter is shot to hell with dope, and he broke up his hotel room and Negulesco's place in two nights; he has developed a mania for breaking windows."

Bob was again hospitalized at Kingston. When Elizabeth visited him there, he told her he wanted some paints — any kind would do. Taking him at his word, she brought three little cans of ordinary carriage paint, one light blue, one forest green, the other black, with a square of canvas. With the black paint Bob brushed a window and bars, and beyond, floating in the distance, upthrusting blue mountains amidst a field of green.

Elizabeth asked Bob, who attached great importance to the titles of his paintings, what he called this sketch. He answered:

"Paradise."

It was there, on October 24, 1930, that Robert Winthrop Chanler — the artist who had been driven to spend too much of his gigantic energy in sloughing off the burden of his inheritance — died, aged fifty-eight. His larger-than-life mold threatened to mar even the dignity of his funeral. Margaret's son, Richard, who was studying engineering at Harvard, foresaw that there would be a difficulty getting the specially built coffin — over seven feet long and of massive width — through the entrance to the Chanler vault in Trinity Cemetery. A hasty measurement confirmed this fear, and a more manageable casket had to be procured.

Bob's inherited fortune went to his daughters, but there were private benefactions, too. His library of more than five hundred art books, many of them rare and costly, was left to the Library of Decorative Arts at Cooper Union. And by blind bequest ostensibly to the attorneys, $50,000 was left in a trust to ensure that Clemence Randolph should have an income for life.

44 | "ALWAYS KEEP A LITTLE GOLD ON HAND"

During the 1920s Archie kept up his psychic investigations, although he was warned that he risked losing his way and blurring the line that separates conscious reality from the subconscious realm. This eventually happened to Archie. After years of testing his "X-faculty," he had become its tool. Straying too frequently and too far down subliminal lanes, he was finding it increasingly difficult to come back; and sometimes he did not, and the hallucinations became fixed.

Indications of this began to show up publicly during the 1920s. When Archie issued his final publication — a volume of the published reviews of his books, "both literary and psychological," bearing the title, *British and American Reviews of the Prose, Poetry, and Plays of John Armstrong Chaloner* — the preface contained this revealing statement: "The Author — though utterly unknown to the reading Public — is recognized by Reviewers in Great Britain and the United States — from the Thames to John O'Groat's Land in Britain, and the Atlantic to the Pacific over here — and recognized as a Poet and Dramatist — a blank verse dramatist — of very high class."

Archie meant every word of it.

In January 1928, he came to New York for the purpose of informing the American Association for the Advancement of Science about his amazing discovery that by psychic power he could change the color of his hair. He found the convention had adjourned the day before he arrived, so he decided that a press demonstration would do just as well.

The newsmen were ushered along a winding passage to a room at the back of the third-rate hotel where Archie was staying for reasons of economy. At the bellboy's secret knock, the door opened, and the representatives of the press were invited to enter. Even the most blasé were startled by the apparition that welcomed them. Over a tattered flannel nightgown, yellow with a green stripe, Archie had pulled a pair of red tights. About his waist a pair of gray flannel drawers was tied like a Masonic apron, and another pair of red drawers dangled gracefully down his back like a cavalier's cape. Physically he appeared fit despite his sixty-five years.

By way of preliminary, Archie stated that the millennium was at hand, and that he had been chosen by the spirit of the Prophet Elijah — acting through Napoleon, Charlotte Corday, and several others — to conduct the grand windup in New York City — a second Sodom and Gomorrah, given over to abominations like Prohibition and the tango. In order to awaken the city, he had come to demonstrate his magical power to change his hair from white to "black walnut." He invited the newsmen to observe his hair: it was luxuriant and undeniably white. Then he doused his hair in a wash basin full of water and gave it a vigorous toweling to show that there was no secret preparation on it.

He then commenced combing his hair steadily for half an hour with a chip of black walnut wood, all the while explaining the magical process in highly religious language. Although Archie's hair did begin to look somewhat darker, one reporter suggested that the accumulation of natural oil on the comb had produced the effect. Archie rejected the hypothesis. It was magic from Elijah, he said, and he'd give a thousand dollars to anyone who could account for it. "The millennium is here," he pronounced in closing.

As the embarrassed reporters sidled out the door, trying to avoid the eyes of the old man in the grotesque attire, his voice followed them down the hall: "A thousand dollars! A thousand dollars!"

This was Archie's last major encounter with the press. Back in Virginia he sank deeper into hallucinations, but gently, inoffensively, while still maintaining a workable relevancy with the people around him.

By the 1920s time seemed to be drawing Willie closer to home associations. Living in Paris, he made himself an information bureau and relayer of news about the friends and relatives who were constantly passing through France, going to or returning from cures and desultory travels.

His relationship with Beatrice remained cordial, although their separation was complete. Women had never been of primary interest to Willie; action, or a chance for action, was what truly seduced him, not feminine allure. He continued to be protectively fond of Beatrice, even though her interests bored him.

To the new generation of Chanlers, Uncle Willie had an air of mystery, with his great mantle of a cape and his stumping pegleg, but he also intimidated them. All their parents' generation seemed to have lived on a scale larger than their own, but Willie's amplitude was vast, beyond all the others.

When Maddie Aldrich, Margaret's daughter, went to the Sorbonne for graduate study, Willie invited her to a luncheon at Prunier's. When they entered, the entire restaurant staff bowed practically to the floor, and Willie was ushered without a word to the choicest table. Willie, who was on a strict diet, informed his niece in a tone that brooked no refusal: "Now, I am going to order the luncheon that I should like to enjoy, and you are going to eat it."

The meal began with oysters and stout, moved on to soup with Madeira, then to fish and white wine, pheasant and Bordeaux, and so through course after course, while Willie beamed in satisfaction, taking occasional sips of mineral water. Maddie had been subsisting on student fare — mainly snacks and sandwiches — and she struggled through the Gargantuan menu, trying to pay attention to the stream of advice being ladled out by her formidable uncle. It was mid-afternoon, it seemed to Maddie, before they were at last bowed out obsequiously and she was able to escape to her room and collapse.

Yet Willie's concern for his nephews and nieces was genuine and Conrad Chapman he especially admired and confided in. His older son, Willie, persisted in stuttering, which worried him, and he thanked Elizabeth and Jack Chapman for their efforts to correct the habit. Ashley, his younger son, worried Willie for different reasons — he had no vices!

In 1926 Willie's health took a turn for the worse, with what appeared to be a bad attack of gout. He tried the south of France, basking in the sun, but obtained no relief, and so returned to Paris, where he was confined to bed. In May he wrote Margaret that the doctors now thought it was some sort of infection. A month later, Willie wrote to Beatrice: "I think I told you that I had ten injections (one every other day) of a certain anti-streptococcus serum which certainly did me good. And now I am taking 12 more injections of different serums, as before, two days apart. The doctor (and believe me, he is one of the best in France) believes that when the second treatment is finished the bug will be killed. Then comes the long slow work of recovering my strength. The calf of my good leg for example has come down to the size of the handle of a tennis racket. . . ."

The former man of action fretted at his incapacity, and the petty business cares that occupied his time — two stone quarries and an ochre mine in the Midi, all marginal enterprises. How far they were from the grandiose undertakings he had projected in his buccaneering days. He tried to get his building stone used by Paris architects, without success, although he did provide the cornerstone for the new American church on the Quai d'Orsay.

Willie passed the period of his brother Wintie's death and turbulent burial in sickness, suffering constant pain and subsisting on miserable diets. His health and affairs both improved somewhat during 1927 and 1928, and he made periodic trips to the United States, only to suffer renewed illness and financial difficulties as the Depression set in.

Preoccupied as he was with business and personal frustrations, the return of Franklin Delano Roosevelt to political activity, after emerging from his contest with paralysis, aroused Willie's combativeness again. He was eager to put his counsels at the service of the newly elected Democratic governor of New York, but unfortunately his letter focused solely on his preoccupation with Jewish conspiracy. His letter drew a prompt reply, in which Roosevelt said that any letter Willie sent to him at the Executive Mansion would be opened by him personally, but this reassurance that Willie's correspondence would remain confidential was apparently not sufficient to persuade Willie to impart any of the promised valuable information.

In 1925 he had published a novel entitled *The Sacrifice*, under the pseudonym Robert Hart, which embodied in fictional form his belief that Jewish conspirators were planning to take over Western culture and government. Since that time, his feelings had only deepened, and at the time of writing Roosevelt he was in confidential communication with anti-Jewish Arab leaders, such as the Grand Mufti of Jerusalem.

During the 1920s Willie learned that his old friend Ludwig von Höhnel was struggling to survive on a hopelessly inadequate pension which postwar inflation was destroying altogether. Willie established a generous annuity for his friend, which he arranged to have continued even if he died first. It was faithfully paid to von Höhnel until he died in Vienna in 1942.

Willie's interest in family news became pronounced during 1931. In December he wrote to Elizabeth about those of their kindred who had passed through Paris: ". . . The other day Alida blew in like a tornado on her way to the Holy Land for Xmas, and thence to Egypt where she intends to spend the winter for her bronchitis; and she told me that her winters in Rome had been bad for her throat — I suspect, *entre nous*, that they had been bad for her pocket book; for you know that converts to the Sainte Religion are considered fair game on the grounds that no person can be really converted until he or she proves it by continually giving money. She looked reasonably well and in hilarious spirits. She was so pleased to see me that, before her departure (she was only here for nine hours) she sent me a nice little calendar — but it was for '31 instead of '32! Time has no meaning for dear Alida. . . .

"I suppose of course you saw Lewis before going south; it looks to me as if at length he has become a real convert to Bahaism — at least it keeps part of his mind occupied; and as you know, he loves to make speeches. A woman friend of mine went to one of the meetings and told me she cried at seeing such a fine man talk such bunk. . . . But I have no criticism to make, for anything that leads to even a little mental activity keeps the dear boy in good health. Over here he has his racing which takes him in the open air and gives him great interest; and then he reads a great deal of extremely light literature — he absolutely refuses to read anything serious, as he says it tires him. On the whole I think he is as well and as happy as he is meant to be; and that gives me great satisfaction.

"Beatrice is in much better health and is going shortly for her cure at Berne, which lasts I believe six weeks. . . . As for me, I am happy to say that my stomach seems to be at length very much better. But I suffered and am still suffering from repeated attacks of what doctors call 'gout' in my only good foot, which has kept me in bed for over a month lately. . . ."

The Depression was making inroads on Willie's income. He regretted that "things over here look as bad as in New York; though the French are a logical, brave people, who are accustomed to ups and downs and do not become hysterical when passing through a crisis whether in war or peace. In giving me advice on my coming of age, Uncle John Astor [grandson of the original John Jacob Astor] told me always to keep a little gold on hand in case there should be trouble and the banks should be closed for a few weeks. I am now following his advice and have a few hundred dollars in $5 and $10 American gold pieces. Uncle John said that there were certain daily expenses which were absolutely necessary — for example, the payment of servants, subordinates, etc. And it seems to me that this advice was sound. So if I were you, I would do what I have done. But don't talk about it to other people; because it might cause a little panic and withdrawals of money from the banks; not that I have any too great confidence in the stupid men who control our banks to-day."

Willie apprehended certain aspects of the world's economic and political turmoil acutely enough. In 1933 he predicted to his son that a war would erupt shortly in Spain, in a showdown between the Fascists and

Leftists. "The fight will be a tough one," he forecast, "and I think the military will win: but it will be a near thing." He also predicted another world war growing out of the conflict in Spain, and "should it be Armageddon, as I think it will, the anti-Christ will be Hitler, not Mussolini or anybody else."

In 1933 Franklin Delano Roosevelt had been elected President of the United States, the New Deal was in the making, and a world monetary conference was about to convene in London. Willie saw danger, and he alerted Elizabeth: "You have heard of Roosevelt's 'brain trust.' Some say he is guided by these people; others not. I hope not. For several of them — Tugwell, Bullitt, Berle and Moley — are extreme Socialists; and the curiously named Mordecai Ezekiel, whom no one seems to know, cannot care much for the U.S. Constitution. Some of these men are going to London. Now, it may interest you to know that there is a very strong organization in England called the 'Fabians,' and that nine members of the British Cabinet belong to this sect. The present leader of the Fabians is a Jew named Israel Moses Sieff; and I got passed to me the secret plan of the Fabians, which is to Bolshevize, not only Great Britain, but the U.S.A. — of course not exactly in the Russian Soviet form; but in a manner (as I said I have read the detailed plan) a little more adapted to the Anglo-Saxon mind, but which will result in the absolute loss of individual independence. . . ."

There was a postscript, thanking Elizabeth for a book about Talleyrand, whom Willie said he had always looked upon as a time-server and turncoat. However, Talleyrand "certainly kept France's flag flying," whereas the current politicians in Paris "Have lowered it in an unconscionable way. Anyway, I believe that with our present rapid means of communication, and with the centralized Jewish control of world affairs, it would be impossible for another real Talleyrand to appear."

A month later Willie wrote again, a letter filled with affection for the Chapmans and thanking them for the Talleyrand book: "He was a great old rascal, but certainly a great man. He reminds me very much of Themistocles as described in *Plutarch's Lives*; but Themistocles committed suicide in the end. I fancy Talleyrand was too lazy to do so."

His birthday on June 11, 1933, with Lewis was Willie's last. When John Jay Chapman died in November, Willie could only passively sympathize with Elizabeth, for he himself was gravely ill. He declined to alarm the family, however, and it was only at the end of February 1934 that Conrad Chapman, who had been with his uncle throughout the winter, notified

Beatrice that Willie had been dreadfully ill for weeks. On March 4, 1934, before Beatrice was able to reach his bedside, William Astor Chanler died in Mentone, on the Riviera.

By the desire of the family, his body was brought home, and at Margaret's behest he was given full family funeral honors in St. Mark's-in-the-Bouwerie. The service was attended by representatives of learned societies, fellow explorers, grizzled Spanish War veterans, ex-gunrunners, Tammany cronies, Cuban diplomatic and military dignitaries, and by George Galvin. Von Höhnel, forgotten relic of vanished imperial Austria, sent a heartfelt eulogy from Vienna, and the family turned out in all its branches. Even the members who were not speaking to each other joined in paying tribute. Willie's excitements had been theirs, they had shared in his fame; his shortcomings and his fantasies they were burying with him. Among all those gathered to say good-bye one feeling prevailed: try as they might, it was impossible to think of Willie Chanler as old.

All did not go as Margaret intended, however. She suspected that Alida meditated some profanation of the ritual, and indeed, Thomas Addis Emmet, Alida's youngest son, showed up with a large floral cross which Alida had secretly blessed and doused with holy water. During the confusion at the tomb, uptown at Trinity Cemetery, Margaret picked up the offensive bouquet and dumped it behind a wall. But after the mourners had departed, someone — no one ever knew who — recovered the disdained cross, brought it to the open vault, and laid it on Willie's coffin. The feat furnished the subject of a family ballad:

> In St. Mark's-in-the-Bowery, where Guthrie intones
> His weird incantations o'er Stuyvesant bones
> With theatrical spotlights of purple and blue
> And crimson and amber of delicate hue
> The Chanlers were gathered by Margaret's will
> To pay their last honors to dear Uncle Bill.
>
> From brother and sister from nephew and niece
> Comes many a fine horticultural piece
> On lily, sweet peas, gladiolus, and rose
> The deep amber spotlight religiously glows,
> When Aunt Alida's Tommy comes staggering in
> With a great floral cross reaching up to his chin.

Now Alida thought that her late atheist brother
Would roast in damnation of some sort or other
Unless e'er his dust was consigned to the grave
She made one last effort his soul for to save
So she'd taken the cross to be blessed by a priest
And its blossoms were seared by the mark of the beast.

But at the commitment Aunt Margaret stood
In the lee of the flowers, so placed that she could
Sniff the odor Papistical coming across
With a strong reek of Rome from Aunt Alida's cross
So she solemnly strode and removed the offence
And laid it away by a neighboring fence.

But after she'd gone, through somebody's fault,
The cross was put into the family vault.
So distilled papal poison will ever disturb
The repose of the Chanlers beneath the stone curb;
And the atheist William has found his last home
Amid flowers aspersed by the minions of Rome.

— Lawrence Grant White

45 | "IN THIS WAR NOBODY IS GOING TO GET HURT"

At The Merry Mills, Archie had drifted into a fantasy world, calmly, serenely, contentedly. He scarcely bothered about the abysmal muddle into which his affairs had fallen. He passed his days wandering through his fields and woods, chatting with the unpaid farm hands, or visiting neighboring estates, where he was always welcome. On Sundays he attended his church in a spirit of cheerful humility.

He continued to make haphazard benefactions when the means came to hand, although some misfired. In 1927 he offered to finance an expedition under the auspices of the Smithsonian Institution to observe an eclipse of the sun from a location in Norway. Professor S.A. Mitchell, director of the University of Virginia Observatory, came to The Merry Mills, at Archie's invitation, to discuss cost estimates and technical details. He arrived, as requested, at evensong, and was rather startled to be ushered into a room draped in black, where sat his host under a spotlight. Archie proceeded to entertain his guest by impersonating great figures of history, not omitting Napoleon. Every time the professor attempted to discuss the estimates, Archie drowned him out. The show went on for hours. The dazed doctor did not dare attempt to escape, because of the ferocious baying of the "burglar alarm" dogs outside as they circled the house in the darkness. When he was finally dismissed with punctilious courtesy, the reeling astronomer staggered back to his observatory and the expedition was never mentioned again.

Archie had long been sensitive to the danger in which isolated country houses stood from marauders. Dutchess County was terrorized in the early 1920s by the depredations of the Candle Gang, an organized band of house breakers, Sylvania being one of the houses entered. Margaret was besieged in Rokeby one night, until a posse of sheriff's men arrived to rescue her. The episode moved Archie to urge his sister to fortify Rokeby as he had fortified The Merry Mills, for her own preservation: "I had all my solid shutters — just like yours — covered on the inside with galvanized sheet iron — both upstairs & down — for a jointed ladder could be brought by the thieves, & the second story windows reached & entered with ease. The galvanized iron has a rather attractive effect, & need not, unless you prefer, be painted. It is folded up in daytime & covered by curtains at night anyway. This is my gesture to prevent you all from being murdered in your beds. Affectionately yours. P.S. Pass it on to the Chapmans etc."

The following day he followed up this advice with further details about armored doors, burglar-proof locks, and recommendations to bar and armor the cellar windows.

Archie was proud of any distinction earned by members of the family, and particularly praised Richard Aldrich's *Musical Discourse*, a collection of his music criticisms, when it appeared in 1929.

It was Margaret who kept closest in touch with her erratic "ex-brother," as Archie sometimes still styled himself. Elizabeth was again being troubled by recurrent illness, and had purchased a house in Charleston, where she and Jack spent the winter months.

Archie's financial situation at length reached the point of desperation, and he appealed, through his lawyers, for a family loan. But the Depression was drastically reducing the incomes of all, so they had Morris, the family lawyer, write to Archie: "If a judgment is taken against Mr. Chaloner and his income is attached so that he will not have enough to live on, they will be then inclined to contribute the necessary amount so that he will have enough to live on, but the amount to be contributed and how it will be done will be decided when the occasion arises."

The situation was further complicated by Archie's failure, or inability, to carry out his obligation to maintain St. Margaret's Home properly. Bills for repairs and upkeep went unpaid, and Margaret had to come to the rescue repeatedly. Finally, in December of 1932, she decided to visit The Merry Mills and see for herself how matters stood.

She traveled south by automobile, stopped over briefly at Archie's estate, drove on to Richmond, and there took the train to Charleston, to visit her sister. From Charleston she wrote her son, a student at Harvard: "I don't think he [Archie] has any sense of financial responsibility at all; has just drifted into the habit of shelving it; lives in old clothes and no comfort with some five people hoping for wages while the lawyers handle his income 'for taxes and

mortgage interest' as he expressed it. I naturally was only casual in my discussion of money-matters, saying we could not [afford to] go to town until
January etc etc. He was not in the least irritated, said the Sheriff is a kind
friend and will not hold a sale if some money is sent by Kosman [Chaloner's
lawyer], otherwise (laughing) 'You see how little I have that they could realize on.' He saw me in his bedroom lying on a low armchair with a rug over
his leg which was on a chair I think. His hair is very white, was not brushed,
and he had a patch over one eye. I stayed an hour and a half, making
Richmond at dusk. The darky who talked to William [her chauffeur] said
nobody is paid. I was received by a white man who looked at first as if he
thought I had come to make trouble, but who was soon telling me that 'The
General' has no money for gasoline or anything else. As his only pleasure in
motoring is to go as far as Washington and back of an evening, or rather
night, it must come somewhat expensive. I have no idea whether the general
stands for Armstrong or Buonaparte. It is a great consolation to have been,
because of the pleasure I gave, and because I now know just what I am dealing with."

The full story Margaret did not confide to paper. She had been
appalled by the condition of her brother's house. It was cluttered with the
debris of years — stacks of newspapers, clippings pasted on the walls, books
in tumbling piles thick with dust, framed reviews of his books, pictures of
people whose names he had forgotten, wallpaper peeling, scrawled placards
tacked to the doors ("Pls keep this d closed"). There was a bust of
Napoleon in the library, an engraving of the emperor over the mantle, and
a row of cheap plaster Napoleons in the hall. Heaps of Napoleonana
spilled from bookcases. In Archie's bedroom unopened parcels were
strewn about, with disorderly mounds of legal papers, and sheaves of messages transmitted by his subconscious. Surrounded by this indescribable
clutter, Archie vegetated cheerfully. He was by no means incapable mentally,
but retreated frequently to his subliminal world of fantasies. The only
touch of neatness in his appearance was his hair, which, although uncombed,
gave evidence of being trimmed regularly.

Margaret had confided her observations to her son rather than to her
husband, because her husband had recently had a serious heart attack and was
in no condition to cope with Chanler problems.

Margaret's trip to The Merry Mills set off rumors that she had taken over
Archie's affairs. She scotched those immediately, but did inquire whether the
hospital in Charlottesville had been paid for a long stay Archie had made there.

It had not, and Margaret paid the bill, just in time it turned out, for word came that Archie had become very ill, and Margaret had him taken back to the hospital. She also arranged for Beatrice to go and stay with him since she felt unable to leave Richard.

From Charlottesville Beatrice telephoned Margaret that the doctor's diagnosis of Archie's illness was "cancer in the spine, the most painful kind. There is also cancer at the base of both lungs, not painful, but mercifully likely to hurry the end. It may be seven months, or two months, or ten days."

Margaret withheld the news from her husband, who was recovering very slowly. Elizabeth wrote Archie a long, chatty letter: "We often talk of old times, & you play a great part in these reminiscences. Every time you enter some story, it is to the tune of pipes & timbrels! When Owen Wister talks of you, it is always the same thing — your wit, your flashing quickness, your altogether delightfulness as a companion, or as a mere contribution to the sparkle of some dinner table.

"Those were great days, the days of our youth. What I miss most in the intercourse with young people nowadays, is their lack of interest in conversation *per se*. It will come back in a generation or two, but it flags today. And that was our chief pleasure in life!

"This letter does not demand an answer. It is just to take you my love & to tell you how sorry I am that you are ill."

Too feeble to write himself, Archie dictated the reply to "Dearest Elizabeth," quoting with unconcealed feeling Wister's praise, and adding, with unquenchable conviction: "My health is decidedly better. I have had no more damnable pain and the doctors say I am to have none. I will give you a secret. You can tell it to Margaret — it is rather over the third sister's — Alida Emmet's head — who flopped to Romanism. Great times impend, and a wonderful international role awaits J.A.C. which will put the Chanler family to the historical front for all time. It is liable to occur any day."

Since Richard Aldrich's recovery was progressing satisfactorily in the spring of 1935 Margaret came to relieve Beatrice at her brother's bedside. Letters of sympathy had poured in, including a note from Castle Hill, in the well-remembered perfect script:

"Dear Archie,
"Mary Lewis has told me that you have been speaking very kindly of me, and that she thinks you would like to have a message from me. I send it from my heart. . . . I have thought of you so constantly for a long time, and night

and morning since your illness I have remembered you in my prayers. . . . Anything that I could do to please you I would do so gladly.

"I am sending you a charming photograph that I have kept all these years. I wanted so much for Elizabeth to have it, but I know she would not like it to come from me. So perhaps you would give it to her, if you think best.

"Please remember, dear Archie, anything that you would like me to do I would do gladly. I pray God to keep you close to Him.

AMÉLIE"

The photograph was one of Archie as a college student.

By a great effort, he scrawled out a response to this voice from another age, but the writing was so chaotic that the nurse transcribed it. It read:

"Princess Pierre Troubetskoy
"Castle Hill, Cobham, Va.

"Dear Princess,

"Thanks for your kind note and the sub-graduate photo of me for Elizabeth.

With long life, health, and happiness for the Prince and yourself.

J.A. CHALONER"

It was the last message written with his own hand. Margaret prodded relatives to come and make the oldest of the family feel that his place among them was secure. His mind remained clear and alert for the most part, and a nephew was surprised to find how entertaining and acute a talker his Uncle Archie could be.

In one conversation Margaret asked Archie whether he thought there would be a second world war. Instantly his manner changed. Pulling himself up in the bed, he drew up his knees and hugging them said earnestly: "There is going to be a hell of a war! And I am to be in charge. I have my men drilling now — out there."

He nodded toward the window and named an astronomical figure. Then with a sweet smile, he said: "But in this war nobody is going to get hurt."

Two days later, on June 1, 1935, he died. He was seventy-two.

Archie had requested that he be buried at The Merry Mills, beside the pool. His family preferred that he be buried in the churchyard of Grace Episcopal Church in nearby Keswick. Two years later, the rector of the church wrote Margaret inquiring whether anyone intended to put up a

Captain Winthrop Chanler with the Allied Expeditionary Force at Neufchateau, France. Photo July 1918.

Theodore Roosevelt and the cast of "A Children's Revolution," a play for children written by John Jay Chapman and produced as a benefit for a French soldiers relief fund organized by Beatrice Chanler. Willie Chanler, Jr., is at Roosevelt's left.

The Knickerbocker Club, New York City. A dinner in belated honor of Hubert W. Chanler's coming of age. From left: Lewis Chanler, Willie Chanler, Bob Chanler, Hubert Chanler, Lawrence Grant White, John Jay ("Jack") Chapman, Wintie Chanler and Richard Aldrich. John Winthrop Chanler, father of the Astor Orphans, was a founding member of the Club. Photo April 1924.

John Jay ("Jack") Chapman, Charleston, South Carolina. Photo ca. 1931.

Mrs. Stanford White (left) and Elizabeth Chapman arriving at Rokeby for the wedding reception of Maddie Aldrich and her husband Christopher Rand. Elizabeth is in mourning for her husband, who had died a few months before. Photo June 1934.

The Army Officers Training program at Plattsburgh, New York. This program for college-educated volunteers attracted an aging Lewis Chanler (left), and his young cousin Hamilton Fish. Of different political parties, both had recently served in the State Assembly from adjoining districts. Photo 1916.

Julie Olin Benkard at about the time she married Lewis Chanler. Photo ca. 1921.

Lewis Chanler. Photo ca. 1925.

Lewis Chanler (in white fedora) with a horse from his racing stable outside Paris. Photo ca. 1932.

Margaret Aldrich with her dog Lucky on the front steps at Rokeby. Photo ca. 1930.

Richard Aldrich. Photo ca. 1925.

Margaret Aldrich on the front porch at Rokeby. Photo 1945.

"The House of Fantasy," the two houses Bob Chanler consolidated into one great studio and residence on East 19th Street, New York City.

"Porcupines." A screen painted by Bob Chanler, that suggests his love of animals. Photo 1914.

Bob Chanler and his mistress Clemence Randolph. Photo ca. 1915.

Bob Chanler, standing in front of the house in Woodstock, New York, that he gave to Clem Randolph. Clem is seated in front with her left hand extended to pet a cat; behind the cat is Bob's second mistress, Lousie Hellstrom; to the left, smoking a pipe, is the artist Louis Bouché. Photo ca 1925.

At Arden House, Harriman, New York, the wedding of Edwin D. Morgan, Jr., the oldest grandchild of Alida and Temple Emmet, to Nancy Whitney, daughter of Cornelius Vanderbilt Whitney and Mrs. W. Averell Harriman. From left: groom, bride, bride's father, Alida Emmet, bride's mother, and Temple Emmet. Photo 1949.

Margaret Aldrich, at Rokeby, bids a visitor goodbye. She was in mourning for her son, Dickie, and died herself three months later at 92. Photo December 1962.

Alida Emmet in animated conversation in the drawing room of her Stony Brook house. Then 91, she died there at age 96. Photo Christmas 1964.

Rokeby, a view of the west elevation and the tower. "In my end is my beginning."
Photo ca. 1975.

stone marker: "I do not like to think of so wonderful a man lying in a nameless grave. Everyone here who knew him loved him."

Margaret promised that the family would remedy the omission before the end of the year, but wished to consult with Elizabeth regarding the inscription. The stone was placed, across the churchyard from the stone that Archie had placed over the grave of John Gillard, the man he had shot. The epitaph reads: "Blessed is the man who considereth the poor and needy."

The Virginia countryside missed "The General," and none more than the legatees of his will. Among those listed in a recent codicil were the entire staff of The Merry Mills — supervisor, farmer, cook, and laborers, with their wives and children; all were left the full amount of their accrued unpaid wages and a present of cash besides. But when the estate was proved, it was found to be bankrupt. Farm, home, and the remnants of Archie's personal property were auctioned off, but the proceeds could not pay the obligations. His inheritance in trust funds, being untouchable, went to his sisters and only surviving brother, Lewis, and to the heirs of those siblings who had died before him.

One legacy that did accomplish its object was the Chaloner Paris Prize Foundation. A year after his death, the trustees obtained court permission to change the terms of the award, allowing it to be given for study in this country, instead of exclusively abroad. The Fund is still in operation, subsidizing talented young artists just as Archie intended.

46 | "TAKE A DRAFT ON YOUR FAITH"

One member of the Chanler circle who had dropped from sight in the years after Bob's death was his former wife Julia. The family had never known very much about Julia, and they had never taken pains to learn. They were hardly aware, for instance, that she had written three novels in German, that she painted very well, or that she numbered among her devoted friends many distinguished musicians and not a few artists.

Shortly after Bob's death in 1930, Julia had made a break with all her former associations. She notified her daughters that she was retiring to a suite in the National Hotel in Lucerne, and she wished them neither to see nor to write to her from then on. The daughters did not visit, but they did, now and then, write, although no reply came.

In May 1936, Julia's younger daughter, Julia, was in Aix-en-Provence with her husband, when she had a dream in which her mother told her that the next day she was to undergo an operation and that she did not expect it to succeed. But she was content and at peace, she said, because her father was coming to fetch her. In the dream her mother went on to say that she had wished to see her daughter, to give her her blessing and tell her of the love she had never been able to express adequately. Then she asked Julia not to come to the funeral, because she would be the only stranger there, and the resemblance between them would disturb her friends.

The next morning Julia told her husband about the dream, and they decided to wait and see what happened. At eleven o'clock that evening, Julia was paged. It was the manager of the National Hotel calling from Lucerne. He proceeded with great embarrassment until Julia interrupted and said she knew that her mother did not wish her to come, either then or later, and she would abide by her mother's wish. She did ask that he send her her grandmother's prayer books. Julia Chanler died, and her daughter received the prayer books. She did not attend the funeral, a fact which caused comment but for which she offered no explanation.

After her husband's death in 1933, Elizabeth Chapman recruited Mark A. DeWolfe Howe to prepare a volume on her husband and assisted him in his work. She died a few months before *John Jay Chapman and His Letters* was published to admiring reviews, initiating a positive reevaluation of Chapman as a moralist and critic that was soon amplified by Edmund Wilson and others.

Once this memorial project approached completion, Elizabeth put her affairs in order and settled down to die. She was not morbid, merely calmly resolute. She considered her work in life completed, and she was content to depart. Some time before Chapman's death, they had moved into a smaller house on the grounds of Sylvania, a cottage they named Good Hap, leaving the main house to their son, Chanler Armstrong Chapman, and his wife and children. Elizabeth had always been "sensible" about money. She liked comfort and elegance, but not luxury, and she hated extravagance. She had always contributed liberally to philanthropies, never less than ten percent of her income and usually closer to twenty. When traveling in Europe she was always scrupulously careful not to allow herself to be cheated, as just another "rich American." Now, in her widowhood, in 1935, she took her leave of worldly matters by disposing of her entire income except for $5,000 a year for the next five years — the allowance she was reserving for her own necessities, her total income at that time being some nine or ten times that amount. Her capital, Sylvania, everything, she transferred to her heirs.

In the late spring of 1937, Conrad Chapman, her stepson, cabled word from London of his forthcoming marriage there, and Elizabeth steeled herself to make one more Atlantic crossing. Conrad begged her not to come, knowing her hold on life to be tenuous, and she no longer had any friends in London who might care for her. Much against her wishes, she finally yielded to this sound advice. Late in May Conrad received a cable saying that Elizabeth seemed to be sinking. He caught the first ship for New York, but arrived only in time for the funeral. The governess who had lived with the Chapmans for years, Miss Montgomery, described her death: "She willed herself to die. It is strange, but your mother wanted to die. She would say to me when I came in, in the morning, 'I want to die. Don't you want to die?' And I would say, 'No, I do not want to die.' She went into a coma, with no illness that the doctors could find. They kept her alive by intravenous feeding for a few days, and then she just ceased to live."

The will of "Queen Bess" had always been strong. She had allotted herself only enough money to support her for five years and had lived only two of the five, breathing her last at Good Hap on June 5, 1937, aged seventy-one.

Margaret did not attend Elizabeth's funeral, and her absence was almost as startling as her sister's death. The reason she did not was because she herself was under medical care, prostrated by the news of her husband's sudden death in Rome three days before, on June 2, 1937. Richard had seemed fully recovered from his heart attack and had sailed to Europe to attend a reunion with his two brothers and their sister. Shortly after arriving, Richard was stricken again, collapsed, and died. He was seventy-three. So, ironically, Margaret, who had remained behind in order to be close to Elizabeth, was prevented from attending her sister's burial by the shock of her husband's death.

This double bereavement left only Margaret, Alida, and Lewis of the original eleven Chanler children, and Margaret had not spoken to either Alida or Lewis for years. She heard from them indirectly, and heard about them often, through relatives and mutual friends. This persistent estrangement seemed preposterous to some of the younger members of the family; but deeming it required by loyalty to principle, Margaret remained inflexible.

Lewis had adjusted to his banishment from Rokeby without recrimination. Although he was conventional enough, he had always gone his own way and had cared little what people might say. And he was both independent and proud. With all his brothers, including Archie, he had remained friendly if not intimate, and the same with Elizabeth. Alida and the Emmets had been rather outside his orbit, for both Julie's presence and her devotion to Bahaism formed an obstacle, but there was no personal estrangement. Bob had liked Julie and shared her response to Eastern religions, and Lewis had always displayed the most careful courtesy toward Bob's friends.

The breach between Lewis and his children had been quite healed over, thanks in part to the tactful intercession of Elizabeth and Leslie, the wife of Lewis's son Stuyvesant. As Stuyvesant's brother, William, had reported to his Aunt Elizabeth: "Leslie met Papa in Paris, & went to lunch with them [Lewis and Julie], & all went off very nicely, she said. This was a most fortunate thing, as it was a much easier way to 'break the ice' than it would have been here in New York. . . ."

A complete rapprochement followed, and Lewis became a favorite with his daughter-in-law.

Lewis took Julie's absorption in Bahaism with good grace. When she wished to visit the holy places of the cult, Lewis had forthwith embarked with her for Egypt and Palestine. As time went on, the Bahai cause became quite congenial to him, although he did not adhere to it formally. Julie was immersed in it, and ardently sought to further its advance. In order to spread a knowledge of the founder, Abdul Baha, and his teachings, she organized the New History Society, with headquarters in the Chanlers' town house at 132 East 65th Street. Determined to "make Bahaism fashionable," she also organized lectures at the Ritz-Carlton and Park Lane Hotels that drew a smart audience, but eventually led to a separation from the official Bahai organization. Julie and her associates identified themselves as a new group, setting up a Bahai center, bookshop, and meeting place for young people called The Caravan.

To these activities Lewis lent his benign sanction and occasional assistance. His life gradually had settled into a placid and not uninteresting routine. His homes in Paris and New York were well ordered, and his circle of friends was wide. Always a handsome man, his appearance improved as time went by. In Paris, he had his racing stable, and he spent much of his time at his clubs — the Knickerbocker in New York and the Travellers in Paris. Although nursing the grudge of party regularity against Franklin Delano Roosevelt in 1932, Lewis had, before the New Deal was far advanced, become a convert and enthusiastically supported Roosevelt from then on. Occasionally messages recalling the old days in Dutchess County passed between the two men; and Lewis encouraged his son Willie, who was becoming interested in politics, in organizing young people's clubs for Roosevelt. Roosevelt welcomed this approach as a means to overcome the prejudice against the Democratic party as one made up predominantly of "saloon-keepers and the uneducated."

Domestically Lewis became more and more the benevolent grand seigneur. At the dinner table he monopolized the conversation. If, upon returning home from his club, he found Julie still in earnest conference, he would arbitrarily rescue her. First he would boom, "Nearly seven! Aren't you going to dress for dinner?" If the conversation went on, he would repeat the admonition from upstairs. And if that failed to terminate the talk, he would sing out, "Your bath is running!" That always worked because Julie knew that the bath was indeed running and that Lewis would not turn the water off.

When young men came courting Elsie Benkard, his stepdaughter, Lewis would enforce the curfew time by appearing in his long nightshirt at the top of the stairs and singing out cheerfully, "Pretty late, isn't it?"

Lewis liked to quote his brother Willie's injunction, "Take a draft on your faith," and he used the principle in the increasing involvement of Julie with the cause of world peace. In 1932 she was elected president of the Women's Peace Society, and was active in promoting the War Resisters League, whose members were pledged not to fight in the event of a new war. Lewis, although inclined toward pacifism, would not follow his wife all the way in this crusade, believing that under certain circumstances he should and would fight. But he did march in an Anti-War Parade along Fifth Avenue in the spring of 1933 — not in the League's uniform green shirt, as the ranks behind him marched, but impeccably dressed, Homburg-hatted, tall and spare, jauntily swinging his cane.

When the Depression drastically reduced Lewis's income, he gave up the Paris apartment. Although he admitted that he knew nothing about business, and certainly was not going to learn, he felt that somehow the family lawyers had not played fair in springing on him the announcement that his income had been reduced from around $70,000 a year to a paltry $21,000. He suspected some mismanagement and he grumbled as he and Julie put severe economies into effect. Yet even after trimming expenses, the East 65th Street house retained an indispensable "skeleton staff" of cook, butler, parlor maid, and Julie's personal maid.

Lewis kept himself in trim by strenuous exercise, daily walking twice around the reservoir in Central Park. Once in a while he would encounter his former wife, Alice, who also sunned herself in the park; Lewis would blush bright red and stride past without a sign of recognition. He could never understand why Alice had not remarried. "I thought she was going to marry a duke," he told his son. "I thought that was why she consented to a divorce."

He was cheered by his sons' success. Stuyvesant had done well in banking, and William, a lawyer, in 1937 was appointed Corporation Counsel of New York City by Mayor Fiorello LaGuardia. This particularly pleased Lewis, for it seemed to carry on his own legal-political career.

Year after year, Lewis grew into the most nearly aristocratic of all the Chanlers — aristocratic in the sense that he viewed life and people with the detachment and freedom of a man conscious of his superiority and therefore at ease with all classes. He had long been disabused of illusions regarding his sister-in-law Daisy, but he maintained an even disposition toward her with patrician indolence. He was disinclined to write letters, but when Daisy's memoirs, *Roman Spring*, appeared, he penned a long letter of complaint to his sister Elizabeth, indignant about many of her allusions to Wintie's family.

Lewis had been a persistent pipe smoker all his adult life, convinced that the habit was harmless, whereas smoking cigarettes was not. When he became bothered by an apparently abscessed jaw, his doctor diagnosed a dental infection. But a thorough examination revealed cancer, already so far advanced that no cure could be expected. To cover his doctor's original error, Lewis falsified the date on which the trouble had started. To Julie he gallantly pretended that recovery was certain, although he knew that his time was short. He was more open with his son Stuyvesant, assuring him that "I am perfectly willing to pass out with a smile — much better than staying on as an invalid."

The family reciprocated his pretense of eventual recovery, although they knew the truth. On July 31, 1941, Lewis wrote a brief note to Stuyvesant:

"Dear Stuyve: Don't bother to call up. I am going to the hospital for a course of treatments on my jaw. I hate the idea but there it is. Your aff Father. Best to Leslie."

Still pretending, he returned to the hospital several times, and was there on February 28, 1942, when Julie found him in good spirits. He greeted the doctor affably and seemed on the point of making a speech, but growing drowsy, drifted off to sleep, and his life ebbed away. He was seventy-two.

And again the family, who had never shirked a fight, became embroiled in a conflict over where Lewis's funeral should be held and where he should be buried. Stuyvesant Chanler, as his father's heir, was determined that the ceremony should be held in St. Mark's-in-the-Bouwerie, of which Lewis had been a warden. Julie, the widow, was firmly resolved that Lewis should be buried with Bahai rites. And the bishop of New York was adamant that no cult service should be held in his sanctuary. To complicate matters further, the Masons — Lewis had been a 33rd degree Mason — expected to participate ritually, while the Bar Association and numerous political dignitaries expressed a desire to attend or be represented. A message of condolence came from the White House, and by order of New York's Governor Herbert H. Lehman the flags on state buildings were flown at half-staff.

Finally a compromise arrangement was worked out: the funeral would take place in St. Mark's, with the Episcopal service, and a Bahaist would be permitted to recite a simple prayer, while the Masons and other interested delegations would be accommodated appropriately.

The resulting crowd overflowed the church, and the pews reserved for the family were quickly filled. Margaret, starchily erect, arrived late; nothing would have kept her from attending the funeral of the brother with whom she had not communicated for the last twenty years. The relatives watched tensely as an usher led her to the only vacant seat remaining — in the front pew, beside her equally excommunicate sister, Alida Emmet. While onlookers held their breath, the sisters stoically ignored each other; and when forced to share the same hymn book, did so, each holding one half and directing her gaze pointedly in the opposite direction.

Midway through the service, a side door opened, and a diminutive man wearing a white headpiece suggesting a chef's hat, tripped up the pulpit steps and delivered a monologue that completely mystified the Masons in their regalia, the frock-coated politicians, and all other non-Bahaists present. The coffin was so lushly buried in flowers that the effect was theatrical rather than religious, but the consensus was that Lewis was receiving a proper sendoff.

He was not to lie in the family vault. Julie's wishes prevailed, and he was buried in her family's plot at Glen Cove. But in a way he was linked ancestrally there, too, for Julie's grandfather, S.L.M. Barlow, had been the beloved friend of Lewis's grandfather Sam Ward.

47 | "IS LOVE DIMINISHED?"

It was Margaret who grieved most deeply for Lewis: he had been her nursery companion, and attached to Rokeby and its associations as only she was herself. Every room in the mansion spoke of Lewis — Lewis as a boy, lording it over his "twin sister" — Lewis as an eager law student, spending happy weekends alone in the house with Jex, the dog — Lewis accepting his nominations for lieutenant governor and governor of the state on the porch — Lewis as a voice in the affairs of the church at Red Hook, and as the leader of the Chanler Democratic Club of Barrytown — Lewis, Lewis, everywhere. But principle must take precedence over affection, and Margaret was not supple, not pliant: her faith, when given, was given whole, entire, undivided, and unwaveringly; and as a result, her life was becoming a wasteland of frustrated affection.

She had cut herself off from so many dear to her because of their transgressions against the concepts upon which she believed the purity — indeed, the sanity — of society rested — the concept of family. Her very sense of being more and more isolated from friends and kindred caused her to cling the more tenaciously to her rejections, and even suggesting the possibility of giving way would produce in her an almost panic reaction.

Alida had long wanted to heal the breach with her sister, but her ill-timed, furtive attempts had only widened it. Once, when staying at Sylvania, Alida had offered to accompany Olivia, Elizabeth's daughter-in-law, on a round of neighborhood errands, even though a stop at Rokeby was included. Alida protested that she would wait in the car while Olivia dispatched her business in the house, "and Margaret will never know."

But while her niece was inside the house, Alida, who was addicted to impulses, got the idea that this might be the psychological moment to "break the ice." Darting into the hall, she dropped her card on the table, and skipped back to her seat before Olivia returned. Some time later a housemaid noticed Alida's card and took it to Margaret, who instantly guessed what had happened, and in a blinding rage she dashed off a furious note to Temple Emmet: "Let there be no more of these papal invasions!" read the stormy interdict, which went on for pages. Emmet was completely baffled, knowing nothing of what had caused it, and the Emmet household cried out against their aunt. No one was more astonished by the uproar than Alida herself, when it was all recounted to her.

After seeing the cause of women's suffrage triumph, Margaret had taken up the cause of militant prohibition, and had waged a bitter fight against repeal of the Constitutional amendment outlawing the traffic in alcoholic liquors. Two of her brothers, Willie and Robert, had destroyed themselves by drink, she believed, and she lumped rum with Romanism as twin menaces in her stern appeals for retention of the prohibition laws. She would have no appeasement, no halfway measures, no yielding to the specious arguments of Americans "who go to the Vatican for their religion, to France for their expensive wines, to Carlsbad for their expensive cures." The scenes in the hard-drinking, "scofflaw" society around her she deplored, and she preached her own doctrine of piety and self-discipline.

If with regard to the conventions, social observances, and private morality Margaret was an anachronism in the "Roaring Twenties," in other respects, especially politically, she was much in tune with the times, even advanced in her views and sympathies. During the Thirties she ardently supported the New Deal, not merely because of friendship with President Roosevelt, but because of her pronounced liberalism. She was a close friend of Franklin Roosevelt's mother, Sara Delano Roosevelt, and visited often at Hyde Park. Social legislation she took to heart, and one of the only two times her own daughter ever saw her in tears was at the defeat of a New Deal measure in Congress.

The second time Maddie saw her mother cry was after the death of her Scots maid, Ellen Dalton, known universally as Ella. Ella had succeeded Mary Meroney as the dominant personality of Rokeby's domestic staff. Silent, white-haired, always dressed in black, she moved about the house energetically, running "a tight ship." The family thought that Ella, who was well educated, had been probably Margaret's closest friend: both were austere, brusque in manner, unsentimental, yet warmly affectionate underneath, and they understood each other perfectly. Ella died while Margaret and her family were touring in Europe in 1921, and Bob's daughter Julia, as the only family member at Rokeby, had been obliged to arrange the funeral. Several years afterward, Maddie came upon her mother sitting silent and alone, weeping. The astonished girl asked what could be the matter, and the answer was a sob: "I miss Ella!"

Margaret once confided to her daughter that she believed all the Chanlers felt most at ease with friends of a slightly inferior social class. They had friends of their own class, of course, some dear and trusted ones; but the most intimate were a class somewhat below themselves. To Maddie that explained Ella.

From her childhood, Margaret had been taught to abhor idleness. Always, actively or meditatively, one should occupy one's self with either good works of self-improvement. "I have tried for many years to live my life in relation to what I call Productive Time," she wrote. "I have considered as Productive Time all household cares, hospitality, correspondence, reading, and study; the conducting of societies, public speaking, and the intake of music or other art. . . .

"I have considered as unprofitable time certain relaxations, like aimless conversation with those that talk about people; card playing in the daytime; the reading of desultory books or magazine articles; and the multiplication of activities chosen because of companionship with those who are conducting them. . . ."

Changes came rapidly in Margaret's personal life during the Thirties. In 1934 had been the marriage of Margaret's daughter to Christopher Rand, a writer. Then in 1939, Margaret's only son, Richard Chanler Aldrich, had married Susan Kean Cutler, linking the Chanlers and Aldriches with the Hamilton Fish family on the southern reaches of the Hudson. Margaret's hopes were centered upon young Dick: he was to carry on at Rokeby, preserving unbroken the family ownership that General Armstrong had envisaged when he built the rugged old house. Dick's wedding present was the formal announcement of his mother's intention to leave Rokeby to him, with all its contents; to Maddie, as an equivalent, was to be left the New York house.

The arrival of grandchildren in both families pleased Margaret immensely: they ensured the line of succession, of family and of Rokeby. And she needed these reassurances as more and more rifts occurred in the family web. In 1940, Lewis's son Stuyvesant decided to build a house at the renamed

Orlot. In view of Orlot's proximity to Rokeby, Stuyvesant's wife, Leslie, wrote to Margaret making clear her loyalty to Lewis, under banishment from his boyhood home.

"My dear Aunt Margaret,"
"Feeling as I do, I think it best not to come to Rokeby while you are there. I love Stuyve's father so much it is impossible for me to feel comfortable with someone who has treated him with so much unkindness, and in his own old home where he is not allowed to come.

"While he was in good health and spirits one could treat his banishment from Rokeby with a certain levity, though it was never really very funny — but now that he is so ill, so brave and without hope, I cannot bring myself to do other than write you this letter, as I should have done many uneasy months ago. Hard hearts are catching, you know, and mine is like a stone.

Yours ever,
LESLIE CHANLER"

Margaret answered with dignity, but also self-justifying rationalization:

"My dear Leslie:
"Many thanks for your consideration in sending me what must have been a sad and difficult letter for you to write.

"Of course I will neither go to Orlot or telephone your house. So far from forbidding his presence at Rokeby have I been, that twice within recent years Stuyve's father has had communications from me letting him know that as far as I am concerned his desertion has never taken place. He decided during the World War to vanish out of my life. I realized this as time went on without seeing or hearing from him. Somewhat to my surprise the lines of separation held when I was at death's door with mastoiditis in 1922. . . . People must marry into a family without knowing much about what has gone on before, and I do not want you to think that I am annoyed with you. Especially when in this neighborhood should you both be able to forget the hideous strain somewhat, and it is therefore better for you not to see your affectionate

AUNT MARGARET"

The obstacle, of course, had been Lewis's refusal to go where his wife, Julie, would not be received. The practice that Margaret had resorted to from youth — shutting out of her mind whatever was too agitating — had caused her to invert the issue and lay the initiative for the estrangement, and responsibility for the suffering it had entailed, squarely upon Lewis.

During all the estrangements, Rokeby had been kept sedulously open to all Margaret's nieces and nephews, without reference to any differences she might be having with their parents. And this free association with the new generation of her family had been a joy and a consolation to her. Family was bedrock.

Ironically, it was Lewis's death in 1942 and the funeral that led to a reconciliation between the surviving sisters. The spectacle of the women sharing the same hymn book but not facing each other seemed so ridiculous that one niece finally blurted out that she was tired of shuttling back and forth between Rokeby and Stony Brook to see both aunts, of whom she was equally fond, and that the time had come for Alida and Margaret to mend their quarrel. It took another decade, but then the sisters discovered that each had moderated her theological views in minor but crucial ways. In the Chanler way, without ado, recrimination, or apologies, the two came together and picked up just where they had left off forty years before.

The first encounter took place on neutral territory, at the Colony Club in New York. Margaret spent several hours with her sister catching up on decades years of gossip. Alida was charming and Margaret was amiable, and the visit was successful. On the drive home, a niece asked Margaret her impression of Alida, after all these years of separation. Margaret thought a moment, then burst out: "That hideous old woman!" Gradually it came out that she had been mentally picturing her sister as the beautiful, youthful matron she had been, not a woman of eighty. The reconciliation was permanent, the threads being picked up without further comment.

In 1939 public recognition of Margaret's public service had come in the form of a special Congressional gold medallion for her work during the Spanish-American War. Members of both the Aldrich and Roosevelt families gathered at Hyde Park on December 17 for luncheon and then President Roosevelt ceremoniously handed the medal to "one of my very old friends and close neighbors." Recalling that as a schoolboy he had tried to enlist in 1898, but had been prevented by an attack of mumps, Roosevelt joked that the medal was going to "the one who got there." He read from the act authorizing the medal and a similar posthumous award to Anna Bouligny,

Margaret's associate, that the two women "at their own expense went to Puerto Rico and nursed military patients . . . establishing six hospitals and treating 142 men without the loss of a single life among their charges."

It was a handsome tribute, and in a clear voice Margaret expressed her appreciation. Her son beamed as photographs were taken of his mother with the President who had been boosted into political life with Chanler help. In reporting the event, the newspapers listed Mrs. Aldrich's many public activities — Red Cross organizer, former president of the Women's Municipal League, founder and president of the girls' branch of the Public Schools Athletic League, a director of the Legal Aid Society, vice president of the Dutchess County Health Association and the Red Hook Nursing Society, trustee of Christ Church in Red Hook, and other positions of public concern.

Another World War came, and armies of young men died. Margaret's son served in the Navy, and numerous nephews and cousins were active in the military forces. On February 9, 1944, during the Italian campaign, a bomb, accidentally dislodged from an American bomber flying north over Florence, exploded in the garden where Lina Cavalieri was sitting, ending her life. She was seventy, and since her retirement from the stage had been reported to be a member of the inner circle around Mussolini. Her death was not mourned at Rokeby.

In June 1945, another echo of bygone days sounded when Amélie Rives died at Charlottesville at eighty-one. She had continued to turn out books and plays until 1930, with diminishing success. Prince Pierre Troubetskoy had died a decade before, only a year after Archie.

Then in 1946 Beatrice Chanler, Willie's widow, succumbed aboard a train on the way to her Maine summer home. During World War II she had been active in relief work, particularly as president of the Friends of Greece. For her service she was posthumously awarded the Order of the Phoenix by the Greek government, and her funeral was delayed to give time for the decoration to be flown from Athens and placed, with her Legion of Honor cross, upon her coffin. Margaret deeply felt her loss, for she had always liked this public-spirited sister-in-law.

Margaret had become quite deaf, and devised her own ways of coping with the handicap. To use the telephone, she would ring a number, and when the person answered, would say what she had to say, and hang up. In church, when she thought the rector had preached long enough, she would shut off her hearing aid and loudly whisper a line from Donne: "If the Preacher tedious be, God takes the text and preaches patience." As her friends died, she found herself attending more and more funerals, until one time she overheard two women speculating in loud whispers "who would be next." Believing that she was totally deaf, they wondered aloud "whether Margaret wouldn't be the next to go." After that she avoided funerals.

With small children she had the knack of pleasing, and she was devoted to her grandchildren. She would read to them, starting with the Victorian-age children's books that she had read, then juvenile stories, and on to Scott, Dickens, Cooper, and Shakespeare — all the classics that lined the walls of Rokeby library to the ceiling. Her tolerance had grown broader and her tactfulness was sometimes surprising. Her Hungarian cook had a boy about the age of her grandsons, and Margaret included the boy in her nightly readings. Once, when reading *Barnaby Rudge*, she skipped over several passages. Her grandsons, who had lost the thread of the story, asked her why she did it. Privately she told them that she had omitted the strongly anti-Catholic talk, so as not to give pain to the cook's little boy. Later she paid for the child's education in a good Catholic preparatory school and through college.

But though her religious tolerance had broadened, she remained firm in her defense of the usages of her own Low Church Episcopalianism. Margaret's defense of her principles suffered a heavy blow when Maddie and Christopher Rand were divorced, and Maddie remarried. Margaret maintained communication with her daughter, but she refused to meet the second husband, Byron DeMott, or to acknowledge the marriage. Letters from Rokeby to Maddie were addressed to "The Mother of the Rand Children," at the proper street number in Santa Barbara.

In 1958 Margaret's idiosyncratic memoirs, *Family Vista*, were published by the Dutchess County Historical Society; they were "dedicated to my Descendants: May their Hearts beat high for Faith, Family and Opportunity."

In December 1952 Daisy Chanler had died in New York at a stalwart ninety-one. Until her eightieth year she continued to ride, plaintively pleading to be allowed to jump "a few little fences," although her eyesight was failing. Death finally unseated her, and she was laid to rest beside Wintie at Geneseo. Then in 1955 Alice Chanler, Lewis's first wife, died; she had lived to be eighty-seven. And in 1961 Lewis's second wife, Julie, died at age seventy-eight.

The lionesses of the pride were proving tougher than the Chanler lions. On October 31, 1960, Margaret turned ninety. The event demanded a party, and the delighted nonagenarian described the festivities at Rokeby to one of Wintie's daughters:

"Dearest Beatrice:
"I must tell you about the celebration of the fact that I am now ninety years old! . . . We had a luncheon of 20 . . . Laura [White] represented your father, Chanler Chapman his mother, Stuyve Chanler his father, and so on. One child or grandchild from each of us. I get confused with too many people so limited it. My sister-in-law Amey Aldrich [Richard's sister] gave me the most wonderful present. She brought on from California my only daughter! . . . ."

One year later, on November 5, 1961, fate dealt Margaret perhaps her severest blow, when her son, Richard, died suddenly. All her plans had to be revised: Rokeby was left to her son's three children, who had been imbued with its spirit from their toddling days.

The months thereafter passed in diminishing activity. Margaret traveled to New York to help Amey Aldrich celebrate her own ninetieth birthday, the elder Margaret taking a quiet pride in her seniority. At home, Margaret kept in touch with events, watched over the farm, wrote letters to the newspapers, prodded the rector, and received such visitors as came out of ancient friendship or modern curiosity.

Loneliness often weighed upon the erect, unbending old woman. Where was the world she had known? So many graves, and in the house so many voices audible to her alone when she turned off her hearing aid. The estrangement from Lewis still hurt. Yet she did not complain, but went about her affairs, her mind clear, current, and inquiring to the last. And so it was a surprise to everyone when, in the spring of 1963, before the frost was out of the Rokeby field, she briskly took to her bed and in her last show of impatience died. The date was March 19, and she was well advanced into her ninety-third year.

Her funeral was held with the rites she approved in Christ Church, Red Hook, and then she was taken to the Chanler vault in Trinity cemetery, to rejoin her parents.

After her death, among her papers, was found a sonnet that revealed something of the silent anguish with which she had lived. Written in pencil, it read:

Must I then hate him since that horrid tale?
He told me bears were underneath my bed;
I believed everything he ever said.
A woman made him sin, and he would quail
At the sight of me — is love diminishèd?
He knew 'twas wrong — his wife was not yet dead;
But my great love for him need never fail.

Now he is gone to rest and I alone
Continue our companionship on earth,
A comfortless old age — to see him young,
Doing great things in law, and then among
State government, will always make me prone
To love one who was near me in our birth.

Nov. '62 — L.S.C.

"L.S.C." — Lewis Stuyvesant Chanler — the brother she had loved best.

48 | A NEW WORLD

Alida alone was left. Alida, the child who had clutched her father's hand that day in 1876 when the family had first arrived at Rokeby — lovely, scatterbrained, chattering Alida, for whom family business had been "over her head" — Alida had outlived them all.

Temple Emmet had died in 1957 at eighty-nine, shortly after Alida and he had celebrated sixty years of marriage. After Margaret's death in 1963, Alida's birthdays glided by with tranquil regularity — ninety-two, ninety-three, ninety-four. She had taken to receiving visitors in her bedroom, but on festive occasions she would don a striking gown and join the company downstairs, alert and full of fun. Children, grandchildren, great-grandchildren surrounded her, with a multitude of nieces, nephews, and cousins.

To them she provided a vision of the old life at Rokeby. She would speak of the house, how she had known it as a child and then as a young woman, eager to escape. The grief she had suffered at the death of her playmate, Egerton, was still vivid to her. She would tell of the sing-songs with her sisters and brothers in the home parlor, and the setter bitch that howled — of Cousin Mary Marshall, sad, resigned, and stern — of the rules of etiquette — and Old Black Jane, sweeping the billiard room — Hade the coachman, and falling off ponies — the awesome guardians, seldom seen, always felt — the servants — William the butler who borrowed the children's savings and did not pay back — the shock of her brother Marion's death at St. Paul's — the goats and rabbits and fights around the dinner table — the governesses — Mr. Bostwick, the tutor — Mary Meroney — the high-bred manners, and the voices, those Chanler voices . . .

It had been a long, long time.

At ninety-five Alida looked striking in her portrait as one of a gallery of great American ladies that was published in *Life* magazine. At ninety-six her birthday came and went . . . and then, almost without preamble, the flame flickered out.

The date was August 31, 1969, and so utterly was she of a vanished world that the newspapers found little to say about Alida Beekman Chanler Emmet except that she had been the last surviving member of New York's once-famous original "Four Hundred." The "Four Hundred?" What was that? But what was "society" any more?

The door of Rokeby stood open to a new world.

FOR FURTHER READING

GENERAL:

John Armstrong, Jr., 1758–1843: A Biography
     By C. Edward Skeen. Syracuse: Syracuse University Press, 1981.

The Astors
     By Harvey O'Connor. New York: Alfred A. Knopf, 1941.

Sam Ward: "King of the Lobby"
     By Lately Thomas. Boston, Houghton Mifflin Company, 1965.

A Pride of Lions: The Astor Orphans
     By Lately Thomas. William Morrow & Company, New York, 1971.

Three Saints and a Sinner: Julia Ward Howe, Louisa, Anne and Sam Ward
     By Louise Hall Tharp. Boston: Little, Brown and Company, 1956.

At the Top of Their Game
     By Robert H. Boyle. Piscataway, NJ: Winchester Press, 1983.

RELATING TO ARCHIE:

Four Years Behind the Bars of "Bloomingdale," or the Bankruptcy of Law in New York
     By John Armstrong Chaloner. Roanoke Rapids, NC:
     Palmetto Press, 1906.

Scorpio No. 1, Containing "A Poet-Caravan" and Other Sonnets
     By John Armstrong Chaloner. Roanoke Rapids, NC:
     Palmetto Press, 1913.

The Quick or the Dead? A Study
     By Amélie Rives. Philadelphia: J.B. Lippincott Company, 1888.

"Johnny Jackanapes, the Merry-Andrew of The Merry Mills: A Brief
Biography of John Armstrong Chaloner"
> By J. Bryan III. *Virginia Magazine of History and Biography* 73, 1
> (January 1965).

RELATING TO WINTIE:

Roman Spring: Memoirs
> By Margaret Terry Chanler. Boston:
> Little, Brown and Company, 1934.

Autumn in the Valley
> By Margaret Terry Chanler. Boston:
> Little, Brown and Company, 1936.

Winthrop Chanler's Letters
> By Winthrop Chanler. Collected by his wife Margaret Terry Chanler.
> New York: privately printed, 1951.

Some Letters from "Chan," 1886–1926, for a Chosen Few
> By Winthrop Chanler. Collected by Amos Tuck French.
> Chester, NH: privately printed, 1939.

Roosevelt: The Story of a Friendship, 1880–1919
> By Owen Wister. New York: The Macmillan Company, 1930.

RELATING TO ELIZABETH:

John Jay Chapman, and His Letters
> By M. A. DeWolfe Howe. Boston: Houghton Mifflin Company, 1937.

Victor Chapman's Letters from France, with Memoir
> By Victor Emmanuel Chapman. Edited by John Jay Chapman.
> New York: The Macmillan Company, 1917.

The Selected Writings of John Jay Chapman
> By John Jay Chapman. Edited with an introduction by Jacques
> Barzun. New York: Farrar, Straus & Cudahy, Inc., 1957.

John Jay Chapman: An American Mind
> By Richard B. Hovey. New York: Columbia University Press, 1959.

RELATING TO WILLIE:

Through Jungle and Desert: Travels in Eastern Africa
> By William Astor Chanler. New York: Macmillan and Company, 1896.

Quest for the Jade Sea: Colonial Competition around an East African Lake
    By Pascal James Imperato. Boulder, CO: Westview Press, 1998.

Over Land and Sea: Memoir of an Austrian Rear Admiral's Life in Europe and Africa
    By Ludwig Ritter von Höhnel. Edited by Ronald E. Coons,
    Pascal James Imperato, and John Winthrop Aldrich. New York:
    Holmes and Meier, forthcoming.

RELATING TO LEWIS:

From Gaslight to Dawn: An Autobiography
    By Julie Chanler. New York: New History Foundation, 1956.

RELATING TO MARGARET:

Family Vista: The Memoirs of Margaret Chanler Aldrich
    By Margaret Chanler Aldrich. New York:
    The William-Frederick Press, 1958.

RELATING TO BOB:

The Art of Robert Winthrop Chanler
    By Ivan Narodny. New York: William Helburn, Inc., 1922.

RELATING TO ALIDA:

Point of Departure: An Adventure in Autobiography
    By Ralph McAllister Ingersoll. New York:
    Harcourt, Brace & World, Inc. 1961.

ACKNOWLEDGEMENTS

The principal manuscript sources consulted for this book include the following.

The Margaret Livingston Aldrich Papers, at Rokeby; the Elizabeth Chanler Chapman and John Jay Chapman Papers, at Rokeby; the Robert Winthrop Chanler Papers, courtesy of Sidney Ashley Chanler; the Lewis Stuyvesant Chanler Papers, at Orlot; the William Astor Chanler and Beatrice Chanler Papers, at the New-York Historical Society, at Rokeby, and in the custody of William Astor Chanler, Jr.; the John Jay Chapman Papers, at Rokeby and at Houghton Library, Harvard University; the Winthrop and Margaret Terry Chanler Papers, at Houghton Library, Harvard University; the John Armstrong Chaloner Papers, at the Alderman Library, University of Virginia, and the Perkins Library, Duke University; the Robert Winthrop Chanler Album, Archives of American Art, Smithsonian Institution; the Rives Family Papers, Alderman Library, University of Virginia; the George E. Galvin Collection of documents, photographs, and artifacts, at Rokeby; the Stanford White Letterbooks, Avery Library, Columbia University; the S.L.M. Barlow Papers, Henry E. Huntington Library; the Franklin Delano Roosevelt Papers, at Hyde Park; the Theodore Roosevelt Papers, at Houghton Library, Harvard University; "Over Land and Sea," a manuscript memoir by Ludwig von Höhnel, at Rokeby (soon to be published as *Over Land and Sea*).

The staffs of the following institutions provided invaluable help: New-York Historical Society; New York Public Library; Henry E. Huntington Library; Museum of the City of New York; New York Society Library; Franklin Delano Roosevelt Library; Houghton Library, Harvard University; Alderman Library, University of Virginia; San Francisco Public Library.

In 1971 Lately Thomas acknowledged the generous and unreserved assistance of the various heirs, descendants, associates, and friends of the Chanlers, without whose help his research would have been impossible. In particular he named the last two survivors of the eight Chanlers, Margaret Livingston Chanler Aldrich and Alida Beekman Chanler Emmet. He also explicitly thanked the Aldrich family, the present proprietors of Rokeby, including myself; my brother, Richard Aldrich; my sister, Mrs. Rosalind Fish Aldrich Michahelles; my mother, Mrs. Richard Chanler Aldrich; and my aunt, Mrs. Byron DeMott.

Other family members included Mrs. William Christian Bohn; Mr. Porter R. Chandler; Rear Admiral and Mrs. Hubert Winthrop Chanler, of Sweet Briar Farm; Mrs. Lewis Stuyvesant Chanler, Jr.; Mr. and Mrs. William Astor Chanler, Jr.; Mr. Sidney Ashley Chanler; Mr. William Chamberlain Chanler; Mr. Chanler Armstrong Chapman and his wife, Mrs. Helen Chapman, of Sylvania; Mr. and Mrs. Conrad Chapman; Mrs. Charles H. Clarke; Mr. Christopher Emmet; Mr. Thomas Addis Emmet; the Rev. Allie W. Frazier, Jr.; Mrs. Julia Chanler Laurin; Mr. and Mrs. G. Francklyn Lawrence; Mrs. Kiki Randolph Minervini; Mr. William Platt; Mrs. Kenneth Robertson; Mrs. Julia Ward Stickley; Mrs. Pauline Petchey; Mrs. Lawrence Grant White; Mr. Peter White.

Thomas also thanked the historian Allan Nevins, John C. Willey, and Robert Lescher.

Many of these individuals have continued to provide help and encouragement during the years since. In addition, I must also thank the following individuals for their support and contribution: Jedediah Tecumseh Steele; Theo Steele; Clelia Steele; Judith Steele May; Frances McAndrews Steele; Anne Older; Margaret Mirabelli; Elizabeth Backman Potter; Bronson and Evelyn Chanler; David S. Chanler; Edwin D. Morgan; Winthrop S. Emmet; Margaret Kinnicutt Goodman; Benjamin LaFarge; William A. Chanler III; John Winthrop Chanler; David Pickman; Benjamin Swett; John Jay Chapman; Victor W. Chapman; John Chanler Trenholm; Monica Laurin von Nagel; Pascal James Imperato, M.D.; Professor Ronald E. Coons; George E. Galvin, Jr.; Henry Wiencek; Robert H. Boyle; and David Garrard Lowe.

I also wish to salute my wife Katharine and children, Laura and Daniel Middleton and Meg and Kit Aldrich, for being so tolerant of this quest which has lasted longer than the children have been alive.

— John Winthrop Aldrich

INDEX